James L. Patton
Museum of Vertebrate Zoology
University of California
Berkeley, California 94720

MacClade

MacClade

Analysis of Phylogeny and Character Evolution

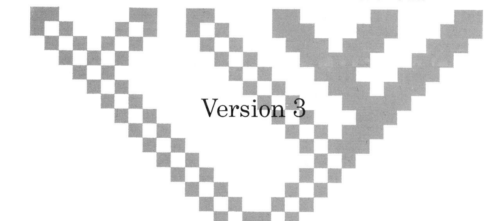

Version 3

Wayne P. Maddison
University of Arizona

David R. Maddison
Harvard University

Sinauer Associates, Inc. • *Publishers*

SUNDERLAND, MASSACHUSETTS, U.S.A.

MacClade Version 3

Copyright © 1992 by Wayne P. Maddison and David R. Maddison.
All rights reserved. To order or for information address
Sinauer Associates, Inc., Sunderland, Massachusetts 01375 U.S.A.

ISBN 0-87893-490-1

Printed in U.S.A.

5 4 3 2 1

TABLE OF CONTENTS

PREFACE

MacClade began in 1985 when one of us (WPM) began to explore drawing and interacting with trees on the screen of an Apple Macintosh™ computer. From these initial explorations sprang MacClade version 1.0, which was released in June of 1986 (W. Maddison, 1986). It contained the central features of the Tree Window — namely, tracing of characters with fixing of the states at branches, rearrangement of branches of the tree using the computer's mouse, and a feature like Trace All Changes. It was primitive in other features.

MacClade version 2.1 was released in March of 1987 (Maddison and Maddison, 1987). It added the full Macintosh user interface of menus and dialog boxes, incorporated a built-in text editor, and added user-defined matrices of state-to-state distances ("step matrices").

Version 3 incorporates many new features beyond those found in version 2.1; some of the most noticeable are the specialized data editor, the chart window, acceptance of polytomous trees, and support for molecular data. For those of you who have used version 2.1, Chapter 1 gives a brief overview of some important differences between version 2.1 and version 3.

Many people aided in the development of MacClade. We would like to thank H. W. Levi and E. O. Wilson, who gave us support and encouragement, and the freedom to work on MacClade when we should have been working on our theses. Some of the recent work on MacClade was done while WPM was a Natural Sciences and Engineering Research Council of Canada Post-doctoral Fellow, in Monty Slatkin's lab, and while DRM was a Alfred P. Sloan Foundation Post-doctoral Fellow, in R. C. Lewontin's lab; we thank them for their support.

We thank all those who reviewed pre-release copies of MacClade for us, and tested its functioning. Foremost among these was Willem Ellis, who searched long and hard for bugs in the program, and provided us with many thoughtful reports on MacClade. David Swofford, Robert O'Hara, Jenny Chappill, and Todd Disotell also deserve special note for their efforts in keeping us informed about MacClade bugs. Others who found bugs or gave suggestions include Belinda Chang, Jonathan Coddington, Chuck Crumly, Mike Cummings, Michael Donoghue, Jim Doyle, Sharon Gowan, Mike Hammer, Toby Kellogg, Jean-François Landry, Jim Malusa, Santiago Madriñan, Ted Oakes, Norm Platnick, and Jim Woolley. We are grateful for the encouragement we received from those testing the program, especially Michael Donoghue, David Swofford, Willem Ellis, and Mike Cummings.

We would like to thank specifically several people who had an impact on the content of MacClade: David Swofford, who was always there for lively discussions about phylogenetics programs, and who provided programming advice, suggestions for improvement, and code for the random number generator; J. S. Ashe, whose interest in the charts summarizing statistics over multiple trees convinced us that it was worth the effort to include; Scott Edwards, whose desire to see the distribution of transitions and transversion over the length of a DNA sequence inspired the inclusion of the Restrict Changes feature in the Character Steps charts; Allan Wilson and Linda Vigilant for inventing circular trees.

For comments, suggestions and discussion that contributed to this book, we thank Helen Amerongen, Leticia Avilés, David Baum, Michael Donoghue, Willem Ellis, Joe Felsenstein, Daniel Fisher, Larry Gall, Junhyong Kim, Michael Sanderson, and David Swofford.

We are very grateful to Michael Donoghue, Walter Fitch, Arnold Kluge, James Lake, Diana Lipscomb, and Mark Stoneking for supplying electronic versions of data files which form the basis of some of the example data files distributed with MacClade.

MacClade would not have arisen if it were not for Apple Computer's development of the computer and graphical interface that made it possible. We also thank them for supporting our work with a generous award.

Throughout the long gestation period of this current version of MacClade, Andy Sinauer has been incredibly patient and tolerant of the many delays. We also thank Joe Vesely, Carol Wigg, and Roberta Lewis for their efforts.

Finally, we would like to thank Leticia Avilés and Helen Amerongen, for their support through many long hours of programming, and for their endurance of horrendous phone bills.

Wayne P. Maddison
Department of Ecology
  and Evolutionary Biology
University of Arizona
Tucson, AZ 85721

David R. Maddison
Harvard University

current address:
Department of Entomology
University of Arizona
Tucson, AZ 85721

Part I

Introducing MacClade

1. INTRODUCTION

MacClade

This book is both a manual for the computer program MacClade, describing its features and potential uses, as well as a portrayal of a phylogenetic approach to studying diversity and evolution. It is relatively easy to see the diversity of living organisms, but it has proved more difficult to see that diversity in terms of its history; the slow development of a thoroughly phylogenetic perspective in biology attests to this challenge. Together this book and program present methods for analyzing and exploring phylogenetic hypotheses, including hypotheses about character evolution. MacClade is one attempt to give our mind's eye phylogenetic lenses, to help us think about and see lineages and evolution.

Some of the chapters and sections of this book (especially Chapters 3–6) discuss phylogenetic principles in general, and indeed the book could be read solely for its presentation of phylogenetic theory. Much of the rest of the book (especially Chapters 7–20) is devoted to MacClade itself. In this introductory chapter, we give a brief overview of MacClade's capabilities, followed by a summary of the chapters in this book, as well as information on citing MacClade, earlier versions of the program, future versions of MacClade, reporting bugs, and acquiring technical data about the program.

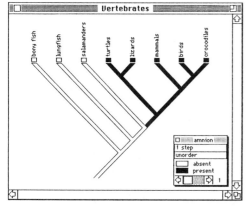

Examining character evolution on a tree in MacClade's tree window

MacClade provides an interactive environment for exploring phylogeny. In MacClade's tree window, hypothesized phylogenetic trees or cladograms can be manipulated and character evolution visualized upon them. To manipulate the tree, tools are provided to move branches, reroot clades, create polytomies, and automatically search for more parsimonious trees. Character evolution is reconstructed on the tree and indicated by "painting" the branches. Alternative reconstructions of character evolution can be explored. Summaries of changes in all characters can be depicted on the tree. As trees are manipulated, MacClade updates statistics such as treelength and the results are depicted in graphics and charts.

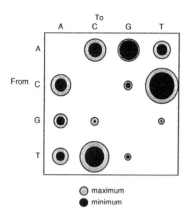

A chart showing the relative frequencies of reconstructed changes between bases on a tree, with area of circle proportional to frequency of change

		1	2	3	4	5
		amnion	temp.fene	hemipenes	gizzard	lat.sphen
1	rayfinned fish	absent	none	absent	absent	not
2	frogs	absent	none	absent	absent	not
3	turtles	present	none	absent	absent	not
4	lungfish	absent	none	absent	absent	not
5	salamanders	absent	none	absent	absent	not
6	crocodiles	present	two	absent	present	ossified
7	lizards	present	two	present	absent	not
8	birds	present	two	absent	present	ossified
9	mammals	present	one	absent	absent	not
10	snakes	present	two	present	absent	not
11						
12						

MacClade's data editor

MacClade provides charts summarizing various aspects of character evolution on one or more trees, as well as charts comparing two or more trees. For example, the charts can show the number of trees of each length, the number of characters on the tree with different consistency indices, and so on. It has a number of charts specifically designed for DNA/RNA sequence data, including one showing the number of changes on the tree at first, second, and third codon positions, and a chart of the relative frequencies of various transitions and transversions.

In MacClade's data editor, systematic and comparative data are entered and edited. The editor has numerous features for manipulating rows, columns, and blocks of data, and for recoding data. Assumptions about how character states transform into one another can be applied.

We will not detail MacClade's additional capabilities here. At the start of each of the Chapters 9 through 20 is a brief summary of the features described in the chapter. By browsing through these, you will get a more complete overview of MacClade's features.

If we had to admit a grand purpose to all of these features, it might be "to help biologists explore the relationships between data and hypotheses in phylogenetic biology". We envisage MacClade's use by biologists of many backgrounds. For example, suppose:

1. A systematist is working on the phylogenetic relationships of snail species. She enters data for 100 morphological characters and 20 taxa in MacClade's data editor, saves the file, and reads it into Swofford's PAUP. PAUP is used to find parsimonious trees, but to her surprise, the resulting trees separate two species she had thought closely related. By moving back to MacClade, examining alternative trees by hand, and using the charting functions, she discovers that the unexpected result is due to the influence of two characters of the nervous system. This not only provokes her to examine those characters in more detail, but also to gather molecular data. The molecular data set, on 60 taxa and 1500 nucleotides, is too large to get exact solutions from PAUP. PAUP's heuristic algorithms, combined with her ability to suggest and examine alternative trees in MacClade, convince her that the most-parsimonious trees for both data sets agree that the two species are not sister species. Although she had no intention of looking at fossil species, she realizes that this result suggests that their peculiar shared morphology might be primitive and old. By using the stratigraphic character type in MacClade, she discovers the minimum age of the ancestor in which the morphology was apparently derived was Paleocene, much older than the group of predators against which the morphology was thought to be a defense.

2. A population biologist has been studying the adaptive advantages of larval dispersal strategies. Although his past studies have fo-

cused on measuring risks and fecundities at two study sites in the Gulf of California, he realizes that his hypotheses could be tested by seeing if it accurately predicts a species' strategy according to its ecological position. After talking to a phylogenetic biologist, he reluctantly admits that his question is actually one of phylogenetic correlation between ecology and strategy. He finds a collaborator working on the phylogeny of the group, and together they use MacClade to map the evolution of larval dispersal strategies on the phylogenetic tree. He discovers that the correlation between strategy and ecology is not nearly as strong as he would have hoped, but he notices on MacClade's character tracing that the two groups on the phylogenetic tree with a special dispersal strategy also have the most species. His study shifts to an examination of the influence of dispersal strategy on speciation and extinction. After accumulating known phylogenies from numerous groups and exploring them with MacClade, a clear correlation emerges between speciation success and the special dispersal strategy. Itching to get back to his study sites, he discovers that his newly acquired familiarity with trees can be applied to his populations to examine patterns of dispersal and gene flow using reconstructed gene trees. He uses MacClade's random tree and random character generation to formulate null models to test his population hypotheses.

3. A molecular biologist studying cell surface proteins in a herbivorous insect suspects that a particular domain might be involved in binding secondary compounds made by the host plants. A direct chemical approach to demonstrate binding proves difficult, but the genes coding for this protein have been sequenced in several dozen related species. Using MacClade to help reconstruct the phylogeny of the species and to chart how evolutionary changes of amino acids are distributed along the length of the protein, she finds that this domain is indeed the most rapidly evolving. Furthermore, by comparing the phylogenies of the insect and the plant host using Page's COMPONENT, she makes a convincing case that one of the insect groups arose with a shift to a new plant host that had powerful and diverse secondary compounds. Not only did MacClade reconstruct many amino acid changes along that branch of the insect phylogenetic tree, but it also showed that changes in other amino acids were concentrated in the clade of insects living on the noxious hosts. With such evidence that the domain was evolving in response to host secondary compounds, the molecular biologist faced with renewed vigor the direct chemical approach to examining the binding.

4. An evolutionary biologist teaching a basic evolution course wants to introduce students to phylogenetic reconstruction. In a live demonstration MacClade is used first to help students picture phylogenetic trees in their minds' eyes. Then, the concept of fit between a tree and a character is shown via MacClade's character tracing.

Students are given an example data set, and let loose. Soon they are moving branches around with increasing rapidity, treating the search for parsimonious trees like a video game, competing against one another for shorter trees. In the process they discover that grouping by derived similarity will gain them shorter trees. One of them notices that one character disagrees with most of the remaining characters on whatever tree they can find. Indeed, on the parsimonious trees this character shows many cases of convergence. Another character is found that is similarly convergent, and students discuss what evolutionary processes might lead to the two characters having correlated evolutionary changes.

These scenarios illustrate the varied uses of a phylogenetic perspective, and of MacClade in making it accessible. We hope that whether or not you use MacClade, you will find in reading this book a new appreciation for the importance of phylogenetic studies.

Learning how to use MacClade

MacClade is a large and complex program. If you are just getting started with MacClade, we advise you to follow through the examples in Chapter 2, "**A Tutorial Overview of MacClade**". This will guide you step by step through simple data files, and thereby introduce you to some of the basic functions of MacClade.

Chapters 7 through 20 of this book will provide more detailed guidance. Although we hope that many of MacClade's features will be obvious from the program itself, some important ones will not. So that you may discover these features, and thoroughly understand MacClade's analyses, we strongly recommend that you at least glance through Chapters 7 through 20.

Part II of the book, comprising Chapters 3 through 6, concerns phylogenetic theory. "**A Phylogenetic Perspective**" outlines how phylogenetic analysis, such as that provided by MacClade, can be of value in answering various biological questions. "**Introduction to Phylogenetic Inference**" discusses methods of inference of phylogenies, and of patterns and processes of character evolution. "**Reconstructing Character Evolution Using Parsimony**" describes the assumptions and methods MacClade uses in reconstructing character evolution. A chapter by Daniel Fisher, "**Stratigraphic Parsimony**", briefly describes the principles of stratocladistics. We recommend that you read the relevant sections of these chapters before using MacClade to study character evolution.

Part III contains fourteen chapters (7 through 20) that provide detailed information on using MacClade.

Chapters 7 through 9 introduce the basics of using MacClade and of file management. "**Using MacClade on your Macintosh**" gives an overview of hardware and software requirements, installation, memory management, the help facility, and setting preferences. "**Managing Data Files**" tells how to create, open, and save data files. "**Importing and Exporting Text Files**" describes how to share files with HENNIG86, PHYLIP, and other programs.

Detailed information about manipulating data, assumptions, and trees is provided in Chapters 10 through 12. "**The Data Editor**" tells how to use MacClade's data editor to enter and edit data. "**Assumptions About Characters**" details the various assumptions used in MacClade's calculations, such as weighting of characters and how states transform one to another. "**Trees and Tree Manipulation**" introduces MacClade's tree window, and how trees can be manipulated, stored, and retrieved.

Chapters 13 through 18 focus on analysis of character evolution and the relationship between the character data and the tree. In "**Tracing Character Evolution**", methods for reconstructing the ancestral states (and thereby pathways of character evolution) are discussed. In "**Basic Tree and Character Statistics**", simple statistics of treelength and indices such as the consistency index are outlined. MacClade's charting facility is described in "**Charting Tree and Character Statistics**". Use of continuous-valued characters is explained in "**Continuous Characters**". The next chapter discusses "**Patterns of Correlated Character Evolution**", particularly the concentrated-changes test for phylogenetic character correlation. MacClade's randomization facilities, which can be used in various statistical tests, are discussed in "**Generating Random Data and Random Trees**".

Several of MacClade's features specific to molecular data are described under "**Using MacClade with Molecular Data**". In this chapter we also give some examples of MacClade's applications to molecular data.

The chapter "**Recording Your Work: Printing, Graphics, and Text**" gives strategies for keeping records. Printing facilities are described there.

The remaining sections of the book include an appendix on file format, an appendix on using MacClade and PAUP together, and Indices.

Conventions

Throughout this book, menu items and dialog boxes will be shown in **boldface** type. Buttons in dialog boxes will be shown in the font Helvetica. Important comments will be flagged with labels, as follows:

WARNING: *Important warnings are indicated in this fashion.*

NOTE: *Notes, shortcuts or tips are indicated in this fashion.*

EXAMPLE: *Exercises using the Example files included with MacClade are indicated in this fashion.*

How to cite MacClade

The computer program MacClade is not just a calculating tool. As with any published paper, it contains new ideas, implicit suggestions, and new methods. MacClade is distinct from works published on paper in that new ideas and methods presented are in a form that can be immediately used by researchers and students; it responds actively to a user instead of passively to a reader. Use of ideas in this book or in MacClade must be acknowledged as with any other published paper. (This may seem obvious; we mention it only as history suggests that it is not.) MacClade should also be cited in your Materials and Methods as a source of the calculations or output used in your papers.

Despite the scientific content of MacClade and other phylogenetic programs such as HENNIG86 (Farris, 1988), PAUP (Swofford, 1991) and PHYLIP (Felsenstein, 1991), some journal editors may object to placing a citation to a computer program in the Literature Cited. However, as the 21st century approaches, we think this attitude will become rarer. We recommend the following citation, which can be used both for the program and this accompanying book:

Maddison, W. P. and D. R. Maddison, 1992. MacClade: Analysis of phylogeny and character evolution. Version 3.0. Sinauer Associates, Sunderland, Massachusetts.

Earlier versions of MacClade

Previous versions of MacClade are numbered 1.0, 1.01, and 2.1. Any other version of MacClade, such as 2.65, 2.87, 2.97, 2.99, 3 Beta 9.9, were pre-release test versions that we showed at meetings or distributed to a few colleagues to test for us. (The easiest way to determine if a copy is a test version is to choose **About MacClade** under the menu. If "Release Version" appears in the dialog box, or the version number is 1.0, 1.01, or 2.1, it is not a test version.) Test versions were distributed *for testing only,* under the condition that no results be published based on those versions, as they have bugs in many parts of the program, including the algorithms that give basic results such as tracing of character evolution and treelengths. Unfortunately, copies of the test versions have been circulated, and some people may have test copies without realizing it.

Thus we repeat: DO NOT USE RESULTS FROM ANY TEST VERSION IN PUBLICATIONS. Except when we have indicated otherwise, results from test versions should not be trusted. We expect that any analyses done with test versions will be redone with the officially released version 3 of MacClade.

Differences between MacClade 3 and 2.1

MacClade version 3 is different in many ways from version 2.1. Most striking, perhaps, is the spreadsheet editor for entering data, which allows an intuitive means of row and column editing, copy/pasting, adding footnotes to any cell in the matrix, and so on. The raw text files of MacClade 3 follow a different format than those of earlier versions. This new format, called NEXUS, is also the format used by version 3 of PAUP. MacClade 3 automatically saves files in the correct format. This allows you to enter data without worrying about details of where semicolons and periods and the like need to be placed in the NEXUS file.

MacClade 3 can read data files in the formats used by versions 1.0, 1.01, and 2.1 (but it may not understand the formats used by test versions of MacClade).

The 80 taxa by 200 character limit on earlier versions of MacClade has been increased significantly (to 1,500 taxa and 16,000 characters).

Editing of assumptions has been made much easier, in part through a graphic dialog box for editing user-defined character types as matrices or character state trees. Trees can now have polytomies, and can be edited with a more powerful, more graphic set of tools. Trees no longer have to include all taxa in the data matrix, characters can be traced in color, the old Show Changes summary mode has been expanded and unlocked. A charting facility has been added that generates various tables or bar charts to summarize characters or trees. Publication-quality trees can be produced with choice of fonts, angle of taxon names, tree shapes, and so on. Many other features have changed; if you are familiar with version 2.1, and version 3 behaves unexpectedly, then check the rest of this section, and in the remainder of this book.

Version 3, in contrast with version 2.1, maintains the data file, including the user-defined types, type sets, weight sets, trees, and character names, in the computer's memory (RAM) while you move between the data editor and tree window. In version 2.1 the editor and tree window were like separate programs, and in transferring to the tree window, the program would reread the file from the disk.

MacClade no longer has built-in fonts with male/female symbols. Please write to your favorite typeface company to lobby for biological symbols.

Differences in calculations or assumptions

MacClade 3 will give results different from version 2.1 in some circumstances.

MacClade 3 treats Dollo characters differently from version 2.1; if two states of a Dollo character might otherwise be placed at the root with equal parsimony, MacClade 3 will place both states at the root, whereas version 2.1 will place only the lower-numbered state there.

User-defined type characters with polymorphisms of more than two states are treated differently by MacClade 3, which will use the lowest number of steps from one state to any other state as the number of steps required within a terminal taxon should the first state be reconstructed at the taxon's base.

The type called "reversible" no longer exists in version 3. This type was used instead of ordered and unordered for binary characters in MacClade 2.1 because there is no useful distinction between ordered and unordered types for binary characters. However, the reversible type can be dispensed with if one realizes that calling a binary character either ordered or unordered gives the same results. In version 3 it is expected that you will use unordered or ordered for binary characters.

Future plans for MacClade

Our plans and your suggestions

Among the planned improvements for future versions of MacClade are:
— Modular and extensible program format (see below)
— Full incorporation of continuous-valued characters into the program, with editing in a spreadsheet data editor
— Better tools for sequence alignment
— More ways to display the tree in the tree window
— Better interface for charting facilities and tree printing
— Likelihood and other statistical techniques
— A better editor for character state symbols and names
— Better interface for getting and storing trees and tree files
— Full System 7 support

We would *very* much like suggestions from you, whether they concern user-interface features (e.g., tree appearance on screen), or new sorts of calculations (e.g., a new correlation test, new charts).

Adding your own calculations

One of our long-term goals is to make MacClade capable of being expanded by the user. We cannot hope to incorporate all of the phylogenetic calculations that have been and will be developed, but we can build means by which new calculations can be added as modules to MacClade. In the future this may involve the use of System 7's Apple Events to pass information from MacClade to stand-alone modules.

At present, MacClade has some primitive tools that allow access to some of MacClade's memory structures. These allow you to write programs that run under Multifinder or System 7 alongside MacClade and do calculations using the same tree and data that MacClade is using. For details of how to do this, please contact us.

Reporting bugs

We have extensively checked and tested the main algorithms in MacClade in an attempt to ensure that no faulty results will be generated; in various parts of this book we have described our checking procedures. We hope that no such bugs remain, but there will remain, we are sure, a number of bugs having to do with screen display and occasional crashes. If you think you have found a bug in MacClade, please report it to us.

To correct a bug, we need the following information:

1. A description of the problem. This includes a list of *all* the steps that led to the bug. If at all possible, try to repeat the problem yourself until you know the exact sequence of steps that reliably lead to the bug. Without knowing an exact sequence of events that reproduces the bug, there is a good chance we cannot find the bug and fix it.

2. We also may need an *exact* copy of the data files or tree files involved, as many bugs appear only with specific files. Therefore, a copy of the files should be saved. (If we do borrow your files, they will be kept strictly confidential, and will be discarded once the bug is fixed.)

3. Your name and address (e-mail if possible).

4. Exact version number of MacClade used (see **About MacClade** in the menu).

5. Model of Macintosh.

6. Amount of memory (RAM) in your Macintosh.

7. Version number of system (see **About Finder** or **About this Macintosh** in the menu when in Finder).

8. If not using System 7, were you using Multifinder?

9. If using Multifinder or System 7, how much memory was allocated to MacClade (determined by selecting MacClade in the Finder and choosing **Get Info**)?

10. Any other possibly relevant information about data file format (such as standard, extended, DNA, etc.), number of taxa and characters, type of printer, and so on.

To report a bug, send the above information to one of us, Attention: Bug Report (our addresses are listed in the Preface).

You may find that you are not sure whether you have discovered a bug or simply don't understand how MacClade is supposed to function. We would like to hear from you even if the problem is only that MacClade's intended behavior was not made clear to you. We suggest that you first reread the appropriate sections of this book to see how MacClade was intended to behave.

Technical information and availability of source code

MacClade 3 was developed and compiled using Symantec's Think Pascal™ version 4.01, except for some sections in assembly language.

If you would like more technical information about MacClade, some details about the functioning of MacClade's algorithms are given in Chapter 5 and the various other chapters concerning them. If you want further information on the algorithms or other technical details, please contact the authors. The source code for those parts of the program that deal directly with the calculations of results are available from us, so that they may be examined by the scientific community.

2. A Tutorial Overview of MacClade

As an introduction to MacClade and some of its capabilities, we offer the following tutorial. It will guide you step-by-step through some simple data files. (We will assume basic familiarity with the operation of a Macintosh; if you need help with basic operations, see your Macintosh manual.) Those already familiar with MacClade may want to skip this chapter.

As you work through the tutorial, remember that MacClade 3 has four main windows. The *Data Editor* is an editor in which the taxa are named, and their states in various characters are entered. In the *Tree Window* trees are built and modified, and their relationship to the character data explored. You can move between the data editor and tree window using items in the **Display** menu. MacClade cannot show both windows at the same time; thus at any given time MacClade is either in data editing mode or tree analysis mode. The *Character Status Window*, requested in the **Display** menu, lists the characters in the data file, and various assumptions about each character (its weight, assumptions about transformations from one state to another, and whether the character is currently included or excluded). This window not only lists these assumptions, but also allows you to change them. The character status window also lists statistics relating the characters to the current tree (e.g., their consistency indices) when the tree window is in use. When the tree window is on the screen, the *Chart Window* can be requested from the **Chart** menu to show various summary statistics about the characters and their evolution according to the tree. By exploring each of these windows you will introduce yourself to many of MacClade's features.

Tree manipulation

Vertebrates

Open the MacClade Examples folder. Double-click on the Vertebrates data file to start MacClade. The data file will take you straight to the tree window, and you will be presented with a phylogeny on the screen, as in the following figure. (If you are presented with a data matrix instead, the file has been altered — try selecting **Go To Tree Window** from the **Display** menu.)

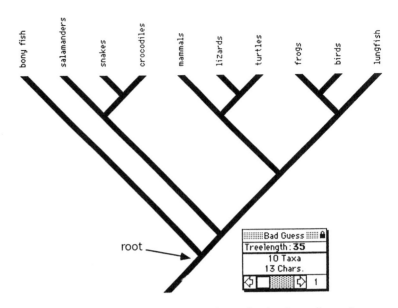

More accurately, what you see is one hypothesis about how the ancestral vertebrate lineage split and evolved, leading up to the major living vertebrate groups. As its name ("Bad Guess") implies, it is almost certainly wrong. The branch at the bottom of the tree, representing the ancestor of the taxa, is called the **root** of the tree.

To see how the traits of vertebrates have evolved according to this hypothesis, choose **Trace Character** from the **Trace** menu. You should now see the evolution of the amnion traced onto the screen.

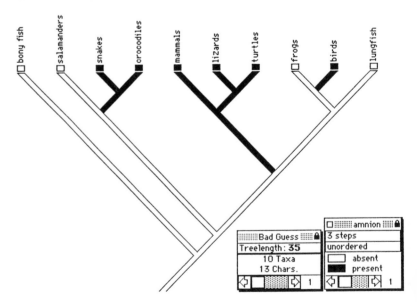

Look at the legend in the lower right of the tree window. Note that the character amnion has two states: "absent" or "present". According to this phylogeny, the amnion (portions of the tree shaded in black) arose three times. This is also indicated in the legend at the far right, where it indicates that there were "3 steps" of evolution in this character. (If you have a color monitor, then the states might not be symbolized by white and black, but by colors, most likely yellow and blue.) These three arisals are shown in the diagram below:

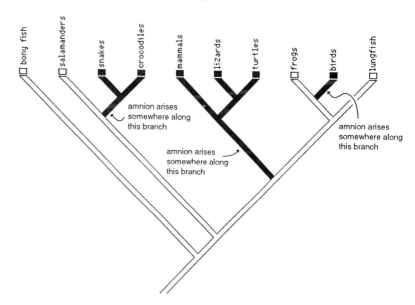

That the amnion arose three times independently (and thus that the amnions of snakes, mammals, and birds are **analogous**) seems unreasonable, as it is a complex explanation of the observations, and a simpler explanation is available. It seems more reasonable to presume that the amnion arose only once, in an ancestral tetrapod vertebrate, and that it was passed on to descendants of that ancestor (and thus that the amnions of snakes, mammals, and birds are **homologous**, having been derived from a common ancestor).

N O T E: *Here MacClade shows the amnion arising at the start of a branch. MacClade does this for convenience only. The evolution of the trait might have happened anywhere along the history of the branch.*

Now, let's alter the phylogenetic hypothesis slightly. Move the snakes + crocodiles over so that they now are next to the mammals + lizards + turtles. To do this, move the mouse's arrow pointer over to the branch just below the snakes + crocodiles, click down on the mouse, and, while holding the mouse button down, drag the diamond over to the branch just below mammals + lizards + turtles:

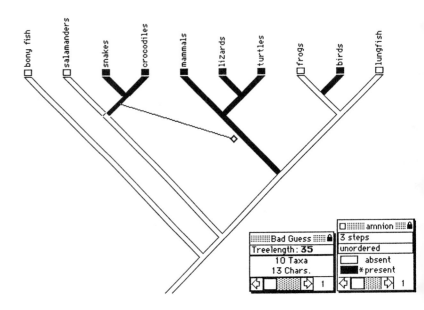

When the mouse is over the latter branch (this you can tell as the branch will change shades), let go of the mouse button. The snakes and crocodiles should have moved over beside the mammals + lizards + turtles.

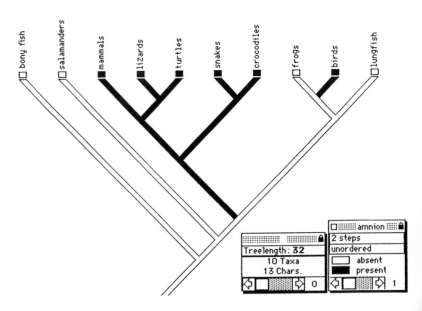

According to this new hypothesis, the amnion arose only twice; that's better, as it is a simpler explanation.

In the second box from the right is a line that reads "Treelength: 32". The **treelength** is a statistic that gives an indication as to how well the tree fits the data. The longer the treelength, the worse the fit; the shorter the treelength, the better the fit. The treelength is simply the sum, over all characters, of the number of evolutionary steps in each character on the tree. For the tree on the screen, the number of steps in the first character is 2; the number of steps in the second character is 3 (to scroll to see the second character, click once on the lower, right-hand arrow in the character legend at the far right); in the third character, 5; and so on. The treelength is thus $2 + 3 + 5 + \cdots = 32$. Shorter treelengths mean that, in general, the tree fits the characters well, that is, that the tree does not require one to presume multiple independent arisals of traits.

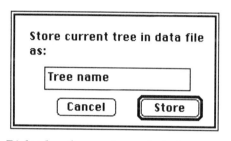

Dialog box for naming and storing trees

Once you have found a tree you would like to save, store it in the file with the **Store Tree** command of the **Trees** menu. In the dialog box that is presented to you, enter a name for the tree and press **Store**. You can re-examine the stored tree when you want using the **Trees** command. (You may want to save the modified file, with its new stored tree, to disk so that you can see your tree the next time you open the Vertebrates file. You would do this using the **Save File** command of the **File** menu. However, if you do save the file to disk, it will no longer be in its original condition, making it more difficult for others to follow this tutorial.)

To see other options for tree manipulation, select the **Tools** menu. You will notice the menu is a palette with various small icons, which represent tools for your use. Choose the tool that looks like this: , then click this tool on a branch in the tree. The tree will be rerooted where you touched it (unless you touched the tree at or near the root, in which case rerooting wouldn't make any difference).

Try some other tree manipulation tools. will ask MacClade to try rearranging branches in the clade above the branch touched, in order to search for alternative trees that are more parsimonious according to the data set. will destroy the branch touched and so yield a polytomy from a dichotomy. Play with the other tools to see what they do. MacClade lists the function of the tool in the small window at the bottom of the palette. See Chapter 12 for a more detailed description of these tools.

Once you have finished exploring the tree manipulation tools, use the **Trees** dialog box in the **Tree** menu to choose the "Another Guess" tree. Trace character 1 onto the tree by scrolling to it using the arrows in the character legend. You should see the following:

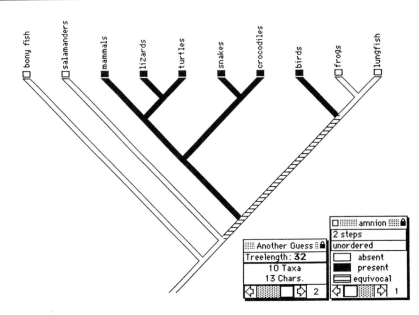

Of course, if you were really serious about examining the evolution of this character, you would do it with a phylogenetic tree that was well supported by available evidence (clearly this one is not!). But this example is just for practice, so bear with us.

For the branches with horizontal striping (the "equivocal" pattern) the evidence is ambiguous as to how the characteristics evolved. The ancestors along these branches might have had amnions, but they might not have; either possibility is equally parsimonious. When you click on a striped branch (do this now), MacClade indicates this uncertainty by placing a question mark in the legend box on the right beside each state that could be along that branch.

In this case, there are two possible patterns of character evolution; that is, two patterns that equally simply explain the distribution of the amnion in living vertebrates. They are:

1. The amnion arose independently in the mammals-to-crocodile clade and the birds;

2. The amnion arose only once, but was later lost in frogs and lungfish.

To see these two possibilities, you can use one of the several tools MacClade provides for manipulating and examining the tracing. These are stored in the palette in the **Tools** menu. Select the paintbrush tool ( ). Click the paintbrush tool on the box in the legend to the left of "present", as shown in the following figure.

The paintbrush should turn black (![brush]), indicating that it "contains" your selected state. (If you have a color monitor, and colors are used to indicate the states, then the paintbrush will turn the color of the state; otherwise, a filled paintbrush will always be black, an empty one white.) Now click on one of the equivocal branches. In doing this, you are fixing the state of the branch; you are telling MacClade: "Show me the evolution of the amnion assuming that organisms along the branch I touched had an amnion". You should see the amnion arising once and being lost once. Now, undo what you just did by choosing **Unfix All** from the **Trace** menu. Next, click the paintbrush tool on the box in the legend to the left of "absent". Now, when you click the paintbrush on the same branch, you should see the amnion arising twice.

There are many other features to help you analyze character evolution which we will introduce in other chapters (see especially Chapter 13).

Entering data

Now let's examine the data that you have been analyzing. Go to the **Display** menu and choose **Go to Data Editor**. This will take you to a data editor that should look something like this:

		1	2	3	4
		amnion	appendages	body covering	thermoreg.
1	ray finned fish	absent	fins	derm.scales	poikilotherm
2	frogs	absent	legs only	smooth	poikilotherm
3	turtles	present	legs only	epid.scales	poikilotherm
4	lungfish	absent	fins	derm.scales	poikilotherm
5	salamanders	absent	legs only	smooth	poikilotherm
6	crocodiles	present	legs only	epid.scales	poikilotherm
7	lizards	present	legs only	epid.scales	poikilotherm
8	birds	present	legs&wings	feathers	homeotherm
9	mammals	present	s only /legs&wi	hair	homeotherm
10	snakes	present	?	epid.scales	poikilotherm
11					
12					
13					

Vertebrates

On the left of each row are the names of the taxa. Along the top of each column are the names of the characters, and in the matrix itself are the names of the character states possessed by each of the taxa for each of the characters. If you want to change the data, click on the cell of the matrix you want to edit, and type in the new data. For instance, click on the cell in the first column (amnion) beside "salamanders" and type "present" if you want to claim that salamanders have an amnion.

Now let us make a new data file. In the **File** menu choose **Close File.** If MacClade asks you "Do you want to save changes before closing?", respond "No". MacClade will then present you with a list of files you might open. Instead of opening any of them, choose the New button to start a new data file. You will be presented with a blank data matrix with one taxon and one character:

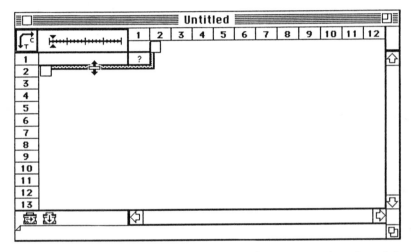

The thick gray border with a box at each end represents the edge of the matrix. To enlarge the matrix so as to add taxa, place the cursor over the bottom edge of this heavy border, as shown above (note the ⬍ cursor), click and drag down. When you let go, MacClade will add more taxa. To make new characters, place the cursor over the right-hand heavy border, click and drag to the right. Add at least 5 characters, and at least 3 taxa.

Now fill in taxon names in the wide column at the left hand side. To enter the name of the first taxon, click on the cell beside the number 1, and type in the name. Continue for the other taxon names. Now enter character state data in the body of the matrix. Enter character state data as 0's, 1's, 2's, and so on. For now, we will name the states 0, 1, 2, and so on. If you want to use names like "absent", "present", "red", "blue", and so on in the matrix, refer to Chapter 10 to learn how to prepare the data file for entering character state data by full names, as we did in the Vertebrates example, or for using other symbols such as ACGT. Chapter 10 also explains many features of the editor not included in this Tutorial.

Specifying assumptions

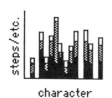

▾ Character▾	Type▾	Weight▾	States
☑ 1.	unordered	1	2
☑ 2.	unordered	1	2
☑ 3.	unordered	1	2
☑ 4.	unordered	1	2
☑ 5.	unordered	1	2
☑ 6.	unordered	1	2
☑ 7.	unordered	1	2

Selecting character 3

Once you have typed some data into the new matrix, you can set the assumptions used for the characters. Choose **Character Status** from the **Display** menu. In this window are listed the characters and information about them. To practice changing assumptions, click on the row for character 3, then go to the **Change Type** submenu in the **Assume** menu and select **Ordered**. This will change the type of character 3 from unordered to ordered. (The difference between an unordered and ordered character is described in Chapter 5.) Now try excluding character 5 from subsequent analyses. To do this, select character 5 in this window. Then choose **Exclude** from the **Change Inc Exc** submenu in the **Assume** menu. The check mark on the left will change to an x and the character type will be listed as "(excluded)". Character 5 is now excluded from any tree analysis.

Now try going to the tree window (using the **Go To Tree Window** menu in the **Display** menu) and playing around with trees. (Don't forget to give names to all of the taxa first!)

Charting results

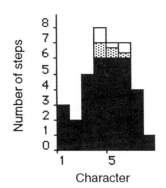

Lower-middle icon of
Character Steps/etc. dialog box

Lower-left corner of the chart

We can now briefly explore some of MacClade's charting facilities.

Close the current file, and open the file Amblygnathus in the Morphological Examples folder. This file contains morphological data on a group of ground beetles (Ball and Maddison, 1987). Go to the tree window, and choose **Character Steps/etc.** from the **Chart** menu. In the dialog box that appears, there are six large icons; touch on the lower-middle icon.

When you press Chart, MacClade will present you with a chart summarizing the number of steps in each character over the 21 most-parsimonious trees that are stored in the data file. The 28 characters will appear along the horizontal axis, the number of steps along the vertical axis.

In the chart that appears, most of the bars are solidly filled (with black or a color, depending on your monitor), indicating that those characters have the same number of steps on all 21 trees examined. For seven of the characters (4, 5, 6, 19, 21, 22, and 27), however, part of each bar is solid, part is grayed, and the top is white. The number of steps in these characters varies over the 21 trees. The solid part of the bar indicates the minimal number of steps across trees, the gray part the average number, and the white part the maximum number. For example, the chart indicates that character 4 has between 6–8 steps, with an average number of 7 steps.

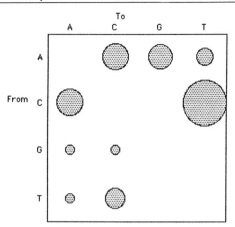

Chart showing the relative numbers of
reconstructed changes from A to C,
A to G, and so on.

To explore another sort of chart, close this file, and open the file Marsupial Wolf in the folder Molecular Examples. This file contains DNA sequence data for the cytochrome b gene for various marsupials (Thomas et al., 1989). In the tree window, choose **State Changes & Stasis** from the **Chart** menu. In the dialog box that appears, press Chart. This asks MacClade to make a chart of the relative frequencies of each kind of nucleotide change for the DNA sequence data over the tree on the screen, as reconstructed by parsimony. The chart presented should look something like the one shown on the left. Note the relative abundance of C to T changes.

Concluding remarks

You have now seen some of the major parts of MacClade. Other features that you may quickly need include printing (Chapter 20), and the ability to custom-make your own assumptions about how character states evolve one to another (Chapter 11). Examples of some features useful for molecular data are presented in Chapter 19.

N O T E: *As you explore MacClade, be aware of the power of the Option key. When you hold down the Option key, menus and cursors may change to give you access to features not otherwise available. These features are described in their appropriate places throughout this book.*

Part II

Phylogenetic Theory

3. A Phylogenetic Perspective

A primary goal of MacClade is to help biologists understand the implications phylogeny has on their studies of molecules, development, function, adaptation, ecology, speciation, and biogeography. It is now well recognized that phylogeny can inform such studies by supplying an historical perspective (e.g., Rosen, 1976, 1978; Eldredge and Cracraft, 1980; Lauder, 1981, 1982, 1988, 1990; Fink, 1982; Ridley, 1983, 1986, 1989; Wanntorp, 1983a; Larson, 1984; Dobson, 1985; Felsenstein, 1985a; Greene, 1986; Huey, 1987; Huey and Bennett, 1987; Ritland and Clegg, 1987; Sessions and Larson, 1987; Wake and Larson, 1987; Coddington, 1988; Futuyma, 1988; O'Hara, 1988; Sillén-Tullberg, 1988; Gittleman, 1988; Carpenter, 1989; Donoghue, 1989; Golding and Felsenstein, 1990; Losos, 1990; Wanntorp et al., 1990; Baum and Larson, 1991; Brooks and McLennan, 1991; Harrison, 1991; Harvey and Pagel, 1991; McLennan, 1991). Our goal in this chapter is to introduce the nature of a phylogeny, and to review briefly some of the insights that might be gained from phylogeny. Readers unfamiliar with the basic concepts and vocabulary of phylogenetic biology might want to consult Chapter 4.

What is phylogeny?

The central image of this book and MacClade is that of the **phylogenetic tree** or **phylogeny**. In introducing the concept of a phylogeny, we will begin by focusing in on the individual organisms that comprise a living species.

Imagine that we were examining four living butterflies, shown at left, which are but a small part of a population.

Four butterflies

The genes in these four butterflies came from their parents in the preceding generation. Each butterfly individual, being a diploid organism that reproduces sexually, will have two parents. We can show their parents below them, connected to them by lines indicating a passage of genes.

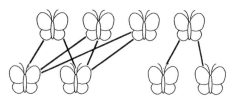

Four butterflies (top row),
connected to their parents (bottom row)

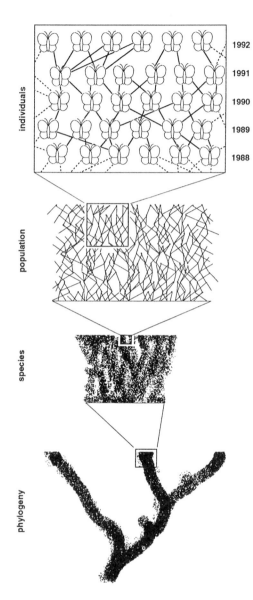

Levels of detail in genetic history:
From individuals to the phylogenetic tree

These parents, of course, received their genes from their parents, and so on. On the top left is shown a somewhat broader view of the population, over five generations. This shows the parent-offspring inheritance lines connecting the butterflies, with dotted lines drawn to butterflies out of the picture.

But this is only a small part of the full set of breeding relationships within the population. If we step back further, we would see this sub-population as it fits within the entire population. Further back still, we could see that this population is a piece of an entire lineage or **species**.

A species of sexual organisms is like a bundle of genetic connections. For many of our purposes we need not concern ourselves with the exact nature of species, as long as they are delimited so as to have a more or less tree-like history of descent, as described below. However, the reader should realize that different authors have different definitions of the word "species" (e.g., Simpson, 1961; Mayr, 1963; de Queiroz and Donoghue, 1988; Nixon and Wheeler, 1990), with some authors preferring to define species in terms of past genetic connections, others in terms of forces currently keeping the members cohesive, others in terms of expectations of future cohesion, and others in terms of the means by which we can distinguish them. A species concept focusing on past genetic connections is most easily integrated into phylogenetic studies, and is the one we will lean toward here.

Finally, as we step back and look more broadly across organisms and deeply in time, we would see that this species forms one branch on the **phylogenetic tree** of species of this particular group of butterflies. The ancestral lineage of these butterflies split to give rise to two descendant lineages. This process of **speciation** was repeated to give rise to three extant species. The genetic history of the species therefore takes the form of a tree as this branching process happens again and again. The tree is not without its failures, for some lineages are terminated by **extinction** (as is the small branch near the base of the right-hand lineage at left).

Thus, the entangled individual parent–offspring lines, visible in the upper-most picture, form the ties that bundle together individuals into the species lineages in the phylogeny, as shown on the bottom. As these parent–offspring lines are routes of genetic inheritance, they, and the lineages of organisms they form, are the conduits for the passage of traits, both molecular and structural, between organisms.

But we should not think that within the bundles, below the level of the species, history is entirely tangled and reticulate without any trace of trees. In fact, the history of genes within a species is entirely tree-like. The problem is that there are many different interwoven trees, one for each non-recombining piece of the genome.

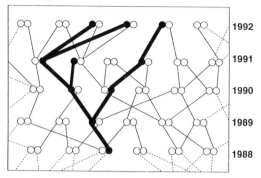

The fate of one gene copy in the butterflies

The interwoven nature of gene trees can be seen from the diagram at left, which shows the same few related butterflies over the past five generations. Specifically, it is showing the inheritance of a single locus of the genome. Although the usage is not general, for our discussion we will use the terms "locus" and "gene" to mean a section small enough such that there is no recombination within it. Each butterfly is represented by two circles, one for each of its copies of this gene. Highlighted in thick lines is the inheritance of a single copy from the 1988 generation. It left one descendant in 1989, two in 1990, three in 1991, and three in 1992. Its history is purely tree-like, for any copy of the gene will always have only a single ancestor in the previous generation (assuming no recombination within it) regardless of how many copies it leaves in the following generation. If we were to follow the history of all of the copies of this locus in the species, we would find a single grand gene tree that would appear reticulate only because it would fold over itself so as to make two copies pass through every diploid individual. If we were to look at a different locus somewhere else in the genome, we would find likewise a grand gene tree. It would be a gene tree of a different form, however, because recombination would make the other locus's ancestry trace through the alternative parent in many instances.

A phylogeny is the branching history of routes of inheritance. If the routes of inheritance represent the passage of genes from parent to offspring, then the branching pattern depicts a gene tree or gene phylogeny. If the routes represent the descent of species lineages, then the branching pattern depicts a species phylogeny. At both the level of species trees and gene trees, the passage of genetic information is constrained to their branches. The form of these trees is therefore one of the dominant and indispensable facts of evolutionary history.

Comparisons broad and deep

What is it that we can learn by studying many organisms comparatively that we cannot learn by studying only *Caenorhabditis elegans*? In particular, what can we learn by studying many species and thinking phylogenetically?

Comparative biologists have long recognized that broad comparisons can uncover illuminating patterns. Some important processes may leave traces too difficult to detect in narrow studies of the here and now. One might hope that knowledge from the small time-slices of many microevolutionary studies would sum to a complete understanding of evolutionary processes, but this is not necessarily the case. Microevolutionary studies may be too shallow to detect some patterns that could be detected by examining phylogeny deeply and broadly. In general, study of small-scale patterns will not necessarily extrapolate easily to understanding of large-scale phenomena. If a 12-inch ruler is thrown on the ground in random locations, one might hope that, *on average*, the ground curves down away from the center of the ruler, but one could not expect to have sufficient sample size to show this and so prove the curvature of the earth. Indeed, if the earth were like a golf ball with enough large dimples, one might get the impression that the earth is concave! One must get off one's knees and look greater distances to see the overall pattern.

It is not enough, however, merely to look broadly. If comparative studies are to yield evolutionary explanations instead of mere descriptions of extant variation and covariation, they need to consider the *history* of evolutionary events (Eldredge and Cracraft, 1980; Ridley, 1983; Felsenstein, 1985a; Donoghue, 1989; W. Maddison, 1990; Brooks and McLennan, 1991; Harvey and Pagel, 1991). If evolutionary biology is to study evolution, it must consider events through time. This is true whether one is studying the evolution of molecules, development, structure, behavior, or ecological relationships.

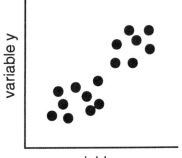

variable x

As we stand on our leaf of the tree of life, we look across to all of the other leaves and try to see patterns. We might notice a broad-scale pattern that species with large values of variable x, for instance, tend to have large values in variable y. We might plot a scattergram as shown at left, calculate a correlation coefficient and judge that there is a significant correlation between variables x and y. This might lead us to propose a hypothesis about evolutionary process: for instance, that species with large values of variable x (having to do with distribution of the species' resources, perhaps) are selected to have large values of variable y also (having to do with mating systems, perhaps).

However, such an approach has a serious flaw, as has been recognized for the last decade (e.g., Clutton-Brock and Harvey 1977; Ridley, 1983; Felsenstein, 1985a). If the species plotted are phylogenetically related so that the upper-right cloud of points is a clade, and the lower-left cloud of points is a separate clade, as shown in the figure to the left, then there is no reason to believe these two variables are causally related to one another, except insofar as both are constrained to have evolved along the phylogeny. It could be that y is large in the upper clade because of any of the many other features in which the two clades differ, or perhaps only by chance. It is as if there are only two data points, one of which has large x and y, one of which has small x and y. Knowing the phylogeny, we realize that there is much weaker support for the notion of a causal connection than we had thought, because each of the species within each of the clades cannot be considered an independent data point supporting the correlation.

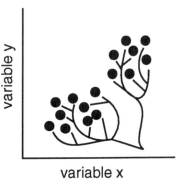

variable x

Although this flaw has been well-recognized, and comparative biologists have developed methods to consider phylogeny when seeking correlations between characters, it must be said that comparative biology has yet to thoroughly absorb a phylogenetic perspective. This is seen especially in the term "phylogenetic effects". Comparative biologists that recognize the problem with the simple scattergram correlation sometimes explain that the correlation is inflated by speciation generating "false" replicates with the same combination of traits passively inherited from a common ancestor. Such a correlation is said to be due in part to the effects of adaptation, and in part to the effects of phylogeny. There is therefore an attempt to partition the correlation or covariance into the component due to adaptation (or function, or whatever else) and the component due to phylogeny.

We feel that this perspective, even though it takes phylogeny into account, remains burdened by its non-phylogenetic beginnings. If we take a thoroughly phylogenetic view of correlation, instead of a scattergram view, the concept of "phylogenetic effects" becomes unnecessary. Phylogeny on its own does not produce any correlation between characters beyond that expected by chance, when our chance expectations are formulated appropriately with the tree in mind. First, as evolutionary biologists we should be seeking correlation in *events*, in character changes (or lack thereof), not just correlation in the results of evolutionary history. Second, the chance expectations must be *constrained by the phylogeny*. If two characters change once each, on the same branch or in close sequence one after the other on the phylogenetic tree, then their nested distribution is simply not a significant correlation (in the sense of "association over that expected by chance"). It would be a departure from chance expectations if we thought species were not related by a phylogeny but instead each independent from every other, but that is not a relevant null model. The correlation calculated from the scattergram is based on an irrelevant null model, and so was simply the wrong correlation to calculate. It is not so worthy of dissection into components, except to understand the mistakes we might have made. "Phylogenetic effects" are like Ptolemaic epicycles, corrections to an explanation that began with the wrong model.

The scattergram approach cannot be simply tidied up by admitting to phylogenetic effects; it must be replaced by a new, more thoroughly phylogenetic paradigm. And the need for a change is not limited to bivariate scattergrams. Other comparative methods that use organisms from different species, such as multivariate ordinations or pairwise sequence comparisons, all suffer from similar difficulties when they address questions of evolutionary processes and events by comparing laterally from species to species instead of via phylogeny.

We do not mean to say that an evolutionless scattergram of the standing variation among extant species is irrelevant. It may, for instance, be a heuristic device to suggest the possibility of certain processes. However, nature's genetic processes worked vertically, and so should our methods and hypotheses. If we are to ask how and why creatures differ, we must incorporate into our thinking from the start that these creatures arose via phylogenetic trees, and that their differences and similarities are to be explained by processes of change (or lack thereof) along the lineages of the phylogenetic tree. Looking only broadly at extant forms, without modeling (at least implicitly) their history, will not accurately tell us how they came to differ.

This focus on evolutionary history has been called "tree thinking" (O'Hara, 1988), by virtue of the tree-like form that phylogeny usually takes. Tree thinking is not a minor addition to the toolbox of evolutionary theory; it is a commitment, an abiding concern, to understand organisms through their history. Even within species, it will change the way we do evolutionary biology. With the new DNA sequencing technology, for instance, gene trees within populations hold the promise of shedding light on many population-level processes, including migration and population fluctuations (Avise et al., 1987; Slatkin and Maddison, 1989; Felsenstein, in press a,b).

The remaining sections of this chapter discuss some of the applications of phylogenetic analysis in biology. These sections are intended to be concise reviews of the various fields. Readers new to phylogenetic analysis may prefer to begin with introductory material provided in the papers cited.

Speciation and extinction

Phylogeny is in large part the history of branching (speciation) and extinction; theories of speciation and extinction should therefore depend very much on a phylogenetic perspective. Speciation and extinction can be studied both on the large scale, for instance in macroevolutionary studies of diversity in various clades, and on a small scale, for instance in the study of particular cases of hybrid zones.

Macroevolutionary studies can use relative success of groups to examine natural selection at the species level (Vrba, 1980; Cracraft, 1985; Mitter et al., 1988). Basic to this enterprise is an understanding of what are the various lineages and their descendants, that is, what is the phylogeny. Consistent association of a particular feature (e.g., limited dispersal, herbivory) with large clades might indicate a role of this feature in promoting speciation or limiting extinction (Vrba, 1980; Mitter et al., 1988; Farrell et al., 1991). Pairwise comparisons of sister clades provide a controlled test of such species-selection hypotheses (Mitter et al., 1988), since the sister clades are of the same age and starting conditions. Non-sister clade comparisons can also be done, if a time dimension can be relied upon (Gilinsky, 1991). Species selection might also be discovered by examining the asymmetries in sizes of clades in phylogenetic trees (Savage, 1983; Slowinski and Guyer, 1989; Guyer and Slowinski, 1991; Hey, 1992) and comparing them to expectations from null models of speciation (Harding, 1971; Simberloff et al., 1981; Savage, 1983; Simberloff, 1987; Slowinski and Guyer, 1989; Maddison and Slatkin, 1991; Guyer and Slowinski, 1991; Hey, 1992). These tests may indicate significant asymmetry, but they do not directly examine what features are responsible for a clade's success.

Phylogenetic study either at the species, population, or gene level could inform microevolutionary studies of speciation (Wiley, 1981; Wiley and Mayden, 1985; J. Lynch, 1989; Harrison, 1991). In studies of hybrid zones, for instance, a crucial question is whether an apparent hybrid zone is actually a hybrid zone of secondary contact, or whether it is a cline representing primary contact (Thorpe, 1984). To answer this question historical information is needed. Species-level phylogenies can indicate the appropriate players, that is the very close relatives, that need to be considered in any proposed scenario. They could also help to indicate the status of characters involved in reproductive isolation — has one of two contacting species responded with a derived courtship display, or do they both show divergence from ancestral states? Phylogenies of genes within the species, now becoming available through the ease of sequencing, can not only elucidate the structure of gene movement during speciation and at a hybrid zone (e.g., Harrison, 1991; Slatkin and Maddison, 1989, 1990), but also could help to trace past population sizes (Cann et al., 1987; Felsenstein, in press a,b) that play a critical role in speciation theories. Here, coalescent theory (Kingman, 1982; Tavaré, 1984) is vital. If the genes of one species coalesce rapidly as one looks backward in time, while its sister species' genes take longer to coalesce, then we have evidence that the first species may have arisen via narrower bottlenecks in population size.

Evidence on the nature of the speciation process — for instance, whether character change is concentrated at speciation events (Eldredge and Gould, 1972) — might come from phylogeny. In stochastic models of character change there is a choice between assuming change is proportional to the temporal duration of phylogenetic lineages (a gradualist view) or is independent of temporal duration (perhaps a punctuated equilibrium view). Examining the distribution of changes on a phylogeny may help test the predictions of these models (Lemen and Freeman, 1989; Mindell et al., 1989; Sanderson, 1990). Of course, any direct paleontological tests of these models require a phylogenetic reconstruction — including the lineages, speciation events, and character changes.

Combined with geographic and character data, phylogenies can also elucidate patterns of character displacement and migration in connection to speciation, testing such hypotheses as the *in situ* differentiation of ecomorphs in *Anolis* lizards (Losos, 1990).

Character evolution: Adaptation, constraint, and rates

Evolution does not consist only of branching and extinction of species lineages (cladogenesis); these lineages undergo genetic and phenotypic change to yield the many forms of organisms seen (anagenesis). Studies of how and why characters evolve can focus on various forces or parameters of character evolution. Such studies also depend on a phylogenetic perspective. We will divide our discussion into three topics: adaptation, constraints, and rates.

In studies of character evolution, perhaps the most basic function of a phylogeny is to help reconstruct a character's history — what changes might have occurred, and in what lineages (Lauder, 1981; Fink, 1982; Ridley, 1983; Greene, 1986; Donoghue, 1989; Baum and Larson, 1991; Swofford and Maddison, in press). Given an inferred phylogeny, and the observed characteristics in extant taxa at the tips of the phylogeny, criteria such as parsimony can be used to select a reconstruction of character evolution on the phylogeny (Farris, 1970; Fitch, 1971; Hartigan, 1973; Sankoff and Rousseau, 1975; Swofford and Maddison, 1987; W. Maddison, 1989, 1991; Rinsma et al., 1990; Strauss, in press). Such reconstructions of character change can be used as the basis for various evolutionary studies. Clearly, it is easier to explain evolution if you have some idea as to what happened during evolution (O'Hara, 1988), that is, what it is that needs to be explained (Donoghue, 1989). The characters examined do not need to be molecular or morphological; they could be behavioral (Packer, 1991; Langtimm and Dewsbury, 1991), physiological (Huey and Bennett, 1987), ecological (Futuyma and McCafferty, 1991), or geographical (Cann et al., 1987). Making such reconstructions of character evolution might be considered the central feature of MacClade. Other computer programs that reconstruct ancestral states on phylogenetic trees include CLADOS (Nixon, 1992) and most programs that search for parsimonious trees (e.g., PAUP [Swofford, 1991]).

One simple use of these reconstructions is to check that the history indicated is consistent with a proposed explanation (Greene, 1986; Coddington, 1988). Proposed explanations often make claims about the direction of evolution, or the context of arisal of a trait. For instance, an adaptive explanation that a trait arose in response to some selective pressure would be imperiled should the phylogeny suggest that the occurrence of the supposed selective pressure actually followed the trait's arisal (Greene, 1986; Coddington, 1988; Baum and Larson, 1991), just as a proposal that a change in developmental program yielded a new structure would be imperiled should the phylogeny suggest the structure arose before the change in developmental program. Perhaps a trait was viewed as highly adaptive and thought to have been derived one or more times, but then phylogeny indicated that, contrary to expectations, it was lost occasionally (Coddington, 1986; Donoghue, 1989).

A phylogenetic perspective can uncover a consistent, repeated pattern in the evolution of a trait. For instance, a particular structure may have arisen in each of several independent lineages after members of the lineage evolved a particular behavior. Such correlations between the evolution of one character and that of another can be important to establish the adaptive significance of a trait, at least insofar as "adaptation" refers to the forces at work in the trait's original fixation in lineages as opposed to the forces involved in the trait's maintenance (Gould and Vrba, 1982; Coddington, 1988). Correlations can also establish the constraining effect that one character can have on another. Methods to study the phylogenetic correlation of one trait with another have attracted attention especially in the last decade (Clutton-Brock and Harvey, 1977, 1984; Harvey and Mace, 1982; Ridley, 1983, 1986, 1989; Stearns, 1983; Felsenstein, 1985a; Cheverud et al., 1985; Huey and Bennett, 1987; Pagel and Harvey, 1988; Burt, 1989; Bell, 1989; W. Maddison, 1990; Gittleman and Kot, 1990; M. Lynch, 1991; Harvey and Pagel, 1991). These methods have been referred to collectively as "the Comparative Method" (Ridley, 1983; Felsenstein, 1985a; Harvey and Pagel, 1991; Bell, 1989), although this name is misleading given the many other methods in phylogenetic biology that are also comparative. (It is rather like calling analysis of variance "the Statistical Method"!)

Some of these correlation methods seek patterns in character change (Ridley, 1983; Felsenstein, 1985a; Huey and Bennett, 1987; W. Maddison, 1990); others seek patterns in character variation (Harvey and Mace, 1982; Stearns, 1983; Cheverud et al., 1985; Grafen, 1989; Bell, 1989; Gittleman and Kot, 1990). Though this distinction may seem minor, and indeed some methods like Felsenstein's can be described either way (e.g., Grafen, 1989), it represents a rather deep difference in viewpoint (W. Maddison, 1990). Whatever their goals, methods that partition variation, if they are not based on models of evolutionary processes and events, risk yielding results that merely describe instead of test process. We should not be seeking a static correlation of occurrences of states, even if we can improve the accuracy of its estimation by using phylogenetic information to compensate for the non-independence of points. Rather, we should seek the correlation of character *changes*. Of course, an evolutionary, dynamic model of character evolution may direct us to study patterns of character variation. But our methods must be motivated by a dynamic view, and not merely taken from the standard statistical toolbox, because the notion of "correlation" depends on the exact evolutionary process hypothesis tested. As W. Maddison (1990) noted, constraint can yield different patterns of character correlation than can adaptation. Nonetheless, all of the authors cited above agree on one point despite their differences in approach: correlations between characters should be sought in the context of phylogeny, and the dependencies between data points created by the common histories of phylogeny cannot be ignored.

"Constraint", defined as the reduction or restriction of certain evolutionary changes in certain contexts, can be approached phylogenetically. Tests have been developed to determine whether character changes are clustered (Sanderson, 1991) or concentrated in particular regions of the phylogeny (W. Maddison, 1990). Such tests might be used to show, for instance, that one character evolves a particular state more readily when in the context of a permitting state of a second character. Similar tests might be applied to the question of whether characters develop a "burden"; that is, they become less likely to change because other characters subsequently evolved come to depend on them as a developmental and functional foundation (Reidl, 1978; Donoghue, 1989).

One set of constraints on morphological evolution comes from development (Maynard Smith et al., 1985). If phenotypes move in evolutionary time through an adaptive landscape, their movement is not completely free, but rather constrained by developmental mechanisms to a "highway system" by which some phenotypes may be inaccessible and others more distant than they might otherwise appear. One would hope that consistent patterns in character evolution seen in phylogenetic trees might reflect not only the topography of the landscape (adaptation), but also the highways to which movement is restricted (constraint). Of course, determining which is responsible will not always be easy (Wake, 1991).

To detect such patterns, testing for a correlation between characters is not necessarily our goal. Instead, we may be looking for consistency in the pathway taken — for instance, from state A, state B is almost never evolved, whereas state C (perhaps solving the same adaptive problem) is. Our methods to determine consistency in the pathway taken need much work. Several methods (Lanave, et al., 1984; Ritland and Clegg, 1987; Barry and Hartigan, 1987; Hendy, 1989; Williams and Fitch, 1990; D. Maddison, 1990; Janson, 1992) attempt to discover parameters relating to the relative probability of changes between states. Should we find consistent rules in the pathway character evolution has taken, then we may learn something about the forces or constraints involved. These methods can estimate parameters that might apply either to individual characters or to whole suites of characters. They are discussed in more detail in the next chapter.

The parameters of interest may involve not the specifics of what character states change to what other states, but rather they may involve overall rates of change and convergence. The literature on evolutionary rates is extensive, especially for molecular characters (e.g., Gillespie, 1986), in part because clock-like behavior could have implications for phylogeny reconstruction (Felsenstein, 1988a, and references therein). Among the questions that can be asked is whether different groups of organisms or different classes of characters differ in their rates of homoplasy (e.g., Sanderson and Donoghue, 1989).

Correlation between phylogenies

While processes such as adaptation can yield correlations between different characters on a phylogenetic tree, other processes can yield correlations between the phylogenies of different organisms. For instance, two species with a close ecological relationship, such as a parasite and its host, might have congruent patterns of phylogenetic branching because they have evolved and speciated together (Brooks, 1981, 1985, 1988; Mitter and Brooks, 1983; Farrell and Mitter, 1990; Hafner and Nadler, 1990; Page, 1990a,b; Ronquist and Nylin, 1990; Brooks and McLennan, 1991). Even species without such intimate ties might show congruent phylogenies because they have speciated similarly following successive fragmentation of their common habitat (Rosen, 1976, 1978; Platnick and Nelson, 1978; Simberloff, 1987; Brooks and McLennan, 1991). For studies of cospeciation and biogeography, a central focus is the development of techniques for comparing the forms of phylogenetic trees (Goodman et al., 1979; Brooks, 1981, 1990; Page, 1988; Farrell and Mitter, 1990), such as those implemented in the computer program COMPONENT (Page, 1989, in press).

The parallelism of species phylogenies with the fragmentation of their habitats or hosts has an analogy at the genetic level, with the species being like the geographical area and the species' genes being like the inhabitants of the area (although this analogy is not quite apt, given that genes are components of species and not independent). As the species divides into two, its inhabitants (genes) find themselves divided into two gene pools. With continued speciation the original species has yielded a full branching phylogeny of descendant species. As each of the genes of the genome was passed down on either side of these successive speciation events, its own history unfolded as a branching gene phylogeny. Although one might expect that each locus in the genome would have a gene phylogeny exactly concordant with the species phylogeny containing it, this is not necessarily the case (Goodman et al., 1979). If you took a gene from each of two sister species, it is unlikely that their most recent common ancestral gene would have been found exactly at the time of divergence of the two species, but more likely at some time before, in the ancestral species. If the common ancestral gene was far enough back in time, it might have occurred even before previous speciation events as well. With disturbing probability, this can allow the gene to have a different branching pattern than that of the species and other genes (Pamilo and Nei, 1988; Takahata, 1989). Species of sexual organisms are like communities of genes, and an understanding of species phylogeny will involve the reconciliation of the phylogenies of many separate genes into an aggregate phylogeny that describes the branching events in the bulk of the genes. On occasion, there will not be a single simple phylogeny that explains the bulk of the genes, for the genes of species of hybrid origin will have their ancestry either in one or the other of the lines that hybridized (Sneath et al., 1975).

There will be some special genetic elements that behave as renegades, differing drastically in their history from the majority of the genome, due to special mechanisms such as horizontal transfer (Doolittle et al., 1990; Kidwell, in press). The number of transfer events might be estimated by comparing the element's phylogeny with the genomic phylogeny (Valdez and Piñero, 1992), just as the number of host shifts might be estimated by comparing the parasites' phylogeny with that of their hosts, or the number of geographical dispersal events might be estimated by comparing a species phylogeny with the proposed history of their inhabited areas (Brooks, 1981, 1990; Wiley, 1988; Futuyma and McCafferty, 1991).

Discordance between host and parasite phylogeny might also be explained as due to hidden speciation and extinction (Page, 1988), much as discrepancies between a gene phylogeny and the species phylogeny can be explained by duplication of gene loci, passage of multiple loci through speciation events, and extinction of some of the loci (Goodman et al., 1979). Methods to quantify the required amount of hidden duplication and extinction have been developed in the molecular context (Goodman et al., 1979); this work is applicable as well to the study of hosts and parasites or biogeography (Page, 1988, 1990a,b).

Whether species are following the same path through history because of tight coevolution, or merely because of their sharing a similar habitat, is of course an important question. To answer such questions, comparison of both the phylogenies and the character evolution in the different groups needs to be made (Brooks and McLennan, 1991). If the phylogenies are more or less congruent, and phylogenetic changes in host defenses coincide with changes in parasite offenses, then an arms race is indicated. Little work has been done, however, on how one might statistically test correlated character evolution between different phylogenies.

Molecular evolution and population genetics

The explosion of comparative molecular data has not only given more data with which to reconstruct phylogeny, but also more characters whose processes of evolution might be the subject of study. Many of the comments above on how phylogeny can and needs to be considered in investigating character evolution also apply to molecular characters. One advantage of sequence data is that, with certain qualifications, different nucleotide sites might be expected to have more or less the same evolutionary behavior, allowing data from different sites to be summed. In part for this reason, molecular data have been the focus of theoretical work on understanding the parameters of character evolution (Gojobori et al., 1982; Fitch, 1986; Barry and Hartigan, 1987; Nei, 1987; Ritland and Clegg, 1987; Rempe, 1988; Gillespie, 1989).

With increasing frequency such theoretical work uses a phylogenetic perspective to examine the evolution of multiple sequences. The non-phylogenetic analytical approach from which molecular evolutionists have had to escape is not the scattergram but the pairwise comparison. Pairwise comparisons of sequences are popular but often do not suffice, insofar as they ignore the fact that some species (or genes) have a more recent shared history than do others. Ignoring the non-independence of the different sequences can yield poor estimates of parameters like population size (Felsenstein, in press a), just as ignoring non-independence of taxa yields poor estimates of character correlation.

One special problem with molecular data is that of alignment. Unless one wishes to align sequences for purely functional comparisons, sequence alignment is implicitly an historical reconstruction, as one is reconstructing the history of insertions, deletions and substitutions. These historical events took place on a gene tree or phylogeny, and without considering phylogeny one cannot accurately assess how many insertion or deletion events a particular multiple-sequence alignment would have required. This point has been well recognized by Sankoff (1975), Sankoff and Cedergren (1983), Feng and Doolittle (1987), Felsenstein (1988a), and Hein (1989), who have advocated aligning sequences in the context of, or simultaneously with, the reconstruction of phylogeny.

Phylogenetic theory has usually taken the luxury of restricting its consideration to strictly branching phylogenetic histories. However, phylogenies can have reticulations — anastomoses — through hybridization, recombination, and horizontal transfer. These problems may be particularly acute in some plants where hybridization is feared rampant, in bacteria where horizontal transfer could be common, and below the species level where sex and recombination occur. While there may be some hope in detecting these processes with morphological characters, using conflicting apomorphies as evidence (Bremer and Wanntorp, 1979; Wagner, 1983; Wanntorp, 1983b; Nelson, 1983; Funk, 1985; but see McDade, 1990), there is a much better chance with molecular characters because of the discrete inheritance and linear sequence of DNA (Sneath et al., 1975). A short segment of DNA may have a unique branching phylogenetic tree as its history, but this history may differ from other pieces of DNA because of the process of recombination. Each nucleotide base must have a strictly tree-like history, but even adjacent bases could have had different phylogenetic histories (Sneath, 1975; Hudson and Kaplan, 1985; Hein, 1990a). For example, as the mitochondrial DNA of humans lacks recombination, it has a single phylogenetic history, including a single ancestral copy, by necessity present in one of our ancestors (Cann et al., 1987). But in our nuclear genome, there are presumably thousands of short segments of DNA with separate phylogenetic histories, each traceable to separate ancestral pieces of DNA, spread through a number of ancestral humans. Whenever one piece of DNA suggests a phylogeny different from another piece, one of the anastomosing processes (gene flow, hybridization, recombination, gene conversion, lineage sorting) may be implicated. In plants, for instance, comparison of phylogenetic trees from chloroplast and nuclear DNA has provided clear evidence of hybridization (Reisberg and Soltis, 1991).

Methods to compare gene phylogenies and species phylogenies have been discussed above in the section "Correlation between phylogenies".

Methods to measure rates of recombination or gene conversion were initially done with only partial reference to phylogeny (Sawyer, 1989; Stephens, 1985; Hudson and Kaplan, 1985). Newer methods use phylogeny more directly to find recombined or converted regions (Koop et al., 1989; Hein, 1990a). Hein's (1990a) method in fact attempts to reconstruct the separate gene trees for adjacent recombined regions.

Population genetics processes are also approachable phylogenetically (Avise, 1989). If the phylogeny of genes taken from different members of a species is known, then it may be used to infer gene flow (Slatkin and Maddison, 1989, 1990; Maddison and Slatkin, 1991), effective population size (Felsenstein, in press a,b), phenotypic effects of mutations (Templeton et al., 1987, 1988), or natural selection (Golding and Felsenstein, 1990; McDonald and Kreitman, 1991; Hey, 1991). The history of population subdivision and branching can be approached by estimating phylogenies of genes within these populations (Avise et al., 1987), but caution needs to be taken because different genes may have phylogenies differing from each other and from that of the populations, as their splits may extend deeper than the splitting of the populations (Tajima, 1983; Pamilo and Nei, 1988; Takahata, 1989, 1991; Wu, 1991). This is a problem not only in understanding population histories, but also in reconstructing phylogenies among closely related species.

Gene phylogenies within species are not the only useful phylogenies for addressing population genetics processes: between-species phylogenies also can play a role. For example, selection within species may be detectable using between-species phylogenies (Golding and Felsenstein, 1990). In general, between-species phylogenies must have the power to test theories about population genetic processes, at least if population genetics has any long-term importance to evolution. That is, if our theories of genetic process are to explain successfully biological evolution and diversity, they must yield predictions consistent with our observed phylogenetic patterns. We might note, however, that M. Lynch (1989) legitimately makes the converse statement (see also p. 40).

Paleontology

One field where evolutionary history is obviously central is paleontology, and explicit consideration of the history of phylogenetic branching is important to paleontological inferences (Cracraft, 1981; Novacek and Norell, 1982; Fisher, 1991; Doyle and Donoghue, in press). A phylogeny can indicate deeper-than-observed minimum ages to groups by the simple principle that if one lineage has been observed in old strata, its sister group's lineage must be at least that old (Hennig, 1966; Norell, 1992). This combined approach to aging groups is resulting in a revised view of the eutherian mammal diversification (Norell, 1992). By the realization that the full phylogenetic tree needs to be considered instead of a ranked (possibly paraphyletic) classification, a phylogenetic approach to extinction may also challenge notions such as that of a 26-million-year cycle (Patterson and Smith, 1987; Smith and Patterson, 1988).

Paleoecology depends on reconstructions of an organism's structures or habits that are at least partially based on knowledge of close, perhaps extant, relatives. While it may be sufficient to adopt a phenetic view ("predict states of a taxon by those of taxa similar to it"), one should attempt phylogenetic use of criteria like parsimony or maximum likelihood to predict unobserved states. One could trace the evolution of the character (Chapter 13) and see what states are assigned to the incompletely known fossil groups.

Outside of evolutionary biology

Branching histories are not restricted to evolutionary biology. A branching process of phylogenetic descent is seen not only in the descent of species, genes, and geographical areas, as we have already discussed, but also in the descent of cell lineages in development, human languages, and manuscript traditions. Phylogenetic techniques derived in biology have been applied to the study of languages and manuscript traditions (Platnick and Cameron, 1977; Cameron, 1987; Lee, 1989), and one might imagine biogeographical or population-genetic techniques being applied to the study of cell migration in development. Of course, developments in these other fields could also be imported into phylogenetic biology. Phylogenetic biology may provide theory even to philosophers, where a "tree thinking" approach may clarify such philosophical issues as the nature of individuality (de Queiroz, 1988).

Going both ways

We have discussed how phylogeny is important in answering questions in evolutionary biology, but it is expected that the interplay between history-oriented phylogenetic theory and process-oriented evolutionary theory will go both ways. We might ask, how can the other biological disciplines help us better reconstruct phylogeny? Certainly discussions of processes and rates of character evolution have been used to argue in favor of one or another method of reconstructing phylogeny (Felsenstein, 1988a). But any of the other fields discussed above could have an impact on how phylogeny is reconstructed. For instance, developmental biology will supply phylogenetic biologists with important data to deal with character coding in continuous characters, character state ordering, and other problems with morphological data. Molecular biologists might inform phylogeneticists regarding biases in transitions versus transversions, and the expected frequency of horizontal transfer and various genome rearranging events, information that could be critical in properly reconstructing phylogeny from molecular data. The exchange of information to and from phylogenetic biology is discussed further in Chapter 4.

4. INTRODUCTION TO PHYLOGENETIC INFERENCE

MacClade's focus is inferring evolutionary history and understanding its implications. In this chapter we provide an introduction to relevant terms and a theoretical background.

Trees and their terms

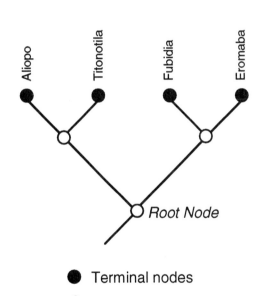

Root Node

● Terminal nodes
○ Internal nodes

A diagram depicting a phylogenetic tree has a simple form of branching lineages. The point at which a lineage branches or ends is referred to as a **node** (also sometimes called a vertex). Between the nodes are the **internodes** or edges. A tree is therefore composed of nodes and internodes. A tree is rooted if it has a node that is designated as the **root**. With the root so designated the tree has polarity, and one can speak of nodes being **ancestors** or **descendants** of one another. In this book we will sometimes refer to nodes above or below other nodes, meaning nodes descendant or ancestral, respectively, following MacClade's usual tree orientation with time proceeding from bottom to top. Some of the nodes are at the tips of branches with no descendants— these are the **terminal nodes**, and they correspond to observed taxa. These observed taxa could be individual genes, or individual species, or they could represent higher taxa such as genera or families. Nodes ancestral to the terminal nodes are **internal nodes**; they generally refer to unobserved (hypothetical) lineages, unless a claim is being made that an observed taxon is an actual ancestor. In MacClade, the term "root" is used specifically for the internal node that is the most recent common ancestor of all other nodes in the tree, as shown at left. (Note that PAUP 3 uses "root" to refer to an ancestor just below the most recent common ancestor; Swofford, 1991.) As shown in the diagram at left, MacClade draws an internode dangling below the root even though there is no node at its bottom end. This dangling internode is drawn to yield a larger object for ease of manipulating the root node and also to suggest the tree's connection with the rest of the tree of life.

Nodes always have only one immediate ancestor unless there is reticulation or hybridization. (Reticulate trees cannot be directly represented in MacClade.) In a fully **dichotomous** tree each node has exactly two descendants. A **polytomous** node has more than two descendant nodes. There are at least two interpretations of a polytomous node (W. Maddison, 1989; see Chapter 12), one in which it represents uncertainty in relationships and another in which it represents multiple simultaneous branching.

Branch { Node / Internode

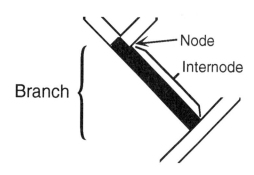

Branch { — Node / Internode

In MacClade the term **branch** is used to refer to a node plus the internode immediately below it. In MacClade's graphical style this would be drawn as shown in the bottom left figure.

Because it is difficult to display graphically all of the required information about a node in the small region of the node itself, MacClade sometimes uses the whole branch to display information that actually refers to the node at the top of the branch. For instance, in tracing the evolution of a character, MacClade shades the whole branch to indicate what character states are reconstructed at the node at the top of the branch (see the section "Interpreting the character tracing" in Chapter 13). The user must be aware of such distinctions: although MacClade treats the branch as a single graphical unit, the information displayed on the branch sometimes refers to the node at the top of the branch (e.g., Trace Character's indication of states on a node) and sometimes refers to the internode of the branch (e.g., Trace All Changes' indication of changes that occur along the internode).

A **monophyletic group**, called a **clade**, consists of an ancestor and all of its descendants. Because our collections from tropical forests are still incomplete and time machines are not yet available, we can never have in front of us *all* of the descendants of a common ancestor. Thus when a claim is made that a recognized group, for example "birds", is monophyletic, it means that there exists a clade of which the known birds represent the only and all of the sampled members. Usually, it is convenient to use a qualified concept of monophyly that restricts itself to the sample of organisms under consideration (e.g., the set of taxa in your data file): a group of these organisms is monophyletic if it has a single most recent common ancestor that is not also an ancestor of organisms in the sample that are not included in the group. This definition is more useful than the one that began this paragraph not only because it is applicable to samples of organisms. It also avoids complications within species by disallowing the designation "monophyletic" for groups whose most recent common ancestors are not unique to them, as can happen in phylogenies with reticulations (for instance within species, de Queiroz and Donoghue, 1990). In terms of nodes on a tree diagram, a **clade** includes a node and all nodes descendant from it.

The **ingroup** is a set of taxa, often assumed monophyletic, designated as being the focus of interest, as compared to the **outgroups**, which are brought into the analysis to provide a broader phylogenetic context to aid in determining the root of the ingroup or ancestral states (Farris, 1972, 1982; Watrous and Wheeler, 1981; Maddison et al., 1984). In MacClade no distinction is made between ingroup and outgroups; it is up to you to formulate and maintain your own distinctions as you work with the program. A **taxon** is one or a group of species (or genes, or other entities), and might be either a clade in your tree, or a taxonomic unit placed in terminal position on the tree (a **terminal taxon**, or "OTU", or

"EU"). As should be clear from context, sometimes we will use the term "taxon" to refer specifically to a terminal taxon.

Not all authors would agree precisely with our definitions of terms concerning trees, for the tree diagrams used throughout phylogenetic biology have different meanings to different authors (for discussion see Nelson, 1974; Platnick, 1977; Hull, 1979; Eldredge and Cracraft, 1980; Nelson and Platnick, 1981; Wiley, 1981). A branching diagram in the form of a tree might be interpreted to represent:

1. *The hypothesized phylogenetic history, with lines representing lineages descending through time and branch points representing speciation events.* If the diagram places two observed species on separate terminal branches next to one another, this means that they share a common ancestor unique to them, and neither is the ancestor of the other. If one had been an ancestor, it would have been placed directly at an internal node of the tree diagram. Thus, the diagram depicts both recency of common ancestry *and* whether or not observed taxa are ancestors.

2. *The relative recency of common ancestry of the observed taxa.* This interpretation differs from interpretation 1 in that the tree diagram is silent on the issue as to whether any of the observed taxa might be ancestors of other observed taxa. By placing several observed taxa in a clade, the diagram claims only that these taxa share a common ancestor not shared by other taxa outside the clade. Even though each observed taxon is placed in terminal position on the diagram, separated from the internal nodes by an internode, the internode leading up to the terminal node might or might not have existed in nature — no claim is made either way. That is, the diagram allows the possibility that the observed taxon might actually be the ancestral lineage represented by the internal node to which it is connected.

3. *The hierarchical distribution of shared, derived, homologous character states (synapomorphies).* A "clade" in the diagram represents not necessarily a group of taxa sharing uniquely a common ancestor, but rather a group of taxa united by concordant synapomorphies; the internode below the clade represents the evolutionary derivation of these synapomorphies. Although this interpretation does not speak of lineages and speciation, it is evolutionary insofar as it summarizes evolutionary changes.

4. *The hierarchical distribution of shared characteristics.* Various characteristics are more or less general in their distribution and it is presumed that their generalities form a nested hierarchy. This hierarchy might arise by branching evolution, or by the laws of ontogeny, or by some other cause. Placing taxa in the same "clade" does not necessarily mean that they share an evolutionary

innovation, but rather that they share a similarity. This interpretation makes no claims about evolution.

How are MacClade's tree diagrams to be interpreted? Although you may be able to use MacClade regardless of which of the four interpretations you prefer, our perspective (and MacClade's) is very much one of lineages, ancestors and branching. As such, the appropriate interpretations are 1 or 2.

The distinction between interpretations 1 (recency of common ancestry and ancestral status) and 2 (recency of common ancestry only) has been considered an important distinction (Nelson, 1974; Platnick, 1977), because the difficulty of finding evidence that a species is ancestral leads some authors to prefer remaining silent on the ancestral status of species. However important this distinction may be, we do not view MacClade as dealing solely with one or the other interpretation. Indeed, in the context of MacClade it is difficult to maintain a crisp distinction. First of all, a diagram or hypothesis need not be completely specific nor completely silent on the issue of ancestry. Perhaps you know of derived characteristics for some species, and can therefore make strong claims that they are not ancestral, while for other species you have no evidence about their status as ancestors. A tree diagram might be annotated to indicate which species are claimed to be terminal, and which species might be either ancestral or terminal. Second, as soon as you indicate that an observed taxon is in ancestral position (as can be done in MacClade), the tree at least partially commits itself to claims about ancestral status. Such a claim might be supported by stratigraphic parsimony (Fisher, 1991, 1992). Third, and perhaps most common and most subtle, as soon as MacClade reconstructs a change on a terminal branch, and you accept this reconstruction as a working hypothesis, then the tree can no longer be considered silent on the issue of ancestry. The change on the terminal branch implies that the terminal branch exists, that is, that the observed taxon is in fact terminal and not ancestral, and therefore it would be inconsistent both to accept the hypothesis of change and simultaneously to allow for the possibility that the taxon was ancestral. Fourth, various of MacClade's features, such as the concentrated-changes character-correlation test, and the random generation of characters on the tree, assume that changes can occur on terminal branches. If you use these features, you are assuming that the tree is fully specific about ancestral status, that is, that *all* observed taxa that are not explicitly placed as ancestors are actually terminal.

Various terms have been applied to the various interpretations of tree diagrams (Platnick, 1977; Eldredge and Cracraft, 1980; Wiley, 1981; Hendy and Penny, 1984), but since their usage varies we will tend to avoid making fine distinctions. The term "phylogenetic tree" has been used for interpretation 1, the fully specific hypothesis of branching of ancestors and descendants, but sometimes the term is used to refer to the history itself (not just our hypothesis of it). "Cladogram" has been used variously for interpretations 1, 2, 3, and 4, while "synapomorphy diagram" has been used for 3 and 4. To avoid misleading readers accustomed to a particular interpretation of these words, especially "cladogram", and for the sake of compactness, we will most commonly use the word "tree" when we refer to the structures displayed by MacClade. Occasionally we will use the term "phylogenetic trees" to refer to our hypothesis about phylogenetic history or even to refer to the history itself. We apologize to the reader for any confusion this may cause. It should be clear from the context whether we are referring to the history (e.g., in most of Chapter 3), the hypothesis (e.g., in this chapter), or either. As discussed, a "phylogenetic tree", as we use the term, may have some elements of both interpretations 1 and 2.

Characters and their terms

A **character** can be viewed as a set of alternative conditions, called **character states**, that are considered able to evolve one to another. Thus the character "eye color" might consist of the states "eyes blue" and "eyes red", and it is assumed that red eyes can evolve into blue eyes and vice versa. A goal of phylogenetic analysis might be to discover how these different conditions might have evolved into one another: which is the ancestral condition, whether and where convergence has occurred, and so on. The decision as to what states can be considered part of the same character (i.e., what conditions represent transformations of one another; what conditions are homologous) may be made prior to a phylogenetic analysis, or it may be made simultaneously (Sankoff and Rousseau, 1975; Patterson, 1982). Simultaneous decisions about phylogeny and which features can be considered states of the same character are generally not made in computer phylogenetic analysis, as available programs usually require specification of states and characters beforehand. One exception is simultaneous sequence alignment and phylogeny reconstruction with molecular data (Sankoff and Rousseau, 1975; Hein, 1989).

Within the context of a particular group of organisms, an **apomorphy** is a character state derived within the group, while a **plesiomorphy** is the ancestral character state (the state at the most recent common ancestor of the group). A derived character state shared by members of a group is a **synapomorphy** of the members of the group, and an **autapomorphy** of the group. When a character state evolves more than once in different branches of the tree, there is **homoplasy**. That is, homoplasy is similarity that cannot be directly attributed to common ancestry. If the character is of a state, then it changes, then reverses to its original state, the process is called **reversal**. If the state evolves separately on different branches of the phylogenetic tree (branches that are not in ancestor-descendant relationship) the process is called **convergence** or **parallelism**. The concept of homoplasy can be made slightly broader by saying that whenever a character evolved with more changes or more costly changes (in the sense of "cost" used in a parsimony analysis) than the minimum conceivable, then homoplasy is implied.

Coding character states

Before a collection of data, perhaps consisting of illustrations of mouth parts, leaf shapes, or molecular sequencing gels, can be used in computer-based analysis, the data need to be **coded** in a form acceptable to the computer program to be used. Coding the various forms of a character as states is a crucial but often under-appreciated step of phylogenetic analysis (Meacham, 1984; Pogue and Mickevich, 1990; Stevens, 1991). A character may naturally be **discrete-valued** ("red", "blue", "green"; "absent, "present"), or it may have gradations of value and be **continuous-valued** (0.197, 0.231, 0.224, 0.258). Even if it is a continuous character, it may be coded for convenience as if it were discrete, with certain ranges of values grouped together as one state (e.g., Archie, 1985; Stevens, 1991). Even when a character seems discrete, it may have states whose separation is not as clear as one would like. Decisions made in coding the character will have an effect on all later stages of phylogenetic analysis.

A clear distinction should be made between how states should be coded in theory, and what codings can be accepted by the available computer programs. For instance, before computer programs could accept multistate characters, characters were decomposed by additive binary recoding (Sokal and Sneath, 1963), often with unexpected consequences in implicitly ordering the states. Before computer programs could accept polymorphic taxa, these may have been coded as having missing data (Nixon and Davis, 1991). Attempts to use certain assumptions about character evolution often required special coding methods when those assumptions were not directly available in the computer programs. For instance, additive recoding (e.g., O'Grady and Deets, 1987) is needed when programs can not directly handle character state trees. The "X-coding" of Doyle and Donoghue (1986) attempted to capture special assumptions about transformability between states, but now the assumptions can be approximated by step matrices (see below). Even now there are some situations that available computer programs do not directly handle, and recoding remains an important option. (Note for instance the discussion about ancestral polymorphisms below and in Chapter 5.) Please take the time to learn the full capabilities of MacClade before recoding your data: it can handle missing data, polymorphic or uncertain states, multistate characters with various assumptions about transformations, characters with as many as 26 discrete states, and, in a limited way, continuous-valued characters.

Polymorphisms and missing data

A given terminal taxon may be **monomorphic**, having a single state ("A"), or **polymorphic**, having multiple states ("A and C"), or of **uncertain** state ("A or C"), or its condition may be completely unknown (**missing data**). In MacClade, each of these codings is allowed, but it is important to consider certain dangers of coding polymorphisms and missing data.

Before you fill your data matrix with codings of terminal taxa having multiple states (polymorphisms), you should think carefully about the cautions given by Nixon and Davis (1991). Although they phrase their objection to polymorphisms in terms of missing data codings, their main point holds whether the polymorphism is coded as missing data or directly as can be done in MacClade. The potential difficulty arises when a terminal taxon is polymorphic in more than one character. If the terminal taxon had been decomposed into monomorphic component parts, it might be seen that the state distributions of the two characters interact, such that some combinations of states are not parsimonious combinations for the most recent common ancestor of the terminal taxon under any potential arrangement of the component parts. Leaving the taxon intact but polymorphic hides the problems and allows the algorithms to use these combinations despite the fact that they are not parsimonious. This problem is another incarnation of the problem discussed by Maddison et al. (1984:96) concerning unresolved outgroups and by W. Maddison (1989) concerning the length of trees with soft polytomies. In every case, an unresolved region of the phylogeny is analyzed without adequately considering interactions between characters.

With terminal taxa the question is, should one always avoid polymorphic codings and either infer an ancestral state for the taxon or decompose it and use the monomorphic component parts? Using an inferred ancestral state would avoid the problem, could the inference be well defended. Decomposing the taxon could also be done, but its success depends on how well the component parts are known. For instance, perhaps your knowledge that a genus is polymorphic comes from studies that were able to identify specimens only to genus. Decomposition could not then be done effectively. Success of decomposition depends also on whether you are prepared to take on the task of analyzing the components' phylogeny at the same time as the rest of your taxa. (What if the polymorphic terminal taxon was "Insecta"?) In some circumstances, you must simply admit that you have incomplete information, and leave the taxon coded as polymorphic. After all, assuming one lacks precise information about the monomorphic components, there is a most-parsimonious interpretation of evolution within polymorphic terminal taxa, and this is what MacClade allows. Unless one is also inclined to fear that goblins rearrange the furniture when one is out of the room (see Sober [1983, 1988]), one can provisionally be satisfied with the parsimonious interpretation. Finally, decomposition may be inappropriate if reticulate evolution dominates within the taxon (for instance, with a species) and it is therefore not decomposable into monophyletic groups. Nonetheless, the points raised by Nixon and Davis (1991) do give one good reason to try to avoid polymorphic codings if possible.

A second problem with coding a character as polymorphic in a taxon has to do with limitations on the algorithms for reconstructing ancestral states. These algorithms assess alternative assignments of ancestral state to internal nodes. In most existing algorithms, including those in MacClade, the alternative assignments are mutually exclusive; that is, the internal node might have either state "yellow" or state "red", but not both at the same time. This prohibits ancestors from being polymorphic.

As described in Chapter 5, this restriction can be avoided if the character is coded so that its states refer to species and not to individuals (see Mickevich and Mitter, 1981; Farris, 1983:27). "Eye color yellow" is a character state of a salamander, not of a population or species of salamanders; "All individuals with yellow eyes" could be the character of the species. The character referring to species-states would have three states, all yellow, all red, and polymorphic. By using characters coded at the species level, the algorithms can allow ancestors to be polymorphic.

Is MacClade's ability to code a character as polymorphic ("0&1") in a taxon in the data matrix therefore not useful? We have just discussed how a polymorphic coding might be better decomposed into components, or that a polymorphic coding should be changed to a single-state coding reflecting the species-level condition of being polymorphic. However, there are reasons not to decompose or recode polymorphisms. If the terminal taxon is a higher taxon and the "polymorphism" amounts to uncertainty about the terminal taxon's ancestral state, then decomposition may be impractical and recoding inappropriate. If the terminal taxon is a species, then recoding may be impractical (too many states, step-matrix calculations too slow) and decomposition inappropriate. We will therefore often be forced to code the characters in a less-than-ideal way. At the very least, coding polymorphic taxa as polymorphic ("0&1") is better than coding them as having missing data. Finally, it may be best to save a copy of the data matrix with polymorphisms listed by organism-states so that the data file might be better used when better algorithms come out in the future that do allow ancestral polymorphisms.

Coding a taxon as having missing data in a character should also be done with caution. The character state possessed by a taxon may be unavailable either because the state is not known, or because the character is simply inapplicable to the taxon (e.g., feather type in a crocodile; Platnick et al. [1991]; Nixon and Davis [1991]). The missing data coding in MacClade is intended for the former case, when the state is simply unknown. Coding an organism as having missing data because the character does not apply to the organism can lead to implications of impossible ancestral states (Platnick et al., 1991; W. Maddison, in press). This can lead to an unjustified choice of trees, whenever such inapplicable codings are not isolated to a single group on the tree (W. Maddison, in press). When the character is inapplicable to a taxon, in general it would be better to code it as having an extra state "not present". The missing data coding would be better restricted to those circumstances in which the organism is presumed to have one of the character states, but which one it has is simply not known because of incomplete information.

Inferring the tree

Now that we have introduced the vocabulary of trees and characters, we can discuss a central problem of phylogenetic biology — the reconstruction of evolutionary history. This involves first the reconstruction of the past genetic connections of organisms (the phylogenetic tree). Reconstructing the phylogenetic tree is no simple task, but at least we know where to start. The echoes of phylogenetic history arrive to us in the traits of the organisms it has produced.

Similarities and differences among organisms have long been recognized as the primary evidence with which to reconstruct phylogeny, but exactly how this evidence is to be used has been the subject of considerable debate. The members of a clade share uniquely among themselves that branch of the tree that is their most recent common ancestor. Any new characteristics that evolved on that branch will mark the members of that clade, while species not part of the clade, that is, species not descended from this common ancestor, will lack these characteristics. By this logic Hennig (1966) argued that a clade can be recognized if its members share characteristics that are derived within the larger group of species being considered; that is, they have **synapomorphies**.

The clarity of this logic is unquestionable, but it does not fully prepare us for the real world. Character state distributions do not align themselves neatly into nested sets delimiting more and more restricted clades: some characters disagree with others as to what monophyletic groups they suggest. Convergences and reversals serve to make members of different clades appear to be marked by the same apomorphy, or members of a clade sometimes to lack the clade's insignia. Some criterion by which to balance conflicting evidence from different characters is therefore needed.

If our goal is to find scientific hypotheses that can most simply explain the observed data, then we might apply the criterion of **parsimony** to the conflicting evidence, and choose the tree that requires the least amount of convergence and reversal amongst the characters (Edwards and Cavalli-Sforza, 1964; Camin and Sokal, 1965; Farris, 1970, 1983; Fitch, 1971; Sober, 1988). A measure of the amount of evolutionary change required by a tree, therefore indicating the amount of convergence and reversal, is the **treelength**. Treelength is calculated by the weighted sum of steps in the characters (Chapter 14). It therefore depends on whether we weight characters differentially, and on what models we have about character evolution (discussed below in the section on "Inferring the history of character change", and in Chapters 5 and 14).

Parsimony methods bear some relationship to Hennigian argumentation (e.g., Wiley, 1981:139). For instance, grouping by characteristics determined to be derived by outgroup analysis can be justified by parsimony considerations (Farris, 1982; Maddison et al., 1984). However, when convergence and reversal make evidence from different characters conflict, then the subtle balancing that can occur in parsimony decisions may not have any simple parallel in Hennigian argumentation.

It is not always a trivial task to determine the tree with the minimum treelength. The methods used to search for the most-parsimonious tree or trees (for there are often many more than one tree with minimal treelength) depend upon the size and complexity of the data matrix. For smaller, simpler data matrices, one can use methods that guarantee the discovery of all most-parsimonious trees, such as branch-and-bound (Hendy and Penny, 1982; Swofford, 1991); these methods are available in several computer programs. For larger, more complex matrices, less-thorough heuristic searching methods can be employed using computer programs. Methods used by programs such as HENNIG86 (Farris, 1988), PAUP (Swofford, 1991), and PHYLIP (Felsenstein, 1991) begin by generating one or more starting trees, and rearranging the branches of the trees in hopes of discovering trees of smaller lengths. For the most complex matrices, multiple searches may be required to find the most-parsimonious trees (D. Maddison, 1991a; Maddison et al., 1992).

MacClade can be used to find parsimonious trees, but its automatic search capabilities are not as well developed as those in other programs.

Parsimony methods are not the only class of methods used to infer phylogenies. Four others commonly discussed in the literature are:

1. Distance techniques such as least-squares methods (Fitch and Margoliash, 1967; Cavalli-Sforza and Edwards, 1967; Bulmer, 1991), UPGMA (Sokal and Sneath, 1963; Sneath and Sokal, 1973) and Neighbor Joining (Saitou and Nei, 1987). These methods reduce the data to a matrix of distances between taxa, and build a tree from this matrix. This is a heterogeneous assemblage of methods

united by their use of pairwise distance matrices rather than by their goals or biological assumptions.

2. Maximum likelihood estimation (Edwards and Cavalli-Sforza, 1964; Edwards, 1970; Felsenstein, 1973, 1981b, 1992; Thompson, 1975, 1986; Barry and Hartigan, 1987; Kishino et al., 1990; Goldman, 1990; Weir, 1990). These statistical methods choose the phylogeny for which it would have been most likely to observe the data, under a particular stochastic model of evolution. To date these methods have focused on molecular and genetic data.

3. Methods based on invariants (Lake, 1987; Cavender and Felsenstein, 1987; Cavender, 1989; Jin and Nei, 1990; Sankoff, 1990; Sidow and Wilson, 1990, 1992; Navidi et al., 1991). This method calculates the value of a formula relating relative frequencies of various patterns of distributions of nucleotides, and chooses the tree that most closely matches the value of the formula predicted by a model of nucleotide sequence change.

4. Compatibility analyses (Le Quesne, 1974; Estabrook et al., 1976; Meacham and Estabrook, 1985). In these methods, which are closely related to parsimony methods, trees are constructed to maximize the number of characters that show no extra evolutionary changes (homoplasy) upon the tree.

While some work has been done determining the behavior of the methods under a few simplistic models of evolution for small numbers of taxa (e.g., Felsenstein, 1978b, 1979, 1981a; Sourdis and Krimbas, 1987; Sourdis and Nei, 1988; Hendy and Penny, 1989; Saitou and Imanishi, 1989; Fukami-Kobayashi and Tateno, 1991; Hasegawa et al., 1991; Hillis et al., 1992; Nei, 1992; Sidow and Wilson, 1992; Fitch and Ye, 1992), the behavior of each method under more realistic models that might be relevant for a particular data matrix is essentially unknown (Farris, 1983, 1986).

Each of these methods has advantages and disadvantages. Each can succeed or fail, depending upon the nature of the evolutionary process. Simple parsimony methods fail under some conditions in which some branches of the tree are much longer than other branches, as parsimony tends to group the long branches together, even if they do not belong together on the correct tree (Felsenstein, 1978b; Hendy and Penny, 1989). Most of the simulation studies use model trees with greatly unequal branch lengths, and show this behavior of parsimony (see review by Nei, 1992). UPGMA tends to fail if a molecular clock is not obeyed (see Felsenstein, 1988a; Nei, 1992; and references therein). Distance methods in general use a transformation function to convert the observed distances to transformed distances; the methods can fail if assumptions used to derive the transformation functions are violated (see examples given in Nei, 1992). Likelihood methods may also fail if the stochastic model used in the method is incorrect, although the behavior of likelihood methods when their assumptions are false has not been thoroughly investigated. For further details on the pros and cons of each of the methods, the reader is referred to the reviews by Felsenstein (1982, 1988a) and Swofford and Olsen (1990).

Character polarity

Since Hennig (1966), there has been a focus in phylogenetic systematics on character polarity and derived character states, because of the understanding that only shared derived traits indicate recency of common ancestry. However, exactly what is character polarity and what it is useful for are often poorly understood. Various statements about character evolution might be interpreted as statements about character polarity:

1. *State 0 is ancestral in the study group, and wherever state 1 occurs, it is derived from 0, and 2 derived from 1, and 0 is never derived from 1 nor 1 from 2.* This amounts to claiming that the character is irreversible with ancestral state 0. To some systematists, the notion of character polarity amounts to this strong statement of universal ancestral-derived relationship; we call this **global polarity**. (For this example, we chose state 0 arbitrarily as ancestral. The ancestral state need not always be designated as state 0, and we could have called the ancestral state "1" or "2".) One could imagine a weaker assumption about polarity, in which one specified not an absolute direction to evolution, but rather a tendency (perhaps stating that gains were twice as likely as losses).

2. *State 0 is ancestral in the study group.* This is a much weaker statement of character polarity, one that can be justified by outgroup analysis (Maddison et al., 1984), and which allows subsequent reversals to state 0; thus the ancestral-derived relationship of states 0 and 1 is not necessarily universal throughout the study group. This is **basal polarity**, as only the polarity of a basal change in the study group is specified.

3. *States 0, 1 and 2 form an ordered sequence,* such that it is two steps from 0 to 2 or 2 to 0, and one step between 0 and 1 or between 1 and 2. This is not a statement of character polarity or direction, since it does not say whether 0, 1 or 2 is ancestral, but it is a statement about character state **ordering**. It is important to understand that an ordered character does not imply which state is ancestral, and that a statement of ancestral state does not necessarily imply ordering or irreversibility (Meacham, 1984; Mabee, 1989).

Rooting the tree

If no presumption about global or basal polarity is made, then an entire tree can be rerooted on any of its branches, with each of these rerooted trees being of equal length. Ideally, our methods of tree inference would allow us to choose which of these branches is the ancestral branch — that is, which branch is the root of the tree. In the absence of an inferred root, we are left with a collection of candidate rooted trees, which in sum form a kind of consensus hypothesis typically called an "unrooted tree" (see example, p. 289).

Assumptions of global or basal polarity provide the power to choose the root of the study group tree, and to affect the reconstruction of the character's evolution. These assumptions make some tree rootings more parsimonious than others. It is perhaps obvious that assumptions such as character irreversibility can help root the tree, but milder assumptions about global polarity, such as those embodied in asymmetrical step matrices, can also have the power to choose the root of the tree (Maddison and Maddison, 1987; Wheeler, 1990).

Polarity assumptions are not, however, the only assumptions or evidence that can help choose a root to the tree. Indeed, we expect that the majority of studies in the future will infer phylogenies without explicit assumptions about character polarity. Two methods have been proposed for rooting trees that avoid specification of character polarity. First, if one incorporates into a tree inference not only the study groups but also any outgroups, then the root of the study group tree will be the branch that connects to the outgroups (Farris, 1972). Such an analysis will require assuming some phylogenetic structure, namely what groups might be considered outgroups and what groups comprise the study group. At no point in the analysis would one actually make an explicit assumption about ancestral states. In some circumstances including outgroups as extra taxa is equivalent to use of assumptions about character polarity, if the outgroup data are condensed into a claim about basal polarity (Maddison et al., 1984). However, in other circumstances, particularly when outgroup relationships are uncertain, it is better to avoid specifying character polarity and instead include all the outgroup taxa along with the study group during tree inference (Maddison et al., 1984). Second, by analyzing the composite phylogeny of duplicated genes, the point at which subtrees of separate gene copies attach to one another can indicate the root of the species tree (Iwabe et al., 1989). One can extend this method, and choose the root of a species tree to minimize the number of duplications and extinctions of genes required to fit a gene tree within the species tree (D. Maddison, unpublished). That is, for each candidate species tree, one can fit the contained gene tree so as to minimize the required number of duplications and extinctions of genes. One can then choose the rooted species tree with the minimum number of duplications and extinctions on the inferred gene tree.

How can you specify polarity or outgroups in MacClade? MacClade has no facility to specify directly basal polarity by designating which states are ancestral, as with PAUP's ANCSTATES command. Therefore, to use an assumption about ancestral states, you must use outgroups, for instance by entering a hypothetical taxon that has the proposed ancestral states, and maintaining it near the base of the tree as an outgroup. You can specify global polarity by setting a character's type to irreversible or an asymmetrical, user-defined type. Finally, you can incorporate observed outgroups directly into the analysis and maintain them near the base of the tree. MacClade has no facility to enforce the designation of some taxa as outgroups. Therefore, if some of your taxa are outgroups, it is your responsibility to maintain them apart from the ingroup and impose any phylogenetic structure within the outgroups you wish to assume.

Branch lengths

Although the first concern in reconstructing a phylogenetic tree is to determine the order of branching events that gave rise to the taxa, a second concern might be to reconstruct the lengths of the branches of the tree. Branch length is a term whose meaning varies in the literature. It can refer to:

1. The length in time between the node just ancestral to the branch and the node terminating the branch.

2. A parameter indicating the probability or expected amount of character change on the branch.

3. The actual number of evolutionary changes along the length of the branch.

4. The actual number of differences between the characters in the organisms at the start of the branch and the end of the branch. (This can differ from the previous if there is more than one change on the branch — evolution from A to G to A along a branch implies two actual changes but no net difference from start to end of branch.)

5. The reconstructed number of evolutionary changes along a branch.

To know branch lengths in the first sense would probably be most generally useful to evolutionary biology, but these time lengths are not easy to come by. Paleontological data can give us minimum ages of nodes. Molecular data can date nodes but at the cost of assumptions about the rates of molecular evolution.

In maximum likelihood estimation of trees, branch lengths in the second sense often come included as part of the estimated tree. In parsimony analyses, branch lengths tend to be derived secondarily, after trees are reconstructed. One way to estimate 2 to 4 would be to reconstruct ancestral states and use a reconstruction of character evolution to calculate probabilities, changes or differences. However, parsimony reconstructions usually underestimate the actual number of changes along the branch (Felsenstein, 1985a; Saitou, 1989). Parsimony reconstructs parallel changes on sister branches, or multiple changes along a single branch, as a single change. Various algorithms have been devised to estimate the first three sorts of branch lengths listed above, and these generally assume a stochastic model of evolution that allows one to estimate and incorporate the number of hidden changes into the estimate of branch length (Fitch and Bruschi, 1987; Hendy and Penny, 1989; Fitch and Bientema, 1990; Olsen, 1991; Tajima, 1992).

In parsimony-based computer programs, the branch length usually refers to the number (or amount, if weighted) of reconstructed changes on the branch. The number of reconstructed changes on a branch is sometimes taken to be an indication of support for the clade above it, with longer branches taken to provide greater evidence for the monophyly of the members of the clade. However, this interpretation is problematical, in part because the branch length is usually ambiguous as a result of equally parsimonious reconstructions of change, and in part because this ignores interactions between characters (see pp. 47, 119).

Character evolution: History versus models

It is along the branches of phylogenetic trees that the traits of organisms have evolved. As discussed in Chapter 3, study of phylogenetic character change is important in evolutionary biology. Such study can seek either a narrative description of the history of change, or a model of the process of change. In the remainder of this chapter, we will discuss these two, distinct aspects of our hypotheses of character change.

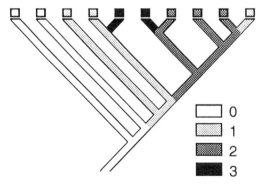

Hypothesis about the evolution of a particular character on a phylogeny (states of the character are indicated by shades)

- □ 0
- ▨ 1
- ▨ 2
- ■ 3

Imagine we have inferred a phylogeny for our study group. We might wish to know how a particular trait of interest evolved along the lineages of this phylogeny. We might propose a hypothesis of the pathways of change of the characteristic, as shown on the left. This hypothesis states that the ancestral lineage of the organisms had state 0 (indicated by white), with a later lineage evolving to state 1 (light gray), and then to state 2 (dark gray), and so on. This is a hypothesis about the **history of character change**: that is, what actually happened, lineage by lineage, during the course of evolution. It is a hypothesis about the history of the pathways taken by characters from one state to another through the course of evolution. In later chapters we will speak of "**reconstructions** of ancestral states", or "**tracings** of character evolution", or "a **mapping** of the character on the tree". These phrases are interchangeable; they amount to hypotheses of the history of character change.

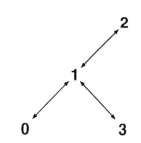

A possible-pathways model
(character state tree)

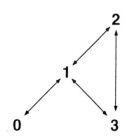

Another possible-pathways model
(character state graph)

It is important to distinguish between what happened, and our models as to how evolution in general happens. For instance, we might have reason to believe that some changes between states are possible while others are not. This would be a **possible-pathways model**. For example, in the possible-pathways model pictured on the left, a direct change from 0 to 1 is considered possible, but a direct change from 0 to 3 is not.

A possible-pathways model such as the one pictured at left, without closed circuits, can also be called a **character state tree**. However, if circuits are present, then the more general term of **character state graph** is appropriate. The most extreme character state graph in terms of the pathways allowed connects every state directly to every other state. Such a graph depicts the model underlying unordered characters, for which a change from any state to any other state can occur in a single step.

Although character state tree diagrams look like little phylogenetic trees linking character states, they are not, and they differ in the fundamental sense that phylogenetic trees purport to show what actually happened in evolution, while character state trees show what can in general happen in evolution. There has been some confusion on this point. The term "transformation series" has been applied to both the actual history of character change (e.g., Liebherr and Hajeck, 1990) and possible-pathways models (e.g., Mickevich and Weller 1990). There is also variation in the meaning of "character phylogeny", although the term is not as widely used. Hennig's use (1966:95) appears to correspond to the actual history of character change. Mickevich (1982:461) equates the term to a possible-pathways model; Mickevich and Weller (1990) use it as synonymous with the history of character change.

Hypotheses about what happened and what in general might happen, though fundamentally distinct, have an intimate relationship: in order to reconstruct the history of what happened, we need to assume something about what in general could happen, and in order to formulate theories about what in general happens in the evolutionary process, we may need to know something about what actually happened in evolution. Obviously one needs to step gingerly to avoid circularity, but it can be done, and we will now consider further the principles of inferring the history and the processes.

Inferring the history of character change

Now we will consider how to reconstruct the history of character change. We will presume that the phylogenetic tree is known, and that we have a character whose states are known in the taxa sampled. Our goal is to reconstruct the history of character changes along the branches of the phylogeny.

For a study group, with known phylogeny, there are numerous ways a particular character could have evolved resulting in the states observed in the terminal taxa. For example, for the following phylogeny,

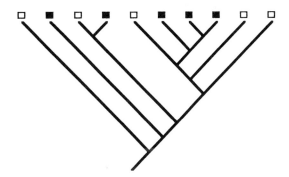

two possible historical reconstructions that would lead to the observed states are:

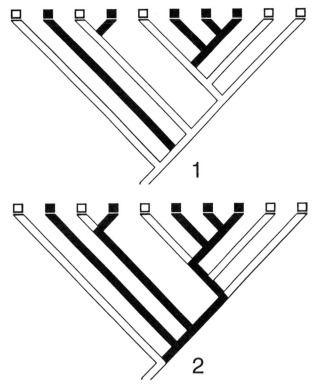

Assuming our goal is to reconstruct the history of character changes during evolution, how do we choose among these two and the hundreds of other possibilities?

One could imagine several methods of inference. Statistical methods such as **maximum likelihood** inference have been discussed in the context of reconstructing phylogenetic trees, but have been little explored in the context of reconstructing the history of character changes. These statistical methods explicitly assume a probabilistic model of character evolution in order to make historical inferences.

Currently, the most commonly used numerical method to reconstruct ancestral states is based on the criterion of parsimony. In its most basic form, **parsimony** chooses the historical reconstruction with the minimum number of evolutionary changes (Farris 1970, 1983; see also Chapter 5). We would thus choose reconstruction 1, as it entails 3 changes, over reconstruction 2, as it involves 5 changes.

Parsimony methods can incorporate some notions about evolutionary process even if they are not explicitly statistical. For example, you might assume that character evolution follows a character state tree as discussed above, or you might assume that Dollo's law (Farris, 1977) applies to a character. These assumptions place constraints or weights on the reconstructed character changes, and therefore alter which reconstruction is judged most parsimonious. The weight placed upon a particular sort of change is called its **cost**.

When changes are weighted in this way, the quantity that parsimony calculations attempt to minimize in judging reconstructions is the summed cost of all the changes. This summed cost is referred to as the number of **steps** in a character. (When weighted and summed over all characters it is the **treelength.**) Even though the term "step" would seem to connote a single discrete evolutionary change, in MacClade and PAUP "step" is used in a more general way as a unit of cost. A single evolutionary change might be measured as costing 1 step, or 2 steps, or even 1.31 steps (since MacClade allows continuous-valued costs). Further details concerning changes, steps, and lengths are given in Chapters 5 and 14.

Among the key assumptions used in a parsimony analysis therefore are the assignments of relative weights or costs to each type of change. The costs assigned to each type of change can be summarized in a **cost** or **step** **matrix** (for further details see Chapter 5). Although the term "cost matrix" (D. Maddison, 1990) is more general and perhaps more appropriate, we will use the term "step matrix" following recent use (Swofford and Olsen, 1990; Swofford, 1991). If we assign a cost of g to each gain of black, and a cost of l to each loss of black, we would have the step matrix shown on the left.

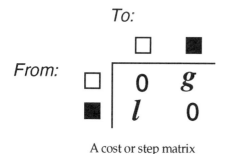

A cost or step matrix

Under this step matrix, reconstruction 1 entails a total cost of $3g$, and reconstruction 2 entails a cost of $4l + g$:

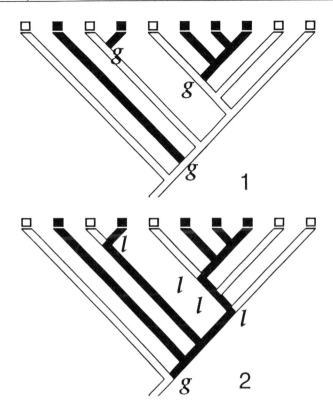

The upper reconstruction would be considered more parsimonious than the lower reconstruction if $3g$ was less than $4l + g$. Thus, if l and g were both 1, the upper reconstruction would be more parsimonious. If g were 2 and l were 1, the lower would be more parsimonious. Of course, there might be another reconstruction that is even more parsimonious.

Even after one has fully specified the assumptions behind a parsimony analysis, there remains the issue of how to find the reconstruction that is most parsimonious. Various algorithms have been devised to find the most-parsimonious reconstruction; these are used by MacClade and are described in detail in Chapter 5. Often there will be more than one most-parsimonious reconstruction — in fact, there can be several thousand reconstructions of equally low cost.

$$0 \longleftrightarrow 1 \longleftrightarrow 2 \longleftrightarrow 3$$

linearly ordered states

To:

From:		0	1	2	3
	0	0	1	2	3
	1	1	0	1	2
	2	2	1	0	1
	3	3	2	1	0

Step matrix derived
assuming linearly ordered states

To:

		0	1	2	3
From:	**0**	0.90	0.04	0.02	0.04
	1	0.08	0.80	0.10	0.02
	2	0.04	0.06	0.85	0.05
	3	0.20	0.12	0.08	0.60

Model specifying probabilities
of change between states

Where does the step matrix come from?

We have just discussed parsimony methods that find reconstructions of character change that minimize the total cost of character changes, where costs are measured implicitly or explicitly according to a cost or step matrix. The step matrix is therefore an assumption used in the reconstruction. We will here consider the sources from which this step matrix might be derived, in order to emphasize that it is based on a model of how evolution happens.

In the discussion above we described character state trees and character state graphs as possible-pathways models of character evolution. Assuming that our character evolves according to a possible-pathways model, then the cost of presuming a state i to a state j change could be the number of evolutionary steps implied on the model. For example, if one assumed that the states were linearly ordered, then the number of steps between states 0 and 1 is 1, between states 1 and 3 is 2, and so on, implying the cost or step matrix shown on the left.

The step matrix might be derived instead from a **probabilistic model** that specifies the relative probabilities of change between states. The table to the left, for example, specifies that a branch beginning with state 0 has a probability of 0.90 of ending at state 0, 0.04 of ending at state 1, 0.02 of ending at state 2, and 0.04 of ending at state 3. The probabilistic model, and the costs derived from it, might be applied universally throughout the tree. Alternatively, it may be adjusted for each branch of the tree, for instance to reflect variation in the time length of different branches (MacClade cannot do this, by the way).

To derive a step matrix from the probability model one could suppose that the more likely a change, the less it costs. One possible conversion function is:

$$\text{Cost} = -\text{ natural logarithm of the probability}$$

(Felsenstein, 1981a; W. Wheeler, 1990).

Indeed, if a step matrix is used whose costs are derived from a transition probability matrix using the above logarithmic formula, then a most-parsimonious reconstruction of ancestral states will be more than a parsimony estimate. It will also be a Bayesian probability estimate, because the ancestral state reconstruction that minimizes the sum of negative logarithms of probabilities is also maximizing the product of probabilities of the implied change (or lack thereof) along the branches (D. Maddison, 1990, in preparation; see also W. Maddison, 1991). The step matrix, however, might look rather unfamiliar to users of parsimony, since it will have the diagonal elements non-zero. It will cost something not to change! (MacClade does allow diagonal elements

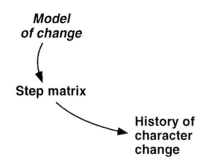

Model of change

Step matrix

History of character change

to be non-zero, and therefore can make Bayesian ancestral state reconstructions in addition to more typical parsimony reconstructions.)

Whether from a possible-pathways model or a probabilistic model, we could view the step matrix, used for inference of the history of character change, as emanating from some model of change. Thus some model of how evolution in general happens is used in reconstructing the history of character changes. This is true even for phylogenetic analyses that assume characters are unordered. For an unordered character, the model of evolution says, in a sense, that anything can happen.

Analyzing characters on their own trees

An often-heard proscription is that characters that are analyzed in the light of a reconstructed phylogeny should not have been used to reconstruct the phylogeny (Coddington, 1988; Brooks and McLennan, 1991). The phylogeny, it is said, should have been derived independently from the characters later analyzed. This proscription is not followed universally, however, for many authors place tick marks on tree branches indicating interpreted evolutionary changes in characters that were used to reconstruct the tree.

Although the problem is sometimes characterized as one of circularity, it is better characterized as one of bias (W. Maddison, 1990; Swofford and Maddison, in press). As noted by W. Maddison (1990), the inclusion of characters in reconstructing a phylogenetic tree will tend to reduce their own inferred number of convergences and reversals, at least if parsimony was used in reconstructing the tree. This biasing effect may in fact not be serious, and it may be conservative with respect to the evolutionary hypothesis investigated.

Of course, the better supported is the phylogeny by independent characters, the more confidence we will have in our character analysis. A phylogeny well-supported by independent characters would be preferred. However, Swofford and Maddison (in press) note that it is important to consider characters in the reconstruction of the phylogeny if they have a substantial contribution to make, even if those characters are later analyzed using the phylogeny. If you are reluctant to include characters you will later analyze, you should at least perform a sensitivity analysis to see what influence these characters would have had on the phylogeny. If addition of these characters significantly changes the phylogeny reconstructed, and thus casts doubt on the phylogeny reconstructed without them, then that phylogeny is probably not strongly enough supported to be enforced as a background assumption in the character analysis. (See the discussion on acceptable assumptions later in this chapter.)

Inferring models of character change using phylogenies

In the previous section on reconstructing the history of character changes, it was noted that the assumed matrix of costs used by parsimony implies a model of character evolution. What if your focus is not the history but rather the model of character evolution? In this section we will turn the previous discussion upside down by considering how models of character change may be derived using phylogenetic trees.

Models of the process of character change could be obtained from outside of systematics from such sources as developmental biology or molecular biology. For instance, developmental studies may indicate the nature of gene changes required to change one structure into another, and thereby suggest the relative probabilities of change. Alternatively, we may seek to use phylogenies to uncover the patterns of character change that would then allow us to formulate models of change (Chapter 3). MacClade can help with phylogenetic inference of models of character change.

Phylogenetic methods use the distribution of character states on reconstructed phylogenies to infer the parameters of models of character change. Maximum likelihood approaches to estimating parameters of character change have been briefly discussed by Barry and Hartigan (1987) and Ritland and Clegg (1987); Hendy (1989) has described a least-squares method applicable to simple data for small numbers of taxa. Derivation of stochastic models of change has been more of concern with molecular sequence data (previous citations and Gojobori et al., 1982; Lanave, et al., 1984; Fitch, 1986; Nei, 1987; Rempe, 1988) than with morphological data (e.g., Janson, 1992), in part because it seems more reasonable to presume constancy of models across nucleotides or amino acids than across numerous morphological characters.

To infer relative probabilities of change using a parsimony-based technique, several methods are possible. The simplest, used by MacClade's **State Changes & Stasis** chart (see Chapter 15), involves first reconstructing the history of character change and then extracting frequencies of each type of change. For example, the following inferred history of character change shows four 0→1 changes, one 1→0 change, and four 1→2 changes:

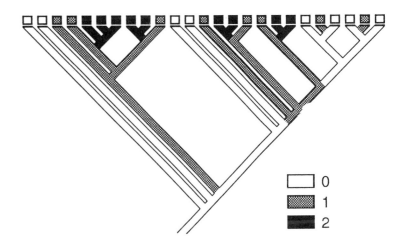

One could graphically represent these relative frequencies of changes using the following "bubble diagram":

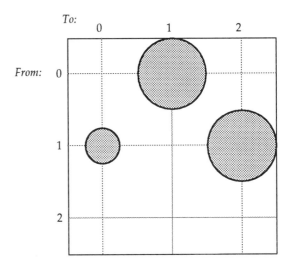

Here, the area of each circle represents the relative frequency of that kind of change. Thus, 0→1 and 1→2 changes are more frequent than 1→0 changes; other changes were inferred not to have taken place.

One may wish to interpret this bubble diagram as an estimate of the parameters of a probabilistic model of the process of character change. The reconstructed frequencies of changes would be interpreted as estimating the actual probabilities of changes. There are several difficulties with this interpretation; we will mention only three here. First, the sample size is rather low (only 9 changes in all were inferred). In order to increase the sample size, one would have to examine changes on a much larger tree (in which case one would have to assume constancy of process across more lineages) or over multiple serially homologous characters, such as along a DNA sequence (in which case one would have to assume constancy of process across characters). Second, if the history of character change was reconstructed using the principle of parsimony, as it is in MacClade, then the bubble diagram may distort the probabilities because it seeks the reconstruction minimizing change. This distortion would be especially noticeable if one were using parsimony reconstructions to try to estimate the relative frequencies of branches with change as opposed to stasis — branches on which no change is reconstructed. An example of parsimony's distortion is given on p. 288. Third, this estimation method contains an inherent bias arising from the way parsimony counts costs. This bias, which we will call **step-matrix bias**, was recognized by Mickevich (1982; Mickevich and Weller 1990).

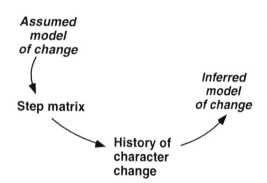

The parsimony method used in the reconstruction method depends on an assumption of a step matrix, and that step matrix itself is derived from an assumed model of change. Clearly the assumed model of change can bias the reconstructed frequencies of change, and thus the inferred model of change.

(This method need not involve circular logic, if for instance the input model of change supplies a general constraint on the inference, while the output model of change is a more detailed hypothesis about process; see p. 68.)

In an attempt to avoid this bias, Mickevich (1981, 1982), as part of her Transformation Series Analysis, introduced a numerical method that did not begin with a step matrix or character state tree, but rather derived character state trees during the course of the analysis from the distribution of character states on a tree. This method is not based on the reconstruction of character change, and makes no explicit mention about background hypotheses that direct the inference; in fact, it attempts to avoid them. Mickevich and Weller recently (1990) provided a description of a modified version of this method. They seek the character state tree that "predicts the exact sequence of [cladogenetic] events" or that "exactly map[s] the hierarchy of events depicted by the cladogram" (Mickevich and Weller 1990:148-149). If an exact mapping is not possible (as there is convergence), then their goal is to choose the character state tree that maximally reflects the hierarchy implied by the cladogram. Unfortunately, they do not provide three critical elements required for an adequate justification of the method: a clear, mathematical definition of maximal reflectance, a proof that the algorithm described maximizes reflectance, and a justification for using reflectance to choose among hypotheses (D. Maddison, in preparation). The method could also be sanctioned if it could be shown (perhaps through simulations) that it is a reasonably successful estimator of models of change. This has not yet been done.

Without clearly justified procedures that avoid an initial specification of step matrices or similar assumptions, it would appear that we are forced to use such assumptions. Although step-matrix bias is a problem, it need not be devastating. While the nature of the step matrix may obscure the true nature of change between character states, it does not necessarily hide it completely: some aspects of the relative frequencies of change can be detected despite the obfuscation created by step-matrix bias (D. Maddison, in preparation). However, no fully satisfactory parsimony-based solution has been proposed. For this reason, we must treat parsimony estimation of process models with caution. We should note, however, that all estimation procedures, statistical or not, will have something analogous to step-matrix bias, insofar as they need to make assumptions that can affect the results. We cannot fully escape our assumptions, but neither are we so fully bound by them that we can learn nothing new.

Should we rely on historical reconstructions?

Methods to estimate parameters of character evolution can be grouped into two categories. Some, like those just described, reconstruct character changes on a phylogenetic tree, then use these changes to estimate parameters, such as the probability of different sorts of changes, whether two characters are correlated in their changes, and so on. Ridley (1983), Huey and Bennett (1987), W. Maddison (1990), Pagel and Harvey (1989), and Sanderson (1991) all describe methods that begin by making a reconstruction of the history of character change, and then proceed to use that reconstruction to make an inference about evolutionary process. On the other hand, other methods avoid making a reconstruction of changes, and instead directly test for parameters using the observed distribution of character states, the form of the tree, and some stochastic model of evolution to relate them. Felsenstein (1985a), Barry and Hartigan (1987), Ritland and Clegg (1987), and Golding and Felsenstein (1990) all have described methods that estimate parameters of character evolution without at any point actually reconstructing the history of changes. For instance, a stochastic model can yield a likelihood, which is the probability of obtaining the observed data given the particular tree and parameters of character evolution. By seeing which parameters yield the highest likelihoods, possibly comparing them with likelihood ratio tests, estimates of those parameters can be obtained. At no point is a reconstruction made of character change. In fact, these procedures legitimately sum probabilities over all possible scenarios of character change (even the least parsimonious).

The problems of relying on an historical reconstruction of character change are several. First, one tends to forget the error and ambiguity in the reconstruction of ancestral states (see Chapter 5; Felsenstein, 1985a; W. Maddison, 1990; Swofford and Maddison, in press). Second, one needs to be careful that the methods that reconstructed the ancestral states use assumptions consistent with the assumptions used in any subsequent estimation procedure based on the reconstructed states. One would not want to build a statistical test based on an elaborate stochastic model, only to apply it to ancestral states reconstructed using a method inconsistent with that model. Because of these problems, the direct methods that avoid the historical reconstruction have advantages.

This does not mean, however, that we should abandon making historical reconstructions of character change (and perhaps therefore abandon much of MacClade's use!). First, the history of evolution might be considered just as legitimate a subject of study as are the processes of evolution. Second, in many studies it is important to estimate the sequence of evolutionary events (Donoghue, 1989). As long as the possible errors are considered, the reconstruction can be important in understanding evolutionary processes. It serves at least the heuristic purpose of suggesting patterns, even if those patterns are later confirmed statistically by methods that avoid historical reconstructions. Third, direct methods that avoid historical reconstructions tend to require detailed stochastic models that may not be known to us. Fourth, for many estimations we may want to make, direct methods are simply not yet invented, and we may find the indirect, historically based methods easier to concoct. As Felsenstein (1985a) has noted, it is probably better to use phylogeny crudely than to ignore it entirely. Fifth, in some circumstances simulation studies have shown that reconstructions of character change can be used in statistical methods without too much danger. W. Maddison (1990) and Martins and Garland (1991) both used simulations to confirm that correlation tests based on parsimony reconstructions of ancestral states behave themselves reasonably well statistically. D. Maddison (in preparation) concluded the effects of step-matrix bias were not all-obscuring. Slatkin and Maddison (1989) found that a parsimony-based statistic, the minimum number of migration events, was a reasonably good estimator of gene flow.

If one does estimate parameters of character evolution using historical reconstructions of change, then it is important to be concerned about these issues. It would be best to test for any possible biases. If you use MacClade's State Changes & Stasis chart, for instance, to estimate probabilities of various changes, you could try to set up null models and do simulations using MacClade's randomization and random data generation facilities to see how the parsimony reconstructions may be affecting your estimates (see the example given on p. 288).

Multiple solutions

When one infers models using historical reconstructions, then ambiguity in the historical reconstruction can lead to ambiguity in the model inferred. On occasion, the data at hand will not speak for a single historical reconstruction. There may be equally well supported trees, or equally well supported reconstructions upon each tree.

Parsimony-based methods generally provide an objective function (cost or length) by which one can judge the relative merits of trees or character reconstructions. This is one of the strengths of parsimony analyses, as compared to, for example, cluster methods based on distance matrices. One can examine and select a collection of acceptable trees or character reconstructions based on the objective function. But the multiple solutions that often result create problems in analyzing character evolution, as different trees or character reconstructions may favor different notions about the history and models of character change.

While some believe it fruitful or necessary to find ways to eliminate some of the solutions (Brooks et al., 1986, Carpenter, 1988), we believe it important to accept the diversity of solutions that are supported by the data. Unless one is to choose solutions arbitrarily, then multiple equally supported solutions will continue to be a common result of phylogenetic analyses. Indeed, we feel it important that the full diversity of equally supported solutions be consciously sought (D. Maddison, 1991b) especially as more is learned about confidence limits on phylogenies (Cavender, 1978, 1981; Templeton, 1983; Felsenstein, 1985b,c; Sanderson, 1989).

Tools need to be developed that can more readily examine multiple trees and multiple character reconstructions, and summarize and present results to the biologist. This necessity has been one of the prime motivating factors behind MacClade's charting facilities, which will examine multiple trees and character reconstructions, and behind MacClade's tracing features that indicate ambiguity. But for aspects of character evolution beyond those examined by MacClade, few tools are currently available for automatic processing of multiple solutions. This is an important area for future development.

What assumptions are acceptable?

Let us return to the issues of assumptions and circularity. We have discussed hypotheses about processes of character change and how they could be both used as assumptions for phylogenetic analysis, and tested by phylogenetic information. There is a clear danger in such activities of assuming what one tries to show. In recognition of this danger, it has been urged that one should, as much as possible, avoid making assumptions about evolutionary processes while reconstructing evolutionary history, so that the reconstructed phylogenies can supply independent tests of evolutionary process theories (see Platnick, 1986a and references therein). Mitter (1981) notes that among zoological systematists "there is widespread (but not universal) agreement that ... systematic methods should be as free as possible from assumptions about how evolution works, since these assumptions are in general not testable without reference to systematic results." This sensible prescription might suggest that there should be an imbalance of trade between phylogenetic biology and evolutionary process theory — that phylogenetics should export cladograms to process theory for use there as assumptions, and yet be reluctant to import assumptions about the processes of evolution. (Reluctance to use process assumptions is by no means universal, however [Felsenstein, 1988a; Harvey and Pagel, 1991].) Since MacClade gives you opportunities to use elaborate assumptions in opposition to this prescription, a word on the use of assumptions is in order.

Circularity can happen. One might assume a process, reconstruct the phylogeny, then use the phylogeny as evidence for the very process assumed. However, while process assumptions invite poor science, they do not require it. Care can be taken that the phylogeny is used to test process theories other than the ones that went into it. Thus, process theories used as assumptions place limitations on the uses of the reconstructed phylogeny (Platnick, 1986a). The assumed process theories might concern different and better-established aspects of character evolution, or less specific aspects, than those derived from the study. In some circumstances, the process theories will merely provide a bias, like the step-matrix bias discussed earlier, that can to some extent be escaped. In the sequence of assumed process theory → tree → inferred process theory, the inferred process theory is no more forced to be the same as that assumed than are the trees at two stages of an iterative process like successive approximations character weighting (Farris, 1969) doomed to be identical. The reader is referred to Hull (1967) for further discussion of circularity in systematic biology.

Another, perhaps more important, complaint against a particular process assumption is that it may not be well enough supported. On the one hand, we should not blindly accept current beliefs about the evolutionary process. On the other hand, it must be conceivable for process theories to be well-enough supported to use as assumptions, otherwise physicists would still be worrying about what a galvanometer measures, and we could not apply what we have learned from experience. Our task is therefore to set criteria that would tell us whether a process theory is sufficiently supported to graduate into an assumption for use in subsequent analysis.

Within a parsimony framework, the use of particular assumptions about character evolution is comparable to the use of outgroups. Outgroup analysis allows systematists to enlarge the taxonomic scope of their parsimony considerations from the local (ingroup) to global (ingroup plus outgroups; Engelmann and Wiley, 1977; Maddison et al., 1984). Using special assumptions about the mechanisms of character evolution allows systematists to enlarge the scope of their parsimony considerations to include previously acquired biological theories. As noted by Farris (1983:23), assumptions about mechanisms of change can result in improved phylogenetic hypotheses "if the postulated mechanisms can themselves be corroborated by other sources of evidence".

Imagine a systematist who has what we will call the *local data*, observations of character states in a set of taxa. A parsimony analysis treating all the characters as unordered, assuming any state can transform to any other state in one step, yields a cladogram requiring 20 evolutionary steps. However, one of the characters has states 0, 1 and 2, and the systematist has developmental information suggesting there is one genetic change between states 0 and 1, one between 1 and 2, but two between 0 and 2. Redoing the analysis with this character treated as ordered results in a different cladogram requiring 24 steps. This is an expected difference: ordered characters always require at least as many, usually more, steps than unordered characters.

Application of the assumption of character ordering yielded a result that seemed slightly less parsimonious according to the local data alone. Indeed, the local data themselves might have cast doubt on the theory of character state ordering, had we been using them to test the theory of ordering instead of subjecting them to ordering as an assumption. In this case, the fact that ordering requires more steps may have been viewed as evidence that the character does not seem to behave as an ordered character. We are faced with a choice between believing the theory of ordering, or believing what the local data seem to be telling us. When will the external theory be well enough supported to be believed and applied against the local data? Two criteria must be satisfied:

1. The process theory that gives us the imported assumption must be backed by enough evidence that the local data cannot severely cast doubt on the theory in general. If the evidence previously acquired to support the process theory is so weak that the theory would have been untenable had the "contradictory" local data been known earlier, then the assumption cannot be used. In outgroup analysis a similar situation holds when the previous data supporting assumed outgroup relationships are so weak that the current data targeted at the ingroup could actually overturn the assumed outgroup relationships.

2. The imported assumption must be sufficiently constraining or have sufficient ramifications that it cannot be easily dismissed as locally inapplicable by adding a few *ad hoc* assumptions. In the example of character state ordering, one could accept that in general developmental systems require these states to be ordered, but dismiss the applicability of this theory by an *ad hoc* assumption claiming the system is different in the few species being studied. Whether a local dismissal of the external theory is parsimonious depends on the sort of *ad hoc* assumptions needed to allow the local exception. If the external theory is a simple empirical generaliza-

tion (e.g., "In all cases observed to date, medium evolves between small and large"), and there is no understanding of the mechanisms underlying it, then it can be dismissed locally with ease, regardless of the number of cases observed in its favor. Farris (1983:25) noted, when talking of the assumption of irreversibility, "... if the evidence for irreversibility was originally based on character distributions, then it would be quite unwarranted to analyze further cases as to force them into conformity with irreversibility"; we would rather say "based *only*." Without any understanding of mechanism, we can easily invent a single factor that would render the rule inapplicable in our case, and thus only a single *ad hoc* assumption is needed to dismiss it. It may then be more parsimonious to dismiss as inapplicable the external theory and let the local data have their way. To be enforceable, the external theory must therefore be backed by a sufficiently detailed understanding that dismissing it locally would require many *ad hoc* assumptions. In our example, if the developmental system were well understood in the group of organisms studied, then dismissing the character state ordering may require casting doubt on many developmental studies, and it would be more parsimonious to accept the theory's applicability and so force a few more evolutionary steps in the local data.

The greater the evidence supporting the external theory, the greater the complexity and mechanistic understanding behind it, the more strongly the theory can be enforced as an assumption. One implication of this analysis is that models of the probabilities of various character changes like those discussed in the previous section, if they are derived solely from reconstructed frequencies of changes, cannot be justifiably returned for use as assumptions for phylogenetic analysis. To do this, some understanding is needed of why the frequencies are as they are.

This analysis does not by any means cover all cases. For instance, an assumption may, instead of making one's local data seem more complicated, make one's local data seem less complicated. Perhaps a genetic study would tell us that red toes and blue toes, although they appear different, are in fact different phenotypic expressions of the same genes due to differences in temperature during development. In this case we could code organisms with red and blue toes as having the same state, and not need to count evolutionary steps between them. How well supported does such an assumption of sameness need to be? Surely one could not simply invent the assumption, without evidence, to compress one's local data at whim; there must be some reluctance to create a generalization dismissing apparent data. One of the greatest challenges that phylogenetic biology faces in the future is the development of methods to make decisions of this sort, which have to do with the coding of phenotypic characters (see discussion of coding, p. 46).

We have tried, using parsimony arguments, to convince the skeptic why certain process assumptions will sometimes be justified. When particular process assumptions are justified, we are not only licensed to use them, but we should feel compelled to use them in order to achieve a solution that is globally parsimonious considering both our local data and the rest of biological knowledge. By avoiding process assumptions at all costs, we might hope that we are constructing cladograms that are pure and untainted by process assumptions, and so can be legitimately used to test any evolutionary theory. Instead, however, if there is good evidence that certain processes are occurring that would distort the hierarchy we recover, then by ignoring these processes we obtain cladograms that have little power to test *any* evolutionary theory, by virtue of their being the wrong hierarchy; that is, incorrect estimates of history. (The correctness of the historical estimate is especially important when we use phylogenies to examine characters other than those that went into the reconstruction of the cladogram. For these studies, we depend on the cladogram being an estimate of history, not just a summary of the pattern of distributions of characters that are no longer part of the question.) Only if we never manage to learn anything about the evolutionary process (a sad thought) can we legitimately continue to ignore it.

The above discussion was worded as if to suggest that it is conceivable to avoid process assumptions. Some workers (e.g., Felsenstein, 1978; Sober, 1988) would argue that one cannot be silent on the issue of process. They would suggest that new process assumptions generally replace old ones, instead of being elaborations or additions. If the use of a new assumption about process results in a different phylogenetic tree, then it is fair to say the constellation of assumptions before incorporation of the new one was not merely neutral with respect to the new assumption, but rather denied it. If we use methods because we believe they stand a reasonable chance of reconstructing evolutionary history, then in using a method, we implicitly assume that the evolutionary process is such to allow the method to succeed. By this view, the issue is not whether process assumptions should be used, but what are the correct process assumptions to use.

Parsimony versus other criteria

In MacClade, parsimony is used both in judging the phylogenetic tree and in reconstructing the history of character change. The justification of parsimony methods in phylogenetic biology is currently a matter of much controversy (see summary provided by Sober 1988). However much we might hope that parsimony is merely a neutral methodological principle, it does guide us to choose some hypotheses over others, and it will guide us incorrectly in certain circumstances (Felsenstein, 1978b; Hendy and Penny, 1989). In general, we know that if evolution behaves according to some well-defined rules, parsimony methods will not be consistent estimators of phylogenies; we also know that there exist other models of evolutionary process under which parsimony methods will be reliable estimators (Felsenstein, 1979; Sober, 1988). The models of evolution investigated to date are overly simplistic and unrealistic (Farris, 1983). As parsimony's status under more realistic models is unknown, no argument for or against it is overly compelling. Of course, the same statement could be made of any other method of inference. All methods proposed to date would have their assumptions violated at least occasionally, and it remains to be seen how often they are violated and which method is most robust to violations in its assumptions.

Though the controversy may eventually be resolved, it should not be expected to result in a single, universally applicable answer to the question of whether parsimony, maximum likelihood, or some other criterion should be preferred. Some classes of characters may have a statistical behavior that is both well known and consistent enough across taxa and characters that fully statistical methods like maximum likelihood could be justifiably applied. Subsets of DNA sequences may eventually fall into this category. In contrast, other characters may not fall into classes with known statistical behavior, and indeed their behavior may be the object of study. Many morphological characters whose genetic and developmental basis is not well understood might fall into this category.

We cannot simply ignore morphological, behavioral and other characters whose statistical behavior is not well understood. For one thing, despite their detractors, morphological characters persist in informing us about phylogenetic relationships (Hillis, 1987; Donoghue and Sanderson, 1992). And even if we were (1) to show convincingly that some molecular characters were well-behaved phylogenetically and (2) to decide always to place primary confidence in these molecular characters for phylogeny reconstruction, our goal is not merely a phylogenetic tree relating the few tens of thousands of specimens sequenced. When a specimen from a single species of a genus of orchids is chosen for sequencing, we will legitimately assume, on the basis of morphological characters, that other members of the species and the genus will fall with it on the phylogeny. Not only will we rely on morphology in this case, we need to rely on it, otherwise our molecular phylogenies will be powerless to inform us about the evolution of the vast majority of specimens and species on earth that remain and will remain unsequenced. Molecular phylogenies can at best be thin skeletons on which the majority of organisms are arranged by morphological characters. Finally, there is another reason we cannot ignore characters whose statistical behavior is not well known. Many of the most fascinating biological questions concern the evolution of morphological, behavioral or other characters each of which has unique characteristics. We would be hard-pressed to justify assuming an explicit statistical model of their evolution in order to reconstruct their history. For these characters, parsimony-based methods may always be a reasonable place to begin understanding their evolution. Of course, if robust non-parametric phylogenetic statistics can be developed, then perháps even for these characters fully statistical methods may eventually be preferred.

Alternative methods such as parsimony and maximum likelihood need not always be kept separate. One could imagine likelihood methods applied to molecular characters to reconstruct the phylogeny, then parsimony used to interpret the evolution of morphological characters, whose statistical behavior is not well known, in the light of the reconstructed phylogeny.

5. Reconstructing Character Evolution Using Parsimony

The pathways and patterns shown by character evolution hold an important key to our understanding of evolutionary processes, as discussed in Chapters 3 and 4. Could we see into the past, we would want to know which characteristics transformed to which others, how often, in what lineages and at what times, and in what contexts. Patterns in these events might indicate what forces cause characters to change or remain stable, including forces arising from other characters possessed. Of course, in most cases we will have to be satisfied with inferring the history of character evolution indirectly. With this aim, a number of methods have been developed to use reconstructed phylogenetic trees along with the observed character states of organisms to infer the states of ancestral lineages and their changes through time.

In this chapter we describe parsimony-based methods to reconstruct character evolution. After explaining exactly what we are trying to reconstruct, we will discuss separately the assumptions that specify how parsimonious is a reconstruction, and the algorithms that find what reconstructions are most parsimonious under those assumptions. We will describe the algorithms as they are implemented in MacClade, in order to document MacClade's calculations. The reader is referred to the review by Swofford and Maddison (in press) for additional discussion of parsimony reconstructions of character evolution.

Some statistics about trees and characters are derived from parsimonious reconstructions of character evolution. These include the number of steps in a character, the treelength, the consistency index, and so on. In this chapter only the calculations of number of steps and changes are described, since their calculations are intimately tied up with the reconstruction algorithms. Chapter 14 discusses the treelength and other indices.

Goals, assumptions, and algorithms

In reconstructing character evolution, our **goal** is to reconstruct the character states of hypothetical ancestors throughout the phylogenetic tree (Chapter 4, p. 57). In particular, the usual practice is to estimate the states of the hypothetical ancestors at the nodes or branch points of the tree, because these provide convenient reference points (see Chapter 4 for a discussion of nodes and branches).

We will assume that character evolution is being reconstructed on a particular phylogenetic tree. That is, the phylogenetic tree has already been reconstructed, and is no longer an issue.

Under various **assumptions** about the nature of changes between states, including the number of steps between states, parsimony methods seek to reconstruct ancestral states by choosing the states at the branch points that require the minimal number of steps on the tree. Thus, parsimony together with the assumptions provides a **criterion** for choosing among character reconstructions.

But there are many possible reconstructions, and finding the reconstruction or reconstructions with the minimum number of steps is not always an easy task. Various **algorithms** (computational procedures) have been developed that accomplish this task of finding the most-parsimonious reconstruction.

Ancestral states and reconstructions

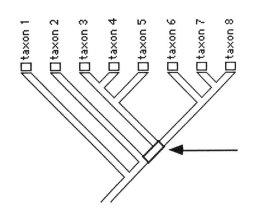

The result of our inference is an assignment of states to each node in the tree, indicating those states that can be placed at the node parsimoniously. If we had a phylogeny as shown at left, with all taxa observed to have the white state, then obviously the assignment of the black state to the branch marked by the arrow is not parsimonious, since that would require one white-to-black change and two black-to-white changes. There is only one parsimonious assignment to this branch: the white state.

A state can be placed at the node parsimoniously if it allows the observed states in the taxa to be evolved in as few as possible evolutionary steps. If more than one state can be placed parsimoniously at a node, the node's assignment is said to be *equivocal*. The set of all the states that can be parsimoniously assigned to a node is called the node's **MPR set** (Swofford and Maddison, 1987; the name refers to the fact that these states occur in the Most-Parsimonious Reconstructions). The purpose of MacClade's Trace Character facility is to shade the branches to indicate the nodes' MPR sets.

An equivocal assignment is indicated in MacClade by shading a branch with a horizontally striped pattern. For the unordered character shown traced onto the tree below, there are four branches shaded with the equivocal pattern:

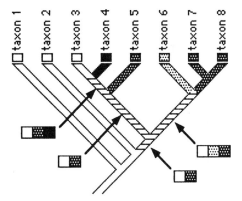

Two of the nodes have three states in their MPR sets, and two have two states:

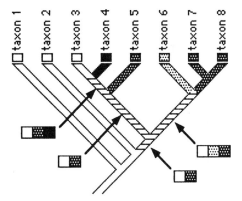

There happen to be six equally parsimonious **reconstructions** for this example; that is, there are six most-parsimonious resolutions of the equivocal regions in the tree above. (Other examples may have from one to billions of equally parsimonious reconstructions.) A reconstruction is a set of assignments to the nodes such that each node is assigned only one state. You can think of it as one particular scenario for the evolution of the trait in question. The diagram above doesn't directly tell you about such individual reconstructions. For example, looking at the above figure you might think that the following was a parsimonious reconstruction, since it chooses one state from the MPR set at each of the nodes:

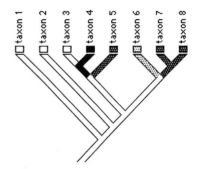

In fact, this is not one of the parsimonious reconstructions. It indicates five evolutionary steps, but only four are needed. There are 36 (=2x2x3x3) different reconstructions that can be obtained by choosing states from MPR sets, but only six of them are parsimonious. The six reconstructions that are parsimonious are:

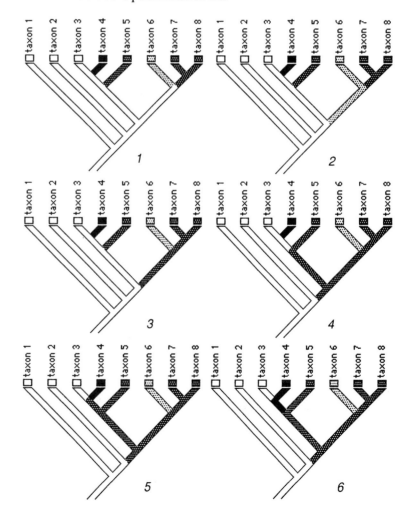

Each one of these reconstructions shows four evolutionary steps. The problem with the first reconstruction we showed was that, although the one internal branch could be black, it could not parsimoniously be black at the same time that the other internal branches were white.

The meaning of "reconstruction" given above is a very specific one — a fully resolved (lacking ambiguity) scenario for the evolution of the character, node by node, on the tree.

The nature of a reconstruction of character evolution is discussed also on pp. 57 and 241–245.

Assumptions about character evolution

For a given character, various assumptions about transformation between states are possible. You may believe that the states follow a linear transformation series, or that gains are more difficult than losses, and so on. In order to select parsimonious reconstructions, we need to consider these assumptions, for they will influence how parsimony is quantified. It is not enough to say "minimize evolutionary steps", because perhaps transformations between some states involve more evolutionary steps than do others.

In MacClade these assumptions are specified by **transformation types**. A transformation type indicates certain rules about transformations between states. By specifying a character is of a particular type, MacClade will use that type's rules in reconstructing the character. For example, if you specify a character is of the **ordered** type, then MacClade will assume the states evolve along a linear transformation series, while if you specify the character is of the **unordered** type, then MacClade will allow any state to transform to any other in a single step.

Which transformation type is assigned to a character will clearly affect the reconstruction of character evolution, and the number of steps of evolution required for the character on the tree (see Swofford and Maddison, in press). For example, a reconstruction that requires fewer steps than any other under the assumption that a character is unordered may suggest changes of all sorts, from every state to every other state. Under the assumption that character states are ordered, some of these changes would require multiple steps, and this particular reconstruction might no longer be the most parsimonious.

These transformation types are essentially specifications of intra-character weightings, or the costs of presuming a particular type of change. Thus, if you assume a character to be ordered, you are weighting some state changes more highly than others. For example, a change in an ordered character between states 0 and 1 would count as one step, whereas as change between state 0 and 8 would be weighted eight times as much (that is, it would count as eight steps), and a change from 7 to 4 would count as three steps. If you assume a character to be unordered, you are weighting all state changes equally, such that a change between states 0 and 1, 0 and 8, or 7 and 4 each would count as one step. A brief introduction to choosing these weights is given in Chapter 4.

Given the variety of weights that could be applied, many transformation types are possible. MacClade supplies five predefined transformation types: **unordered, ordered, irreversible, stratigraphic** and **Dollo**. These predefined transformation types can be characterized as follows.

Unordered

For characters designated as unordered, a change from any state to any other state is counted as one step ("Fitch parsimony"; Fitch [1971]; Hartigan [1973]). Thus, a change from 0 to 1, or from 0 to 8, or 7 to 4, are each counted as one step. A five-state unordered character can be represented diagrammatically as shown at left, where change between any two states involves only one step (i.e., only one line has to be traversed in the diagram).

Nucleotide sequence characters might, as a first approximation, be considered as having unordered states, with a transformation from any one base A, C, G, or T to any other base being one step. Alternatively, step matrices may be used as described below to impose a higher cost for transversions.

Ordered

0 — 1 — 2 — 3 — 4

For characters designated as ordered, the number of steps from one state to another state is counted as the (absolute value of the) difference between their state numbers ("Wagner parsimony"; Farris [1970], Swofford and Maddison [1987]). Thus, a change from 0 to 1 is counted as one step, from 0 to 8 as eight steps, from 7 to 4 as three steps. A five-state ordered character can be represented diagrammatically as shown at left. In this diagram, the number of steps in the change between any two states is equal to the number of lines on the path between the two states; thus, from 1 to 4 is three lines or three steps. Morphological characters in which one state is intermediate between others (medium between small and large; 5 leaflets between 3 and 7) might reasonably be considered ordered characters.

Irreversible

0 → 1 → 2 → 3 → 4

For characters designated as irreversible, the number of steps from one state to another state is counted as the difference between their state numbers, with the restriction that decreases in state number do not occur ("Camin-Sokal parsimony"; Camin and Sokal [1965]). Thus, a change from 0 to 1 is counted as one step, from 0 to 8 as eight steps, but changes from 1 to 0 or 8 to 0 are impossible. Multiple gains are allowed, no losses are allowed. A five-state irreversible character can be represented diagrammatically, as shown above.

Stratigraphic

Characters assigned this type are treated as indicating stratigraphic age, with each state representing a stratum, based on Fisher's (1982, 1988, 1992) notion of stratigraphic parsimony. The oldest stratum is coded by state 0; younger strata are coded by successively higher states. The reconstruction of states at ancestral nodes that MacClade provides is therefore in some sense a reconstruction of the ages of ancestors. Clearly, descendants cannot be older than ancestors and so stratigraphic characters are irreversible. Ancestral ages are assigned using Fisher's (1992) criterion to minimize the instances in which the tree implies that a fossil should have been found in a stratum but wasn't. As a default, one step is counted for each absence in a stratum, but different costs can be assigned to absences in different strata. For instance, a lineage implied missing from an extensive and well-known stratum might count more heavily against the tree than a lineage missing from a poorly known stratum. Further details on the interpretation of this character type are discussed below in the section on finding parsimonious reconstructions.

The stratigraphic character type allows paleontologists to determine how well a phylogenetic tree agrees or disagrees with stratigraphy, using a sort of "stratigraphic parsimony". A phylogenetic tree disagrees with stratigraphic data when it suggests fossils should occur in some strata but they have not yet been found there. Therefore a parsimony-based approach might prefer those trees that minimize the amount of fossil record that is absent from the known stratigraphic record, but that the tree indicates should exist (i.e., that minimizes *ad hoc* hypotheses of missing fossils). Fisher's (1982, 1992) formal criterion is implemented in MacClade's stratigraphic character type. An early application of stratigraphic parsimony is that of Doyle et al. (1982).

Dollo

For Dollo characters, the number of steps from one state to another state is counted as the difference between the numbers given to the states, with the restriction that each increase in state number occurs only once (Farris, 1977). Thus, a change from 0 to 1 is counted as one step, from 0 to 6 as six steps, but gain of 1 or 6 can happen only once each on the tree. Multiple losses are allowed, multiple gains are not. One possible use for Dollo characters is in restriction site data (e.g., DeBry and Slade, 1985), where state 1 (site present) might be thought difficult to gain but easy to lose. Thus a two-state Dollo character for restriction site data might be represented as shown on the left.

MacClade 3 assumes, as did MacClade 2.1 (Maddison and Maddison, 1987), what Swofford (1991) calls the "unrooted" Dollo assumption. That is, MacClade does not assume that there was a gain from state 0 to state 1; it assumes only that there was no more than one gain from 0 to 1, no more than one from 1 to 2, and so on.

Step Matrices

In addition to the predefined transformation types discussed above, MacClade users can specify their own assumptions. You can do this by indicating how many steps it is for a transformation from each state to each other state.

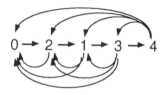

For instance, suppose you had an assumption that transformation between states followed the pathways indicated on the diagram at left. This supposes that for increases in character state (which might be thought of as gains) the character behaves as an ordered character, with one step between 0 and 1, three steps between 0 and 3, and so on. For any decrease in character state, there is one step. Thus, you may believe gains have to be accumulated, but any loss can be accomplished in a single step (perhaps by deletions or modifiers). You can take this diagram and translate it into the matrix at left. This matrix claims that there are no steps between 0 and itself, four steps from state 0 to state 4, one step from 4 to 0, and so on.

To:

	0	1	2	3	4
From: 0	0	1	2	3	4
1	1	0	1	2	3
2	1	1	0	1	2
3	1	1	1	0	1
4	1	1	1	1	0

This matrix format for indicating distances between states and the algorithm that uses it (Sankoff and Rousseau, 1975; Sankoff and Cedergren, 1983; Maddison and Maddison, 1987) are very flexible, and with it you can code all sorts of elaborate assumptions such as asymmetry in number of steps between gains and losses, and so on. The predefined transformation types unordered, ordered and irreversible can be written in this format:

unordered

	0	1	2	3	4	5
0	0	1	1	1	1	1
1	1	0	1	1	1	1
2	1	1	0	1	1	1
3	1	1	1	0	1	1
4	1	1	1	1	0	1
5	1	1	1	1	1	0

ordered

	0	1	2	3	4	5
0	0	1	2	3	4	5
1	1	0	1	2	3	4
2	2	1	0	1	2	3
3	3	2	1	0	1	2
4	4	3	2	1	0	1
5	5	4	3	2	1	0

irreversible

	0	1	2	3	4	5
0	0	1	2	3	4	5
1	∞	0	1	2	3	4
2	∞	∞	0	1	2	3
3	∞	∞	∞	0	1	2
4	∞	∞	∞	∞	0	1
5	∞	∞	∞	∞	∞	0

In Chapter 4 is a discussion of the source of such step matrices.

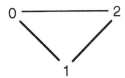

Distances that satisfy
the triangle inequality

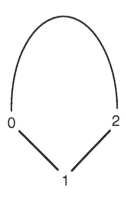

Distances that violate
the triangle inequality

Violating the triangle inequality It is possible to define a matrix of state-to-state distances that disobeys a fundamental property of distances called the "triangle inequality". The name is derived from the fact that triangles in Euclidean space have the property that the length of one side is always less than the sum of the lengths of the other two sides. More generally, the triangle inequality states (more or less) that the shortest distance between two points is a straight line. For instance suppose the direct distance from state i to j is more than the distance from i to k plus k to j. This means that the shortest distance between two states is not a straight line; that is, there is an indirect route that provides a shortcut. A transformation type matrix that contains such a shortcut is said to violate the triangle inequality.

For example, in the illustration above to the left, distances between states satisfy the triangle inequality, as the distance from 0 to 1 and then to 2 is not shorter than the distance from 0 directly to 2.

However, in the illustration below to the left, the triangle inequality is violated, as the distance from 0 to 1 and then to 2 is shorter than the direct route from 0 to 2.

Whether or not a matrix implying such distances is nonsensical and internally inconsistent depends on exactly how you interpret it. Suppose the matrix says the distance from state i to j is 5. If you take this to mean that a transition from i to j costs five steps regardless of the time taken to accomplish the transition, 10 years or 10,000,000 years, then the matrix must be considered self-inconsistent. It is claiming that one can go between i and j in a certain number of steps whereas in fact the matrix itself allows a more parsimonious transition through an intermediate. However, if the matrix's claimed cost for a transition is qualified by a time limitation, the inconsistency can be avoided. For example, a change between two states i and k may be unlikely over a short time period (perhaps the length of a branch on the tree), in fact much less likely than an i to j or j to k change. But over a longer time interval, the likelihood of an i to j change followed by a j to k change makes an i to k change more likely. Thus, if the matrix was presumed to reflect the probability of changing over the time span of short branches, violation of the triangle inequality would not make the matrix self-inconsistent. This latter view of a step matrix is rather different from the traditional parsimony view in which time is no factor. Whenever there are violations of the triangle inequality, however, it would seem we are forced into this view if we want to avoid inconsistency. If we want to maintain a standard parsimony view in which time is not considered, then we must accept the inconsistency of step matrices that violate the triangle inequality.

Violations of the triangle inequality are particularly troublesome when terminal taxa are polymorphic. The algorithms for reconstructing ancestral states count steps from one end of a branch to the other; they do not imagine interpolated changes along a branch, with the exception of changes within a polymorphic terminal taxon. When a terminal taxon is polymorphic, MacClade allows changes to occur *within* the terminal taxon, even though there is no "branch" there. If you view a step matrix as indicating the cost of changes over the time span of a branch, which you might do to avoid inconsistency when the triangle inequality is violated, it is not clear how costs are to be assessed to implicit changes within terminal taxa.

Character state trees

Assumptions about the evolution of a character can also take the form of a character state tree. This tree, for instance, says that to evolve from state 1 to state 5, state 3 is a necessary intermediate. In MacClade, character state trees are reversible and unrooted, meaning that transformations from 5 to 3 are also possible.

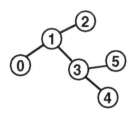

A character state tree

To some people a character state tree such as that shown at left means that character state 0 was ancestral, and it then evolved to state 1, then 1 evolved to 2 and 3, and 3 evolved to states 5 and 4. Such an interpretation would be that the tree directly shows the actual history of character change. An alternative interpretation is that it shows only the possible pathways that evolution could have followed. Thus the tree says that if evolution were to proceed from state 0 to state 5, it would have to pass through states 1 and 3. Evolution could go from state 4 to state 5, but would have to pass through state 3. State 0 need not even be ancestral.

Of the two interpretations, clearly the possible-pathways model (see Chapter 4) is more appropriate than the history of change for our purposes. Were we to suppose we already knew the history of character change, there would be little point in reconstructing character evolution using the character state tree as an assumption. Instead, the character state tree as an indication of possible pathways is perfectly appropriate as an assumption to constrain (but not completely specify) our conclusions about character evolution.

Ancestral polymorphism

MacClade's algorithms used for reconstructing character evolution assume that for each character there is only one state at each point on the tree's branches. That is, ancestral species are presumed to be monomorphic. The only place where polymorphism is allowed is in the terminal taxa (although see Chapter 4 and the cautions of Nixon and Davis, 1991). For ancestral branches MacClade sometimes shows an equivocal pattern representing more than one state, but this does not mean that such a branch is polymorphic. Rather, it means that any of the states represented could by itself be placed on that branch with equal parsimony.

The implicit assumption that ancestors can have only one state at a time may or may not be appropriate. It is perhaps most questionable for molecular characters in which a polymorphic condition is quite conceivable and may even be observed. For instance, suppose that two sister species are observed both to be polymorphic at a nucleotide site, both having A and G. The unordered character parsimony algorithm will presume that their immediate common ancestor was monomorphic, either for A or G, and that the alternative base was independently derived in the two species. In such a situation we might prefer to suppose the ancestor was also polymorphic and the polymorphism was simply maintained in the two daughter species.

The assumption of ancestral monomorphism is rather harsh, but it does simplify parsimony calculations. If ancestral polymorphisms were allowed, one could explain any character distribution by supposing a highly polymorphic ancestor with successive loss of states, or by supposing convergence, or in many other ways. Thus one would have to balance gains, retention of polymorphism, and loss in deciding which reconstruction of evolution is preferable.

Polymorphic ancestors have been incorporated into parsimony reconstructions of ancestral states by Farris (1978) and Felsenstein (1979) who proposed parsimony calculations that minimize fixations after a single gain of a polymorphic condition, and by Cavalli-Sforza and Edwards (1967), Rogers (1984), and Swofford and Berlocher (1987), who minimized amount of gene frequency change. The latter criterion uses data (gene frequencies) very different from those used in MacClade. Neither the "polymorphism parsimony" of Felsenstein and Farris or the "frequency parsimony" of Swofford and Berlocher are available in MacClade 3.

Maddison and Maddison (1987; included in "Read Me First" file on disk in September 1987, and in manual after January 1989) proposed a method to allow ancestral polymorphisms using step matrices. They suggested recoding the data to represent *population or species states* instead of organismal states (see p. 48). For instance a binary character that could exist monomorphically as states 0 or 1, or polymorphically as [0,1] gets recoded so that its new states are 0 and 2 for the monomorphic cases and 1 for the polymorphic case. Then one can choose or make a transformation type that indicates how many steps are required between one population state and any other. Perhaps the simplest assumption is that there is one step for any gain or loss of a state and no penalty for retaining polymorphisms; the recoded character could then be treated as ordered. This logic can be extended to a three- and four-state character. (For more than four organism states, the number of population states becomes larger than 26, the most states allowed by MacClade.) If one believed it to be one step for any gain of a state and one step for any loss, with no penalty for retaining polymorphisms, a user-defined type with the following matrix of steps could be used for a three-state character:

To:	0	1	2	01	02	12	012
From: 0	0	2	2	1	1	3	2
1	2	0	2	1	3	1	2
2	2	2	0	3	1	1	2
01	1	1	3	0	2	2	1
02	1	3	1	2	0	2	1
12	3	1	1	2	2	0	1
012	2	2	2	1	1	1	0

Thus it is 2 steps to go from condition 0 (monomorphic for 0) to 012 (polymorphic for 0, 1, and 2), but 3 steps to go from 0 to 12 because states 1 and 2 would need to be gained and state 0 lost. To implement this in MacClade, a new recoded population character could be made that codes the population states 0, 1, 2, 01, 02, 12, and 012 to be represented by states with symbols A, B, C, D, E, F, and G (for instance).

The original organismal character might lead one to superimpose various weights to changes. For instance, the step matrix for population transformations might be:

To:	0	1	2	01	02	12	012
From: 0	0	2	4	1	3	3	2
1	2	0	2	1	3	1	2
2	4	2	0	3	3	1	2
01	1	1	3	0	2	2	1
02	3	3	3	2	0	2	1
12	3	1	1	2	2	0	1
012	2	2	2	1	1	1	0

if the original three-state organismal character was constrained to evolve in an ordered sequence. That is, if to change from state 0 to state 2, one had to go via state 1, then to go from population state 0 to state 02, three steps are required: first, evolve 1 from 0; then, evolve 2 from 1; then, lose 1. This would be appropriate, for instance to model the transition from an XXO species to an XXXY species by two chromosome fusions (W. Maddison, 1982): first, one fusion occurs to give XXY, then another to give XXXY, and the intermediate XXY and the original XXO need to be lost.

Users interested in exploring other ideas about retained polymorphism may want to investigate some of the options of Felsenstein's (1991) PHYLIP computer package or Swofford and Berlocher's (1987) FreqPars.

Finding the most-parsimonious ancestral states

The problem of reconstructing the character states of ancestors using the principle of parsimony can be phrased as the following question: Given the form of the phylogenetic tree, the states observed in the terminal taxa, and the assumptions regarding character evolution, what assignments of states to the internal nodes of the tree require the fewest evolutionary steps? In this section we will describe algorithms to find what states can be parsimoniously assigned to each node of a tree. We will not consider algorithms to resolve individual reconstructions in cases of ambiguity; these are described in the following section.

In some cases it may be intuitively obvious how states can be most parsimoniously assigned to ancestors. For instance if all the extant members of one clade share state 1, then it is simplest to suppose all of the ancestral members of the clade also had state 1. In other cases it may not be so easy. Thus a number of algorithms have been developed to find the most-parsimonious reconstruction of ancestral states on a tree (Farris, 1970, 1977, 1978; Fitch, 1971; Fitch and Farris, 1974; Hartigan, 1973; Moore et al., 1973; Sankoff and Rousseau, 1975; Wagner, 1981; Rogers, 1984; Sankoff and Cedergren, 1983; Swofford and Berlocher, 1987; Swofford and Maddison, 1987; W. Maddison, 1989, 1991; Rinsma et al., 1990; Strauss, in press). Some of these are reviewed by Swofford and Maddison (in press). These different algorithms have been written to handle different restrictive assumptions they impose on character evolution. For instance, the algorithm of Farris (1970), completed by Swofford and Maddison (1987), reconstructs character evolution under the assumption that states are linearly ordered.

In the following sections the algorithms, as formulated in MacClade, are described. In these descriptions we will imagine that we are assigning states to the nodes of the tree. The nodes are the branching points; between them are the internodes or edges (see Chapter 4). Graphically, MacClade colors a node and the internode beneath it together as a single unit, though a change between one node and the next could have occurred anywhere along the internode between them.

The algorithms of MacClade are exact in that they find (barring bugs) all and only the most-parsimonious assignments of character states that can be made to every node of the tree. There are two known exceptions to this: for user-defined type characters in which some taxa are polymorphic with more than two states, and for characters in which polymorphic observed taxa are made ancestral, MacClade may not give all most-parsimonious assignments. These problems are discussed below.

What information is used?

A parsimony reconstruction of character evolution uses three sources of information: the phylogenetic tree, the character states observed in the extant and fossil taxa, and the assumptions about character evolution. Whether the whole phylogenetic tree, or only part of it, is used in reconstructing ancestral states has been a matter of some confusion.

In phylogenetic systematics a distinction is made between the ingroup or study group, consisting of the descendants of a particular ancestor, and the outgroups, consisting of groups closely related to but not descendant from this ancestor (e.g., Watrous and Wheeler, 1981). In order to determine which traits are derived (apomorphic) and thus indicate monophyletic groups within the ingroup, the states of outgroups have been classically used to reconstruct ancestral states (Stevens, 1980; Watrous and Wheeler, 1981; Farris, 1982; Maddison et al., 1984). Outgroup analysis has been a popular method to determine character polarity for this purpose, and so it is not surprising that its use has been extended to trace pathways and patterns of character evolution in general (e.g., Ridley, 1983; Mooi, 1989). These authors have suggested that one could reconstruct ancestral states by applying outgroup analysis stepwise, working from the bottom of the tree toward nodes higher and higher up. In our context, one could think of outgroup analysis as basing the state reconstruction of an internal node entirely on information from the node's sister group and cousins, that is, from terminal taxa below and beside the internal node, without any information from the node's descendants. In terms of the algorithms, using sequential outgroup analysis to estimate ancestral states would be like using only the states from the "uppass" of the algorithms (see "How the algorithms work", below). While such an estimate may be adequate for special purposes, such as to help obtain a parsimonious reconstruction of phylogeny within the ingroup (Maddison et al., 1984), it is not adequate in general as an estimate of the ancestral state because it fails to take into account evidence from the descendants of the internal node of interest (Maddison et al., 1984:89).

One might take an exactly opposite approach — reconstruct a node's state using only information from its descendants. After all, if one tests a reconstruction by comparing its implications about what data are expected against observed data, then one might argue that the state at an internal node has implications only about its descendants, since only these are biologically derived from the ancestor. However, this would be confusing biological derivation with logical derivation. An outgroup's (cousin's) states give us evidence about the state at an internal node, because the states at the internal node's sisters and cousins might suggest a state at the internal node's ancestor, which might in turn suggest states at the internal node itself.

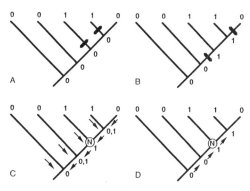

Both MPR's (A and B)
and Farris's (1970) method (C and D)

The states of both descendants and cousins can influence what is the parsimonious reconstruction of an internal node's states. The need to consider information evenly from above and below a node is well illustrated by the behavior of Farris's (1970) algorithm, which finds only some of the most-parsimonious reconstructions for ordered characters (Swofford and Maddison, 1987). In the example to the left, there are two equally parsimonious reconstructions, one in which state 1 is gained twice independently (tree A at left) and another in which state 1 is gained then later lost (tree B). Farris's (1970) algorithm first proceeds downward on the tree, assigning sets of states to the nodes according to the preferences of the clade above the node, as shown in tree C. In particular, note that state 1 is assigned to the node N. Because the pass back up the tree (tree D) can only resolve ambiguities remaining from the downpass, information from below node N has only a secondary role in determining N's state since it cannot overrule the decisive assignment of 1 to N. The priority given to the clade above N prevents the discovery of equally parsimonious compromises which are disfavored above N but favored by the part of the tree below N. Information from all parts of the tree needs to be considered evenly for all optimal reconstructions to be found, at least under many assumptions of character change.

Because MacClade considers the whole tree when reconstructing ancestral states at any given node, it does not shade the outgroup node the same as would be achieved using the "outgroup algorithm" of Maddison et al. (1984), which considers the outgroup in isolation from the ingroup (see Maddison et al., 1984:88).

How the algorithms work

Each of these algorithms works in a similar way. Each moves through the tree, distilling information as it goes, in order to arrive at estimates for the states at each node. Information from above and below the node is distilled and combined to yield the estimate. Thus the state estimated for a node will depend on the information distilled (1) down through the clade of the node's left descendant, (2) down through the right descendant's clade, and (3) up from the part of the tree below and beside the node. These three sources of information converge at the node and indicate its state, as shown at left.

In practice this distilling process is done in two or three passes up and down the tree. The details of the process differ with the different assumptions used. As an example, let us choose the algorithm for unordered characters.

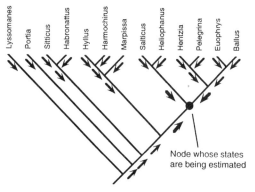

Node whose states
are being estimated

Algorithms distill information
through tree

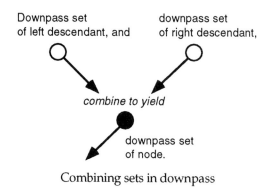

Downpass set
of left descendant, and

downpass set
of right descendant,

combine to yield

downpass set
of node.

Combining sets in downpass

The algorithm first makes a pass down the tree from the terminal taxa to the root (we will call it the **downpass**). As it proceeds down the tree, the algorithm visits each node and calculates a set of states that can be appropriately assigned to that node. This set will be called the **downpass set** of the node, because this is the set of states preferred by that part of the tree above the node. To calculate this set of states, the algorithm uses the sets already calculated from the two nodes immediately above (descendant from) the node being visited. The unordered algorithm uses the following calculation: a node is assigned the set of states that are present in both state sets of the two descendant nodes if there are any such; if no states are present in both sets above, the node is assigned the union of the sets of the two descendant nodes. Once the state set has been calculated for the node being visited, the algorithm can then move down the tree to the node's immediate ancestor and perform the calculation on it. The algorithm continues down until it eventually arrives at the root. The downpass set at a node can be seen by holding the Option key and touching the list-states tool on the branch when a character is traced in MacClade.

The states assigned to a node on the first downpass of the algorithm are not necessarily the most-parsimonious assignments to the node according to the whole tree. When we arrive at a node on the downpass, only the nodes descendant from it have been used in the calculation of the visited node's states. Thus, the states assigned on the downpass are most parsimonious according to the clade above it, but may not be most parsimonious according to the whole tree since the state calculations have not yet considered nodes below the visited node. There is one exception to this result, in that there is one node for which the downpass states are most parsimonious. By the time the algorithm gets to the root, it has considered the entire tree, and the states assigned to the root are indeed the most-parsimonious states according to the whole tree.

We want to know eventually, for every node, the set of states that can be most parsimoniously assigned to it according to the whole tree. Because the downpass algorithm guarantees whole-tree parsimony for the states assigned to the root, one way to achieve our goal would be to reroot the tree at each node, each time performing the downpass algorithm ending up at the new root, and thus finding the whole-tree parsimony state sets for each node. Effectively, MacClade does this, but there is a much more efficient way besides actually rerooting the tree and performing a whole new downpass each time (Swofford and Maddison, 1987; Swofford and Maddison, in press).

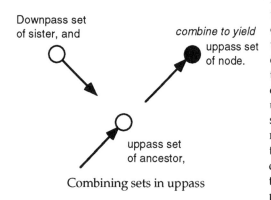

Downpass set
of sister, and

combine to yield
uppass set
of node.

uppass set
of ancestor,

Combining sets in uppass

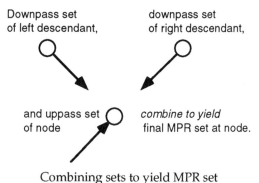

Downpass set
of left descendant,

downpass set
of right descendant,

and uppass set
of node

combine to yield
final MPR set at node.

Combining sets to yield MPR set

After doing a single downpass, MacClade does another pass going up the tree (the **uppass**). The set of states assigned on the uppass will be called the **uppass set** of the node. This is the set of states preferred by that part of the tree below the node. The uppass state set of a node is calculated from the uppass set of the node below it (its ancestor) with the downpass set of the node beside it (its sister node), using the same calculation for combining state sets as for the downpass. The root has no uppass set. A node immediately descendant from the root gets its uppass set directly from the downpass set of its sister, since its ancestor (the root) has no uppass set. The uppass set at a node can be seen by holding the Option key and touching the list-states tool on the branch when a character is traced in MacClade. If {1} is indicated as the uppass set, then the node is most parsimoniously assigned state 1 according to the part of the tree below this node, that consists of the node's immediate ancestor, the node's sister node, and parts further away.

Once this second pass has been completed, we now have information distilled from all parts of the tree surrounding any node. For each node we know the opinion of its right-descendant clade as to what states the node should take (the downpass set of the right-descendant node), we know the opinion of its left-descendant clade (the downpass set of the left-descendant node), and we know the opinion from below the node (the uppass set of the node itself). These three opinions are then combined in a calculation that results in the final state set for the node (Swofford and Maddison, 1987). This calculation condenses three state sets into one. For unordered characters, it chooses those states occurring in the greatest number of the three sets. The set of states assigned is the set of all most-parsimonious states for the node, and will be called the **MPR set** of the node. We will emphasize the fact that it is found by the final pass of MacClade's algorithms by occasionally calling it the final MPR set of the node.

As MacClade is doing its calculations, it displays different cursors to indicate at what stage of the calculations it is in. When it is finding which states occur in the taxa in the tree, is shows ⛎. ⛎ is shown when assigning downpass sets to terminal nodes. For some character types, cursors ⛏, ⛏, and ⛏ are displayed for the downpass, uppass and final passes, respectively. For step-matrix type characters (including those with character state trees), MacClade displays ⛏, ⛏, and ⛏ for the downpass, uppass, and final passes, respectively. While calculating the minimum or maximum conceivable number of steps in the characters, it shows ⛏.

Polytomies When a polytomy is encountered, the algorithm needs to combine information from multiple nodes to yield the information placed at the polytomous node. The combining methods are described below in the context of each character transformation type. The method differs depending on whether the polytomy is treated as multiple speciation ("hard") or uncertainty ("soft"), as discussed by W. Maddison (1989) and below. The reader should refer to the section on interpreting character tracing (p. 243) and the discussion of polytomies (p. 117) for comments on the interpretations of polytomies.

The calculations on polytomies are particularly slow, since MacClade moves through the polytomous region to survey the multiple nodes separately for each character.

Designating observed taxa as ancestors When observed taxa are designated as ancestors, MacClade assumes that the states observed in the taxon are directly on the internal node, except for stratigraphic characters, where special rules apply. For unordered, ordered, and irreversible characters, if the taxon was monomorphic or polymorphic, its states are forced to lie directly on the internal node N. (As noted in Chapter 12, an observed taxon fixed as an ancestor can have only one descendant in MacClade.)

If the observed ancestral taxon had missing data or uncertain states, then N's states are flexible, being assigned in part according to the preferences of surrounding nodes. On the downpass, N acts as a filter of the downpass set from its descendant node. If N's taxon had missing data, the downpass set of N's descendant node is passed directly into N's downpass set. If N's taxon was of uncertain state, then N is assigned a downpass set consisting of those among the possible states at N that are closest to the downpass set of N's descendant. On the uppass, N acts similarly as a filter if its states were uncertain or unknown. On the final pass, the observed taxon, if of uncertain state, is treated temporarily as if it were not set in ancestral position, and N's states assessed using standard algorithms for combining preferences from the observed taxon, its sister node, and N's ancestor. This preliminary state set indicates the preferences from around the tree. N's set is then assigned to include those states in the taxon's possible observed states that are closest to the preliminary state set.

Counting steps The descriptions of the algorithms focus on the problem of finding the MPR sets. However, there are some notes in each algorithm description regarding how the minimum number of steps in the character is counted. The problem of counting steps is discussed toward the end of this chapter, but notes are included here because it is much easier to describe the counting process in the context of the reconstruction algorithms.

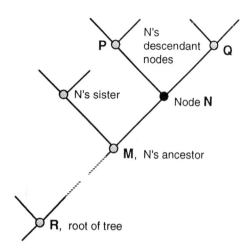

Terms In the following few sections we will give details about the exact calculations used in the algorithms. Generally, the node being discussed will be called N, its two descendant nodes P and Q (assuming N is dichotomous), and its ancestor M. The root of the whole tree will be called R.

The downpass set at N will be called D_N, the uppass set U_N, and the final MPR set F_N. A set of states including only the state t will be indicated as {t}; a set of states consisting of states a through b inclusive will be indicated as {a...b}. The number of elements in a set T is card(T). The smallest element in T will be called min(T); the largest element max(T). The set {min(T)...max(T)}, containing all elements from the smallest in T to the largest, will be called range(T). The set $\mathbf{)}$(A,B) will consist of A∩B if it is not empty; otherwise it is the element in A closest to B.

Unordered characters

Algorithms for unordered characters were first developed and proved by Fitch (1971) and Hartigan (1973); the algorithm is thus occasionally called "Fitch optimization". Hard polytomy algorithms are due to Hartigan; soft to W. Maddison (1989).

As mentioned above, the algorithms combine state sets of nearby nodes.

For unordered characters, designate the combining function by ⊕. The combination of two sets A and B, designated ⊕(A,B), is the intersection of A and B if it is not empty; otherwise it is the union of A and B. The combination of three sets A, B, and C, designated ⊕(A,B,C), is the intersection of A, B and C, if it is not empty; otherwise it is the union of pairwise intersections of the three sets [(A∩B)∪(A∩C)∪(B∩C)], if this is not empty; otherwise it is the union of A, B, and C.

Unordered		
Assignment of <u>downpass set to terminal nodes (card (T) is the number of states in T)</u>:		
State observed for terminal taxon:	Downpass set assigned to terminal node:	Steps counted
One observed state, t	{t}	0
Observed set of states T, uncertain	T	0
Observed set of states T, polymorphic	T	card(T)–1
Missing data	{0...maxstate}	0
Assignment of <u>downpass set to internal node N</u> based on sets at descendant nodes:		
When N has two descendants P and Q, with downpass sets D_P and D_Q: Assign ⊕(D_P,D_Q). *Steps:* One step is counted if a union was required in ⊕.		
When N is polytomous, with k descendants with downpass sets D_1 ... D_K: "Soft" polytomy: Assign union of the smallest sets covering D_1 ... D_K, where a state set S is said to cover D_1 ... D_K if S has a non-empty intersection with each of D_1 ... D_K. *Steps:* m–1 steps are counted where m is the number of states in a smallest covering set.		

"Hard" polytomy: Assign set consisting of those states occurring most frequently among D_1 ... D_K. *Steps:* k–m steps are counted where m is the number of descendant nodes with one of the most frequent states.

When N is an observed taxon fixed as an ancestor, with descendant with downpass set D_P:

When N's observed set of states T is polymorphic or monomorphic: Assign T.

When N's observed set of states T is marked as uncertain: Assign $T \cap D_P$ if it is not empty; otherwise assign T.

When N has missing data: Assign D_P.

Steps: Except if N has missing data, one step is counted whenever $T \cap D_P$ is empty.

Assignment of <u>uppass set to N</u>:

Use same calculations as for downpass, except that when N's ancestor is dichotomous, combine N's ancestor's uppass set with N's sister's downpass set to yield N's uppass set; when N's ancestor is polytomous, combine N's ancestor's uppass set with downpass sets of all of N's sisters to yield N's uppass set; when N's ancestor M is an observed taxon fixed as an ancestor, N's uppass set is calculated using M's observed states and U_M just as T and D_P were used, respectively, in the downpass with taxon fixed as ancestor. (Since the root does not have an uppass set, if N's ancestor is the root, then assign for N's uppass set simply its sister node's downpass set.)

Assignment of <u>final MPR set to terminal node N</u> with observed set T and ancestor M:

When M is a dichotomous or hard polytomous node:

When T is monomorphic: Assign T.

When T is polymorphic: Assign F_M if F_M is a subset of T; otherwise assign $T \cup F_M$.

When T has uncertain states: Assign F_M if F_M is a subset of T; otherwise assign T .

When T is missing data: Assign F_M.

When N's ancestor is a soft polytomous node:

When T is monomorphic: Assign T.

When T is polymorphic, or with uncertain states: Assign $\oplus(T, U_N)$.

When terminal taxon had missing data: Assign U_N.

Assignment of <u>final MPR set to internal node N</u> based on sets at surrounding nodes:

When N is the root: Assign N's downpass set to be the final MPR set.

When N has uppass set U_N and two descendants P and Q with downpass sets D_P and D_Q: Assign $\oplus(D_P, D_Q, U_N)$.

When N has uppass set U_N, downpass set D_N and is polytomous, with k descendants with downpass sets D_1 ... D_K:

"Soft" polytomy: Assign $\oplus(D_N, U_N)$. (Recall node is below polytomy; see p. 243.)

"Hard" polytomy: Use the same calculations as for hard polytomies in downpass, except use sets D_1 ... D_K and U_N.

When N is an observed taxon fixed as an ancestor, with uppass set U_N, and with descendant P with downpass set D_P:

When N was observed monomorphic or polymorphic: Assign observed state(s).

When N had uncertain states, set T: Assign $T \cap \oplus(T, D_P, U_N)$ if it is not empty; otherwise assign T.

When terminal taxon had missing data: Assign $\oplus(D_P, U_N)$.

Ordered characters

Farris's (1970) algorithm ("Farris optimization" or "Wagner parsimony") for ordered characters found only some of the most-parsimonious assignments (see p. 88); it was completed and proved by Swofford and Maddison (1987). The ordered algorithm in MacClade is basically that of Swofford and Maddison. Polytomy algorithms are due to W. Maddison (1989).

As mentioned above, the algorithms combine state sets of nearby nodes.

For ordered characters, designate the combining operator by $\otimes$. It is assumed that each state set contains all states between any two of its states; that is, there are no gaps in the set. (If there are, convert the set to its own range.) The combination of two sets A and B, designated $\otimes(A,B)$, is the intersection of A and B, if it is not empty; otherwise it is $\{max(A)...min(B)\}$ if $min(B)>max(A)$; otherwise it is $\{max(B)...min(A)\}$. The combination of three sets A, B, and C, designated $\otimes(A,B,C)$, is the intersection of A, B, and C, if not empty; otherwise the two sets among the A, B, and C that are furthest apart are found, and the range between them is intersected with the third set's range to yield the assignment. This can also be calculated as:

$$\otimes(\otimes(A,B),C) \cap \otimes(\otimes(A,C),B) \cap \otimes(\otimes(B,C),A) .$$

Ordered

Assignment of downpass set to terminal nodes:

State observed for terminal taxon:	Downpass set assigned to terminal node:	Steps counted
One observed state, t	$\{t\}$	0
Observed set of states T, uncertain	range(T)	0
Observed set of states T, polymorphic	range(T)	max(T)–min(T)
Missing data	$\{0...maxstate\}$	0

Assignment of <u>downpass set to internal node N</u> based on sets at descendant nodes:

When N has two descendants P and Q, with downpass sets D_P and D_Q: Assign $\otimes(D_P,D_Q)$. *Steps:* count the distance between D_P and D_Q if they do not overlap.

When N is polytomous, with k descendants with downpass sets $D_1 ... D_K$:

"Soft" polytomy: Assign intersection of $D_1 ... D_K$, if not empty; otherwise assign the closed interval bounded by the smallest maximum to the largest minimum among the $D_1 ... D_K$. *Steps:* Count the number of steps between the smallest maximum and largest minimum if the intersection of $D_1 ... D_K$ was empty.

"Hard" polytomy: Assign intersection of $D_1 ... D_K$, if not empty; otherwise assign the set of all those states s such that $R_s \leq L_s+1$ and $L_s \leq R_s-1$, where R_s is the number of sets among the $D_1 ... D_K$ all of whose elements are greater than s, L_s is the number of sets all of whose elements are less than s. *Steps:* Choose one such state s and sum the distances from s to each of the sets whose elements do not include s.

When N is an observed taxon fixed as an ancestor, with descendant with downpass set D_P:

N's observed set of states T is polymorphic or monomorphic: Assign range(T).

N's observed set of states T is uncertain: Assign $\blacktriangleright(range(T),D_P)$.

N has missing data: Assign D_P.

Steps: Except if N has missing data, count the distance between range(T) and D_P .

Assignment of <u>uppass set to N</u>:
See description under "Unordered characters".

Assignment of <u>final MPR set to terminal node N</u>:
Define B to be N's uppass set if N's ancestor is a soft polytomy; otherwise B is final MPR set at N's ancestor.

When terminal taxon was observed monomorphic: Assign observed state.

When terminal taxon was observed polymorphic, or with uncertain states: Assign $\blacktriangleright(D_N,B)$.

When terminal taxon had missing data: Assign B.

Assignment of <u>final MPR set to internal node N</u> based on sets at surrounding nodes:

When N is the root: Assign N's downpass set to be the final MPR set.

When N has uppass set U_N and two descendants P and Q with downpass sets D_P and D_Q: Assign $\otimes(D_P, D_Q, U_N)$.

When N has uppass set U_N, downpass set D_N and is polytomous, with k descendants with downpass sets $D_1 \ldots D_K$:

"Soft" polytomy: Assign $\otimes(D_N, U_N)$. (Recall node is below polytomy; see p. 243.)

"Hard" polytomy: Use the same calculations as for hard polytomies in downpass, except use sets $D_1 \ldots D_K$ and U_N.

When N is an observed taxon fixed as an ancestor, with uppass set U_N, and with descendant P with downpass set D_P:

When N was observed monomorphic or polymorphic with observed states T: Assign range(T).

When N had uncertain states, set T: Assign $\blacktriangleright(\text{range}(T), \otimes(\text{range}(T), D_P, U_N))$.

When N had missing data: Assign $\otimes(D_P, U_N)$.

Irreversible characters

Camin and Sokal (1965) have discussed the use of irreversible characters. That part of the algorithm in MacClade that handles uncertainties and missing data is original to MacClade. Polytomies are not allowed for irreversible characters because of difficulties with uncertain states and soft polytomies.

As mentioned above, the algorithms combine state sets of nearby nodes. For irreversible characters, designate the combining operator by $\Rightarrow$. It is assumed that each state set contains all states between any two of its states; that is, there are no gaps in the set. (If there are, convert the set to its own range.) The combination of the sets A and B of two descendant nodes with the final MPR set C at an ancestral node, designated $\Rightarrow(A,B,C)$, is the union of the [intersection of A, B, and C] with the [intersection of the (smaller of the minimum values in A and B) with the (range from minimum value in C to the larger of the minimum values in A and B)]. This can be written $(A \cap B \cap C) \cup ([\min(\{\min(A), \min(B)\})] \cap \{\min(C) \ldots \max(\{\min(A), \min(B)\})\})$.

Irreversible

Assignment of <u>downpass set to terminal nodes</u>:

State observed for terminal taxon:	Downpass set assigned to terminal node:	Steps counted
One observed state, t	{t}	0
Observed set of states T, uncertain	range(T)	0
Observed set of states T, polymorphic	{min(T)}	max(T)–min(T)
Missing data	{0...maxstate}	0

Assignment of <u>downpass set to internal node N</u> based on sets at descendant nodes:

N has two descendants P and Q, with downpass sets D_P and D_Q: Assign intersection of the D_P and D_Q, if not empty; otherwise assign set consisting of the state that is the smaller of the maximum values of D_P and D_Q. *Steps:* If intersection was empty, count steps from smaller maximum to larger minimum.

N is an observed taxon fixed as an ancestor, with descendant with downpass set D_P:

When N's observed set of states T is polymorphic or monomorphic: Assign range(T).

When N's observed set of states T is uncertain: $\blacktriangleright(\text{range}(T), D_P)$.

When N has missing data: Assign D_P.

Steps: Except if N has missing data, count the distance between range(T) and D_P.

Assignment of uppass set to N:
No uppass sets are assigned.

Assignment of <u>final MPR set to terminal node N</u> with downpass set D_N and ancestor M with final MPR set F_M:

When terminal taxon was observed monomorphic or polymorphic: Assign D_N.

When terminal taxon was observed with uncertain states: Assign ▶(D_N, F_M).

When terminal taxon had missing data: Assign F_M.

Assignment of <u>final MPR set to internal node N</u> based on sets at surrounding nodes:

When N is the root: Assign N's downpass set to be the final MPR set.

When N has two descendants P and Q with downpass sets D_P and D_Q, and ancestor M with final MPR set F_M: Assign ↻(D_P,D_Q,F_M).

When N is an observed taxon fixed as ancestor, with set T of observed states and with descendant P with downpass set D_P, and ancestor M with final MPR set F_M:

When T is monomorphic or polymorphic: Assign T.

When T has uncertain states: Assign range(T)∩↻(D_P,range(T),F_M).

When T is missing data: Assign ↻(D_P,{0...maxstate},F_M).

If the result is empty, irreversibility has been violated by the ancestral placement.

Stratigraphic characters

MacClade's implementation of Fisher's (1992) stratigraphic parsimony uses algorithms developed by W. Maddison and described below. *These algorithms are complex, and though they have been intensively examined and tested, they are considered unstable and in certain circumstances may not be completely valid. To document the algorithms' behavior, a test data file showing numerous examples is included with MacClade.* These algorithms are modified from the algorithms for irreversible characters. Users are advised to read the description below so as to be able to interpret better the somewhat unorthodox output MacClade gives with stratigraphic characters. This is especially important because MacClade's tracing of stratigraphic characters does not indicate ages of ancestors in the same way that its tracing of other characters indicates states of ancestors.

Algorithms The basic rules for assigning ages to ancestral nodes are as follows: (1) ancestors must predate descendants; (2) ancestors should be assigned ages so as to minimize implications of missing fossils.

Stratigraphic
Assignment of <u>downpass sets, final MPR sets</u> for all cases except when observed taxa fixed as ancestors:

Use the same algorithms as for irreversible characters, but count steps only as indicated below.

When observed taxa are fixed as ancestors:

Assignment of <u>downpass sets to internal nodes</u> : Treat the tree as if the observed taxa were not fixed as ancestors and use the irreversible character algorithms above.

Assignment of <u>final MPR set to root node N</u> when N is an observed taxon fixed as ancestor, with set T of observed states and downpass set D_N, and with descendant node P with downpass set D_P:

When N is polymorphic (i.e., observed in more than one stratum): Assign
↪(range(T),D$_P$,range(D$_N$+ {max(D$_P$)})).
When N is not polymorphic: Assign D$_N$.
Assignment of <u>final MPR set to internal node N</u> (not the root) when N is an observed taxon fixed
as ancestor, with set T of observed states, and with descendant node P with downpass set D$_P$,
and with ancestral node M with final MPR set F$_M$:
When T is monomorphic: Assign T.
When T is missing data: Assign [F$_M$∩D$_P$]∪[min(F$_M$)...min(D$_P$)].
When T is uncertainty: Assign the state H just below the first gap in T — if H is larger than
min(F$_M$), assign ↪(range(T),D$_P$,range(F$_M$+ {min(H,max(D$_P$))})),
otherwise ↪(range(T),D$_P$,F$_M$).
When T is polymorphic: Assign ↪(range(T),D$_P$,range(F$_M$+ {max(D$_P$)})).

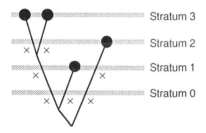

Ancestors placed before descendants

Stratum 3
Stratum 2
Stratum 1
Stratum 0

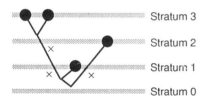

Minimizing stratum crossings

Stratum 3
Stratum 2
Stratum 1
Stratum 0

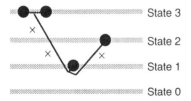

Irreversible character

State 3
State 2
State 1
State 0

Explanation of algorithm Suppose we had a tree of four taxa occurring in various strata, and we drew the branches of the tree so as to indicate possible ages of the various parts of the tree. If at first we only constrained our placement of ancestors so that they were older than descendants, we might end up with something like as shown at left, above.

The x's mark instances where a lineage crosses a stratum without represented fossils. Clearly this reconstruction has more such absences than necessary. There is no point in having two adjacent lineages crossing the same stratum if by moving their common ancestor above the stratum only one crossing would be required. The most-parsimonious assignment of ages to ancestors would therefore push all branch points as high a possible, so that the number of lineages crossing strata would be minimized, as at left, middle.

The rule is therefore that one pushes the ancestors as high as possible without violating the principle that ancestors must predate descendants. The rule for irreversible characters is the same except that ancestors and descendants are allowed to coexist on the same state. Thus an irreversible character would have its ancestral states reconstructed as shown at left, below.

In this figure the x's represent not the crossing of strata but changes from one state to the next. The number of x's is the same as the number of stratum crossings counted above since a stratum crossing is required every time a descendant is assigned to a younger stratum and there is not an observed ancestor to represent this crossing, just as a character state transition in an irreversible character is required every time a descendant is assigned to a higher character state number than its ancestor. Thus, the irreversible algorithm can be used without modification to count the minimal number of stratum crossings and reconstruct stratigraphic ages when none of the observed taxa are treated as ancestors, except an assignment of stratum i to an unobserved ancestral branch point must be interpreted as saying that the branch point was just below the stratum, to avoid the prohibition against coexistence of ancestors and descendants. This is a point worthy of note. When you see that

MacClade assigns stratum i to an ancestral node, do not take this as indicating that MacClade reconstructs the ancestor to have occurred exactly in stratum i, unless the ancestor was an observed taxon considered as a direct ancestor.

If there are observed taxa that are considered direct ancestors, then the number of character transitions that would be counted if age were simply considered an irreversible character cannot be directly used to indicate the number of stratum crossings. The reason for this is that the descent of a lineage from one stratum to the next younger would not have to require an unrepresented crossing of the older stratum if there were an observed ancestor to represent the crossing:

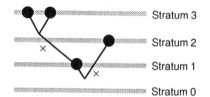

Observed taxon placed as ancestor

With irreversible characters, a state transition would have to be recorded regardless of whether the ancestor was observed or not. This difference can be easily accounted for by modifying the irreversible algorithm so that whenever a taxon is considered a direct ancestor, it can be used to account for a stratum crossing without cost.

MacClade therefore uses the irreversible algorithm with several modifications in order to reconstruct ancestral stratigraphic ages. The modifications concern observed taxa fixed as ancestors. For stratigraphic characters, the state at a node that is an observed taxon fixed as ancestor is reconstructed as if the observed taxon were still terminal. That is, this node is not forced to take the observed stratigraphic ages of the taxon. For instance, if you place an observed taxon known only from higher strata in ancestral position to taxa known from lower strata, MacClade will suppose the observed taxon actually extended deeper, and the actual ancestors were organisms with the exact same states in all non-stratigraphic characters but in lower strata. This is done to avoid ancestors being younger than descendants.

In the above discussion it was noted that an ancestor and its descendant could not coexist in the same stratum. MacClade enforces this, although there are circumstances in which coexistence appears to be allowed.

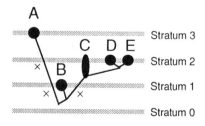

Treatment of ancestor (C)
and descendants (D and E)
found in same stratum

For instance, suppose species C, D, and E were all found in stratum 2, yet C was designated as being ancestral to D and E, as shown on the left. In this case, MacClade interprets the designation of C as an ancestor as not applying only to the members of C sampled from stratum 2, but rather to identical forms just below stratum 2, in the inter-stratum zone between 1 and 2. These ancestral forms gave rise to D and E. This allows MacClade to avoid supposing that an ancestor and its descendants coexisted in stratum 2.

In MacClade's tracing of a stratigraphic character, a branch is shaded with a special pattern (⬍) if it is reconstructed to have multiple states. With other character types, an observed taxon fixed as an ancestor is shaded by the polymorphic or uncertain pattern depending on whether the taxon was coded with the AND or the OR separator (see Chapter 10). With stratigraphic types, it is difficult to determine whether multiple states reconstructed at a node represent uncertainty in the node's position or the spanning of several strata by the node. MacClade therefore ambiguously indicates multiple states with the special pattern.

Counting stratigraphic parsimony The following description gives an outline of MacClade's algorithm to count steps in stratigraphic characters. The original source code should be consulted for full details.

To count stratigraphic parsimony, the total cost of implied but unobserved crossing of strata (missing fossils), MacClade reconstructs ancestral stratigraphic positions then counts implied stratum crossing. After the ancestral states in the stratigraphic character are reconstructed, MacClade begins at the root and finds one resolution of any ambiguity in stratigraphic position. The state so resolved for node N will be called S_N. Each node N is assigned the highest state in its final MPR set, to take maximal advantage of its accounting for crossing strata. As the counting algorithm moves up the tree, it treats each node N as follows. Assume the node ancestral to N is M.

Designating resolved stratum assignments:
  When N is an internal node, but not an observed taxon fixed as ancestor:
    When N is root: Designate S_N to be $\max(F_N)$.
    When N is not root: Designate S_N to be the larger of S_M and $\min(F_N)$.
  When N is an observed taxon:
    When N is observed taxon fixed as ancestor: Designate S_N to be $\max(F_N)$.
    When N is observed terminal taxon: Designation not needed.

Counting steps (these alternatives are not mutually exclusive):
  When N is an internal or external node, and is not the root: If S_M is below the lowest stratum in F_N ($\min(F_N)$), then this implies that N's ancestral lineage crossed the intervening strata. Count the stratum crossings from S_M to $\min(F_N)$, not including the crossing of the stratum $\min(F_N)$, but including the crossing of S_M if its crossing was not accounted for earlier in the tree. Record that S_M's crossing is now accounted for, but that $\min(F_N)$'s crossing has not been accounted for.
  When N is observed taxon fixed as ancestor: Count unobserved stratum crossings for any strata from S_M to S_N that are not included among N's observed strata (if the lowest observed stratum of N is above S_N, then count stratum crossings from S_N to this lowest). S_N, which was designated as the highest stratum in F_N, will be passed to any nodes descendant from N, to which it will be known as S_M (see above). When this value is passed up, it will be indicated that this stratum's crossing has been accounted for if S_N is among N's observed or possibly observed strata, unless its descendant node is reconstructed as having this same state, in which case the stratum cannot be considered accounted for without violating the prohibition against co-occurrence of ancestors and descendants in the same stratum.
  When N is polymorphic observed taxon (i.e., known from more than one stratum): Count unobserved stratum crossings for any strata not included within the taxon's observed strata but that are between the lowest and highest observed crossing.

The most complex part of the counting concerns nodes that are observed taxa placed in ancestral position. If N is an observed taxon fixed as an ancestor, then the strata in which it has been observed are therefore accounted for by observed fossils, and we need not count unobserved stratum crossings. Therefore, where possible, the observed fossils are placed along the branch leading up to the taxon's descendant node. If we have a species B known from strata 0, 2, and 4, and its descendant species C is known from stratum 3, then those samples of species B from strata 0 and 2 can be assumed to be on the line directly ancestral to species C:

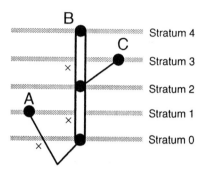

Species A is known from stratum 1, Species B from strata 0, 2, and 4, Species C from stratum 3. Species A and C are treated as terminal, B is considered to be ancestral to C. Three unobserved stratum crossings are required, marked by x's.

Note that in this example the absence of stratum 3 from samples of species B is taken to require an extra stratum crossing.

If species B's stratigraphic position is uncertain, then the algorithm assumes optimistically (for parsimony's sake) that B may be known from each of strata from which samples might possibly derive:

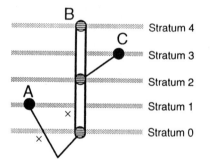

Species A is known from stratum 1, Species B from strata 0, 2, or 4 (uncertain), Species C from stratum 3. Species A and C are treated as terminal, B is considered to be ancestral to C. Two unobserved stratum crossings are required, marked by x's.

If species B's stratigraphic position is completely unknown (missing data) then the algorithm assumes optimistically that B may be known from all strata:

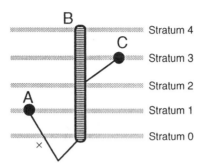

Species A is known from stratum 1,
Species B's strata are not known
(missing data),
Species C from stratum 3.
Species A and C are treated as
terminal, B is considered to be
ancestral to C. One unobserved
stratum crossing is required,
marked by x.

This convention for dealing with uncertain stratigraphic position leads to some difficulties. If many fossil samples are known but none are well dated or correlated, then it may be reasonable to assume optimistically that all strata are represented among the samples. However, if only one specimen is known, but its stratum is not well dated, then clearly we cannot hope that all strata are represented; at most only one stratum is represented by this sample. MacClade follows its convention because it does not yet have the means to indicate in its data matrix both what states a taxon might have in an uncertain character as well as how many states it might have (i.e., "Taxon has exactly one of states 0, 2, or 4", *versus* "Taxon has one or more of states 0, 2, or 4").

Giving different weights to absences in different strata is easily incorporated into the algorithm, because the need to push ancestors as high as possible without violating ancestor precedence does not depend on these different weights. Thus the stratum crossings required are reconstructed the same way regardless of which weights are assigned (unless they are assigned 0), and the only difference is how much we count for each of the crossings so reconstructed.

Dollo characters

A discussion relevant to reconstructing ancestral states for two-state Dollo characters was presented by Farris (1977). The algorithm in MacClade allows multistate Dollo characters. That part of the algorithm in MacClade that handles missing and uncertain data is original to MacClade.

MacClade performs Additive Binary Recoding (Sokal and Sneath, 1963) on Dollo characters. What is described below is the binary version of the algorithm. At each node N is stored two sets: the set recording the last decisive split (E_N), and the set recording the states that would have been assigned to that node were it the root and the clade above it the entire tree (A_N). The E_N set can be thought of as recording what states were on either side of the nearest descendant of N that had non-missing data in both left and right descendant clades. MacClade's algorithms allow only dichotomous trees with all observed taxa terminal.

Dollo

Assignment of <u>downpass sets</u> E_N and A_N <u>to terminal node N</u>:

State observed for terminal taxon:	E_N	A_N
One observed state, 0	{0}	{0}
One observed state, 1	{1}	{1}
States 0 or 1, uncertain, or missing	{}	{0,1}
States 0 and 1, polymorphic	{0,1}	{0,1}

Assignment of <u>downpass sets</u> E_N and A_N <u>to internal node N</u> based on sets at descendant nodes:

Given E_P and E_Q of:		On downpass assign N:	
E_P	E_Q	E_N	A_N
{0}	{0}	{0}	{0}
{0}	{0,1}	{0,1}	{0}
{0}	{1}	{0,1}	{0,1}
{0}	{}	{0}	{0}
{0,1}	{0,1}	{1}	{1}
{0,1}	{1}	{1}	{1}
{0,1}	{}	{0,1}	A_P
{1}	{1}	{1}	{1}
{1}	{}	{1}	{1}
{}	{}	{}	{}

Assignment of uppass set to N:
No uppass sets are assigned.

Assignment of <u>final MPR set to internal node N</u> based on sets at surrounding nodes:
Once the root is reached on the downpass, the set A_R assigned to the root is the most-parsimonious set based on the whole tree, that is it is the final MPR set for R, F_R. The algorithm then can proceed up the tree assigning final MPR sets to all nodes using the E sets of descendants and the final MPR sets of ancestors, as shown below. Assume N has two descendants, P and Q, and ancestor M.

E sets of descendants		Final pass assignments to N for various values of F_M (final MPR sets at M)		
E_P	E_Q	$F_{M=\{0\}}$	$F_{M=\{0,1\}}$	$F_{M=\{1\}}$
{0}	{0}	{0}	{0}	{0}
{0}	{0,1}	{0}	{1}	{0,1}
{0}	{1}	{0}	{1}	{0,1}
{0}	{}	{0}	{0,1}	{0,1}
{0,1}	{0,1}	{1}	{1}	{1}
{0,1}	{1}	{1}	{1}	{1}
{0,1}	{}	{0}	{1}	{0,1}
{1}	{1}	{1}	{1}	{1}
{1}	{}	{0,1}	{1}	{0,1}
{}	{}	{0}	{1}	{0,1}

Once F_N has been calculated for each of the binary factors, they can be recomposed into the final MPR set at node N for the original multistate character.

Assignment of <u>final MPR set (not binary recoded) to terminal node N</u>:
   Assume that the binary recoding has been reversed to obtain the multistate final MPR set at N's ancestor. Define B to be final MPR set at N's ancestor.
   When terminal taxon was observed monomorphic: Assign observed state.
   When terminal taxon was observed polymorphic or with uncertain states: Assign ▶(range(observed states), B).
   When terminal taxon had missing data: Assign B.

Counting steps: No simple method has been described to count steps in a single pass through the tree; MacClade fully reconstructs the ancestral states, then counts steps in the reconstruction.

Step matrices and character state trees

Algorithms for finding the most-parsimonious ancestral states when symmetrical step matrices are used were originally described by Sankoff and Rousseau (1975) and Sankoff and Cedergren (1983). In MacClade 2.1 (Maddison and Maddison, 1987) we extended upon their treatment by allowing asymmetries in distance for gains and losses. Williams and Fitch (1989, 1990) have redescribed the step-matrix algorithm.

In MacClade 3, character state trees are first converted into step matrices and the same algorithms are used as for step-matrix types. This is much less efficient than an alternative method, namely to use additive recoding to break the character state tree into ordered characters.

The algorithm for step-matrix characters follows a similar path through the tree as those for the other character types described above, but differs in that assigned to each node is not a set of states, but rather a number for each possible state. This number records how many steps are required in a section of the tree represented by the node, given that the particular state is assigned to the node. On the downpass, the number records how many steps are required in the clade above the node; on the uppass the number records how many steps are required in the area of the tree below and beside the node. Thus for each possible state that could be assigned to a node, there is a graded scale of goodness, in contrast to the other algorithms in which a state is either included or excluded in a state set as a viable candidate. The algorithm's flexibility, as well as its slowness and other limitations, are due to its keeping records on a graded scale.

The algorithm likewise makes a downpass and an uppass, so that after these passes one has recorded the opinions from the parts of the tree represented by a node's left and right descendants and its ancestor. On the downpass the record for a node N is calculated as follows. Recall that the information to be recorded for N consists of (for each possible state) the number of steps required in N's clade, given that N is assigned this state. So, the algorithm tries assigning each possible state s to N, and for each the minimum number of steps on the left side (N to its left descendant node P and above) and right side (N to its right descendant node Q and above) are added to yield the number of steps required in total in N's clade. The minimum number of steps on the left side, for instance, is calculated by finding the state t assigned to P that yields the lowest sum of steps between N (having s) and P (having t) plus the number of steps required in the clade of P, given P is assigned t. This latter number of steps is available from the information already calculated for P. Thus the records of the two nodes P and Q are combined to yield the information for N. This basic pattern of calculation is followed on the uppass and in the final decision for any given node in which the information for three nodes is combined. After this is done, the states actually assigned to a node are those that require the minimum number of steps according to the whole tree. The minimum number of steps required by the character is directly obtained as part of the reconstruction process: it can be found in the information stored at the node after its final states are reconstructed.

The step-matrix algorithm is therefore conceptually simple. Only one aspect needs particular attention: What to do in terminal taxa that are polymorphic? The following assignments are made:

Assignment of <u>downpass array to terminal node N</u>:	
Missing	0 cost for all states.
Monomorphic	0 cost for observed state, infinity for all others.
Uncertain	0 cost for possible observed states, infinity for all others.
Polymorphic	
Two states, b and c	If a=b, then cost of state a is cost of change a to c.
	If a=c, then cost of state a is cost of change a to b.
	Otherwise, then cost of state a is minimum cost
	among the three possibilities for changes,
	a→b→c, a→c→b, and b←a→c.
Three or more states	If a is one of the observed states, then cost of state a
	is minimum cost of a change from a to
	any other state in polymorphism.
	Otherwise cost of state a is infinity.

For missing data, the assignment allows any states to be placed at the terminal node with no cost within the terminal taxon. For taxa that are monomorphic or multistate uncertain, then any of the possible states are allowed at no cost but unobserved states are prohibited. For taxa that are polymorphic with two states, the above assignment presumes that states b and c might be evolved within the terminal taxon, and it accurately assesses the minimum number of steps required, given state a is placed at the terminal node.

For taxa polymorphic with three or more states, it is very difficult to assess accurately what changes are required within the terminal taxon. For this reason, the assignment indicated above is at best only an approximation. The best approach would be to find the length of the most-parsimonious tree linking all the states observed in the terminal taxon and rooted at state a. This calculation, however, would be involved and slow; MacClade does not do it. Although MacClade might simply ignore steps within these polymorphic taxa and treat them as if they were uncertainties (as PAUP does), instead it assigns steps for putting a state ancestral in the taxon according to the distance to just the single closest other state also observed in the taxon. MacClade does this to avoid assigning states that would imply impossible transitions. If MacClade encounters a terminal taxon polymorphic for three or more states in a user-defined character, it will warn you.

Polymorphic terminal taxa are particularly problematical when the step matrix in use violates the triangle inequality. As noted on p. 82, a matrix violating the triangle inequality might be assumed to be describing the cost for state-to-state transformations during one branch length's worth of time. If we are allowing changes within terminal taxa, as MacClade does when taxa are polymorphic, then there are no explicit branches within terminal taxa. Matrices violating the triangle inequality may therefore behave in strange and inconsistent ways.

All of these calculations use the user-input matrix of the distances from one state to another. When you puts a "∞" in the matrix to indicate the change is prohibited, MacClade treats the distance as infinity (in fact, it stores it as –1). If MacClade indicates that a character requires an infinite number of steps on the tree, then you must have created impossible assumptions, for instance by constructing a step matrix prohibiting any changes.

Fixing states

When the state at a node is fixed to a state of the user's choice in the character traced (by the paintbrush tool), then MacClade forces the downpass, uppass, and finalpass sets at that node to consist of just the fixed state.

If the ancestor of a node N has its state fixed and N's ancestor is either dichotomous or a hard polytomy, then N's uppass set is no longer calculated from the downpass sets of its sister(s) and the uppass set of its ancestors, since the fixing of state at the ancestor effectively insulates N from the effects of its sisters. The uppass set of N is taken from just the state fixed at the ancestor. On the other hand, for soft polytomies, since the ancestral node fixed is treated as just below the basal node of any resolution of the polytomy, the sister's effects are not insulated, and the uppass set at N is calculated from the sisters' downpass sets and the fixed state at the ancestral node.

Since the normal downpass calculations are suspended when a node with fixed state is encountered, the number of steps required locally must be calculated specially. For unordered, ordered, and irreversible characters the fixed state is compared to the downpass sets at each of the descendant nodes. If N is dichotomous or hard polytomous, then the distance from N's fixed state to each of the descendant downpass sets is measured. If N is soft polytomous, then N is actually just below the basal node of any resolution of the polytomy, and the distance need be measured only from N to the downpass set that would have been assigned to the basal node. If N is a terminal taxon, then recall that fixing N's state is assumed to fix a state just below the terminal taxon (see Chapter 13). Steps need be counted from the fixed states to the downpass set that would have been assigned to the terminal node.

For user-defined (step-matrix) characters the downpass information at the node is adjusted so that the cost for assigning the fixed state to the node is calculated as if the node were not fixed (using information from the descendant nodes), while the cost for assigning any other state is infinite.

Assumptions such as irreversibility or the Dollo assumption can be violated by fixing the states at nodes. For irreversible characters MacClade will warn you irreversibility has been violated. If irreversibility is violated, the character tracing treats the character like an ordered, reversible character in the region of the violation. For user-defined types infinite numbers of steps may be required when you make an illegal fixing; MacClade will warn you if an infinite number of steps is required. For Dollo characters MacClade will give *no warning* that you have violated the Dollo assumption.

Continuous characters

The algorithms used for continuous-valued characters are those of Swofford and Maddison (1987) for linear parsimony and of W. Maddison (1991) for squared-change parsimony. The MINSTATE and MAXSTATE reconstructions are derived after a full linear-parsimony reconstruction by selecting either the minimum or maximum values in final MPR sets at the nodes, respectively.

The algorithms for squared-change parsimony in some respects resemble those for step matrices, in that the information stored at each node indicates how good is each state (W. Maddison, 1991). For instance, on the downpass a quadratic function is stored at each node that indicates, for each state that might be placed at the node, the summed squared length required in the clade above the node. It is calculated from the two quadratic functions already obtained for the two descendant nodes. A pass down the tree obtains the downpass quadratic functions at each node; a pass back up the tree obtains the uppass quadratic functions. A final pass combines quadratic functions from above and below each node to yield the quadratic function for the node. This final function summarizes the preferences of the whole tree for the states at the node. The most parsimonious single state at the node comes directly from this function (W. Maddison, 1991).

The linear parsimony reconstruction tends to allow change to concentrate on a few branches; the squared-change reconstruction forces changes to spread out more evenly over the tree. W. Maddison (1991) notes that the squared-change reconstruction can be considered a Bayesian estimate under a Brownian motion model of evolution.

Finding equally parsimonious reconstructions

When there are several equally parsimonious reconstructions of evolution, as in the example in the section "Ancestral states and reconstructions", above, we might want to examine each of them. The initial character tracing that showed equivocal branches did not directly indicate to us that there were six reconstructions nor what they were. We knew only that there was more than one way to resolve the ambiguity. To find all of the fully resolved reconstructions of character evolution, special algorithms are needed to supplement the algorithms described above. Swofford and Maddison (1987) have discussed means by which to examine all the alternative reconstructions.

Algorithms have also been developed that present to the user one or a very few of the most-parsimonious reconstructions. Some of these will be discussed after methods for discovery of all most-parsimonious reconstructions are outlined.

Finding all most-parsimonious reconstructions

MacClade's Equivocal Cycling calculations, which find in sequence each of the equally parsimonious reconstructions of character evolution, are used both in MacClade's Equivocal Cycling display for the traced character and in various calculations, such as for Trace All Changes (minimum-average-maximum) and for the State Changes & Stasis chart (average), which require all equally parsimonious reconstructions to be examined.

The first reconstruction found by Equivocal Cycling is that which places the lowest-valued parsimonious states at the nodes, giving priority to nodes closer to the root. That is, the algorithm first finds the nodes closest to the root that have equivocal assignments (perhaps the root itself). Each such node is assigned the lowest-valued state among its parsimonious assignments (the smallest state in its MPR set). Given these assignments, the algorithm may recalculate the parsimonious assignments to nodes further up, and then looks for the next nodes further up that have equivocal assignments. Each such node is assigned the lowest-valued state among its parsimonious assignments. Given these assignments, the algorithm then moves even higher, away from the root. In this way the algorithm stepwise assigns lowest-valued states, each assignment possibly depending on assignments made closer to the root. It should be understood that if the character is of unordered or step-matrix type, an assignment of a lower-valued state near the root might force assignments of higher-valued states further up the tree. Thus the first reconstruction does not necessarily place at each node the lowest state in its MPR set.

The last reconstruction found by Equivocal Cycling is that which places the highest-valued parsimonious states at the nodes, giving priority to nodes closer to the root. Because assignments to lower nodes affect assignments to higher nodes, the last reconstruction does not necessarily place at each node the highest state in its MPR set.

Between the first and last reconstruction, Equivocal Cycling moves through alternative reconstructions in a particular sequence. Equivocal Cycling moves through higher and higher reconstructions by raising the states at each branch, with the left-most branches changing the fastest (like the 1's digit in a counter), and the right-most branches changing the slowest (like the 1000's digit in a counter). The raising of states is done subject to the constraint that only parsimonious reconstructions are made. Eventually Equivocal Cycling arrives at the last reconstruction.

ACCTRAN and DELTRAN

For characters of unordered and ordered type, ambiguities in character tracings can be resolved so as to choose the assignments that delay or accelerate transformations (see Swofford & Maddison, 1987); these will tend to maximize parallelisms or reversals respectively. The DELTRAN option shows those most-parsimonious assignments that delay changes away from the root; this maximizes parallel changes. In the example illustrated under "Ancestral states and reconstructions", p. 77, tracing number 1 is the DELTRAN tracing, as white is carried as far up the tree as possible. The ACCTRAN tracing, equivalent to tracings from Farris's (1970) algorithm, shows those assignments that accelerate changes toward the root; this procedure maximizes early gains and thus forces subsequent reversals. In the example, the ACCTRAN tracing is:

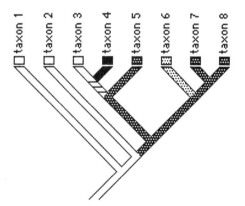

Note that this is not a single, unequivocal reconstruction, but is instead a composite of reconstructions 4–6 combined. This illustrates the fact that ACCTRAN and DELTRAN do not always choose a single one of the most-parsimonious reconstructions.

ACCTRAN and DELTRAN are but two of various methods to select from among the most-parsimonious reconstructions. They should probably not be used unless their treatment of parallelisms and reversals are appropriate for the biological system being considered. Before using them, heed the warnings in the section "Which reconstructions should be examined?", below.

ACCTRAN and DELTRAN reconstructions use the algorithms described by Swofford and Maddison (1987). For both, the downpass of the algorithms is done as normal. For ACCTRAN, MacClade then proceeds up the tree in a final pass that assigns to node N the states in its downpass set that are closest to the states already assigned in the final MPR set in its ancestor M. The closest states consist of the intersection of D_N and F_M if it is not empty; otherwise they consist of D_N if the character is unordered, or the closest element in D_N to F_M if the character is ordered. For DELTRAN, MacClade does a normal non-DELTRAN reconstruction of final MPR sets then moves back up through the tree, reassigning final sets by choosing the states in the original F_N that are closest to the revised F_M. Note that MacClade, unlike PAUP, does not choose the lowest-valued state at the root to begin these processes. Thus MacClade's ACCTRAN and DELTRAN may not fully resolve ambiguity in the ancestral state reconstruction.

There are other options for choosing among equally parsimonious reconstructions of ancestral states. The MINF option discussed by Swofford & Maddison (1987) is not available in MacClade. Two more options are the MINSTATE and MAXSTATE options, which examine the full set of equally parsimonious states at each node, and choose the smallest and largest values, respectively. It can be shown that for ordered characters, choosing the smallest member of each reconstructed state set results in a set of assignments to the nodes that together comprise one of the most-parsimonious reconstructions of ancestral states; likewise, if the largest is chosen. In MacClade, MINSTATE and MAXSTATE options are available with continuous-valued characters, and they are used in the simulation portion of the concentrated-changes character-correlation test. MacClade does not supply a direct way to obtain MINSTATE and MAXSTATE reconstructions for ordered discrete characters, but you can indirectly obtain MINSTATE and MAXSTATE reconstructions by asking for the first reconstruction and the last reconstruction, respectively, using Equivocal Cycling.

Which reconstructions should be examined?

When there are equally parsimonious reconstructions of the character tracing, it would be best to examine all the alternatives in full detail. However, when there are many, this may not be feasible. Which reconstructions you decide to examine will of course depend on the question you are asking. Try, if you can, to examine reconstructions that will give as different answers to your question as possible. ACCTRAN and DELTRAN yield extremes of reversals versus parallelisms. The first reconstruction versus last reconstruction in Equivocal Cycling yield extremes of lowest numbered states versus highest numbered states, with priority given to nodes closer to root. But these particular extremes may not be appropriate for your question.

EXAMPLE: *Consider the character in the example file DELTRAN/ACCTRAN Example. There are 64 equally parsimonious reconstructions of character evolution for this character on the tree. If we are interested in the number of changes from wrinkled (state 2) to smooth (state 0) texture, then we might think to ignore most of the 64 reconstructions, and examine just the DELTRAN and ACCTRAN reconstructions, hoping that these would provide extreme values for the number of wrinkled → smooth changes. There is 1 DELTRAN reconstruction, which displays 0 changes from wrinkled → smooth. There are 2 ACCTRAN reconstructions, which both display 0 changes from wrinkled → smooth. Unfortunately, the DELTRAN and ACCTRAN reconstructions do not provide extreme values, for there exists one most-parsimonious reconstruction of evolution (reconstruction number 64, which can be seen by turning on* **Equivocal Cycling***, and using the* **Go To** *command) for which there are 7 changes from wrinkled → smooth!*

You should think in particular about what reconstructions would be least and most compatible with hypotheses you might be testing, and examine these. In some circumstances, the extremes of most and least compatible may coincide with the DELTRAN and ACCTRAN reconstructions, or the MINSTATE and MAXSTATE reconstructions, or they may not, depending on the biological question you are asking. Again, it is best to examine all reconstructions, if this is possible, especially if you are not certain about what reconstructions are most critically related to your biological question.

Uncertainty in the reconstruction

A reconstructed ancestral state is an estimate. Like any other estimate, its value may have uncertainty.

Equally parsimonious reconstructions

The first expression of uncertainty is ambiguity in the reconstruction; that is, the existence of multiple equally parsimonious reconstructions. Ideally, when faced with multiple reconstructions, one would examine all of them, in order to see if they differ in their implications about that aspect of character evolution of interest (D. Maddison, 1991b). Methods that examine only a subset of the reconstructions should be avoided, if possible (see further discussion in the section "Which reconstructions should be examined?", above).

Confidence

Uncertainty does not end with ambiguity in the reconstruction. Even when the reconstruction unequivocally assigns a single state to a node, this assignment may still be incorrect. Reconstructions of ancestral states are subject to error, as are all estimates of history. The amount of error to be expected or, conversely, the confidence we should have in such reconstructions is not well understood. The reliability of ancestral state reconstructions has not received nearly as much study as it deserves, with the few papers considering the issue for molecular data yielding mixed results (Holmquist, 1979; Goodman, 1981; Kimura, 1981; Tateno, 1990; Hillis et al., 1992). Statistical approaches, which have been applied to investigate the behavior of parsimony methods for reconstructing phylogenetic trees (e.g., Felsenstein, 1978b, 1979), have not been much applied to the problem of ancestral states. Because reconstructions of ancestral states will continue to be used in interpreting evolution (Chapters 3 and 4), it is important that their accuracy be investigated.

It is to be expected that most methods will behave better as rates of evolution are lower. One's confidence in a reconstruction should depend on how many changes seem to have occurred. The fewer the changes, the more confidence one might have, especially if they are spread apart on a large tree.

However, if one's goal is to reconstruct the precise sequence of evolutionary changes in the character, *realize that the precise sequence of changes requires estimation of almost as many parameters as there are data points (observations in terminal taxa)!* It may be the case that summary statistics based on reconstructions of character changes, such as the number of steps or the ratio of gains to losses, can be more reliably used than can the precise sequence of changes in the reconstruction, since the former often requires estimation of many fewer parameters.

Even within the parsimony framework we might investigate confidence, by looking at the number of extra steps required by alternative reconstructions. In some circumstances, this gives disappointing results. For an unordered character and a dichotomous tree, placing a state at any node can give one of four results: it will be a most-parsimonious assignment, or it will be less parsimonious by one, two, or three steps. The worst case (three steps) can occur only if the node is an internal node other than the root and is surrounded by nodes all agreeing on some character state. If the node is the root, then even the worst character state assignment will cost only two steps more than the best, and if the two descendants of the root disagree on their character states, the worst assignment to the root can cost at worst one step more than the best. Thus, for instance, the human mitochondrial phylogeny of Cann et al. (1987), which places Africa on one side of the root and Asia on the other, requires an equal number of steps if either Africa or Asia is placed at the root, but at worst only one extra step (out of more than 40 steps total) if any other continent is placed at the root and geographic location is treated as an unordered character (D. Maddison, 1991b).

Statistics derived from reconstructions

Several statistics concerning the number and cost of changes in a reconstruction have been proposed and are available in MacClade. For individual characters, these are the number of steps, number of changes, consistency index, retention index, and rescaled consistency index. Summed over all characters, possibly weighted by the character weights, these are the treelength, tree changes, and ensemble indices.

Steps

As noted in Chapter 4, the number of steps required in a character is the sum of the costs of each of the character state transformations implied on a most-parsimonious reconstruction of evolution. Except for Dollo characters and stratigraphic characters, MacClade counts the number of steps required in a character during the downpass. For unordered, ordered, and irreversible characters, a running total of steps is kept during the downpass, as indicated in the above descriptions of algorithms. For user-defined type characters, the algorithm calculates for each node the number of steps required in that node's clade by each ancestral state for the clade; once the downpass arrives at the root, the least number of steps required by any state at the root is the number of steps required in the character in the whole tree.

MacClade adds to the number of steps any steps that must have occurred within polymorphic terminal taxa (see "Interpreting the character tracing" in Chapter 13). In general, the algorithms count the minimum number of steps that must have occurred within these terminal taxa and add this to the count of steps for the character. Thus four steps are presumed to have occurred within a terminal taxon polymorphic for states 2, 5, and 6 in an ordered character. Similar calculations can be done for unordered, irreversible and Dollo characters, but for characters of user-defined type it is very difficult to count the minimum number of steps that must have occurred within a terminal taxon if it is polymorphic for more than two states. Details are given in the description above. In these situations MacClade puts a "+" beside the count of steps and treelength to indicate that there is some uncounted length.

In Chapter 14 are explained the calculations used to sum the number of steps for each character into the treelength.

Changes

In an unambiguous most-parsimonious reconstruction of character evolution, a change is required whenever a node has a different state from its immediate ancestor. The number of changes in the character is simply the number of instances in which a change is reconstructed as occurring on a branch. In MacClade, implicit multiple changes within a branch are not counted separately. Thus, if an ordered character shows a 0 to 2 change across a branch, MacClade counts only a single change. It does not suppose that state 1 is a necessary intermediate and count two changes on the branch, 0 to 1 and 1 to 2. Because of this behavior, it may be best to consider the count of changes in each character as the number of *branches* on which the character shows a change in a most-parsimonious reconstruction.

If there is ambiguity in the tracing of character evolution, such that an equivocal assignment is given to some branches, then the alternative reconstructions of character evolution may have different numbers of changes. This can arise, for instance, if one reconstruction allows a single change worth two steps, while another equally parsimonious reconstruction allows two changes each worth one step. In the following figure, an ordered character shows three steps in each of the two reconstructions of character change, but shows two changes in the upper one, and three changes in the lower:

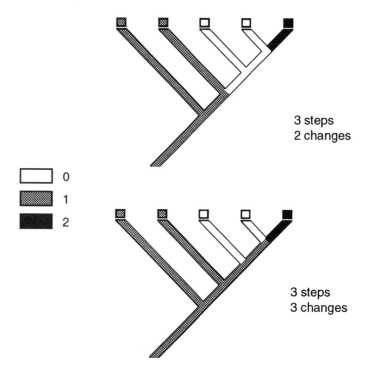

3 steps
2 changes

☐ 0
▨ 1
■ 2

3 steps
3 changes

MacClade uses Equivocal Cycling to try all alternative most-parsimonious reconstructions in the character tracings, and determines the range of number of changes required among these different reconstructions. Therefore MacClade may sometimes indicate a range of changes, for instance "5–7 changes". Changes within polymorphic terminal taxa are *not* counted. (Recall that their costs are counted into the number of steps.) Because it uses Equivocal Cycling, MacClade cannot calculate the number of changes with polytomous trees or trees that have observed taxa fixed as ancestors.

Consistency and retention indices

These indices are derived by scaling the number of steps required by a tree by the minimum and/or maximum conceivable number of steps the character could have in any possible tree. Both single-character and ensemble indices are possible. They are described further in Chapter 14.

Locating and summarizing changes of character state

In several contexts MacClade examines reconstructions of character evolution and locates or counts the changes in character state that are reconstructed as occurring. For instance, this is done to put tick marks on the branches in Trace All Changes, and in the State Changes & Stasis chart to summarize the sorts of changes reconstructed. MacClade's calculations are described here in order to document them. See also Chapter 14 for a discussion of counting the total number of changes in the tree.

Ambiguity in the reconstruction can make difficult the assessment of what changes occurred. If the MPR set at a node has multiple states (an equivocal assignment), then whether a change is placed on the branch between this node and its ancestor may depend upon which of the alternative states is assigned to the node. For instance, in the following example, whether a change is reconstructed on the branch below the clade D-E-F depends on which of the two equally parsimonious reconstructions at right is chosen:

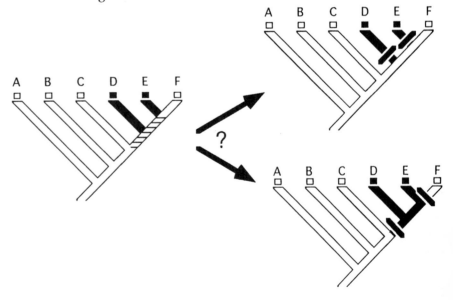

The two reconstructions also disagree on the nature of the changes: the top reconstruction suggests two white to black changes; the bottom suggest a white to black and a black to white change.

In Trace All Changes

In MacClade's Trace All Changes facility, the amount or identities of changes on each of the branches of the tree are marked. To deal with ambiguity in the reconstructions, four different options are offered by MacClade that vary in how they assess whether changes are reconstructed as occurring on particular branches. These are described further in Chapter 13. Note that changes on branches participating in a soft polytomy are never recorded because of difficulties in interpreting these changes. The four different options and their calculations are:

1. Show unambiguous changes only. An unambiguous change is counted as occurring on a branch if the sets of states reconstructed at a node and its ancestor do not overlap at all. This option will show no changes in the example above. If weighted then the distance between these sets is used as the amount of change.

2. Show almost all possible changes (most ambiguous and unambiguous). A possible change is counted if the MPR state sets of a node and its ancestor are not identical. This option will show all four possible changes in the example just above. (The weighted amount of change cannot be calculated, because with this criterion it is not clear what changes are occurring and thus their weights cannot be considered.)

3. Show the maximum amount of change allowed by parsimony. This choice finds all instances in which parsimony allows a change on the branch. For node N and unordered and ordered characters, MacClade compares N's uppass set and downpass set. If these sets intersect, then there are no changes allowed on N's branch; if they do not intersect, then the distance between the sets is the maximum amount of change allowed on the branch. For other character types MacClade performs Equivocal Cycling to examine all most-parsimonious reconstructions to see if at least one of these reconstructions places a change on the branch.

4. Show the minimum-average-maximum amount of change. These calculations are done using Equivocal Cycling to examine all most-parsimonious reconstructions. The minimum and maximum amount of change in the character on the branch are determined by scanning all of the reconstructions. The average is calculated in one of two ways: average over all reconstructions, and average over all classes of changes. In the first option, every one of the equally parsimonious fully resolved reconstructions is examined by Equivocal Cycling (see p. 107). The total number or amount of change on a

branch is summed over all such reconstructions, and divided by the number of such reconstructions. Thus, in the example of six reconstructions shown on p. 77, the branch leading to taxon 3 shows changes in two out of the six reconstructions (numbers 5 and 6), and thus the average amount of change is 1/3 change per reconstruction. In the second option, all distinct classes of change reconstructed on the branch are examined. In the same example, there are three classes of change, either no change (reconstructions 1–4), change from gray to white (reconstruction 5) or change from black to white (reconstruction 6). Two of these classes show a change, and thus the average amount of change is 2/3 changes per class.

In State Changes & Stasis chart

The State Changes & Stasis chart counts the number of instances in which a reconstructed change is from state 0 to state 1, the number from state 1 to state 2, and so on. It therefore counts the number of each sort of character state transformation reconstructed on the tree.

The following options are available to count changes for the State Changes & Stasis chart. As with Trace All Changes, changes on branches participating in a soft polytomy are never counted.

1. Count unambiguous changes only. An unambiguous change from state s to state t is counted as occurring on a branch N if the single state s is reconstructed at N's ancestor and the single state t is reconstructed at N. If the MPR set at either node is equivocal, no change is counted.

    An unambiguous change from s to t is counted as occurring *within* a polymorphic terminal taxon if the terminal node is assigned a single state s but the terminal taxon had also the single other state t. If the terminal node is assigned a single state and the character is ordered, irreversible, stratigraphic, or Dollo, then a series of unambiguous changes are counted if the terminal taxon is polymorphic for more than two states. In this situation it is presumed that changes occurred in an ordered fashion from the assigned state at the terminal node to each of the other states observed in the terminal taxon.

2. Count minimum and maximum changes. MacClade performs Equivocal Cycling to examine all most-parsimonious reconstructions to see in each what changes are reconstructed. In each reconstruction the branches are examined to see what changes are placed on the branch.

    Within polymorphic terminal taxa changes are counted as follows. For unordered characters, changes from the resolved state at the terminal node to each of the observed states in the terminal taxon are counted. Note that this is only one of the possible sets of changes that might have occurred. *Since MacClade does not examine all possible pathways of change within each terminal taxon, it cannot give the exact minimum and maximum number of changes of various sorts,* and therefore gives a warning whenever the taxon has more than one state beyond that assigned to the terminal node. For ordered, irreversible, stratigraphic and Dollo characters, changes within polymorphic terminal taxa are counted as above for unambiguous changes.

After each most-parsimonious reconstruction is examined, MacClade sees whether the number of each type of transformation (e.g., state 0 to state 1) is larger than the maximum found among previous reconstructions, or smaller than the previous minimum. If so, then the maximum or minimum is reset. Thus, MacClade finds among all reconstructions the minimum and maximum numbers of each type or transformation reconstructed.

3. Count average number of changes. MacClade proceeds as for the minimum/maximum algorithm, except that it does not store the minima and maxima while examining the reconstructions, but rather calculates the average, over all the equally parsimonious reconstructions, of the number of each type of transformation.

Polytomies and their difficulties

Soft versus hard

Trees that have polytomous nodes, that is, nodes with more than two descendant nodes, are particularly troublesome in phylogenetic analyses. The polytomies may be interpreted in two different ways (W. Maddison, 1989): (1) as regions of ambiguous resolution ("soft" polytomies), or (2) as multiple speciation events ("hard" polytomies). Although in most cladistic literature polytomies are interpreted in the first sense, most algorithms for reconstructing character evolution that have been presented in the literature and, as far as we know, in other computer programs use the second interpretation, since any daughter nodes of the polytomy that share a state different from that of the polytomy are presumed to have acquired it independently (W. Maddison, 1989). In contrast, soft polytomies represent uncertain resolution, in that the polytomy is taken as indicating a set of alternative dichotomous resolutions. Soft and hard polytomies differ in the interpretation of their display in MacClade, as discussed in "Interpretation of character tracings", in Chapter 13.

Reconstructing character evolution

The description of algorithms above indicated how MacClade reconstructs character evolution on polytomies. For hard polytomies, the polytomy is fixed and MacClade considers each descendant node as independent in assessing what states would be parsimonious. For soft polytomies, MacClade reconstructs character evolution as if the polytomy were allowed to be resolved most favorably for that character.

It is particularly difficult to reconstruct whether a character changed state on the branches arising out of a soft polytomy. For this reason, MacClade indicates no changes on any such branch in its Trace All Changes feature (Chapter 13). The problem arises in that, under different dichotomous resolutions of the polytomy, different changes may be assigned to these branches. Perhaps the best solution would therefore be to resolve the polytomy into all its dichotomous resolutions, reconstruct the changes occurring in each case, and summarize the alternative possibilities by showing the range (over the various resolutions) of the amounts of change placed on these branches. Note, however, that some of the resolutions may be highly unparsimonious with respect to the evolution of the character concerned. As well, there may be variation among resolutions in the changes reconstructed on branches other than those directly involved in the polytomy. Recall that MacClade's character tracings reconstruct evolution on soft polytomies assuming the most favorable resolutions for the characters considered. In the future MacClade may incorporate features to examine alternative dichotomous resolutions and summarize the varying branch lengths, but currently you will have to do this by hand, perhaps by asking MacClade to generate a set of random dichotomous resolutions of the tree (Chapter 18).

Treelength

When MacClade reconstructs character evolution as if a soft polytomy were allowed to be resolved most favorably for that character, it allows different characters to implicitly resolve the polytomy in different ways. This leads to difficulty in interpreting treelengths (W. Maddison, 1989). The problem can be seen by an example. Suppose this were our tree with two characters as shown:

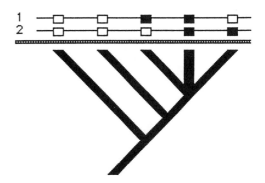

MacClade reconstructs each character's evolution allowing the polytomy to be resolved most favorably for each. Thus, for each of the two characters a different resolution is chosen and one change will be counted as follows:

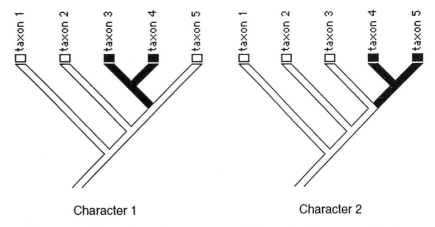

Character 1   Character 2

Summing the number of steps counted for each character will give an apparent treelength of 2, but in fact there does not exist a dichotomous resolution with fewer than three total steps. In general the treelength obtained by summing character steps can be misleadingly low when there are soft polytomies. (For this reason MacClade puts a "+" after the treelength whenever there are soft polytomies, just to warn you that the treelength may be misleadingly low.)

There are two possible meanings of the length of a tree with soft polytomies. One could argue, as did W. Maddison (1989), that the true length of a tree with soft polytomies, that is, the number of steps required by the polytomous tree, should be considered the length of the most-parsimonious dichotomous tree consistent with the polytomous tree. This would be the "minimum number of steps required by the polytomous tree". To find such a most-parsimonious dichotomous tree, a tree search may be required. However, considering a tree with soft polytomies to be simply a summary diagram of a larger number of implied dichotomous trees, one could argue that the treelength of this collection is not the length of the shortest tree contained therein, but rather a set of treelengths. For example, consider the data file called Polytomy Example distributed with MacClade. In the single tree stored in that file, there is a polytomy with five elements. This polytomous tree thus represents 105 dichotomous resolutions. The treelength presuming soft polytomies is given by MacClade as 91+. In fact, the histogram of length of all included dichotomous trees is:

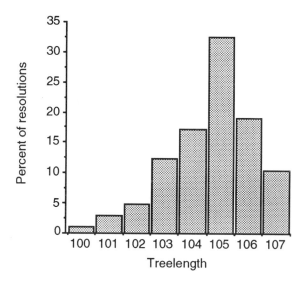

Of the 105 trees, there exists one of length 100, some of length 107, and quite a few (34) of length 105. If one were to ask, "What is the length of that polytomous tree?", one could answer either "100" or "lengths range from 100 to 107, as shown in the histogram above". See p. 286 for further consideration of this example.

Zero-length branches versus consensus trees

In programs like PAUP that reconstruct phylogenetic trees, polytomies can arise either because branches with no support ("zero-length") are collapsed in the course of the search process, or because several different trees are combined into a consensus tree. In both cases, the polytomies should be considered soft, but the two sorts of trees should be treated differently. The reason is that all possible dichotomous resolutions of the polytomy arising by zero-length collapsing should be equally parsimonious, but this is not necessarily the case for consensus trees. Even though the consensus may be compatible with the parsimonious trees that went into it, there may have been other dichotomous trees that would be compatible with the consensus but were not among the most parsimonious. For example, consider the example file Hamamelidae, containing data on plant structure (from Donoghue and Doyle, 1989). The strict consensus tree of the most-parsimonious trees is compatible with about 41,910,000,000,000 dichotomous trees (calculated using the formulae provided by Felsenstein, 1978a), of which only 54 dichotomous trees are of shortest length. After trees are condensed to a consensus, the information as to which dichotomous trees went into it is lost. MacClade might choose as a most favorable resolution (in reconstructing character evolution on a soft polytomous consensus tree) one that was not among the most parsimonious, and you may get a reconstruction of character evolution that would not have been allowed by any of the dichotomous trees that made the consensus. Because consensus trees have lost the information about what trees went into them, reconstructing character evolution and counting treelength on them should be avoided, or at least done with much caution.

Looking at alternative resolutions

Because of the problems with soft polytomies, it is generally advisable to examine alternative dichotomous resolutions of the polytomies. (It is *not* advisable to switch to the hard polytomies interpretation, if the polytomies truly represent uncertainty.) A common situation will be similar to the following. You want to examine the evolution of some particular character, say chromosome fusions, on a phylogeny, inferred using PAUP, based on morphological data. But suppose PAUP (or other tree-searching program) does not generate a single dichotomous tree. Instead suppose it generates a tree with many polytomies due to collapsing of zero-length branches. If you examine the character's evolution on this polytomous tree, your results could be biased by showing too few changes in the character (if you use the soft polytomy option) or too many changes (if you use the hard polytomy option).

There are two ways to solve this problem. MacClade can generate random dichotomous resolutions of the current tree on screen. You might generate a number of such trees and examine the character's evolution on each. Or, you might ask for a chart summarizing the statistic of interest over trees consisting of random dichotomous resolutions of the single polytomous tree on the screen. In doing this, you would be sampling from the set of all possible resolutions, in order to see how the statistic of interest might vary over these resolutions. You might see, for instance, that under some dichotomous resolutions, as few as four steps are required in the character, whereas under other resolutions, as many as eight steps are required.

Another way to solve the problem is to ask a tree-searching program like PAUP not to collapse zero-length branches. However, this could slow down the tree search and use up much more memory. It would be particularly damaging to the efficiency of the tree search if there were multiple equally parsimonious trees, each of which was polytomous (with zero-length branches), as is most often the case.

If a tree-searching program generates multiple equally parsimonious trees, each of which is polytomous, what are you to do? It would be very laborious to place each of one thousand possible polytomous trees on screen, and ask for a chart summarizing the statistic of interest over one thousand random dichotomous resolutions of each tree. Instead you can examine one randomly chosen dichotomous resolution of each of the one thousand possible polytomous trees. (This can be done in MacClade using the Resolve Polytomies button that is found in some of the charting dialog boxes.)

Although examining random dichotomous resolutions of polytomies might be appropriate if the polytomies arose by the collapsing of zero-length branches, it is a dangerous practice if the polytomies arose in the formation of a consensus tree, as described above. It is best to examine directly the trees that went into forming the consensus tree. MacClade's facilities for examining multiple trees and presenting summaries in chart form can be used for these purposes.

Uncertainty in the phylogenetic tree

Rare will be the case that we know a phylogenetic tree with certainty. If there is uncertainty in the phylogenetic tree, how will this affect our reconstructions of character evolution? We have already described reconstructing evolution on trees with soft polytomies, and we advised examining alternative dichotomous trees resolved from the polytomy. If there are multiple equally (or almost equally) parsimonious trees, then reconstructing character evolution on each allows one to see whether the different trees yield different reconstructions of character evolution (D. Maddison, 1991a,b; Swofford and Maddison, in press). MacClade has features specifically designed to facilitate dealing with multiple trees, especially the charting functions.

Maddison et al. (1984) presented a number of simple rules which indicate whether and how much certain changes to a tree might affect a parsimony reconstruction of ancestral states. Though these rules were presented in the context of outgroup analysis, they can be applied in general to reconstructions of ancestral states for unordered and ordered characters:

1. If two terminal taxa that branch from a lineage one after the other have the same state, then changes in the tree above these have no effect on states reconstructed below them, and vice versa.

2. If the entire tree is rerooted, then the states at a node (other than the root) are unaffected.

3. If a single clade is removed from or added to any part of the tree, then the state set at a node before and after the move must overlap, as long as the node itself was not removed.

4. If a single clade is picked up from any part of the tree and dropped somewhere else, then the state set at a node before and after the move must overlap, unless the node was an immediate ancestor of the clade. (In this instance, picking up the clade would destroy the node.) This rule holds for binary characters, but we have been unable to prove it for multistate characters.

These rules provide guidelines for only some simple examples of uncertainty in tree structure; other cases of uncertainty are not amenable to simple rules and will require examination of multiple trees.

6. STRATIGRAPHIC PARSIMONY

by Daniel C. Fisher
Museum of Paleontology
University of Michigan
Ann Arbor, MI 48109

Introduction

The stratigraphic character type in MacClade 3 implements a procedure that is part of an expanded approach to cladistic analysis referred to as "stratocladistics" (Fisher, 1982, 1988, 1991). Use of the stratigraphic character type is briefly described elsewhere in the documentation for MacClade 3, but this chapter offers additional perspective on stratigraphic parsimony and the conduct of stratocladistic analyses. A more detailed discussion of stratocladistics (Fisher, in preparation) will be required to enumerate and defend its assumptions and potential benefits, but this presentation may suffice to guide the user in initial exploration of the method.

Concept of stratigraphic parsimony

The principle of parsimony is routinely used as a basis for hypothesis choice in phylogenetic analysis. The rationale for its use is not undisputed (Sober, 1988), but parsimony has been portrayed as yielding hypotheses that minimize appeals to ad hoc support and maximize explanatory power (Farris, 1983). With morphologic character data, the most-parsimonious hypotheses are those that explain observed character state distribution using the fewest homoplasies. Each homoplasy is treated as an ad hoc hypothesis because it "explains away" (without independent test) a resemblance that would otherwise be taken as supporting an alternative hypothesis of relationship. For a comparable concept of stratigraphic parsimony, we need a means of assessing the extent to which rival phylogenetic hypotheses either agree with, or require us to "explain away", observed patterns of stratigraphic occurrence. One way of evaluating the concordance between stratigraphic data and a given phylogenetic hypothesis is to ask whether the order of occurrence of taxa corresponds to the order that would be predicted from the proposed genealogy, assuming members of different but contemporary lineages, compared over the same time intervals, had roughly equal probabilities of preservation (and recovery). If such correspondence is not observed, we may attribute it to disparities in preservation probabilities, but unless we have independent information on these probabilities, this presumption of disparities is ad hoc — it explains away the offending observation instead of accepting it as a valid test of the proposed phylogeny. Rather than blame preservation probabilities, we should consider the possibility that the phylogenetic hypothesis is in error, especially since the observed temporal order is certain to be the expected one under a competing hypothesis of relationships. Choosing among hypotheses according to a principle of stratigraphic parsimony means favoring hypotheses that reconcile observed and expected patterns of temporal occurrence using the fewest arbitrary statements regarding relative probabilities of preservation.

Definition of parsimony debt

In discussing the basis for hypothesis choice, we refer commonly to the "treelength" of a phylogenetic hypothesis. However, treelength is a sum of two quantities, one related to the number of character states being considered and the other reflecting the ad hoc support required by the hypothesis. The former is constant for a given data matrix; only the latter reflects the merit of this hypothesis in light of observed data. I have referred to this latter quantity as "parsimony debt" (Fisher, 1982). Under equal character weighting, "morphologic parsimony debt" is simply the number of instances of homoplasy required by a given phylogenetic hypothesis. To evaluate the bearing of stratigraphic data on hypothesis choice, I suggest computing an analogous value, the "stratigraphic parsimony debt", reflecting the number of independent discrepancies between expected and observed order of stratigraphic occurrence. MacClade 3 calculates this quantity (or in certain cases, an increment to treelength differing from stratigraphic parsimony debt by a constant value) through use of the stratigraphic character type.

Nature of unit taxa

In a conventional cladistic analysis, the taxa whose relationships are being inferred are assumed to be evolutionary units, whether at a subspecific, specific, or supraspecific level. The same assumption applies in a stratocladistic analysis, but treatment of stratigraphic data introduces an additional dimension, analogous to an additional character, to be considered in the individuation of taxa. At least two responses are possible. One is to argue that any attribution of a stratigraphic range to a taxon is a substantive statement of relationship between earlier- and later-occurring representatives and should be the result of an analysis rather than part of the input. This approach would use as unit taxa only groups of specimens occurring within a "single" stratigraphic interval (in addition to whatever morphologic criteria are applied) and would let ranges emerge at the end of an analysis as summaries of the stratigraphic distribution of clades or portions of ancestor-descendant lineages. This approach allows the analysis to "try out" reconstructions that break up the long-lived taxon as well as ones that maintain its integrity. Alternatively, it may be argued that use of a unit taxon spanning multiple stratigraphic intervals, though it constrains the outcome to some degree, is not in that respect different from any other decision involved in individuating unit taxa. MacClade 3 allows the user to adopt either approach, assigning taxa a single state if they are limited to a single stratigraphic interval, or multiple states reflecting their observed range.

Preliminary assessment and coding of stratigraphic data

The state or states assigned to each taxon are ordered from oldest, 0, to most recent (see p. 80). There is no requirement that the time intervals used be of any particular relative or absolute length; the arguments around which this procedure has been designed rely on order of occurrence. In principle, time can be divided as finely as the precision of radiometric dating or stratigraphic correlation allows, but the number of states allowed by the program is a practical limit. The most conservative application of stratigraphic data will divide time only to the extent necessary to document appearances and disappearances of taxa with unique character combinations, but if stratigraphic data are available with finer resolution, they may be used as well. Taxa should be recorded as occurring in the same interval, or in the same "stratum", as that term is used elsewhere in this manual, unless they can be shown to differ significantly (Marshall, 1990). Coding decisions such as this depend on the certainty of stratigraphic correlation, density of sampling, patterns of occurrence within taxa under study, and representation of depositional environments in available stratigraphic sections. In any case, coding is based on geologic and taphonomic evidence. Such decisions may be nontrivial, but, like decisions on coding of morphologic character states, they represent a level of analysis below phylogenetic inference per se. Stratigraphic data are best drawn from a composite section recording highly corroborated patterns of occurrence within a given region. Ultimately, analyses on a worldwide scale are most useful. The critical aspect of sampling temporal and spatial dimensions is that each taxon have a chance of being recorded, if it existed within a given interval. Since intervals are recognized in terms of actual occurrences of taxa, they are automatically scaled appropriately relative to preservation probabilities. Differential weighting of intervals is possible (p. 207), but this should be used only if the perceived differences affect all taxa within an interval. Lineage-specific differences in probability of occurrence are discussed below.

Computation of stratigraphic parsimony debt

Stratigraphic parsimony debt may be represented graphically by plotting taxa so that their vertical order corresponds to order of occurrence. Taxa are then connected according to the genealogical hypothesis under consideration, with any hypothetical common ancestors placed just prior to their first-occurring descendant taxon. When taxa are limited to single stratigraphic intervals and all stratigraphic states are occupied (unoccupied states might occur if taxa had been excluded without recoding of the stratigraphic character), a phylogenetic hypothesis incurs a unit of stratigraphic parsimony debt for each instance in which a lineage is claimed to have crossed an interval (or "stratum") without representation in the fossil record. The algorithm used by MacClade 3 (pp. 96–101) sums the number of unrepresented interval crossings for an entire tree and reports this as a treelength increment added by the stratigraphic character. In general, this value can be compared directly between competing trees for the same data, as an indication of their relative stratigraphic parsimony. A little experimentation will reveal effects of stratigraphic data and genealogical patterns on debt values. For example, if two sister taxa differ in time of occurrence, interpreting the earlier-occurring one as ancestral to the other yields a lower stratigraphic debt than proposing a hypothetical common ancestor. Stratigraphic parsimony debts range from zero (where each lineage is represented in each time interval in which it is postulated to exist) to a maximum equal to the sum of the lowest stratigraphic state values for each taxon under study (i.e., each taxon is linked by an unrepresented lineage to a hypothetical common ancestor prior to the taxon with the earliest occurrence). There may be instances in which adjustment of stratigraphic parsimony debts is warranted. For example, if the environment in which a particular taxon would be expected to occur is not represented in the stratigraphic sequence recording a given interval, it may be inappropriate to count against a tree the failure of that taxon's lineage to be represented at that position in the sequence. This implies canceling a unit of parsimony debt. If such adjustments are considered (this option is not offered within MacClade 3), they must be handled consistently for all taxa and time intervals.

Stratocladistic analysis

Stratocladistic analysis ranks competing trees in terms of their total (morphologic + stratigraphic) parsimony debts, or a "treelength" that expresses equivalent information. MacClade 3 calculates a stratigraphically augmented treelength as equal to morphologic treelength + stratigraphic increment. The stratigraphic increment, in turn, equals stratigraphic parsimony debt + k, where k reflects any range gaps within unit taxa and any lineages crossing unoccupied intervals. If neither of these exist in the data matrix, k = 0. In either case, the stratigraphically augmented treelength differs from total parsimony debt by a constant value for a given data matrix and represents an equivalent basis for hypothesis choice. As in conventional cladistic analysis, there may or may not be a single most-parsimonious tree. To select the most-parsimonious hypothesis(es), we might in principle examine all competing trees for the same data matrix, but this is of course too time-consuming for most problems. Ideally, stratigraphic debt calculations would be fully integrated into a tree-finding algorithm, but for now, MacClade 3 itself, or MacClade 3 used in conjunction with PAUP 3.0 (Swofford, 1991), allows some of the benefits of stratocladistic analysis to be realized. Other programs can also be used, but common platform and data format make these two a convenient team. Local branch swapping in MacClade 3 integrates morphologic and stratigraphic information, but it does not explore the consequences of making unit taxa ancestors. This can, however, be done "by hand" in MacClade 3. PAUP 3.0 does not recognize the stratigraphic character, but if unit taxa are individuated so that each occurs in only one time interval, and if the stratigraphic data are represented as an irreversible character, an equivalent analysis can be performed, again without considering unit taxa as ancestors.

Another approach is to use PAUP 3.0 to search for trees that are parsimonious morphologically. A tree file recording these can be imported into MacClade from PAUP, all taxa that are attached to a tree by a branch of zero length can be made into ancestors, and the stratigraphically augmented treelengths of these trees can be compared. There may be trees that are less than maximally parsimonious morphologically but that make up for this by being more parsimonious stratigraphically, although there is a limit to how much less parsimonious (morphologically) a tree can be and still be a viable candidate for minimal total debt. This "debt ceiling" is equal to the total parsimony debt of the stratigraphically most-parsimonious of the morphologically most-parsimonious trees. If morphologic parsimony debt is any greater than this value, even a zero stratigraphic debt cannot yield a minimal total debt. This approach requires several steps: searching for morphologically most-parsimonious trees in PAUP, comparing their stratigraphically augmented treelengths in MacClade, determination of the debt ceiling, extending the PAUP search to trees with morphologic parsimony debts up to this limit, and evaluation of their stratigraphically augmented treelengths in MacClade. For simple problems, examination of all trees with morphologic debts at or below the debt ceiling may be feasible. If this number of trees is unmanageable, candidates for minimal total debt may be discovered by tree alterations that include branch swapping and/or making ancestors of selected taxa, with results judged by comparison of stratigraphically augmented treelengths. By combining strongly supported elements of competing trees, alternatives may be found that achieve economies in one debt category (morphologic or stratigraphic) without larger losses in the other. It may be useful to consider trees constructed explicitly to minimize stratigraphic debt or trees that have been generated stratophenetically (Gingerich, 1979).

These may be treated as candidates for minimal total debt or as sources of ideas for tree alteration. Without an efficient stratocladistic search algorithm, there is no guarantee that trees with minimal total debt will be found, but with MacClade 3, any hypothesis can be evaluated and compared with selected competitors.

References

Farris, J. S. 1983. The logical basis of phylogenetic analysis. Pp. 7–36 in N. I. Platnick and V. A. Funk (eds.), Advances in Cladistics, Vol. 2. Proceedings of the Second Meeting of the Willi Hennig Society. Columbia Univ. Press, N.Y.

Fisher, D. C. 1982. Phylogenetic and macroevolutionary patterns within the Xiphosurida. N. Amer. Paleont. Conv. III, Proc., 1:175–180.

Fisher, D. C. 1988. Stratocladistics: Integrating stratigraphic and morphologic data in phylogenetic inference. Geol. Soc. Amer., Abst. Prog., 20:A186.

Fisher, D. C. 1991. Phylogenetic analysis and its application in evolutionary paleobiology. Pp. 103–122 in N. L. Gilinsky and P. W. Signor (eds.), Analytical Paleobiology. Short Courses in Paleontology, No. 4, Paleontological Society.

Gingerich, P. D. 1979. Stratophenetic approach to phylogeny reconstruction in vertebrate paleontology. Pp. 41–77 in J. Cracraft and N. Eldredge (eds.), Phylogenetic Analysis and Paleontology. Columbia Univ. Press, New York.

Marshall, C. R. 1990. Confidence intervals on stratigraphic ranges. Paleobiology, 16:1–10.

Sober, E. 1988. Reconstructing the Past: Parsimony, Evolution, and Inference. MIT Press, Cambridge, Mass.

Swofford, D. L. 1991. Phylogenetic Analysis Using Parsimony (PAUP), version 3.0s. Illinois Natural History Survey, Champaign.

Part III

Using MacClade

7. USING MACCLADE ON YOUR MACINTOSH

MacClade shares with most other Macintosh programs certain conventions – the appearance of windows, drop-down menus, dialog boxes, scroll bars, and so on. We will assume that you have basic familiarity with the Macintosh and so we will not detail all the rules for using menus and editing text, for example. This chapter discusses basic issues of hardware and software requirements of MacClade, how to start MacClade, how to select items from a list, MacClade's help system, messages MacClade may display, and how to set default values for MacClade options.

Hardware and system software specifications

MacClade 3 works on any Macintosh produced since 1987 (that is, the Macintosh Plus, Classics, SEs, IIs, LCs, Powerbooks, and Quadras, among others, but not the Macintosh 128K, 512K, 512KE, and XL). A hard disk is recommended. The amount of memory you will need in your computer depends upon the nature of your data and tree files; see the section "Computer memory and MacClade's limits", in this chapter, for details. In general, 2Mb or more of RAM are recommended if you are running System 6 or earlier, 4Mb for System 7. MacClade will work with any Macintosh-compatible printer that can print graphics (e.g., dot matrix, ink jet, laser); however, some of its tree-printing features require a PostScript® printer.

MacClade requires System 4.2 or later, and is compatible with Multifinder and System 7.

MacClade and anti-viral software

MacClade is compatible with virus-checking software known to us, although some programs, including SAM Intercept® by Symantec may give you a warning that MacClade is attempting to bypass the resource manager. SAM Intercept will do this if you have requested Advanced Protection. The best solution is to click on the Learn button, so that SAM will not warn you again.

Installing MacClade

As with any piece of software, you should make backups of your MacClade disk as soon as possible, and store the master disk in a safe place.

MacClade and associated files are distributed as two compressed files, produced using Bill Goodman's Compact Pro™. If you double-click on the files, select a destination folder, and click on the Extract button, the files will decompress. The MacClade Compressed file contains both MacClade and MacClade's help file; you will need approximately 1Mb available on the disk containing the destination folder to decompress this file. The Examples Compressed file contains the MacClade Examples folder; you will need approximately 865Kb available on the disk containing the destination folder to decompress this file. The examples folder contains files used as some of the examples in this book.

If you wish to use MacClade's help facility, the file MacClade Help needs to be in the same folder as MacClade or in the System Folder.

Using MacClade with Multifinder or System 7

MacClade is compatible with Multifinder and System 7. However, MacClade does not do background processing. That is, you can't switch to another program while MacClade is performing a long calculation, hoping that MacClade will continue to calculate in the background. MacClade 3 is not System 7 savvy, in the sense that it does not take advantage of many of the new features of System 7.

If you are using MacClade and PAUP simultaneously on the same data file under Multifinder or System 7, you may, without realizing it, find yourself working on different versions of the data file in the two programs. See the appendix on using MacClade and PAUP together for instructions on how to avoid this problem.

One final point about using MacClade under Multifinder or System 7 — avoid discarding any currently active data files and tree files and avoid moving them to any other folders or disks while MacClade is still running. This could cause great complications.

Computer memory and MacClade's limits

	Approximate maximum number of standard, DNA, or RNA characters		
Taxa	1Mb	2Mb	4Mb
4	1000	5000	12000
25	500	2000	6000
80	200	800	2500
150	80	500	1400
250	20	300	850
500	•	120	400
750	•	60	250
1000	•	•	160
1500	•	•	75

MacClade 3 can process data matrices with 1500 taxa and 16000 characters, if there is enough computer memory available. It is not easy to give exact limits on how many taxa and characters can be accommodated within a certain amount of computer memory, as it depends upon the number of stored trees, presence of pictures, whether or not you ask MacClade to calculate a chart, and other factors. The table to the left lists the *approximate* maximum number of characters you can have for varying numbers of taxa if MacClade has available 1Mb, 2Mb, or 4Mb of memory (RAM).

Fewer characters could be accommodated if data have more than 10 states per character (protein or extended standard formats). Also note that this is the memory available to MacClade, which will be less than the total memory in the computer.

If you are running under Multifinder or System 7, you have some control over how much memory to allocate to MacClade. Stored in each program is a number indicating how much memory the program will request from the computer for operation. MacClade asks for 1024Kb, an amount that will allow MacClade to work on reasonably large data files (see MacClade's limits above). However, MacClade can function with slightly less memory than this with smaller data sets. Therefore, if you find that MacClade is using up too much memory, try changing MacClade's request by selecting MacClade in the Finder, choosing **Get Info** under the **File** menu, and editing the Application Memory Size. The next time you start up MacClade, Multifinder or System 7 will reserve this smaller amount of memory for MacClade. In contrast, if you find that a data file is too big for MacClade to handle in 1024Kb, then as long as your computer has enough memory, increase the Application Memory Size until it is sufficient for your data file. (Most files included in the Molecular Examples folder require more than 1024Kb. The primate mtDNA and Bird Ovomucoid files require that MacClade be given 1.5Mb of memory, the Kingdoms mtDNA file 2.5Mb, and the human mtDNA file 3.5Mb.)

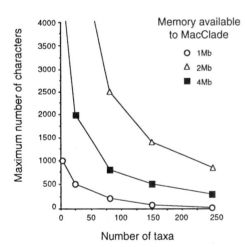

Limits on matrix size in MacClade

When MacClade is running under System 6 or earlier, but not under Multifinder, the Macintosh automatically gives MacClade as much memory as possible. In this context, the only way to increase the amount of memory available to MacClade is to add more memory to your computer!

NOTE: *In the tree window, to see amount of available memory, click on message box at lower left of the window. In the editor, click on the empty space to the right of the ▦ ▦ buttons to see amount of available memory.*

Starting MacClade

 MacClade
program

 Data file
or tree file

 Stationery
pad

 Graphics
file

 Help
file

 Preferences
file

MacClade can be started in several different ways. If you double-click on MacClade in the Finder, MacClade will begin and present you with the **Open File** dialog box which allows you either to create a new file (with the **New** button) or open an existing file (with the **Open** button). MacClade can also be opened by double-clicking on any MacClade file. MacClade files include MacClade data files, tree files, the help file, the preferences file, and MacClade graphics output files.

If you double-click on the icon of a MacClade data file in the Finder, this will start MacClade and open the selected data file. If you select more than one file in the Finder, MacClade will open only one of them. If you select a file in the Finder and give the **Print** command, MacClade will start, open that file, but not print (as MacClade doesn't know what aspect of that file you wish to print).

Data files are any files that contain specifications of the characteristics of taxa; they may also contain trees. In contrast, tree files contain *only* trees. Note that the icons for MacClade's tree files are exactly the same as MacClade's data files. If you ask MacClade to open a tree file, without first having asked it to open a data file, MacClade will give a warning that this cannot be done.

NOTE: *If the icons for your MacClade preferences or graphics files look like blank pages, then this means that the disk has had on it previously an older version of MacClade. In order for the new icons to be displayed, you may need to rebuild the Desktop file for that disk. This can be done by holding down the Option and Command (⌘) keys while the disk is first being read in or as the Finder is first opening; see your Macintosh manual for details. But beware; this action will cause all comments you have entered into the Get Info windows to be lost.*

If you double-click on a **stationery pad** of a data file, MacClade will treat the file exactly as a normal data or tree file, except that it will open the document as a new untitled and unsaved document, leaving the stationery pad untouched on the disk. You will see the stationery pad icon only if you are using System 7.

MacClade's behavior on opening any other type of file varies. If the file opened is the **help file** (MacClade Help), MacClade will open its help window. If the file opened is a MacClade **preferences file**, MacClade will start and use the settings stored in that file as the defaults. If the file opened is a MacClade **graphics file**, MacClade will start, but not open the file. Because MacClade can't actually edit graphics files of this sort (you should do this with your drawing program), it does not process the file.

To open a data file created by another program such as PAUP, see the instructions in Chapters 8 and 9.

Getting help

MacClade's help facility can be called by choosing **About MacClade** in the menu, then pressing the button Help, or by pressing the Help function key on some keyboards. On the left side of the **Help** dialog box is a scrollable list of topics. If you select a topic, a discussion of it will appear on the right. At the end of the list of topics is an index, which has an alphabetical list of subjects indexed to topic number.

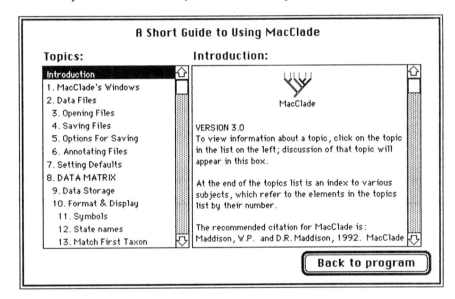

When you request help, MacClade looks for the MacClade Help file. For MacClade to find the file automatically, it must be named "MacClade Help", and it must be located in the same folder as MacClade or in the System Folder. If MacClade can't find the Help file, it will ask you to search for it.

MacClade 3 does not have Balloon Help.

Rules about selecting elements in a list

MacClade uses the standard Macintosh rules for selecting elements in a list. In general, touching on an unselected element, say the third one, will cause other list elements to be deselected, and the third one to be selected:

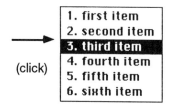

If item 5 were then touched, and the Shift or Command (⌘) keys were *not* held down, item 3 would be deselected and item 5 selected:

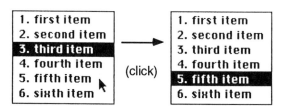

If, however, item 5 were touched while the Shift key was being held down, and the list is one that allows for selection of more than one item, the selection would be extended from 3 down to 5:

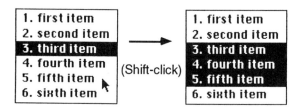

If item 1 were touched while the Shift key was being held down, the selection would be extended from 3 up to 1:

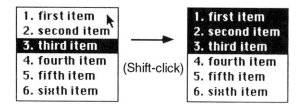

If item 5 were touched while the Command (⌘) key was being held down, item 5 would be added to the current selection:

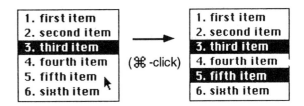

Messages

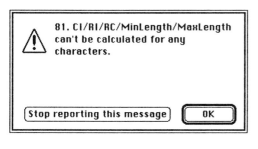

In the course of using MacClade, you may receive various warnings or messages about incorrectly formatted files, or illegal assumptions, or whatever.

If you choose OK, then MacClade will present you with the same warning again, if the appropriate situation arises again. However, if you choose Stop reporting this message, then MacClade will not redisplay that particular message again. This is particularly convenient if you are being warned many times about a particular problem. If you do disable a warning message in this way, there are two ways to tell MacClade to redisplay the message when appropriate: either quit from MacClade and restart the program, or hold down the Option key and choose **Restore Messages** from the **File** menu. All disabled messages will thereby be enabled.

For some of its statistics, such as treelength, MacClade may put an asterisk or other symbol beside the number, indicating that there may be problems underlying the statistic (for instance, that treelength is difficult to interpret with soft polytomies). The infinity symbol (∞) may appear if a number is undefined or negative. When a number is too large to represent with the current options, asterisks (***) may appear. By touching on the number with the pointer, a message may appear that describes the problem. The problem will be discussed in greater detail in the relevant section in this book.

Setting preferences for MacClade's options

MacClade has hundreds of options that may or may not be in effect at any one time. You can choose whether polytomies are to be interpreted as hard or soft, whether treelength calculation is turned on, whether the grid is shown in the data editor, which patterns are used in shading the tracing of character evolution, and so on. You can change these options using various dialog boxes and menu items in MacClade.

How MacClade remembers options

When you begin a new file, MacClade sets the options to the default values. These default values are either the factory defaults, or your own particular preferences. For example, when you start a new file, the data editor will be displayed using the font Geneva, unless you have set your preference to Times, in which case the data editor will be displayed in Times. MacClade stores your preferences in a special preferences file in the System Folder called MacClade Preferences, and refers to this file when the program starts. The means by which you set preferences are detailed in the next section.

When you open an old file, MacClade will, in general, use the values of the options stored in the data file, even if these values differ from your preferences. For example, if you had saved a file in MacClade 3 with Helvetica as the data editor font, then that file will display the data editor in Helvetica, even if the font specified by your preferences is Times. However, MacClade will not always use the values of options stored in data files, for two reasons. First, if the old file was not saved by MacClade 3, then the values of the options may not be stored in the file. The values of most options are included in the data file only when the file is saved by MacClade. Second, there is a set of options whose values are not stored in each file. (The values for these options can only be stored in the program's preferences file.) For these options, the values in use will not change when you open an old file, even if that file was saved when other values where in effect.

There are six groups of options that are not stored in data files. The values for these options are thus preserved throughout a MacClade session, unless you explicitly change their values. They are: (1) the full color and pattern palette, as displayed in the **Branch Shading** dialog box in the tree window's **Display** menu; (2) the **Search Options** available in the **Tree** menu; (3) the **Other Options** from the **Options For Saving** submenu of the **File** menu; (4) the fonts used in printing elements from the **Print Other** submenu of the **File** menu; (5) the items listed in **Save Preferences** dialog box (from the **File** menu) under "tree window display"; and (6) the options in the **Entry Interpretation** dialog box from the **Edit** menu in the data editor. Designating default values is the only way for you to tell MacClade to remember your choices in these six exceptional groups of options, as the values for these options can be saved only in a preferences file, not in a data file.

If you start up MacClade by double-clicking on a preferences file in the Finder, MacClade will use that preferences file for defaults, *no matter what the file's name is.* Thus you can store several alternative preferences files, one for your molecular data, one for your flower morphology data, and so on. To save alternative preferences files, choose the **Save Preferences** menu item from the **File** menu, or press on the Save Preference buttons in the appropriate dialog boxes, then go into the System Folder and rename this preferences file to something other than "MacClade Preferences" (e.g., "MacClade DNA Preferences"). This protects the file from being overwritten the next time you save preferences, and your MacClade DNA Preferences can be accessed as described by double-clicking on its icon. (Under System 7, you might also use stationery pads for data files, as described in Chapter 8. These store most, but not all, preferences.)

Designating preferences

You can tell MacClade what you want its default values to be by using the Save Preferences buttons and menu items. Many dialog boxes in MacClade have a Save Preferences button. Pressing one of these will designate the settings currently chosen in the dialog box to be MacClade's default values. (If you do not designate your own preferences, MacClade will use its own factory defaults.) The preferences will be saved in a file called "MacClade Preferences" in the System Folder.

In addition, preferences for several other options, including some aspects of the editor, chart window, tree window, the default type, and the data format, can be set using the **Save Preferences** dialog box of the **File** menu. To use this dialog box, check off those items you want saved, and press the Save Preferences button; the settings for those items checked will then be saved.

N O T E : *There are two levels of defaults for character types (see Chapter 11). Each data file has its own default type, such that any new characters created will be assigned that type. This file default is set in the **Type Edit** dialog box in the **Assume** menu. There is also a preference for the default type. The factory setting for this program preference is "unordered". Thus, if you create a new file, the default type of any character will be unordered. However, you can change this program preference by first changing the file default in the **Type Edit** dialog box, and then using the **Save Preferences** item of the **File** menu to save the preference. (You cannot do this if the file's default type is user-defined or stratigraphic.)*

N O T E : *To save all current options as defaults, hold down the Option key and choose **Save All Preferences** from the **File** menu.*

Using MacClade with other programs

As you use MacClade on your computer you will find a need to share information between MacClade and other computer programs. Word processors and spreadsheet programs may be used in editing the data file, other phylogenetics programs like PAUP may be involved in analyzing the data, and graphics programs may be used to modify graphics files made by MacClade. Various sections of this book describe how MacClade can share information via files.

We envisage MacClade being used closely in connection with PAUP, a program for phylogenetic analysis developed by David Swofford

(1991). Appendix 2 discusses issues concerning the use of MacClade and PAUP together. Of special concern are slight differences in calculations and file format, and the caution needed in using PAUP and MacClade simultaneously.

Chapter 9 discusses importing and exporting data files from other programs including other phylogenetics programs and sequence alignment programs. Chapter 20 discusses MacClade's saving of results in text and graphics files that can be edited by word processors and graphics programs.

Quitting from MacClade

To quit from MacClade, choose **Quit** from the **File** menu. If you have made changes (such as editing data, rearranging the tree, changing assumptions, and so on) since the last time you saved, MacClade will ask if you want to save the changes before quitting. If you press the Yes button, then MacClade will save changes and quit; if you press No, MacClade will not save the changes and quit; if you press Cancel, MacClade will not save the changes and not quit.

8. MANAGING DATA FILES

In this chapter we review some basic aspects of managing files.

Data files are files that contain a data matrix; they may also contain trees. Tree files contain only trees. For some additional information about tree files in particular, see Chapter 12.

Creating a new MacClade data file

To create a new MacClade data file, MacClade must be running and no data file can be open. There are two ways to ask MacClade to create a new data file. First, you can use the New button in the **Open File** dialog box. This dialog is presented to you when you start MacClade without specifying a data file, or when you choose **Open File** from the **File** menu in MacClade. Thus you can create a new file by double-clicking on the MacClade icon in the Finder, then choosing the New button in the **Open File** dialog box. Second, there is also a **New File** menu item in the **File** menu of MacClade. If the **New File** or **Open File** menu items are grayed, then a data file must still be open; you must close it before attempting to create or open another file. Whether you use the New button or menu item, you will be presented with a blank data editor with one taxon and one character.

To choose the kind of data (standard, extended standard, DNA, RNA, protein) included in the data matrix, select the appropriate item from the **Format** menu (see the section "Data Formats" of Chapter 10 for more details).

Opening an existing data file

How you open an existing data file depends on whether the data file is a MacClade data file (one with a MacClade file icon), or a data file originating from some other source (such as a word processor or PAUP). If the data file is a MacClade data file, it can be opened directly from the Finder by double-clicking on it. The Macintosh will know to start MacClade and will do so automatically. If the data file is not a MacClade data file, or even if it is, you can open it by first starting MacClade, then using the **Open File** item in the **File** menu, then choosing the file in the dialog box. If you are running System 7, you can drop the file onto the MacClade application in the Finder to open the file.

As the file is being read in, you will see a box with a status bar on it showing the progress of the reading. You will also note that the cursor changes as the file is read; each type of cursor indicates which part of the file is being read in; see Appendix 1 for details.

If you decide to abort the reading of a file, hold down the Command (⌘) key and type a period (.).

If MacClade detects that the file being read is not a standard MacClade 3 file (perhaps it is a HENNIG86 or PHYLIP file), MacClade will present you with a dialog box asking you what type of file it is. Select the appropriate file format from the pop-up menu. MacClade can open and understand text files in a number of formats, including those of MacClade 1.0, 2.1, HENNIG86 (version 1.5) and PHYLIP (versions 3.3 and 3.4). Also, some sorts of simple tables can be understood by MacClade. For full details on the files MacClade can import, see Chapter 9.

On opening a file, MacClade will go automatically to either the tree window or the data editing window, whichever was in use when MacClade last saved the file.

NOTE: *If you hold down the Option key while the file is being read, you will be taken automatically to the data editor, even if the file was last saved with the tree window on the screen. If you hold down the Command (⌘) key, you will be taken to the tree window. MacClade checks to see if a key is held down when the cursors change as it is reading the file.*

You can open only one file at a time. If you already have a file open, the **Open File** and **New File** menu items will be dimmed.

As you must open a data file before you open a tree file, MacClade will not allow you to open a tree file first.

The NEXUS file format

Character data, trees, and other information of interest are stored in a MacClade data file or tree file in a very particular format. Generally the MacClade user is not concerned with the internal structure of the data files because MacClade digests this information and presents it to the user in the form of the data matrix in the data editor, a tree, and so on. When you save a file containing these objects, MacClade stores on the disk not the objects themselves, but a textual description of them. The format of this textual description is called the NEXUS format. You do not need to know the details of the format for the most part, as MacClade automatically writes data files in NEXUS format.

The NEXUS format has been designed to make sharing of data between programs as easy and flexible as possible (Maddison, Swofford, and Maddison, in preparation). Swofford's PAUP version 3.0 (1991) uses the NEXUS format, and with a few exceptions, MacClade's data and tree files are completely compatible with PAUP. (See Appendix 2, "Using MacClade and PAUP Together".)

WARNING: *You can easily see a NEXUS file directly by opening it with PAUP's editor, or by viewing it in a word-processing program.* **If you type in or modify the raw text file yourself using a word processor, PAUP, or other program, and try to read it into MacClade, make sure you know what you are doing** *(see Maddison, Swofford, and Maddison, in preparation),* **or you may see some spectacular crashes.** *Because MacClade should write perfect NEXUS files, it expects perfect NEXUS files in return. It thus does not perform extensive error checking on the files it reads in. We recommend that you let MacClade format the NEXUS file for you. If you edit NEXUS files using a word processor, the file must be saved as "Text Only" or MacClade will not even know the file exists. Also, be forewarned that any pictures you have in the data file* **will be discarded** *if you edit and save a MacClade file in most word-processing programs! (See "Annotating your data" in Chapter 10.) (The settings of some display options will also be lost.)*

Adding notes about the data file

A general comment about the data file as a whole can be entered in the window that appears when you choose **About** *filename* from the **File** menu. (In place of "*filename*" will be the name of the file.) You can, for example, include information about the source of the data, including literature citations, or instructions to students. You may also wish to include notes about the characters and taxa, work that needs to be done with the data, and so on. All of the example data files included with MacClade have notes added to them in the About *filename* window. (Notes added to this window will appear in PAUP's main window as the file is being executed.)

To add notes concerning individual taxa, characters, or cells in the matrix, see the section on footnotes in Chapter 10.

Saving files to disk

To save the current data file choose **Save File** from the **File** menu. To save the current data file under a different name (while leaving the last-saved copy on disk under the old name), or to save a brand new file, choose **Save File As** from the **File** menu.

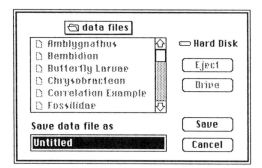

The **Save File As** dialog box

(The dialog box you see may vary depending upon the System you are using.)

To save the current tree file, choose **Save Tree File** from the **Tree** menu. To save the currently stored trees to a tree file under a different name, choose **Save Tree File As** from the **Tree** menu.

MacClade maintains the data file, including the data matrix, user-defined types, type sets, weight sets, trees, and character names in the computer's memory (RAM). Changes you make to these elements (e.g., by storing another type set with the **Store Type Set** command) are maintained in memory and are written to disk *only* when you issue an explicit **Save File** or **Save Tree File** command. Even when you edit the data matrix, the changes are not written to disk before you move to the tree window; they are only held in memory. When you do give a **Save** command, all of the changes you have made and items you have stored are saved to the disk.

To protect your work from system crashes and disk failures, save your file frequently and keep backup copies of your files in more than one place.

NOTE: *If you hold down the Option key and choose **Save Stationery As** from the **File** menu, then MacClade will save the data file as a stationery pad (see p. 136).*

Saving files in other formats

Using the **Export File** submenu, MacClade can write data files in formats other than NEXUS. For instance, MacClade will write HENNIG86 and PHYLIP files so that those programs can be used alongside MacClade. A tab-delimited table representing the data matrix can be written as a simple table file. A text file of descriptions can also be written. These exporting features are described in Chapter 9.

Tree files can also be exported to HENNIG86 or PHYLIP formats using the **Export Tree File** submenu. This feature is described in Chapters 9 and 12.

Results from analyses can also be saved as files, such as graphics files containing a picture of the tree or a chart, or text files storing the information contained in a chart, or the results from the character correlation test. See Chapter 20 for more details.

Altering the way MacClade writes files

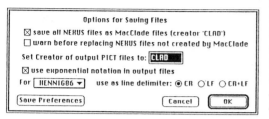

If you want to change the way MacClade writes files, you can use the items in the **Options for Saving** submenu of the **File** menu to make a few changes. Of the two items in this submenu, the **NEXUS Format** item allows you to change the manner in which NEXUS files are formatted; details are given in Appendix 1. The **Other Options** item produces a dialog box in which you can alter the way that MacClade saves a variety of files. We will describe only the first two options here; the others are discussed elsewhere. Setting the creator of PICT files is discussed in Chapter 20, use of exponential notation is described in Chapter 15, and the export line delimiter is detailed in Chapter 9.

On the Macintosh, files are marked as having been created by an application. Thus, if you create a new file in MacClade, and save it to disk, MacClade will stamp its signature onto the file (by setting its creator to "CLAD"). The file then "belongs" to MacClade, it will have a MacClade data file icon, and if you double-click on it in the Finder, MacClade will be opened. If you ask MacClade to save all NEXUS files as MacClade files, then any file that MacClade saves using the **Save File** or **Save File As** commands will have their creator set to "CLAD" (and thus they will have MacClade icons), even if MacClade was not the original creator of the file. For example, if you had a file created in PAUP, displaying a PAUP icon, then you read that file into MacClade and saved it, MacClade would replace PAUP as the creator of the file. If this option is not checked, however, and MacClade was not the original creator of the file, then MacClade will leave the creator as is, if you choose **Save File**. Thus, if a PAUP file is read in and saved in MacClade, its creator would remain PAUP. This will not affect the text of the file as written by MacClade.

Some elements of a data file are ignored by MacClade (such as some types of file comments) and omitted when MacClade rewrites the file. As some of these elements may be valuable to you, you can ask MacClade to warn you before it replaces any files that are not of creator "CLAD".

Reverting to last saved version

To revert to the last-saved version of a file and discard any subsequent changes, hold down the Option key and choose **Revert to Saved** from the **File** menu. This is not available if MacClade considers the file to be unsaved (e.g., a new file).

Closing data files

To close a file, choose **Close File** from the **File** menu. If you have made changes (such as editing data, rearranging the tree, changing assumptions, and so on) since the last time you saved, MacClade will ask if you want to save the changes before closing the file. If you press the **Yes** button, then MacClade will save changes and close the file; if you press **No**, MacClade will not save the changes and close the file; if you press **Cancel**, MacClade will not save the changes and not close the file.

Note that by clicking on the go-away box of MacClade's tree window or data editor (the little boxes at the upper-left that make a window go away), MacClade *does not* close the file. It only closes that window; to close the file you must select **Close File** (or **Quit**) from the **Edit** menu. Conversely, choosing **Close File** does not simply close the front-most window; it also closes the file.

9. Importing and Exporting Text Files

This chapter describes importing and exporting files from and to various other computer programs, including HENNIG86 and PHYLIP. (Because MacClade and PAUP use the same file format, no special importing and exporting between them is needed.) For more details on general aspects of opening, closing, and saving files, see Chapter 8.

SUMMARY OF FEATURES: *MacClade's data and tree files are generally read and written as NEXUS format text files, also used by PAUP 3.0. MacClade can import text files of various other formats, including MacClade 1.0, MacClade 2.1, PHYLIP 3.3 and 3.4, HENNIG86 1.5, and NBRF. It can also import text files with the data matrix formatted as a simple table. MacClade can export to files of these formats and to files of descriptions.*

Importing files

Although MacClade is designed to deal primarily with NEXUS format files, MacClade can read data files written in several other text formats (MacClade 1.0 and 2.1, HENNIG86 version 1.5, PHYLIP versions 3.3 and 3.4, NBRF, and simple tables). If you have a data matrix that is stored in one of these formats, you can import the data file into MacClade as follows. Open the file as you would any other data file (see p. 143 for details). MacClade will detect that the file is not in standard NEXUS format and present a dialog box with a pop-up menu, from which you are to choose the file format. Make sure you choose the exact format. For example, if your file is in PHYLIP 3.4 format, and it contains DNA sequence data, then make sure you select the **PHYLIP 3.4 DNA/RNA** menu item. For more details on importing files of foreign formats, see the appropriate sections, later in this chapter.

If you have data not stored in one of the formats that MacClade understands, you will have to use a word processor to manipulate the data file into an understandable format. It is relatively easy to format files for import into MacClade. Depending on your data and assumptions, you may find it easiest to convert to the NEXUS format for direct reading by MacClade, or you may find it easier to import the data into MacClade via some other format. If you have only the data matrix itself to import, remember that a text file consisting of a matrix by itself may be directly importable by MacClade (discussed under "Simple table files", later in this chapter).

Importing data by hand may be especially common for molecular sequence data acquired from other programs or sequence data banks. Two facts should be kept in mind. First, each sequence must be of the same length (except for NBRF files, for which different sequences can be of different lengths). MacClade does not provide any automatic alignment options. Thus, it would be best to have the sequences pre-aligned. To indicate gaps implied by alignment, use a hyphen, instead of blank spaces. Second, there may be restrictions on the names of the taxa. (Names with spaces may need to be treated in a special way, for instance.)

To import a tree file, choose **Open Tree File** from the **Tree** menu, select the file, and press the Open button. If MacClade cannot quickly determine the file format, it will present a dialog box asking for the format. MacClade understands tree files in NEXUS, PHYLIP, and HENNIG86 formats only.

An imported file will be opened as an Untitled document.

Preparing a NEXUS format file

If you want to convert your file to NEXUS format and you don't want to spend time learning the NEXUS format (p. 355; Maddison, Swofford, and Maddison, in preparation), one simple aid to producing a NEXUS file is to create and save in MacClade a simple NEXUS data file of the same format of data as yours (for instance, DNA data). You can then open up this template file in a word processor. With the word processor, replace the data matrix in the NEXUS file by your own data matrix, and adjust the number of taxa and characters indicated (by adjusting the DIMENSIONS NTAX= NCHAR= line). Or, you can use the following small NEXUS file as a template for producing your own.

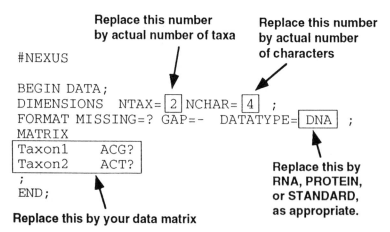

As long as your data matrix is not too strangely formatted, this may be a quick way to convert it by hand to NEXUS format. Be careful that taxon names do not include spaces or other illegal characters, or if they do, are properly protected by quotes (see p. 355). Make sure, if you are using a word processor, to save the file as "Text Only". Further details on the NEXUS format are found in Appendix 1.

Preparing a simple table

Simple table files that MacClade can read consist of the following for each sequence (with no other text): a taxon name (with no spaces or illegal characters, except if properly protected by quotes, see p. 355); a space or tab; the data for that taxon, all on one line, either unseparated or separated by spaces or tabs; a carriage return. You should avoid other text in the file. For further details, see the section "Simple table files", later in this chapter.

Preparing an NBRF format file

You can easily convert molecular sequence data to a MacClade-readable NBRF format by including in the file the following for each sequence:

> >code; taxon name
> one-line comment
> 1 or more lines of sequence, ending in *

No other text should be included in the file. See p. 156 for an example.

Exporting files

Use the **Export File** submenu to choose the format of export. On exporting files, MacClade checks to see if it can successfully write the current file in the requested format. If you ask to export a file to PHYLIP that has only binary characters, or that is of DNA or RNA or protein sequences, then MacClade will (usually) simply export the file. Similarly, files exported to HENNIG86 that have 10 or fewer states per character, with characters of unordered or ordered types, and no polymorphisms or partial uncertainty, will be written by MacClade without any warning. However, other data or assumptions may not be exportable (e.g., if a character is of a character-state-tree type with polymorphisms), and MacClade will warn you to that effect. In such a case, you will have to change your data or assumptions to a form compatible with the other program before requesting exportation.

Line delimiter

By default, MacClade will put a carriage return ("CR"; ASCII value 13) between each line in an exported file. But if you wish to move the file to a non-Macintosh computer, then a carriage return may not be the appropriate line delimiter. For example, if you export an NBRF file and want to move it to a UNIX machine, it may be more appropriate to have a line feed ("LF"; ASCII value 10) between lines. For an IBM PC, a carriage return plus line feed may be most appropriate. You can adjust the line delimiters used by MacClade for each of the exported file types in the **Other Options** dialog box in the **Options for Saving** submenu of the **File** menu. To change the export delimiter for, say, HENNIG86 files, choose **HENNIG86** from the pop-up menu on the left. Then click on the radio button on the right to specify the appropriate delimiter. You can ask MacClade to write carriage returns (CR), line feed (LF), or both carriage returns and. linefeeds.

The software you use to transfer files between computers may automatically translate the line delimiters. Before you adjust the line delimiters within MacClade, you should test out your system to see if your file transferal software automatically adjusts the delimiters. If your software already does this, then you should ignore this option in MacClade.

MacClade 1.0 and 2.1 files

MacClade 3 will import old MacClade files. MacClade will not export files into old MacClade format. MacClade 3 will not import or export files of some test versions of MacClade that were never released for general use (e.g., versions 2.65, 2.87, 2.97; see Chapter 1).

MacClade is not always successful in importing old MacClade files if these files did not comply strictly with the old file formats. MacClade 1.0 and 2.1 would accept files that violated their formats in minor ways. It is therefore possible to have a file that the old versions would accept, but that MacClade 3 will not. An example is the Vertebrates example file distributed with MacClade 2.1, which will not be read properly because one of the tree descriptions is lacking a necessary comma.

PAUP files

With files created for PAUP version 3.0 (Swofford, 1991), you don't have to import or export them in any special way, because MacClade 3 and PAUP 3.0 share the same NEXUS file format (see Appendix 1). However, there are some incompatibilities as indicated in Appendix 2.

If you are using PAUP and MacClade together with Multifinder or System 7, see Appendix 2.

PHYLIP files

Importing

MacClade 3 can understand most PHYLIP 3.3 and 3.4 files (Felsenstein, 1991); it can also import some files from earlier versions of PHYLIP. Because of the ambiguity in pre-PHYLIP 3.4 file formats (caused by the fact that different options in the file mean different things depending upon the PHYLIP program that processes the file), importing PHYLIP 3.3 files is fraught with peril, unless you remove all options, or pay close attention to the following notes.

The first line of the data file must contain only the number of taxa, number of characters, and letters for each of the options. Other numbers, such as required in version 3.3 of PHYLIP's RESTML, are not allowed.

For PHYLIP 3.3 files, MacClade processes options in the following ways:

Option	Code	MacClade's action
ALL	A	*Must be removed*
ANCSTATES	A	Ignores and skips over ancstates line
CAMIN	C	*Must be removed*
CATEGORIES	C	Ignores and skips over two categories line
CLIQUE	C	*Must be removed*
DOLLO	D	Sets all characters to Dollo
FACTORS	F	Ignores and skips over factors line
FREQUENCIES	F	Ignores (molecular sequence data only)
GLOBAL	G	Ignores
HALF JACK	H	Ignores
JACKKNIFE	J	*Must be removed*
JUMBLE	J	*Must be removed*
LENGTH	L	Ignores
LOCAL	L	Ignores
MIXED	M	Sets character types, and stores type set
OUTGROUP	O	Ignores and skips over outgroup line
POLYMORPHISM	P	Ignores
RECONSIDER	R	Ignores
REPLICATE	R	Ignores
ROOTED	R	Ignores
SOKAL	S	Sets all characters to irreversible
THRESHOLD	T	Ignores and skips over line
TRANS/TRANS	T	Ignores and skips over line
USERTREES	U	Reads in trees
WEIGHTS	W	Sets character weights, and stores weight set
WRITE TREES	Y	Ignores

Those options that are marked "*Must be removed*" indicate those options that must be removed from the data file before you import it into MacClade, or MacClade may crash on reading the file.

For PHYLIP 3.4 files, MacClade processes options in the following way:

Option	Code	MacClade's action
ANCSTATES	A	Ignores and skips over ancstates line
CATEGORIES	C	Ignores and skips over categories line
FACTORS	F	Ignores and skips over factors line
MIXED	M	Sets characters types, and stores type set
WEIGHTS	W	Sets character weights, and stores weight set

For a non-molecular matrix, MacClade will read "B", "b", "P", or "p" and set the state equal to "polymorphic for states 0 and 1". For molecular sequence data, it will read the standard IUPAC symbols appropriately.

MacClade presumes that you have allocated 10 characters for taxon names, and so presumes that data for the first character of a taxon begins at the 11th position on the line. In reading in a taxon name, any semicolon, ";", will be converted to an underbar, "_".

If trees follow the matrix, MacClade will read them.

Exporting

MacClade will write the following options, if applicable, into a PHYLIP data file:

Option	Code	MacClade's action
MIXED	M	Writes currently active types
WEIGHTS	W	Writes currently active weights

For version 3.3 PHYLIP files, MacClade will also include the following options, if relevant:

Option	Code	MacClade's action
DOLLO	D	Include if default type for file is Dollo

MacClade will also include any trees in the current data file into the PHYLIP file (and add the Usertrees option for version 3.3 files).

If you choose to export a protein data file, be wary that a program like PHYLIP will not accept extra amino acid states, such as MacClade's states 1 and 2 for serine with the standard nuclear genetic code. If you do have such extra states in your matrix, you should recode them first using the **Recode** or **Search & Replace** commands before exporting the file.

Remember, if you ask to export a file using data or assumptions that MacClade considers incompatible with PHYLIP, MacClade will refuse, and you must revise your data or assumptions before exportation.

HENNIG86 files

Importing

MacClade can import HENNIG86 version 1.5 (Farris, 1988) data files and tree files. Since CLADOS (Nixon, 1992) uses Hennig86's data file format, MacClade can also import files made for CLADOS. It will read in matrices in XREAD commands, trees in TREAD commands, assumptions in CCODE commands, and QUOTE commands. All other HENNIG86 commands are ignored. For MacClade to process trees, they must be in the format that HENNIG86 writes tree files (that is, fairly standard parenthesis notation). MacClade cannot understand trees in Hennig86's newer format that uses symbols such as [ ] / \ { } . Elements in the title line of the XREAD command and in the QUOTE command are added to the About *filename* window in MacClade.

Exporting

MacClade will export data and tree files in HENNIG86 version 1.5 format. It writes XREAD, TREAD, CCODE, and QUOTE commands. Included in the QUOTE command will be any text from MacClade's About *filename* window. If any characters or states have names, MacClade will write these in the QUOTE command. In writing the matrix, MacClade will use "-" for gaps, "?" for missing data. All trees stored in the data file will be written into a TREAD command.

Remember, if you ask to export a file using data or assumptions that MacClade considers incompatible with HENNIG86 version 1.5, MacClade will refuse, and you must revise your data or assumptions before exportation.

NBRF files

Importing

MacClade can read in National Biomedical Research Foundation (NBRF) format. These nucleotide or amino acid sequence files have, for each sequence, one line starting with ">", followed by items that are irrelevant to MacClade, the next line containing the name of a sequence, followed by one or more lines of sequence, ending in "*":

```
>DL; taxon_1
a comment about taxon_1
AGGAAGTACGATCCGGCACA
CAACGGTTTGTTAGCACTTC*
>DL; taxon_2
a comment about taxon_2
TCGGATGTGTCAAGCGCTGG
TTGAGGTGATAATACCTCTG*
>DL; taxon_3
a comment about taxon_3
TAAGGGTCCCGATTATGTGA
GCCACATTAATTGTATTACG*
```

This file format is used by many programs that process molecular sequence data.

Exporting

MacClade also writes out files in National Biomedical Research Foundation format. This is available only for molecular sequence data.

If you choose to export a protein data file, be wary that a program like Jotun Hein's (1990b) TreeAlign will not accept extra amino acid states, such as MacClade's states 1 and 2 for serine with the standard nuclear genetic code. If you do have such extra states in your matrix, you should recode them first using the **Recode** or **Search & Replace** commands before exporting the file.

By default, gaps are included in the NBRF file created by MacClade. If you wish these gaps to be omitted, hold down the Option key before choosing **NBRF no gaps** from the **Export File** submenu.

Simple table files

Importing

MacClade can also read text files that are simple tables of character state data. The format for simple table files for importing is very specific: on each line must be all the data for one taxon, beginning with the taxon name, then a blank space or tab, then the state of the first character, state of second character and so on until the last character, which is followed by a carriage return. Blanks or tabs can be placed between states in the matrix, but they need not be there. The taxon name must have no spaces (use underlines to indicate spaces), unless it is surrounded by single quotes, and states must be listed as single-digit integers (0..9) and letters (A through R excluding I and O), or ACGTU if

DNA or RNA data, or the appropriate IUPAC codes if protein data. The symbol "-" will be treated as a gap, "?" as missing data.

NOTE: *Technically, the taxon name must be a single NEXUS token. See Appendix 1 for details.*

No polymorphisms or partial uncertainties are allowed. There can be comments (surrounded by [ ]) before the matrix begins, and after it ends, but there can be nothing else in the data file.

Here is a simple table file that MacClade can read:

```
[can put comment here]
taxon_1          3 - 2 3 1 3 ? 0
taxon_2          0 0 0 1 2 0 1 2
taxon_3          2 2 3 ? 2 0 1 0
taxon_4          1 2 0 0 0 3 2 1
taxon_5          2 0 2 0 1 2 1 3
taxon_6          3 0 2 0 3 0 1 2
taxon_7          1 0 2 0 0 3 3 2
taxon_8          3 1 0 0 2 0 1
```

Exporting

MacClade allows you to export text files in simple tabular format, by choosing the **Simple Table** menu of the **Export File** submenu. You will be presented with a dialog box in which you choose the format of the table file:

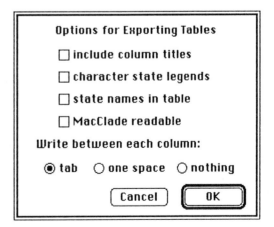

Checking "include column titles" will cause MacClade to insert a title above each column in the matrix. The choice of "character state legends" will write a list of the symbols used in the table and their state names on the left below each character name for transposed matrices, and below the matrix for non-transposed matrices. Part of a transposed table with character state legends looks something like this:

silver spots 0: absent 1: present	0	0	0	0	1	1	1	1	1	1	1
int. 3 micro. 0: absent 1: v. slight mirrors 2: slight mirrors 3: distinct mirrors	0	0	0	1	1	1	3	3	2	3	3

If you choose "state names in table", then MacClade will write full state names for character states if these are available, rather than single-character symbols.

If you choose "MacClade readable", then the table will be of a structure that will allow it to be imported back into MacClade. If this option is chosen, most others (such as "include column titles") are disallowed, as they would make the resulting file unreadable by MacClade.

If the interleave format is set in the **NEXUS Format** dialog under **Options for Saving** submenu in the **File** menu (see p. 357), then the table will be interleaved (unless "MacClade readable" is checked).

Exporting descriptions

If you ask MacClade to export a file in Descriptions format, it will write out the information in the data matrix in telescopic prose. For example, the Descriptions format for the Amblygnathus file included in the Examples folder begins something like this:

seriatoporus-g
m.l. vent. flange present. elyt. micro. isodiametric. body length 6.3-7.0mm. pron. hind ang. rounded. # int sac spines numerous. spine size large. spine loc'n scattered. prostern. process not. head micros. isodiam. elytral vest. 8-9. head & pron color black. clypeal margin ± straight. left mand. apex normal. spermatheca short curve. male lamina width broad. lamina length moderate. lam. apex dir. right. apex shape pointed. m.l. apex form mod straight. m.l. flange bilo not. dorsal flange small. female terg.8 setae absent. sac microtrich. normal. leg color flavous. m.l. vent.-sculp. smooth. elytral color black. m.l. vent.-form tapered. pron. base moderate.

ellipticus-g
m.l. vent. flange present. elyt. micro. isodiametric. body length 4.5-6.2mm. pron. hind ang. subangulate. # int sac spines none. spine size absent. spine loc'n absent. prostern. process ridged. head micros. isodiam. elytral vest. 9 & ap1-8. head & pron color black. clypeal margin ± straight. left mand. apex normal. spermatheca short curve. male lamina width broad. lamina length long. lam. apex dir. right. apex shape pointed. m.l. apex form mod straight. m.l. flange bilo not. dorsal flange small. female terg.8 setae absent. sac microtrich. normal. leg color flavous. m.l. vent.-sculp. smooth. elytral color black. m.l. vent.-form tapered. pron. base moderate.

MacClade cannot read files in Descriptions format.

10. THE DATA EDITOR

Data are entered in MacClade's Data Editor, a spreadsheet specialized for systematics.

You can enter data by selecting a cell in the data editor and editing its contents, add, delete, or move columns and rows, have the data displayed in a number of formats, and so on. Some elements of the data editor are shown in the figure below:

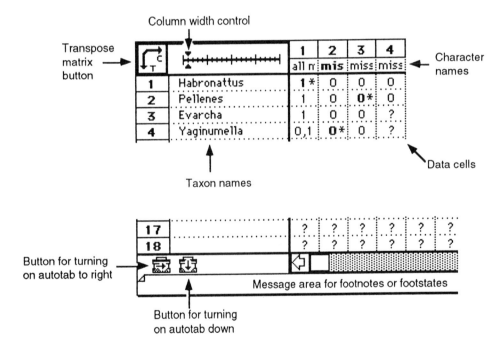

SUMMARY OF FEATURES: *Entering and editing character states in cells of the matrix follow usual Macintosh conventions. A taxon can be indicated as having, for any particular character, a single state, multiple states (polymorphism), uncertain state, missing data, or a gap. Autotab causes the selection to move to the next cell automatically for quickly entering data.*

MacClade allows you to designate a data matrix as having one of the following formats: standard, extended standard, DNA, RNA, or protein. The molecular formats come with predefined and fixed symbols for the states (e.g., A, C, G, T). The standard formats allow you to designate states by default symbols (e.g., 0, 1, 2, ... ,9), by your own symbols (e.g., a, b, c, d ...) or by state names (e.g., red, blue). With extended standard, 26 states are allowed.

Columns and rows in the matrix can be moved, deleted, added, or replicated. A block of the matrix can be selected and filled entirely with one state, or the state of the first taxon. States of a character can be automatically recoded, and a search and replace facility allows data entries to be changed automatically. Taxa can be merged together and redundant taxa filtered from the data matrix. Invariant or excluded characters can be filtered from the data matrix. Nucleotide sequence data can be translated into protein data using a user-defined genetic code; portions of sequences can be moved, reversed, or complemented.

You can change various aspects of the display of the editor, including font of text and column widths; the matrix can also be transposed. The matrix can be drawn so as to place a simple symbol (e.g., ".") whenever a taxon has the same state as that in the first taxon. Footnotes and pictures can be attached to cells in the data matrix.

Creating and editing a data matrix

To create a new data matrix, and enter data, you would generally follow these steps:

1. Start a new file (see p. 143).

2. Choose data format (**Standard, Extended Standard, DNA, RNA,** or **Protein**) from the **Format** menu (p. 162).

3. Expand data matrix to include the appropriate number of taxa and characters (p. 166).

4. Enter taxon names (p. 172).

5. Provide names for characters and states, if you wish (pp. 173, 174).

6. Enter data (p. 178).

7. Save data file (p. 145).

8. Edit and revise data.

Full details for each of these steps can be found in the remainder of this chapter, and Chapter 8.

In any data file in MacClade, only two elements are necessary: names of taxa, and specification of the traits of each taxon. Optionally you can add names of characters and character states, notes about the data, and so on.

The purpose of the data editor is to allow you to create and edit your matrix of character data. These characters are discrete-valued, that is, each character can have up to 4, 10, 25, or 26 discrete states, depending upon the data format chosen. MacClade can also store some continuous-valued characters, but these cannot be edited using the data editor (see Chapter 16 for more detail).

WARNING: *In using the data editor, be careful; most changes you make cannot be automatically undone with an Undo command.*

MacClade can display data to you in several formats. You can give names to the states of a character, and ask MacClade to display the data using those names. You can also use single-letter or number symbols. For example, if you have a DNA sequence matrix, each character has states designated by "A", "C", "G", and "T". For standard and extended standard files you can assign your own symbols. On the screen, the states can be represented therefore either by symbols (e.g., "0", "1", "2", or "A", "C", "G"), or as state names (e.g., "blue", "red").

For example, in the following matrix, the data for each of the five characters are indicated using the symbols "0", "1", and "2".

		1	2	3	4	5
				eye color		
1	taxon 1	0	2	1	0	1
2	taxon 2	0	1	2	0	0
3	taxon 3	1	1	1	1	2
4	taxon 4	0	1	2	2	1
5	taxon 5	1	1	0	2	1

Note that the third character has been given a name.

If we then name the states of the third character (such that state 0 is "red", state 1 is "blue", and state 2 is "green"), and ask MacClade to display the information using state names, we see that the third character is now shown using state names:

⌐c ↓T	▼ ⊢⊦⊦⊦⊦⊦⊦⊦⊦⊦⊦⊦	1	2	3	4	5
				eye color		
1	taxon 1	0	2	blue	0	1
2	taxon 2	0	1	green	0	0
3	taxon 3	1	1	blue	1	2
4	taxon 4	0	1	green	2	1
5	taxon 5	1	1	red	2	1

If we change the symbols used by MacClade for the states to a, b, and c, then all characters (except those with defined state names) are displayed using those new symbols:

⌐c ↓T	▼ ⊢⊦⊦⊦⊦⊦⊦⊦⊦⊦⊦⊦	1	2	3	4	5
				eye color		
1	taxon 1	a	c	blue	a	b
2	taxon 2	a	b	green	a	a
3	taxon 3	b	b	blue	b	c
4	taxon 4	a	b	green	c	b
5	taxon 5	b	b	red	c	b

The underlying data, as stored within MacClade's memory, are the same for each of these three displays. For full details on the relationships between numbers, symbols, and state names, see the section "State numbers vs. symbols vs. names" later in this chapter.

Getting to the data editor

MacClade will automatically open the data editor when a new file is created; this allows you to begin entering data in the new matrix. If you are working with a previously saved file, MacClade will automatically open the data editor if the file was last saved with the editor window open, or if you hold the Option key down while the file is being read.

If you are in the tree window and wish to move to the data editor window, or the editor is hidden under another window and you wish to bring the editor to the front, choose **Data Editor** or **Go To Data Editor** from the **Display** menu.

Data formats

The **Format** menu allows you to choose whether the data consist of standard characters, extended standard, or DNA, RNA, or protein sequences. When you first create a data file in MacClade, it is assumed to be of standard format (unless you have changed your preference for data format using the **Save Preferences** dialog box from the **File** menu), which allows 10 states per character. Extended format differs from standard only in allowing 26 states per character, and in so doing uses more memory. Choosing DNA or RNA format enables some features specifically designed for nucleotide sequence data, and automatically defines some symbols such as A, C, G, T, U. The protein format automatically defines as symbols the IUPAC amino acid codes. For more information about the symbols allowed by various formats, see the section "Editing a cell", later in this chapter.

The maximum number of states allowed per character for each of the data formats is as follows:

Format	Maximum Number of States
Standard	10
Extended	26
DNA	4
RNA	4
Protein	25

You can also include in your data file up to four characters with continuous values. These are edited in a separate editor, as described in Chapter 16.

Changing data formats

You may find you need to change data formats after data have already been entered into the cells. For instance, you may discover you need to switch from standard to extended format because you find a character requiring more than 10 states. If you wish to change formats once data have already been entered into the cells, you should be aware of some limitations.

If the number of states allowed by the new format is less than that allowed by the old format, then MacClade may have to alter the data. For example, if the file was an extended standard format file, with state 15 represented for a character, and you wish to switch it to standard, then MacClade will set state 15 to missing data, as standard format can accommodate only 10 states.

If the states allowed by the new format do not include states indicated in some current user-defined transformation types, then these types will be deleted. For instance, if a step matrix is defined for states 0 through 9 in a standard format data file, the type will be deleted if the data file is converted to DNA format, which allows only four states (0123 = ACGT). Any characters assigned a deleted type will be reassigned the default type.

If you wish to switch a DNA or RNA format to a protein format, then MacClade will translate the nucleotide sequence into an amino acid sequence, using the current genetic code; see Chapter 19 for details of this conversion.

A summary of possible conversions and their limitations follows. Note that two conversions, from protein to DNA or RNA data, are not allowed by MacClade.

		To:				
		Standard	Extended	DNA	RNA	Protein
From:	Standard	✓	✓	-	-	✓
	Extended	-	✓	-	-	-
	DNA	✓	✓	✓	✓	✳
	RNA	✓	✓	✓	✓	✳
	Protein	-	-	✗	✗	✓

✓ :   conversion acceptable
- :   conversion acceptable, except some states may be removed
✳ :   conversion will involve nucleotide to amino acid translation
✗ :   conversion not allowed

WARNING: *If you have data stored in the Clipboard, these data are not converted to the new format until you attempt to paste them into the data editor. If you have a block of nucleotide sequence data stored in the Clipboard, these data are not translated into amino acids when you switch to protein data.*

Selecting and viewing elements in the editor

Selecting a cell

Selecting individual cells

To select an individual cell, so that you may enter data into it, just click on the cell with the arrow tool. The text in the cell will be selected. Just as with most Macintosh text editing, if you type something with the whole cell selected, the cell's contents will be replaced by what you type. If you click on the cell again, you will put the blinking vertical bar (the insertion point) into the cell where you click. The usual Macintosh rules apply to other aspects of editing within a cell, such as placing the insertion point, selecting pieces of text within the cell, and entering new text.

Moving from cell to cell

You can move to other cells by clicking on them using the pointer, or to adjacent cells using the arrow keys. Alternatives to the arrow keys are the Return and Tab keys. The Return key moves to the next cell lower in the column, the Tab key moves to the next cell right in the row. Shift-Return and Shift-Tab move to the next cell above and left, respectively.

To have MacClade automatically move to the next cell after you have typed in a state, select one of the two autotab buttons at the bottom left of the window.

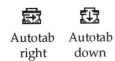

Autotab   Autotab
right   down

If autotab is enabled, then just after you type something into a cell, the next cell will be selected automatically. If you have the button with the right-pointing arrow selected, the cell to the right will be selected; if you have the other one selected, the cell below. When the end of a row or column is reached, MacClade will beep and return to the start of the next row or column. This feature facilitates rapid entry of data. However, while in this mode you can type only one symbol per cell.

Selecting rows, columns, and blocks

Whole rows and columns can be selected by clicking on the number of the row or column. You can also select whole columns or rows using the Macintosh standard Shift-click technique to extend a selection: click on the name or first cell in the row or column, hold down the Shift key, and click on the last cell in the row or column. For example, if you wanted to select a whole character, you can click on the name of the character, hold down the Shift key, and then click on the data cell of the last taxon. Or, you can click on the first taxon's data cell for the character, hold down the Shift key, and click on the data cell of the last taxon.

Selecting a whole column

You can select several rows or columns using the standard Shift-click to extend the selection. You *cannot* make a discontinuous selection using ⌘-click as you can, for example, in the character status window.

You can select a block of the matrix with Shift-click. For example, to select characters 2 through 5 of taxa 2 to 6, click once on the cell for taxon 2, character 2. Let go of the mouse button, and, holding down the Shift key, click once on the cell of taxon 6, character 5. The result should be a selected block, as shown to the left.

A block of cells selected

If a cell or block of cells is selected in the editor, you can also extend the selection using Shift-Arrow key (Shift →, Shift ↓, Shift ←, or Shift ↑). This will extend the selection one row or column over in the direction of the arrow. For example, typing Shift → when the block pictured to the left is selected will extend the selection to include taxa 2 through 6 of character 6. Shift-Option-Arrow key will extend the selection to the edge of the matrix.

You can select the entire matrix quickly by choosing **Select All** from the **Edit** menu.

Once a block of cells has been selected, its contents can be manipulated in various ways, as described in later sections.

Viewing different portions of the matrix

If the matrix is too large to be completely visible in the editor, you can scroll through the matrix using the scroll bars on the right and bottom of the editor.

If **Track Cell** in the **Edit** menu is checked, then MacClade will keep the currently selected cell in view. If a cell is selected, but not visible, and you enter text into it, or you use the arrow keys or autotab to move to a cell that is out of view, MacClade will automatically scroll the matrix until the cell is visible. If **Track Cell** is not checked, then MacClade will not automatically scroll the matrix in this manner.

N OTE: *If you hit the Escape key (esc), you will be presented with a dialog box into which you can enter a character number; MacClade will scroll the data editor so that that character is visible. If you hold down the Option key as you hit the Escape key, then MacClade will take you to a taxon rather than to a character.*

Managing rows, columns, and blocks

This section describes the commands available that add, remove, or merge whole taxa and characters, and how to move blocks of cells.

Adding taxa or characters

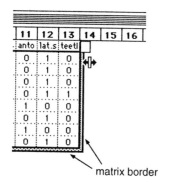

Adding columns by pulling
on the matrix border

When you create a new MacClade data file, there is only one taxon and one character in the matrix. You will immediately need to add more taxa and, perhaps, more characters. You can do this by either grabbing and extending the matrix using the cursor, or by using **Add** in the **Utilities** menu.

Add rows onto the edges of the matrix by grabbing along the lower matrix border and pulling downward. Add columns by grabbing along the right matrix border and pulling to the right.

For example, if you grabbed the right edge of the matrix, and pulled two columns to the right, and let the mouse button go, two characters would be added to the end of the matrix.

To add multiple taxa or characters quickly, use the **Add** dialog box from the **Utilities** menu. If you use the **Add** dialog box, the taxa or characters will be added to the edges of the matrix.

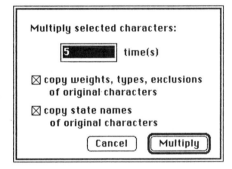

Inserting a column

Multiply selected characters:

5 time(s)

☒ copy weights, types, exclusions
of original characters
☒ copy state names
of original characters

Cancel | Multiply

To insert one or more new columns between two existing columns, move the cursor to the line between the numbers at the top of those columns. The cursor will become a bar with an arrow on it. Then click, and drag to the right the required number of columns. When you release the mouse button, a space will open up and the new columns will be inserted. Follow a similar procedure for inserting rows.

MacClade does not automatically open up new columns or rows to receive columns or rows that are being pasted from the Clipboard. See the section on Copy/Paste, p. 184, for details.

Making duplicates of taxa or characters

If you wish to make a copy of one or more taxa or characters, you can select the rows or columns to be duplicated and use the **Duplicate** command in the **Utilities** menu. If you have selected characters, then the types, weights, excluded/included status, and state names will be duplicated as well. Footnotes and pictures attached to cells will not be duplicated.

If you wish to make more than one copy or to have more control over the duplication, use the **Multiply** dialog box from the **Utilities** menu. Select the rows or columns to be replicated. Choose **Multiply** from the **Utilities** menu. In the dialog box that appears enter the number of times you want the selected rows or columns to be replicated, and press Multiply.

For example, if two rows are selected:

4	lungfish	0	0	0	0	1
5	salamanders	0	1	1	0	1
6	crocodiles	1	1	2	0	1
7	lizards	1	1	2	0	1

and you ask to **Multiply** them two times, the result would be:

4	lungfish	0	0	0	0	1
5	salamanders	0	1	1	0	1
6	crocodiles	1	1	2	0	1
7	salamanders.2	0	1	1	0	1
8	salamanders.3	0	1	1	0	1
9	crocodiles.2	1	1	2	0	1
10	crocodiles.3	1	1	2	0	1
11	lizards	1	1	2	0	1

If you are multiplying characters, you can choose in the **Multiply** dialog box whether or not you want the weights, types, exclusion/inclusion, and state names of the original characters to be copied over to the new characters.

Taxa or characters can also be duplicated manually using **Copy** and **Paste** (p. 184), although some information (weights, types, exclusion/inclusion, and state names of the original characters) may be lost in this process.

Moving rows, columns, and blocks

To move rows or columns, you first need to select the row(s) or column(s) to be moved. When you move the mouse over the numbers of the selected rows or columns, the cursor should change to a hand. You can then drag the rows or columns to the place you want them to be. Rows and columns can also be moved manually using **Cut** and **Paste**, but some information (such as state names) will be lost in the process.

You can move blocks of data cells by first enabling **Block Moves** (in the **Edit** menu). If you select a block of cells and hit an arrow key, the block of cells will be moved over one row or column, leaving missing data in its wake (or gaps, if the data format is DNA, RNA, or protein). If you select a block of cells and move the pointer over it, the pointer will become a hand. You can then click and move the block of cells to their new location. Missing data will be left where the block used to be (or gaps left, if the data format is DNA, RNA, or protein). The movement is constrained so that you can move only within taxa, not between taxa. The movement is also constrained so that you cannot push the block off the edges of the matrix. This constraint is lifted if you hold down the Option key while moving the block. Block moving is illustrated in Chapter 19.

You can also move blocks of data using **Cut** and **Paste** (p. 185).

Deleting taxa or characters

MacClade has several means to remove taxa or characters from the data matrix. To remove taxa or characters by hand in the data matrix, select the *whole* row or column (see "Selecting rows, columns, and blocks" for information on how to select a whole row or column), and choose **Cut** from the **Edit** menu (or press the Delete or Backspace key). To delete rows or columns from the ends of the matrix, grab the border of the matrix (see "Adding taxa and characters"), and push up or to the left to "squeeze" out the unwanted rows or columns. Taxa can also be deleted using the **Filter Taxa** command, which will remove redundant taxa, or the **Merge** command, which will fuse several taxa into one. Characters can be deleted using the **Filter Characters** command, which can remove invariant or excluded characters.

Before deleting taxa or characters from the data matrix, remember that MacClade allows exclusion of taxa from specific trees in the tree window, and allows temporary exclusion of characters in tree calculations. These exclusions are reversible, and may at times be more desirable than deleting forever the taxon or character from the data matrix.

If whole rows or columns are not selected when you choose **Clear** or **Cut** or hit the Delete or Backspace key, then the taxa or characters will not be removed, but any data cells will be emptied (that is, filled with missing data). Note that you cannot clear blocks of taxon or character names in this manner.

Taxa that are deleted in the editor are automatically deleted from the tree in the tree window, from any stored trees in the data file, and from trees in any currently open tree file. States fixed at branches of a character traced in the tree window are lost if any taxa are deleted in the data editor.

WARNING: *For these reasons it is best not to use cut and paste to move a taxon from one part of the matrix to another. If you were to select a taxon Bigidae, choose **Cut**, then go to another part of the matrix, insert a row, then select it and choose **Paste**, you would find that the taxon's states would be pasted into the row. If you then give this new taxon the name Bigidae, expecting that you have simply moved it, you will be mistaken. When you move to the tree window you will find that the Bigidae has been deleted from your trees. The reason is that each terminal taxon in MacClade's trees is associated with a particular row (or column) of the matrix; it is not associated with the taxon's name. A row's (or column's) integrity and association with trees is maintained if it is moved using the hand (see p. 168), or if its taxon is renamed, or if other taxa are inserted into the matrix, but the row (or column) vanishes when it is cut. The new row (or column), even though it has the same taxon name, is treated as a different taxon.*

Merging taxa

If you select two or more taxa (the entire rows or columns must be selected), and choose **Merge** from the **Utilities** menu, MacClade will merge the taxa into one. In the process, any footnotes or pictures attached to the cells of the merged taxa will be removed. This command merges the taxon names together, and merges the character state data using the following procedures:

1. Merge the first two taxa selected, then merge this merged taxon with the next taxon selected, and so forth.

2. For each pair of taxa to be merged, MacClade does the following for each character:

a. If both taxa have missing data, then the merged taxon has missing data.
b. If one taxon has missing data, and the other has a gap, then the merged taxon has a gap.
c. If both taxa have gaps, then the merged taxon has a gap.
d. If one has missing data or a gap, but the other has neither missing data nor a gap, then the merged taxon is set to the states found in the taxon without missing data or a gap.
e. If both taxa are monomorphic or are polymorphic, then the merged taxon is set to the union of the states of the two taxa. If this set has more than one element, the taxon is polymorphic.
f. If both taxa have partial uncertainties, then the merged taxon is uncertain for the intersection of the two sets, if it exists, or for the union, if it does not (MacClade will give a warning if this happens). (*Note*: This procedure may yield different results depending on the order in which taxa are merged.)
g. If one taxa has partial uncertainty, but the other does not, then the merged taxon will take the state of the taxon with certain states. If the intersection of the two state sets does not exist, MacClade will give a warning.

These rules are exemplified by the following table:

States of taxon 1	States of taxon 2	Merged states
?	?	?
?	-	-
-	-	-
?	0	0
-	0	0
0	0	0
0	1	0&1
0&1	0&2	0&1&2
0/1	0/1/2	0/1
0/1	2/3	0/1/2/3, warning given
0/1	0	0
0/1	2	2, warning given

Filtering invariant or excluded characters

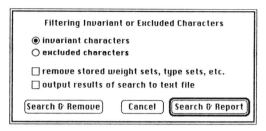

Choosing **Filter Characters** from the **Utilities** menu will present you with a dialog box allowing you to remove or count various sorts of characters.

Using this dialog, you can ask MacClade to search for characters that are invariant or excluded. By pressing on the Search & Report button in the dialog box, MacClade will simply search for such characters, and report on the result of the search. If you press Search & Remove, it will also remove all of the invariant or excluded characters.

A character is considered invariant by MacClade if it has only one state. Missing data and gaps are not counted as states in this definition, and thus the character will be considered invariant if some taxa have state 0, others have missing data, and the remaining have gaps.

Removing invariant and excluded characters will be somewhat slower if there are type sets, weight sets, inclusion sets, or character sets stored. The reason for this is that for every deletion of a character, MacClade has to reprocess these sets so that they continue to apply to the characters intended. Because of the extra time taken by this processing, MacClade gives you the option to throw away type sets, weight sets, and so on, before undertaking removal of characters. This option is valuable only for particularly large data matrices. We suggest that you make a back-up copy of your file, try removing characters without discarding type sets, weight sets, etc., and if this takes too long, stop the process and try again on your back-up, this time discarding the sets.

Filter Characters may be used to strip a data set of characters that are uninformative according to the current assumptions about character transformation. In the tree window, select **Exclude Uninformative** from the **Assume** menu. Then, in the data editor, filter by removing the excluded characters. Exclude Uninformative is described in Chapter 11.

For molecular sequence data, deleting characters (such as, for instance, the invariable ones) can have the undesirable effect of losing the information of the original positions of characters in the sequence. MacClade remembers whether nucleotides were originally in first, second, or third positions of codons, but it does not remember original absolute position. To retain this information, you may want to number the character names automatically before deletion by selecting the character name cells of the spreadsheet and using the **Fill** command in the **Utilities** menu (p. 173).

If "output results of search to text file" is checked, then MacClade will write a text file giving a detailed report of the invariant or excluded characters.

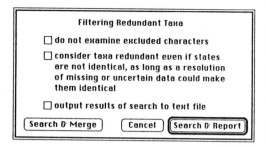

Filtering Redundant Taxa

☐ do not examine excluded characters

☐ consider taxa redundant even if states
   are not identical, as long as a resolution
   of missing or uncertain data could make
   them identical

☐ output results of search to text file

[Search & Merge]   [Cancel]   [[Search & Report]]

Filtering redundant taxa

Using the **Filter Taxa** dialog box from the **Utilities** menu, you can ask MacClade to search for taxa that are redundant. By pressing on the Search & Report button in the dialog box, MacClade will simply search for such taxa, and report on the result of the search. If you press Search and Merge, it will merge together each set of redundant taxa.

If you check the "do not examine excluded characters" box, MacClade will examine only included characters to see if the taxa are redundant; otherwise, it will examine all characters.

If you do not choose "consider taxa redundant even if states are not identical...", then MacClade will consider two taxa redundant only if their states are absolutely identical; otherwise, MacClade uses a slightly broader definition of "redundant". This broader definition is as follows. Two taxa are redundant, if, for each examined character:

1. The states of two taxa are identical, or

2. One has missing data (gaps do not count as missing data), the other does not, or

3. One and only one taxon is partially uncertain, and the states of the certain one form a subset of the uncertain one, or

4. They are both partially uncertain, and the two taxa share at least one state.

Note that if this broader definition of redundant is used, then the result of searching and merging may depend upon the order of the taxa in the matrix. Also, MacClade's Search & Report will then report not the number of redundant taxa, but the number of pairs of redundant taxa.

If "output results of search to text file" is checked, then MacClade will write a text file giving a detailed report of the redundant characters.

Names and symbols

Taxon names

To enter taxon names, click on the cell for the name of the taxon (on the left, beside the taxon numbers, for a normal matrix; see figure at the start of this chapter), and type in the name. Taxon names can be up to 31 characters long; MacClade will truncate if you type in more. Any standard character is allowed in taxon names; thus valid taxon names are "Swainson's Thrush" and "Bembidion sp. 2 (western)". Taxon names cannot consist entirely of numerical digits (e.g., "23" is not allowed, but "23." is).

If you want to increase the width of the column containing the taxon names, grab the right edge of the column and move it.

You can rapidly enter similar taxon names by selecting the block of taxon names and using the **Fill** command from the **Utilities** menu. This action is useful only if the taxon names form a series such as Coleoptera # 1, Coleoptera # 2, etc. (The **Fill** command can also be used to fill character names as described in the next section.)

Taxon names can be italicized by selecting one or more taxon names and choosing **Italic** from the **Display** menu; if the names are already italic, they will revert to plain type. Note that the whole name will become italic, not just a part of it.

Character names

To enter the names of characters, click on the box for the name of the character (on the top, just below the character numbers in a normal matrix; see figure on p. 159), and type in the name. (If you need to make the columns wider to accommodate the names, you can do so using the column width control in the upper left of the matrix — see "Changing the width of columns", p. 191.) Character names can also be edited in the **State Names** dialog box.

Character names can be up to 31 characters in length. Character names cannot consist entirely of numerical digits (e.g., "23" is not allowed, but "23." is).

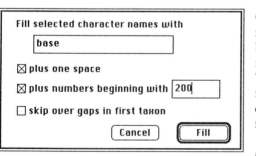

Character names can also be entered by selecting a number of character name cells and choosing **Fill** from the **Utilities** menu. The **Fill** dialog box will allow you to name many characters at once. For instance, you might name 100 characters in sequence "base 200" through "base 299". If "skip over gaps in first taxon" is chosen, then MacClade will use the first taxon as a reference taxon, and not increment the numbers for those characters that have gaps in the first taxon. For example, if the first few bases of the first taxon had the follow bases:

     A C -- C T

and "skip over gaps in first taxon" were chosen, then MacClade could name the characters:

     base 200, base 201, base 201a, base 201b, base 202, base 203.

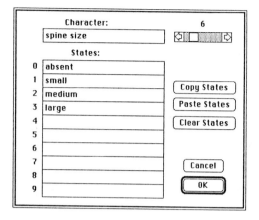

State names

States are represented in MacClade as either single-character symbols (e.g., "0", "1", etc.), or as full names (e.g., "blue", "red"). You can change the single-character symbols as described in the next section.

The names of character states can be added and edited only in the **State Names** dialog box, available in the **Display** menu while you are in the data editor. State names can be up to 31 characters in length. In this dialog box, state names can be copied and pasted from one character to another, by clicking on the Copy States button when the one character is displayed, scrolling to the other character, and pressing the Paste States button. If you press the Clear States button, the state names of the current character will be emptied.

The name of the character itself can also be edited in the **State Names** dialog box.

The scroll bar in the upper-right of the dialog box allows you to move from one character to another.

NOTE: *The right arrow (→) key will take you to the next character; the left arrow (←) key will take you to the previous character.*

For protein data sets, the names of amino acids are predefined within MacClade. If you have **Display State Names** turned on, MacClade will display the state names in the editor, and you can enter these state names instead of the IUPAC code, if you wish.

WARNING: *Do not include within a state name the AND separator (by default "&") or the OR separator (by default "/"), as this will make it difficult for MacClade to interpret entries. If you have two states with the same name, MacClade will interpret a named entry in the matrix as referring to the smaller-valued state.*

NOTE: *If you hold down the Option key and double-click on a character name in the editor, the **State Names** dialog box will appear, allowing you to edit the name or state names of that character.*

If you hold down the Command key (⌘) and click on a character name in the editor, a list of the states of that character will appear with any names assigned to them.

You can also ask MacClade to continually show you the names assigned to a selected character's states using the Footstates option (p. 190).

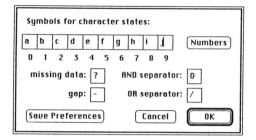

Symbols for states, missing data, gaps, etc.

To use symbols other than "0","1","2"... for states, "?" for missing data, "-" for gap, "&" for the AND separator, "/" for the OR separator, choose **Symbols** from **Display** menu and indicate the symbol to be used for each of these. Symbols defined in this box apply to all characters. The appearance of the **Symbols** dialog box will vary, depending upon the data format. Its appearance for standard format data is shown on the left.

If you press the Numbers button, MacClade will fill the Symbols list with 0 through 9. Changing symbols not only affects how the matrix is displayed, but also how the matrix is saved to the file. Changing symbols will not change the underlying data, however (as discussed in the next section on state numbers, symbols, and names).

You cannot use the same symbol in more than one place (e.g., you cannot use "-" for a state symbol and the gap symbol at the same time). A blank is a valid missing data symbol. Lowercase (e.g., "a") and uppercase ("A") letter symbols are interpreted by MacClade as the same state unless you have defined the two as separate symbols in the **Symbols** dialog.

Symbols for character states in molecular sequence data are provided automatically when DNA, RNA, or protein formats are chosen in the **Format** menu. DNA and RNA data formats come with predefined symbols: ACGT for DNA, ACGU for RNA. Protein data format predefines symbols to correspond to the standard IUPAC symbols for amino acids. These are:

Symbol	Amino Acid	Symbol	Amino Acid
A	alanine	N	asparagine
C	cysteine	P	proline
D	aspartic acid	Q	glutamine
E	glutamic acid	R	arginine
F	phenylalanine	S	serine
G	glycine	T	threonine
H	histidine	V	valine
I	isoleucine	W	tryptophan
K	lysine	Y	tyrosine
L	leucine	*	chain termination
M	methionine		

State numbers vs. symbols vs. names

MacClade refers to states either by their *symbols* or by their *names*. Actually, these are the two modes by which MacClade refers to them in interacting with you. Internally in its own memory, MacClade refers to states simply by *numbers* (state 0, state 1, state 2, and so on) in all of its calculations, and converts state numbers to symbols or names only when it has to communicate with you. The table on p. 179 indicates in one example the correspondence between state numbers, symbols, and names.

Remember that the same state numbers and symbols are used for all characters in the data matrix, but state names are defined separately character by character.

For unordered characters, MacClade's internal numbering is unimportant, but for ordered characters, irreversible characters, Dollo characters, and characters of user-defined types, the internal numbering of states can be important. For instance, this internal numbering of states determines the ordering of ordered characters, and what is a gain versus loss for purposes of irreversible and Dollo characters, and so on. You can discover MacClade's internal ordering of states simply by looking at the **Symbols** dialog box, or the **State Names** dialog box, or the **Recode** dialog box. These dialog boxes list states in the same order as is used internally by MacClade.

Technical details about numbers, symbols, and names For the most part, you can think of MacClade using the symbols but layering over top of the symbols, at your request, your own state names like "red" and "blue". MacClade's internal state numbering system is hidden from the user and usually need not concern you. However, it may be useful to know some basics about the relationship between numbers, symbols, and names so that you can better understand ordered characters and the effects of recoding and other actions that may affect either the data, its presentation to you, or both. This section is provided for those who want such detailed information.

Suppose you started with the following matrix of three taxa and one character, with state names "red" and "blue". Underlying these state names are (suppose) the symbols "a" and "b" which would appear if **Display State Names** were turned off. Underlying everything are the state numbers, which the user would normally not see except if the symbols used matched the state numbers ("0", "1", "2", ...). These state numbers determine the ordering of character states used in ordered characters, irreversible characters, and other circumstances (see p. 203).

As you see it		Underlying state symbols	Underlying state numbers
taxon 1	red	*a*	*0*
taxon 2	blue	*b*	*1*
taxon 3	red/blue	*a/b*	*0/1*

Then, various actions would alter the matrix as follows:

1. Entering data, or using the **Search & Replace** dialog box (p. 188), changes the state numbers MacClade stores for the cell, and therefore the symbols or names MacClade displays to you. If the original matrix above were changed by searching and replacing state "a" by a third state, "c" (whose state name happens to be "green"), then the result would be:

As you see it		Underlying state symbols	Underlying state numbers
taxon 1	green	*c*	*2*
taxon 2	blue	*b*	*1*
taxon 3	blue/gree	*b/c*	*1/2*

2. The **Recode** dialog box (p. 187) changes the state numbers, and therefore the symbols MacClade displays to you in the cell. However, since the correspondence between state numbers and state names is adjusted during recoding, it does not change the state name displayed in the cell, unless states are fused by recoding. If the original matrix above were recoded so as to change red (0=a) to 1 and blue (1=b) to 0 using the **Recode** dialog box, then the matrix would superficially appear unchanged, but the underlying data would be altered:

As you see it		Underlying state symbols	Underlying state numbers
taxon 1	red	*b*	*1*
taxon 2	blue	*a*	*0*
taxon 3	red/blue	*a/b*	*0/1*

3. Changing the **Symbols** list (p. 175) does not change the state numbers MacClade stores for a cell, nor does it change the state names connected to those state numbers, but it does change the symbols that may appear in the cell. If the original matrix above had its symbols changed so as to invert them, making "b" the symbol for state 0 and "a" the symbol for state 1, then we would have:

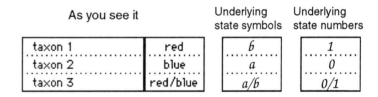

As you see it		Underlying state symbols	Underlying state numbers
taxon 1	red	*b*	*0*
taxon 2	blue	*a*	*1*
taxon 3	red/blue	*a/b*	*0/1*

4. Changing **State Names** (p. 174) does not change the state numbers MacClade stores for a cell, nor does it change the state symbols connected to those state numbers, but it does change the state names that may appear in the cell. If the original character above had its

state names changed from English to Spanish, only the appearance, not the underlying data, would change:

As you see it		Underlying state symbols	Underlying state numbers
taxon 1	rojo	*a*	*0*
taxon 2	azul	*b*	*1*
taxon 3	rojo/azul	*a/b*	*0/1*

Entering data

Entering "0" for taxon 1, character 1

Editing a cell

To enter data into a cell in the matrix, select the cell by clicking on it and type in the symbol or name of a state. Editing the contents of a cell follows standard Macintosh text editing rules.

(For ways to select and move between cells while entering data, see "Selecting individual cells" and "Moving from cell to cell", above.)

Exactly what you type into the cell to indicate a character state depends upon the data file format (standard, extended standard, DNA, RNA, protein) and various other options you can choose. If you type into a cell and MacClade responds with "Bad entry in cell of data editor", you have made an illegal entry; see the section below (p. 183) for explanation.

You can enter a state into a data cell in one of three ways:

1. If you have defined a name for states in the **State Names** dialog box (e.g., "red" or "blue"), and "interpret state names" is checked in the **Entry Interpretation** dialog box from the **Edit** menu, then you can type in the full name of the state. If you have not already named the states using the **State Names** dialog, MacClade won't know what names like "red" or "blue" mean.

2. If you have defined symbols in the **Symbols** dialog box (e.g., "a b c d"), then you can use one of those symbols. If there are predefined symbols (for DNA, RNA, or protein data), then you can use one of those predefined symbols (e.g., "A").

3. Finally, you can use one of the default symbols ("0 1 2 3 4 5 6 7 8 9" for standard data, "0 1 2 3 4 5 6 7 8 9 A B C D E F G H J K L M N P Q R" for extended standard data).

N O T E: *To help you remember which symbols correspond to which named states, you can turn on* **Footstates** *in the* **Display** *menu —*

MacClade will then list the state symbols and names for the currently selected character in the footnote box at the bottom of the editor. See the section "Footstates", below, for an illustration.

If you are using the matching first taxon option (see "Matching First Taxon", below), then if you enter the matching character (e.g., ".") into a cell of the second or later taxon, MacClade will copy into that cell the same states found in the first taxon.

MacClade's interpretation of an entry The following table shows an example in which the user has defined symbols "a" through "z" to be the symbols used for a data matrix (third column). See p. 175 for an explanation of state numbers. The first three columns apply to all characters in the data matrix. The numbers corresponding to the states are given in the first column, the default symbols in the second column, and symbols specified by the user in the third column. The fourth column, which lists state names that have been given to character 1, applies only to character 1. For example, if you wanted to enter state number 1 into a data cell for that character, then you could enter either "blue" or "b" or "1".

Example of correspondence between state numbers, symbols and state names

State number	Default symbol	User-defined symbols	State name of character 1
0	0	a	aquamarine
1	1	b	blue
2	2	c	chartreuse
3	3	d	dark green
4	4	e	emerald
5	5	f	forest green
6	6	g	green
7	7	h	hot pink
8	8	i	indigo
9	9	j	jet black
10	A	k	khaki
11	B	l	lilac
12	C	m	magenta
13	D	n	nut brown
14	E	o	orange
15	F	p	purple
16	G	q	quail blue
17	H	r	red
18	J	s	sienna
19	K	t	tuscan red
20	L	u	umber
21	M	v	vermilion
22	N	w	white
23	P	x	xanthum
24	Q	y	yellow
25	R	z	zinc gray

When you enter data for a cell, and if "interpret state names" is checked in the **Entry Interpretation** dialog box from the **Edit** menu, MacClade first checks to see if you have defined any state names for the character. If so, it checks for state names in the text you have typed. If these do not account for all the text you have typed, MacClade then checks to see if the symbols you have entered are present in your user-defined symbols list (or predefined symbols list for molecular data). If it still has not found a full match, it then looks to see if there is a match between the entered symbols and the default symbols list.

For example, if you entered "9" into a cell of the character shown in the above table, MacClade would first check the state names in the fourth column, and discover that "9" was not a state name. It would then check the user-defined symbols list (third column), and find that it was not in the user-defined symbols list. Finally, it would check the default symbols list, and find that "9" corresponded to state number 9. Having found the state number is 9, MacClade would reassign to that taxon state number 9, which would be represented on the screen by symbol "j" or, if the character was character number 1 and **Display State Names** was turned on, by the state name "jet black".

For protein data, MacClade predefines as state names three-letter amino acid names (e.g., Ala, Leu). You can enter these state names instead of the IUPAC code if you wish.

For DNA or RNA data, MacClade first checks the predefined symbols list, then the default symbols list, as given in the following table.

State number	Default symbol	Predefined symbols
0	0	A
1	1	C
2	2	G
3	3	T

NOTE: *This feature can facilitate quick entry of some sorts of data. For example, if you have DNA sequence data, rather than typing in ACGT, the keys for which are scattered around the keyboard, you could type in 0123 on the numeric keypad. If you are entering a large amount of data, you may wish to place ACGT labels on top of the 0123 keys. Autotabbing can also speed entry.*

Terminal taxa of uncertain state or with polymorphism

MacClade allows a terminal taxon to be given more than one state in a character. There are two interpretations of a taxon coded with multiple states. The taxon's state might be uncertain, being one of the states listed, but exactly which one is not known. Second, the taxon may have been observed to have more than one state. This may occur if the terminal taxon is a species and shows a genetic polymorphism; it may occur if the terminal taxon is a collection of species that show various states and it is not known which is ancestral for the taxon. For either a species or higher taxon, we will speak of such a taxon with multiple observed states as being "polymorphic." The distinction between uncertainty and polymorphism for unordered and ordered characters will not affect ancestral state reconstructions and comparisons between trees. However, uncertainties and polymorphisms may behave quite differently with irreversible, stratigraphic, Dollo, and user-defined type characters. MacClade does not treat taxa coded as having polymorphisms as if they have missing data, unlike the unnamed computer programs described by Nixon and Davis (1991). This distinction can be seen clearly in the different behavior of taxa coded with states 0&2 versus 1&2&3.

N O T E : *MacClade allows a single data matrix to have some entries coded as polymorphisms, and other entries coded as uncertainties. Other programs, such as PAUP 3.0, require uniformity throughout a data matrix.*

Before you fill your data matrix with polymorphisms, you should think carefully about the cautions given in the section "Coding character states and missing data" of Chapter 4.

To indicate in the editor that a taxon is polymorphic, type in the states separated by the AND separator (e.g., "0&1&2", meaning that the taxon has states 0 and 1 and 2). If the state in the taxon is entirely uncertain (i.e., it might be any state), then use the missing data symbol ("?"). If the state in the taxon is partially uncertain (for instance it isn't state 3, but it might be states 0, 1, or 2), then use the OR separator (e.g., "0/1/2", meaning that the taxon has states 0 or 1 or 2). The default AND separator, OR separator, missing data, and gap symbols are "&", "/", "?", and "-", respectively, but these can be changed using **Symbols** dialog box in the **Display** menu.

N O T E : *If you type both AND and OR separators into a cell (e.g., 0/1&2), MacClade will use the right-most separator.*

For DNA and RNA data sets, if you turn on **Use IUPAC symbols** in the **Display** menu, you can enter partial uncertainty using the standard IUPAC ambiguity symbols, if you wish. These symbols and their meanings are:

Symbol	Meaning	Symbol	Meaning	Symbol	Meaning
R	A or G	S	C or G	V	A or C or G
Y	C or T	W	A or T	D	A or G or T
M	A or C	H	A or C or T	X	A or C or G or T = ?
K	G or T	B	C or G or T	N	A or C or G or T = ?

For example, you could enter "R", and MacClade would interpret this to mean "A or G".

If you type in more than one state in a cell, without typing in state separators (e.g., "012"), MacClade will by default assume you mean polymorphism (0&1&2). You can change this default to uncertainty using the **Entry Interpretation** dialog box in the **Edit** menu.

WARNING: *If you enter states using full state names, and you enter more than one state in a cell, you must separate the states by either the AND separator or the OR separator. For example, entering "redblue" is not legal; "red&blue" is.*

If you wish to change a number of polymorphisms to uncertainties, or the reverse, use the **Search & Replace** command from the **Utilities** menu (see p. 188).

Missing data and gaps

As noted above, if a taxon's state is completely uncertain, you should assign it the missing data symbol ("?" as default). In a MacClade analysis, such a taxon is treated almost as if it didn't exist for this character's ancestral state reconstruction.

The **missing data** coding should be used with caution (Platnick et al., 1991; W. Maddison, in press). W. Maddison (in press) points out that coding an organism as having missing data because the character does not apply to the organism (e.g., feather type in a crocodile) can lead to undesirable effects if such inapplicable codings are not isolated to a single group on the tree. When the character is inapplicable to a taxon, in general it would be better to code it as having an extra state "not present". The missing data coding would be better restricted to those circumstances in which the organism is presumed to have one of the character states, but which one it has is simply not known because of incomplete information. Nixon and Davis (1991) note that another use of the missing data coding, for polymorphisms, is also inappropriate. Nixon and Davis suggest that some computer programs that accept polymorphic codings for terminal taxa automatically treat them as if they had missing data; this is not the case with MacClade. These issues are discussed also in Chapter 4.

The **gap** symbol is designed for molecular data, to indicate that there is a deletion and so the particular site does not exist in some organism; it can also be used equivalently for non-molecular data. Missing data and gaps are currently treated identically in MacClade's calculations with phylogenetic trees. The distinction is maintained by MacClade in the data matrices because it is useful for other programs or future versions of MacClade. Treating gaps like missing data can yield problems noted by Platnick et al. (1991) and W. Maddison (in press), and future versions of

MacClade will allow better ways to deal with gaps. One alternative used in PAUP 3.0, treating gaps like an extra character state, can solve these problems but has the other problem of counting adjacent gaps as independent and thus inflating the cost of an insertion or deletion (Swofford, 1991).

Undoing changes made in the editor

If you make a mistake while typing in the entry for a cell, and you have not yet clicked away from the cell or selected a menu item, you can choose **Undo** from the **Edit** menu, and MacClade will revert the contents of the cell to what it was when you first selected the cell.

WARNING: *This is, unfortunately, the only change in the editor that you can undo. You can't undo other changes made in the data editor; so, be careful what you do, and save frequently.*

"Bad entry in cell of data editor"

The bad-cell-entry message is given by the editor when (1) you have typed into a cell something other than a valid character state symbol or name, state separator, or missing data or gap symbol; or (2) you have typed into a cell a valid state name, but "interpret state names" is not checked in the **Entry Interpretation** dialog box in the **Edit** menu; or (3) you have typed into a cell a valid symbol or name to a character state that is not currently allowed because of the transformation type assigned to a character. The first problem might arise if you typed in nonsense characters, such as " [[ )] * + # } " , or if you have typed in a name for a character state such as "small" without having first defined state names using **State Names** in **Display**. Remember you have to define a state name like "small" before using it. The third problem might arise if you type in a "9" to a character currently assigned the type Dollo (in which 9 is not an allowable state), or a "2" to a character assigned a character state tree type defined only for states 0, 1, and 3. MacClade is conscious of the character transformation types assigned to the characters even though you are in the data editor. Generally, the default type assigned is unordered, which will allow any character states allowed by the data format. However, if any of your characters are of user-defined or Dollo types, you should be careful in the editor; these types may not allow a character to have any state. To check what character transformation types are assigned to the characters, choose **Character Status** in **Display**. For more information about character transformation types, see Chapter 5.

If you do encounter the bad-cell-entry message, you will be presented with a choice: either discard the bad cell entry, and carry on as if you never typed the bad entry, or maintain the improper entry, but go back and select the cell with the improper entry, so that you may fix it.

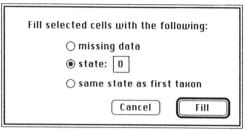

Fill selected cells with the following:

○ missing data

◉ state: ⬚0⬚

○ same state as first taxon

[Cancel] [**Fill**]

Filling a block with data

To fill a region of the matrix automatically, select the region, and use the **Fill** dialog box from the **Utilities** menu. If the region selected includes cells within the matrix, the dialog box will give options as to what state to place in each cell.

You can ask MacClade either to fill the cells with missing data, with a single state, or with the same state as the first taxon. Use state symbols to specify the state, not state names. If you ask MacClade to fill the cells with more than one state (say "012"), then it will fill them only with the first state listed ("0"). You can fill a block of cells with gaps by entering the gap symbol in the box beside "state".

NOTE: *A quick-fill can be done by selecting the block of cells, setting the Caps Lock key, and typing a state symbol or the missing data, gap, or matching character symbol.*

You can also fill a block of data cells with missing data by selecting them and choosing **Clear** from the **Edit** menu.

To fill a block of selected cells with random data, use **Random Fill** in the **Utilities** menu; see Chapter 18 for further details.

1	2	3	4	5	6
amn·	appe	body	ther	int.n	atri·
0	0	0	0	0	0
1	1	2	0	1	1
0	0	0	0	1	1
0	1	1	0	1	1
1	1	2	0	1	1
1	1	2	0	1	1
1	2	3	1	1	1
1	1&2	4	1	1	1

A selected block of cells,
ready to be cut

Copy/Paste

To copy or cut a portion of the matrix, and put it into the Clipboard, select the block (use Shift-click to extend a selection), and choose **Copy** or **Cut** from the **Edit** menu. Remember that **Copy** just places a copy of the selected block in the Clipboard; **Cut** both places a copy into the Clipboard and gets rid of the original selection. Whether **Cut** deletes whole taxa and characters or merely clears the entries in the block's cells depends on whether whole taxa or characters were selected (see p. 165).

To paste, select the region into which you wish to paste, and choose **Paste**. If MacClade thinks that you are trying to paste into a region different in size (different numbers of taxa and characters) from the Clipboard, it beeps.

1	2	3	4	5	6
amn·	appe	body	ther	int.n	atri·
0	0	0	0	0	0
1	?	?	?	?	1
0	?	?	?	?	1
0	?	?	?	?	1
1	?	?	?	?	1
1	?	?	?	?	1
1	2	3	1	1	1
1	1&2	4	1	1	1

Cells after cutting

1	2	3	4	5	6
amn·	appe	body	ther	int.n	atri:
0	0	1	2	0	1
1	?	0	0	0	1
0	?	1	1	0	1
0	?	1	2	0	1
1	?	1	2	0	1
1	?	?	?	?	1
1	2	3	1	1	1
1	1&2	4	1	1	1

Pasting using ⌘-Option-click

To see the size of the block of cells in the Clipboard, hold down the Command (⌘) and Option keys together. A shimmering box will appear on the screen. (If no box appears, then no cells are stored in the Clipboard.) As you move the arrow tool, the shimmering box moves with it. The arrow tool is connected to the top left corner of the box, as long as there is enough room below and to the right for the box to extend in the matrix. If the box is very large, you may see only one shimmering edge (for instance, the left edge of the box). If while the box is shimmering on the screen you click the mouse button, the contents of the block in the Clipboard are dropped (pasted) onto the area of the matrix outlined by the shimmering box.

Moving blocks of data can be accomplished either with **Cut** and **Paste**, or with **Block Moves** (p. 168).

WARNING: *Note that Copy or Cut will place only the character state data themselves into the Clipboard; the character, state, taxon names, character weights, types, footnotes, and pictures in any column or row cut or copied will not be placed in the Clipboard. If you wish to rearrange rows or columns, it would be best to use the technique for moving columns and rows (described on p. 168) rather than Copy and Paste, as moving does retain all character information.*

If you copy data into the Clipboard, then switch data formats, the Clipboard is converted to the new data format when you ask MacClade to paste the data into the matrix. However, if nucleotide sequence data are in the Clipboard, and then you switch to protein data, the matrix itself will be *not* be translated if you ask to paste the data. If the data in the Clipboard contain more states than allowed under the current data format (e.g., the Clipboard data are of extended standard format, and the current file is of standard format) then MacClade will remove all unallowable states, and replace them by missing data.

WARNING: *MacClade will paste only into a pre-existing cell, column, row, or other block of cells of the appropriate size. When you paste columns or rows, for instance, you must first have the correct number of columns or rows ready and selected to receive those pasted. MacClade does not automatically open up new columns or rows to receive the paste. You must make sure not only that the space is available, but also that a block of the exact same size is selected before pasting.*

Copying data from one file to another

MacClade 3 does not have fully developed features for using the Clipboard to copy data from one MacClade file to another, or from MacClade to, for instance, a word-processing program. If you select and copy a block of a data matrix, then move to another MacClade data matrix, you can paste the block into the other matrix (as long as you have space in the other matrix, and paste the block as described above), but all assigned names, weights, and types will *not* be copied. Only the underlying data are copied. If you want to make a modified version of a data file, it would be better to duplicate the file (using **Save As** in MacClade or **Duplicate** in the Finder), then cut unneeded portions out of the duplicate version.

Data matrices cannot be copied from MacClade into another program using the Clipboard. Also, you cannot copy a matrix from another program and paste it into the MacClade data editor using the Clipboard. See Chapter 9 to learn how you can move data matrices to and from other programs.

Reversing or inverting molecular sequence data

If you select a block of cells and choose **Reverse** from the **Utilities** menu, the block of cells will be reversed (that is, the entries for the first and last sites in the selected block will be switched, as will the second and second-to-last, and so on). This works only for DNA, RNA, or protein sequences, and is illustrated in Chapter 19.

Recoding character data

MacClade provides two features that allow you to search and replace, *en masse*, entries in the data matrix: **Recode**, and **Search & Replace**. The simplest tool is the **Recode** dialog box (**Utilities** menu), which allows you to recode many states of the selected character or characters at one time (e.g., change all 0 to 1, all 1 to 0, and all 2 to 1 in the selected characters). The **Search & Replace** dialog box (**Utilities** menu) is more flexible, in that it can also change combinations of states (e.g., change all 0&1 to 2/3), but it can't simultaneously recode many states at one time.

(For recoding DNA/RNA sequence data as protein data, see the "Data Formats" section, above. For taking the complement of DNA/RNA sequence data, see Chapter 19.)

Recoding by either Recode or Search & Replace changes the data for each taxon and character affected. They differ from changing the Symbols list in two ways: they actually change the state numbers stored by MacClade, rather than changing just the symbols by which the states are referred (see p. 175 for discussions of numbers, symbols and names), and they apply only to the characters and taxa requested. Search & Replace differs from Recode in that the former changes only the underlying state numbers; the latter also readjusts the state names so that the recoded cells display the same state names.

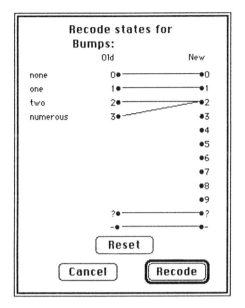

Recode states for Bumps:

	Old	New
none	0● ──────── ●0
one	1● ──────── ●1
two	2● ──────── ●2
numerous	3● ────── ●3
		●4
		●5
		●6
		●7
		●8
		●9
	?● ──────── ●?
	-● ──────── ●-

Reset

Cancel   Recode

The Recode command

If one or more whole characters are selected, you can use the **Recode** dialog box to recode their states.

In the dialog box are two columns indicating state symbols, the left column for the old coding of characters and the right for the new. On the left-most part of the dialog box are the names of the states, which are shown only if the character has names and only one character is being recoded.

Grab the dot corresponding to the old coding of a state and drop it on the dot for the new coding of the state. When you press Recode, all taxa with this old state will be recoded as having the new state (for the selected character(s) only). For example, in this illustration, the user has decided that instead of dividing the character into four states, "none", "one", "two", and "numerous", she or he prefers the coding "none", "one" and "more than one". Therefore states 2 and 3 are fused by making all instances of state 3 recoded to be state 2. After recoding, the user will notice that the state names will be listed as "none", "one", "two-numerous", because MacClade fuses the names of any fused states during recoding. The user can then go to the **State Names** dialog box to change "two-numerous" to "more than one", and the new coding has been achieved.

Whole character(s) must be selected in the data editor before recoding. If more than one character is selected when Recode is called, all of the characters selected will be recoded similarly.

Recode redefines the correspondence between states and their names, so that a taxon will keep the same state name in the character even if its underlying state number and symbol have changed. For this reason Recode can be readily used to try alternative orderings of character states. Suppose you have a character but can't decide whether its states are ordered red, blue then green, or red, green then blue. Using State Names, indicate state 0 is red, 1 is blue, 2 is green. Enter the data as red, green or blue. Try this character as ordered, then compare the results to a recoding in which 1 is recoded for 2 and 2 for 1. This would test the alternative ordering red-green-blue; the taxa would still be listed as having states red, green or blue as you entered.

In the example illustrated above, recoding was used to group together states formerly thought distinct. Though this may be valid if evidence now points to the states actually being the same, recoding is not always the best way to group states together. Suppose, for example, that your species either show no chromosome fusions, or any of several different chromosome fusions. If you wanted to trace chromosome evolution to see which ancestors might have had chromosome fusions (without regard to just what fusions they had), you might recode the character so that the unfused condition is state 0 and all fused states become state 1. This would, however, allow two different fusions to be placed next to one another on the tree with no required character steps, contrary to what is known about the chromosomes. A better approach would be to avoid recoding; leave all the information in the character, but reassign the patterns or colors used by MacClade's character tracing so that all of the fused chromosome character states receive the same pattern or color (as explained under "Changing patterns or shades or colors" in Chapter 13). In this way, the reconstruction uses the character's full information but the shading of patterns in the character tracing summarizes the results as unfused versus fused.

The Search & Replace command

The **Search & Replace** dialog box (**Utilities** menu) allows you more flexibility than **Recode**, but is restricted to making one kind of change at a time.

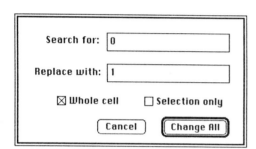

Enter into the "Search for:" box the states you want MacClade to search for, and enter into the "Replace with:" box those states you want them changed to. (You cannot use state names; you must use state symbols in this dialog box.)

If you choose "Selection only", then any changes will be made only to cells that are currently selected; if it is not checked, then changes are made throughout the matrix.

If "Whole cell" is selected, then the only cells that will be changed are ones that match exactly the state set listed in the "Search for:" box. For example, if you had "0" in the "Search for:" box, and "2" in the "Replace with:" box, then MacClade would change cells that contain "0&1" to "2&1" if "Whole cell" is *not* selected, and would not change such cells if it were selected.

Note that changing from a symbol to an equivalent symbol doesn't accomplish anything. For example, if symbols are defined such the first state is -, the second is +, then as - is the symbol for state number 0, changing - to 0 doesn't change the data.

You can also use this dialog box to change all uncertainties to polymorphisms or vice versa by entering the AND and OR separators in the "Search for:" and "Replace with:" boxes. For example, if you entered "/" into the "Search for:" box, and "&" into the "Replace with:" box, then uncertainties would be changed to polymorphisms. If you do change separators in this way, then the "Whole cell" option will be ignored.

Complementing nucleotide sequence data

If you select a block of cells and choose **Complement** from the **Utilities** menu, the bases in the selected block of cells will be replaced by their complements (that is, A will replace T or U, T or U will replace A, C will replace G, and G will replace C). This works only for nucleotide data, and is illustrated in Chapter 19.

Translating nucleotide sequence data

To translate nucleotide sequence data to the corresponding amino acids, choose **Translate to Protein** from the **Format** menu. This is described in detail in Chapter 19.

Editor display options

Displaying state names

To have the data editor display states by their full names, choose **Display State Names** from the **Display** menu. For full state names to appear in the editor, you must have predefined the state names using the **State Names** dialog box (see above). There is an exception to this: amino acid names are predefined for protein data sets.

NOTE: *If you have chosen to display state names in the editor, you should also have "interpret state names" turned on in the* **Entry Interpretation** *dialog box in the* **Edit** *menu; otherwise you may receive many bad-cell-entry messages. By default, "interpret state names" is turned on.*

The following editor is displaying state names.

		1 amnion	2 appendages	3 body covering
1	bony fish	absent	fins	derm.scales
2	turtles	present	legs only	epid.scales
3	lungfish	absent	fins	derm.scales
4	salamanders	absent	legs only	smooth
5	crocodiles	present	legs only	epid.scales
6	lizards	present	legs only	epid.scales
7	birds	present	legs&wings	feathers
8	mammals	present	legs only&legs&wings	hair

Displaying states by their full names affects only the data editor display. In a saved NEXUS file on disk, MacClade writes the matrix using symbols and records the state names elsewhere in the file.

Footstates

Turning on the footstates feature in the **Display** menu will display a list of state names (if any have been defined using the **State Names** dialog box, and for protein data) of the character of the currently selected cell in the box at the bottom.

If you have footstates turned on, you do not have access to footnotes.

If the footstates information is too long to fit in the box at the bottom, you can expand the box by grabbing its top border and dragging it up.

NOTE: *You can quickly see the list of states for a character by holding down the Command (⌘) key and touching on the cell containing the name of the character.*

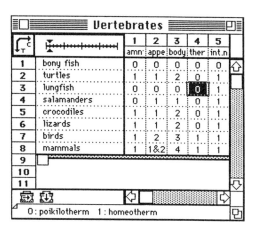

Data editor displaying footstates

IUPAC symbols for DNA and RNA data

If you choose **Display IUPAC symbols** from the **Display** menu, MacClade will display DNA and RNA sequence data using the IUPAC symbols for partially uncertain data (see "Terminal taxa of uncertain state or with polymorphism", p. 180).

Matching first taxon

The data can be viewed in a format commonly used by molecular biologists with the **Match First** dialog box.

Choosing the upper option in the dialog box will make the first taxon the standard; for all other taxa, only those states that differ from that of the first taxon will be shown, otherwise the matching symbol (by default, a period ".") will be displayed:

		1	2	3	4	5	6	7	8	9	10	11
1	Lemur catta	A	A	G	C	T	T	C	A	T	A	G
2	Homo sapiens	.	.	.	.	.	.	.	.	C	C	.
3	Pan	.	.	.	.	.	.	.	.	C	C	.
4	Gorilla	.	.	.	.	.	.	.	.	C	C	.
5	Pongo	.	.	.	.	.	.	.	.	C	C	.
6	Hylobates	.	.	.	.	.	.	.	T	.	C	.
7	Macaca fuscata	.	.	.	.	.	.	.	T	T	C	C	.
8	M. mulatta	.	.	.	.	.	.	.	T	T	C	T	.
9	M. fascicularis	.	.	.	.	.	.	.	.	T	C	C	.

By moving a different taxon into the first position, it will then become the standard. The matching symbol can be changed in the **Match First** dialog box.

Fonts

Change fonts and type sizes of the whole data editor using the **Font** and **Size** submenus in the **Display** menu.

The names of taxa can also be individually italicized. Select the name or names to be italicized, and select **Italic** from the **Display** menu. If the names are already italic, they will revert to non-italic.

Changing the width of columns

Change the width of the left-most column (that listing the taxon names, or, for a transposed matrix, that listing character names) by positioning the cursor over the black vertical line at the right edge of the column. The cursor will change to a hand. Click, and drag the line to its new position.

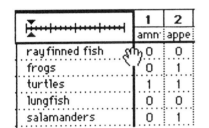

Changing the width of the first column

To change the width of the other columns, use the column width control at the upper left edge of the data editor. To decrease column size, grab the two-triangle control and move to the left; to increase column size, grab the two-triangle control and move to the right.

The column-width control

When you change column width, MacClade will readjust the window size so that only whole columns are shown.

Hiding the grid and column and row numbers

Choosing **Show or Hide** from the **Display** menu will bring forth a dialog box that allows you to remove or redisplay various elements in the data editor. This includes the grid lines shown in the matrix, and the taxon and character numbers.

Choosing character by taxa or taxa by characters

To transpose the matrix (Characters × Taxa as opposed to Taxa × Characters), click on the transpose button in the upper left. The transpose button will vary in appearance in accordance with the current setting (on the transpose button, T represents taxa, and C represents characters).

Transpose button

Annotating your data

You can store text notes or pictures for each cell in the editor, or about the data file as a whole, or about trees (Chapter 12). This section covers attaching information to each cell in the editor; for details on storing longer text notes about the data file or trees, see Chapter 8.

Footnotes

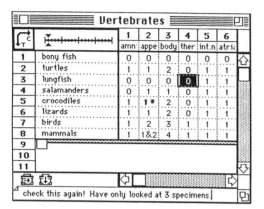

A footnote displayed
for lungfish, character 4

MacClade will allow you to store footnotes to the cells in the matrix. For example, in the matrix at the left, character 4 for lungfish has a footnote attached to that cell, and since this cell is currently selected, its footnote is displayed in the thin strip along the bottom of the window.

To activate the footnote system, choose **Footnotes** from the **Display** menu. Select the cell you wish to footnote. Then click on the little message area at the very bottom of the data editor, and enter the footnote. Footnotes can be attached to each cell in the data matrix, as well as to the cells displaying taxon names and character names. If a cell has a footnote, the entry in that cell will be bold-faced and contain an asterisk. (Note that crocodiles have character 2 footnoted in the figure shown.)

By default, the footnote area has room for only one line of text, but this can be increased by dragging the top of the footnote box up.

N O T E : *To clear the footnotes from a block of selected cells, hold down the Option key and then choose* **Remove All Selected Feet** *from the* **Edit** *menu.*

N O T E : *Option-↓ will pop the insertion point from a matrix cell down to the footnote, and Option-↑ will pop it back up to the matrix.*

Pictures linked to taxa, character names, or data

Illustrations can be linked to the cells of the matrix and displayed on command. Thus you can have a figure of the taxon attached to the taxon name (as illustrated below), or a figure of the taxon's state in a particular character attached to the corresponding cell in the matrix. You might wish to store a map of the geographic distribution of a taxon, or a picture summarizing all the states of a character.

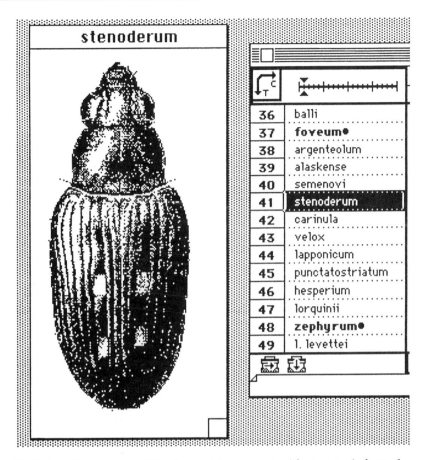

To link a picture to a cell in the matrix, you can either paste it from the Clipboard or import it from a PICT file. To paste the picture from the Clipboard, first put the picture into the Clipboard (perhaps in a graphics application), then select a cell in the matrix, and choose **Paste Picture** in the **Edit** menu. To import a picture from a file, click on a cell, then choose **Import Picture** under **Edit**. In the dialog that appears, choose the name of the file that contains the graphics image. The graphics file must be in PICT format.

To display a picture attached to a cell, select the cell and choose **Show Picture** under **Display**. The moment you move to another cell, the picture window will disappear.

MacClade indicates that a picture is attached to a cell by adding a black circle (●) to the contents of the cell.

For various technical reasons, MacClade requires a fair amount of disk space and computer memory to display, add, and remove pictures. If there is not enough disk space, or the disk is locked, then MacClade will allow you to display the pictures, but not allow you to add more or remove any.

Pictures can also be displayed from the tree window (see "Showing pictures and footnotes" in Chapter 12).

Pictures can be removed from a cell by selecting the cell and choosing **Remove Picture** from the **Edit** menu. All pictures in a block of selected cells can be removed by holding down the Option key and choosing **Remove All Selected Feet** from the Edit menu.

WARNING: *If you have pictures stored in the data file, and edit and save the file with any program other than MacClade or PAUP, you run the risk of losing all of the pictures. For example, Microsoft Word 3.02 and 4.0, FullWrite Professional 1.0, and Word Perfect 1.01 all neglect to save the pictures along with the text. The Save (but not Save As) commands of Baseline's Vantage version 1.5 does maintain the pictures, as does Microsoft Word 5.0 and PAUP. It may be that other programs do save the pictures. Before you edit files containing pictures using any application other than MacClade or PAUP, we recommend that you try saving extra copies of the files first, then see if the pictures are still visible in MacClade. Beware that other alterations to the files may also result in loss of the pictures. For instance, some methods of moving text files along a network will lose the pictures unless you use binary transfer modes.*

When you open the file in PAUP or a word-processing program, you will not see any evidence of the pictures.

For the technically minded, the pictures are stored in the resource fork of the data file, as resources of type PICT. The reason that most word processor programs discard the pictures is that they discard the resource forks of text files.

11. ASSUMPTIONS ABOUT CHARACTERS

In any phylogenetic analysis you may want to apply various assumptions to your characters. You may want to differentially weight, or exclude, some characters, or to apply particular assumptions about the cost of state-to-state transformations. For nucleotide data, you may want to specify which bases are protein coding and which are non-coding. This chapter describes what assumptions you can apply, and how to apply them, in MacClade. Some of the theoretical background for this chapter is found in Chapters 4 and 5, which discuss transformation assumptions in detail.

SUMMARY OF FEATURES: *The character status window lists the characters and whether they are included or excluded, their codon position (if DNA or RNA sequence data), their currently assigned types and weights, and, if requested for the current tree, the character's number of steps and other statistics. The inclusion, type, and weight of a character can be changed using this window. Characters of unordered and ordered types that are uninformative can be excluded automatically.*

Assumptions about the cost of state-to-state transformation can be specified using transformation types. Predefined types are unordered (Fitch parsimony), ordered (Farris/Wagner parsimony), irreversible (Camin-Sokal parsimony), stratigraphic (Dan Fisher's stratigraphic parsimony), and Dollo. Users can specify their own cost matrices or character state trees using the Type Editor.

A listing of current types, weights, or inclusions can be saved to the file as a type set, weight set, or inclusion set, respectively, for later retrieval. A list of characters can be stored in the data file as a character set, for later use to select certain sets of characters (e.g., "Larval characters").

Displaying and changing the current assumptions

To see the assumptions currently applied to the characters in your data matrix, look at the columns in the character status window.

To change the attributes of a character, you first need to select that character. You can do this in one of three ways:

1. Select the row corresponding to the character in the character status window,

2. Select the entire column or row corresponding to the character in the data editor, or

3. Trace the character on a tree, and have the tree window front-most.

Once characters are selected, you can use the various **Change** submenus in the **Assume** menu to change the attributes of these characters. These procedures are detailed in subsequent sections.

Character status window

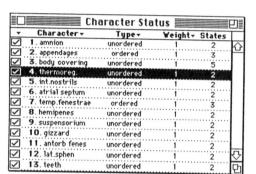

The character status window

The character status window lists the characters in the data matrix, along with various assumptions and statistics that apply to each of them. It is displayed by selecting **Character Status** in the **Display** menu. This window serves two purposes: to inform the user of current assumptions and results, and to allow the user to change current assumptions. Thus, characters can be included and excluded, and their weights and types changed in this table.

NOTE: *If you hit the Escape key (esc) when the character status window is front-most, you will be presented with a dialog box into which you can enter a character number; MacClade will scroll the window so that that character is visible.*

Selecting characters in the character status window

To select a character in the character status window click on its row in the table. It will become highlighted, as shown for character 4 in the figure at left. To select more than one character, first select one character then select another while holding down the Shift or Command (⌘) key. If the Shift key is held down, the selection will include all characters between the first and last selected. If the Command key is down, the selection will include just the characters touched.

The **Select** submenu of the **Edit** menu provides quick ways to select sets of characters. The first five elements of this submenu are **All**, **None**, **Reverse**, **All Included**, and **All Excluded**. If **All** is chosen, the entire table is selected. If **None** is selected, the entire table is deselected. If **Reverse** is chosen, those items already selected will become unselected, and vice versa. If **All Included** or **All Excluded** are chosen, then all the included or excluded characters will be selected, respectively.

NOTE: *The Select submenu is also available by clicking on the title of the column of character numbers or names in the character status window.*

If you are working with DNA or RNA sequence data, the **Select** submenu will include several additional items, namely **Protein Coding**, **Non-coding**, **Every 1st**, **Every 2nd**, and **Every 3rd**. **Protein coding** will select all of those bases that are designated as protein-coding bases, with **Non-coding** selecting those bases that you have designated as non-coding. The last three menu items are based on the defined codon positions; the codon positions are shown in a column titled "Pos". Options for defining coding and non-coding regions, and codon positions, are discussed in Chapter 19.

"All", "None", "Every 1st", and so on, are predefined **character sets**. A character set is, as the name implies, a set of characters. Character sets are used in MacClade solely for selecting elements in the character status window (although they can be used in PAUP for other purposes). To define a character set, select one or more characters in the table. Then choose **Store Char Set** from the **Selection** submenu in the **Edit** menu, give the set a name, and press OK. This new character set will now appear as a new item in the **Select** menu; by choosing this menu item, you will automatically reselect all characters in the character set. You can rename or delete character sets using the **Rename-Delete Char Set** item in the **Select** submenu.

N O T E : *If you hold down the Shift or Command (⌘) key when you choose elements from the **Select** submenu, then the previously selected characters will stay selected, and the newly chosen character set will also be selected. This change in the behavior of the **Select** submenu items is indicated by the presence of a + in front of them (indicating "union"). If you hold down the Option key when you choose items from the **Select** submenu, then the characters selected will be those that were previously selected AND present in the chosen character set. This change in behavior of the Select menu items is indicated by a * in front of them (indicating "intersection").*

Character weighting and exclusion

Changing character weights

MacClade allows you to weight characters differentially, so that more heavily weighted characters contribute more to the treelength. (See p. 265 concerning weighting and treelength; for discussion of weighting see Farris, 1969, 1983; Felsenstein, 1981a; Neff, 1986; Q. Wheeler, 1986; W. Wheeler, 1990.) There are several ways you can change the weight of a character.

Weights of one or more characters can be changed by selecting the characters, either in the character status window, or in the data editor, or by tracing the character, and then selecting a number from 0 to 9 in the

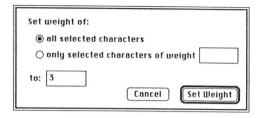

Change Weight submenu in the Assume menu. This will change the weight of the selected characters to the number chosen.

The **Set Weight** dialog box in the **Change Weight** submenu of the **Assume** menu allows you more control of the change in weights. In the dialog box, enter the new weight in the "to:" box. Weights can be integral (0 through 9999) or decimal (0.00 through 99.99).

You cannot mix integral weights with decimal weights; all characters must be weighted in one fashion. To convert integral weights to decimal weights, select **Decimal Weights** in the **Change Weights** submenu of the **Assume** menu. To convert decimal weights to integral weights (for instance, for PAUP compatibility), reselect the same menu item. In converting decimal to integral weights, MacClade gives you two options, to simply truncate (e.g., 3.17 becomes 3) or to multiply by 100 first (3.17 becomes 317). The purpose of the latter option is to preserve accuracy if you must convert weights to integral for use in PAUP, for example. Similarly, in converting integral to decimal weights, MacClade gives you two options, to simply append a decimal (e.g., 61 becomes 61.0) or to divide by 100 first (61 becomes 0.61).

If you press Set Weight in the dialog box in the example shown above, all selected characters would be set to weight 3. If you want to restrict the change, so that only those selected characters that are already of a specific weight, say 2, should be changed to 3, and not the rest of the selected characters, then choose the "only selected characters of weight" option, and type in "2" into the adjacent box. This would cause all selected characters of weight 2 to be changed to weight 3.

NOTE: *The Change Weight submenu will appear if you click on the title of the Weight column in the character status window.*

Double-clicking on the title of the Weight column in the table will display the Set Weights dialog box.

Weight sets

A weight set is a list assigning weights to various characters. Weight sets can be stored to save a particular weighting scheme for all characters, then recalled later when necessary.

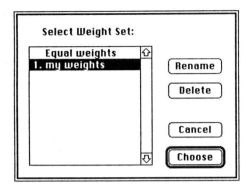

Dialog box to select weight set

The current weight settings for the characters can be named and stored by choosing **Store Weights** from the **Assume** menu. To call up already-stored weight sets, choose **Weights** from the **Assume** menu. With this dialog box, you can also delete weight sets, and rename weight sets.

Creating weight sets based on character statistics You can ask MacClade to automatically produce weight sets in which the weights are functions of the number of changes, steps, the consistency index, retention index, or rescaled consistency index of each character using the **Chart to Weight Set** command, available when the appropriate chart is displayed (see Chapter 15 for details).

Including and excluding characters

Characters in the data matrix can be included or excluded from any analysis. To include or exclude a character, select it in the character status window or in the data editor, and choose **Include** or **Exclude** or **Reverse** from the **Change Inc Exc** submenu of the **Assume** menu. **Include** and **Exclude** do the obvious; **Reverse** includes previously excluded characters, and excludes previously included characters. Included characters are indicated by ☑ at the left side of their rows in the character status window; excluded characters are indicated by ☒ .

Behavior of excluded characters

Excluded characters, for the purposes of MacClade's calculations, don't exist. That is, they are not included in any calculations and you can't trace their evolution. This means that you can have user-defined type characters with polytomous trees, normally not allowed in MacClade, as long as all such characters are excluded. Of course, the excluded characters are not deleted from the data files (unless you explicitly ask MacClade to delete them), and can be included once again when appropriate.

Exclude Uninformative

If this item is selected from the **Assume** menu, when the tree window is visible, MacClade scans the characters to see which ones are uninformative. A character is uninformative if, according to its current transformation type, any possible dichotomous tree would require the same number of steps in the character. *Only unordered and ordered characters are examined.* Also, only currently included characters are examined; excluded characters will remain excluded.

N O T E : *A character is considered uninformative only if it is irrelevant for choosing among trees using parsimony. The character may still be informative for other inferences (e.g., for inferring the relative frequencies of change between states using the State Changes & Stasis chart). "Uninformative" characters may also be informative for choosing be-*

tween trees using maximum likelihood estimation or other techniques not based on parsimony.

Remember that whether a character is uninformative depends on the assumptions you use. Therefore, if you exclude an unordered character as uninformative, you should recheck whether it is uninformative if you later change it to ordered.

MacClade determines whether a character is uninformative by calculating the minimum and maximum conceivable lengths for the character. (See discussion regarding consistency and retention indices in Chapters 5 and 14.) If the minimum and maximum are the same, then the character is uninformative. Since MacClade can calculate both the minimum and maximum only for unordered and ordered characters, **Exclude Uninformative** functions for characters of only these types.

MacClade's **Exclude Uninformative** is calculated over the taxa in the currently displayed tree, and thus is available only from the tree window! A character that is uninformative on a tree with a subset of the taxa in the data file may become informative when all taxa are included in the tree.

If you want to delete uninformative characters completely from the data file, first exclude them using **Exclude Uninformative** in the tree window, then move to the data editor and choose **Filter Characters** to delete excluded characters. Before you do this, however, remember that a character's uninformativeness depends on the taxa in the tree and the transformation type of the character. For molecular sequence data, you may want to use **Fill** to name characters by their sequence positions before deletion (see Chapter 10), so that the original sequence positions can be known after deletion.

Inclusion sets

An inclusion set is a list of those characters that are to be included by MacClade in any calculations. Sets of included characters can be saved and recalled in a fashion similar to weight sets, using items in the **Assume** menu.

NOTE: *MacClade calls the sets indicating inclusion and exclusion "inclusion sets", so that the user can name them positively (e.g., "larval characters") to indicate what is included. However, they are actually saved in the NEXUS file format as lists of what characters are excluded.*

Protein-coding regions

For DNA and RNA data, you can specify which bases are in protein-coding regions, and which bases are the first, second, or third bases of a codon. See Chapter 19 for further details.

Character transformation assumptions

Transformation types

In MacClade, assumptions about how characters evolve are applied by assigning a particular transformation type to a character. Transformation types specify how many steps it costs to go from one state to any other state, and if some transformations are impossible. Transformation types are described in more detail in Chapter 5.

MacClade has both predefined and user-defined transformation types. The predefined types are unordered, ordered, irreversible, stratigraphic, and Dollo. For the user-defined transformation types, the user must first define the transformation type, and then apply it to the character.

Applying transformation types to characters

The type of a character can be specified by selecting the character, either in the character status window, or in the data editor, or by tracing the character, and then selecting the name of the desired type in the **Change Type** submenu in the **Assume** menu (the **Change Type** menu also appears if you touch the "Type" heading in the character status window). This submenu gives as options all available types (at minimum, unordered, ordered, irreversible, stratigraphic, and Dollo). If some of the type names are dimmed (unavailable), then those types are currently prohibited by the situation. For example, the Dollo type cannot be selected if the tree in the tree window has polytomies. See the character status window section, above, for information about selecting elements in the window.

Any transformation types that are inherently directed or polarized (that is, in which there exists at least one pair of states x and y such that the number of steps going from x to y is not the same as from y to x) are *italicized* in the **Change Type** submenu. These characters may provide some evidence about possible roots of the tree. If such a type is currently in use, then a small tree trunk with roots appears beside the message box at the lower left of the tree window.

Types can also be assigned to characters using type sets, as described below.

The default transformation type for MacClade is unordered. That is, if you fail to specify a transformation type for a character, MacClade will assume it is of unordered type. MacClade uses this type as default because it is considered to embody weaker, more conservative assumptions than other types. For instance, designating a character as being of ordered type will often increase the number of steps; it can never decrease it. Unless there is good reason to support the assumption that characters are ordered, it seems better to make the more conservative assumption and to use unordered characters. Of course, if you have good evidence for a transformation type other than unordered, you should use it. See Chapter 4 for more discussion of the use of assumptions.

A user can change a data file's default transformation type by selecting the name of the type in the **Type Edit** dialog box and clicking on the button Set Default. After this, any new characters created are initially assigned this default type. Remember, this is the default type for the current file, not the preference for the default type. To change the preference for the default type, set the file's default type, and then use the **Save Preferences** dialog box of the **File** menu.

Types currently in use have ● in front of their names in the **Change Types** submenu.

Predefined transformation types

MacClade has 5 predefined transformation types: **unordered, ordered, irreversible, stratigraphic,** and **Dollo.** These predefined transformation types can be briefly characterized as follows; they are discussed in more detail in Chapter 5. The section that follows, "The ordering of character states", should be consulted for further explanation regarding ordered, irreversible, stratigraphic, and Dollo characters.

1. **Unordered** ("Fitch parsimony"; Fitch [1971]; Hartigan [1973]) — A change from any state to any other state is counted as one step.

2. **Ordered** ("Wagner parsimony"; Farris [1970], Swofford and Maddison [1987]) — The number of steps from one state to another state is counted as the (absolute value of the) difference between their state numbers.

3. **Irreversible** ("Camin-Sokal parsimony"; Camin and Sokal [1965]) — The number of steps from one state to another state is counted as the difference between their state numbers, with the restriction that decreases in state number do not occur.

4. **Stratigraphic** (Fisher's [1982, 1988, 1992] "stratigraphic parsimony") — Characters assigned this type are treated as indicating

Unordered

$$0 - 1 - 2 - 3 - 4$$

Ordered

$$0 \rightarrow 1 \rightarrow 2 \rightarrow 3 \rightarrow 4$$

Irreversible

stratigraphic age, with each state representing a stratum, or interval of time. Older through younger strata are coded by states of smaller through larger state numbers, respectively. The reconstruction of states at ancestral nodes that MacClade provides is in some sense a reconstruction of the ages of ancestors, though it should be noted that when MacClade shades a hypothetical ancestor as having state i in a stratigraphic character, this does not mean that this ancestor occurred in stratum i, but rather that it occurred *between* strata i – 1 and i. As a default, one step is counted for each absence in a stratum, but as noted below in the section "Defining and editing types", the user can vary the cost of absences in particular strata. Stratigraphic characters behave very much as do irreversible characters, differing mostly in that the cost of each "step" can be varied and in their behavior when observed taxa are fixed as ancestors. This character type is discussed in more detail in Chapter 5.

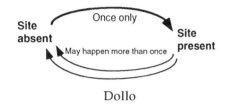

Dollo

5. **Dollo** (Farris [1977]) — The number of steps from one state to another state is counted as the difference between the numbers given to the states, with the restriction that each increase in state number occurs only once.

Dollo characters can include only three states for standard format data files. These states are by default 0–2. For extended and protein data files, states 0–7 are allowed. Dollo characters are not allowed with DNA and RNA format files. MacClade 3 assumes, as did MacClade 2.1 (Maddison and Maddison, 1987), what Swofford (1991) calls the "unrooted" Dollo assumption. That is, MacClade does not assume that there was *exactly one* gain from state 0 to state 1; it assumes only that there was *no more than one* gain from 0 to 1, no more than one from 1 to 2, and so on.

The ordering of character states

For ordered, irreversible, stratigraphic, and Dollo characters there is an implicit ordering or sequence of states. This ordering is used to calculate how many steps are required to go between one state and another; thus for an ordered character it is one step to change 0 to 1, one to change 1 to 2, but two steps to change 0 to 2, because they are ordered in the sequence 0-1-2. In the above discussion we talked of states 0, 1, 2 and so on, but what is the ordering for a DNA data file with states A, C, G, T, or a data file for which you have defined the symbols to be L, C, J, X, P? The order MacClade assumes depends on the sequence of symbols (see the section on symbols, p. 175). If the **Symbols** dialog box lists A, B, C, D as the symbols in that order for states numbered 0 through 3, then MacClade assumes the order of states is A-B-C-D. But if in the **Symbols** dialog box you define the symbols to be A C D B in that order, MacClade will assume that to be the ordering for use with ordered, irreversible, Dollo, and stratigraphic characters.

See the section "State numbers vs. symbols vs. names" in Chapter 10 for a discussion of how you can change the ordering of character states.

User-defined transformation types

In addition to the predefined transformation types discussed above, MacClade users can specify their own assumptions. This can be done by creating and editing new types in the **Type Edit** dialog box, then applying these new types to particular characters.

MacClade's user-defined types can take one of two forms: step matrices or character state trees. Step matrices specify, for each pair of states, how many steps are cost for transformations between these states. A step matrix might specify, for example, that a 0 to 1 transformation costs 1 step, but a 1 to 0 transformation costs 3 steps. Character state trees indicate graphically how transformations between states are constrained to a tree-like graph. Both step matrices and character state trees are discussed in more detail in Chapter 5, and also in Chapter 4.

Step matrices allow you to use a great variety of assumptions. Indeed, it is even possible to define step matrices that indicate the same assumptions as used in the predefined types unordered, ordered and irreversible, as shown on p. 81. However, if you want to use these same assumptions, it is much better to use the predefined types than to build user-defined equivalents, for MacClade handles the built-in types much more quickly and more flexibly than user-defined types. User-defined types have a number of limitations, as discussed below.

The means by which you can create, and edit matrix types and character state tree types are described in the next section.

Defining and editing types

User-defined transformation types are defined independent of any particular characters, then later applied to the characters of your choice. They can be defined and edited in the **Type Edit** dialog box (available in the **Assume** menu). This dialog lists the currently defined types, and allows you to edit existing user-defined types and create new ones. The dialog box looks something like this:

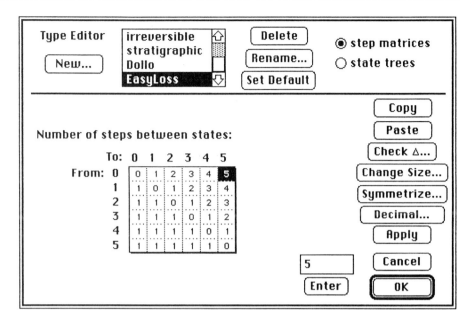

In the list of types, those with a bullet (•) in front of their names are in active use (that is, at least one included character is currently of that type). The one with an asterisk is the default type. The default type can be changed by selecting its name in the list, and clicking on the Set Default button.

There is a limit of 245 user-defined types in each data file.

If the radio button "step matrices" at the upper right is selected, then the list of types will include all available types, even the predefined types and the character state tree types, and for each (except Dollo) the matrix of state-to-state distances of types is shown. Even though the character state tree types are not defined in terms of matrices, a matrix is shown for these to show you what the character state tree implies about state-to-state distances. (However, for character state tree types, you cannot edit them in matrix form.) If the radio button "state trees" at the upper right is selected, then the list includes only the user-defined character state tree types and the predefined types that can be represented as a character state tree. The only predefined type shown is ordered.

If you have a choice of representing a user-defined type as a character state tree or a matrix, choose the character state tree: it is not only much easier to edit, but also other programs such as PAUP are much more efficient at dealing with character state trees than with step matrices. MacClade 3 internally treats the two identically (both slowly).

To create a new type, click on the New button. A dialog box will be presented allowing you to name the type. Type names can be at most 31 characters long; if you type more, MacClade will truncate the name to 31 characters. The new type will be of the matrix or character state tree sort, depending upon whether the dialog box was displaying matrices or trees when the type was created.

You can copy the specifications of a type into a private temporary clipboard with the Copy button. If you then create or select a second type, and then press the Paste button, the specifications of the first type will be pasted into the second type, replacing its previous specifications.

If you press the Apply button, then any currently selected characters in the front-most window below the **Type Edit** dialog box will be set to the type currently displayed in the **Type Edit** dialog box.

If you press OK at the bottom right of the **Type Edit** dialog box, then all editing of types will be accepted and stored in memory; if you press Cancel, they will be forgotten. There is one exception to this. If you delete user-defined types that are in use or that were used in any stored type set, MacClade will set the relevant characters to be of default type. Pressing Cancel after such a deletion will not reset the types of the characters to be the resurrected user-defined type; they will remain of default type.

Step-matrix types

To edit a step-matrix type, select one or more elements in the matrix, and type a new number into the box above Enter to indicate how many steps are counted for a change from one state to the other. You can select multiple elements by holding down the Shift key as you continue to select. When you click on the Enter button (or enter key), MacClade will replace the selected matrix elements with the entered number.

The number of steps you indicate can be either integral (0 to 999) or with decimal points (0.0 to 99.9). Typing uppercase or lowercase i, or the infinity symbol ∞, will signify an impossible transition.

A matrix must be entirely integral or entirely decimal. To convert a matrix from integral to decimal or vice versa, use the Integral/Decimal buttons. MacClade will give you a choice. On converting decimal to integral, MacClade asks if you want to truncate to the next lowest integer (e.g., 9.1 becomes 9) or to multiply by 10 first (9.1 becomes 91). The second option is offered if you want to convert to integral without losing accuracy, for instance to make the matrix compatible with PAUP 3.0. On integral to decimal, MacClade asks if you want to append a decimal point (e.g., 91 becomes 91.0) or to divide by 10 first (91 becomes 9.1).

The matrix has to be big enough to include all states in the characters to which it is applied. That is, if you have a step matrix that indicates the costs for transformations among states 0, 1, and 2 only, MacClade will not allow you to apply it to a character with states 0, 1, 2, 3, and 4. Thus the matrix must be large enough to accommodate the characters. The matrix can be unnecessarily large, in that you can use a matrix that defines costs for transformations among states 0 through 9 even if you apply it to a character with only 3 states. However, using an unnecessarily large matrix will slow down calculations. It is therefore best to adjust the size of the step matrix to fit the characters to which it will be applied. To make a bigger or smaller matrix, touch on the button Change Size and in the dialog box presented type in the symbol of the maximum state.

You can copy and paste already-defined matrices from other types, except that you cannot copy the matrices for Dollo and stratigraphic types.

You cannot edit the matrix if the type shown is predefined or a character state tree type, but you can copy such a matrix and paste it into a new matrix type. The one exception to the rule that predefined types cannot be edited is the stratigraphic type: you can edit this type to a limited extent. The stratigraphic type matrix allows you to alter the cost of an absence in each of the strata.

To make a matrix symmetrical, click on the **Symmetrize** button. You will have three options: copy the lower-left triangle of the matrix to the upper-right triangle; copy the upper-right triangle to the lower-left; or averaging. If averaging is chosen, MacClade will place as the number of steps from i to j the average value of the number of steps from i to j and j to i. If the type matrix originally consisted of integral values, you may wish to ask MacClade first to convert it to decimal values for greater accuracy.

Violating the triangle inequality MacClade does not prohibit types that violate the triangle inequality (Chapter 5), but because violations of the triangle inequality may be unintentional and can have rather strange consequences on the reconstruction of character evolution, MacClade checks for violations of the triangle inequality when a file is read, and reports any to the user. Also, in the **Type Edit** dialog box, you can ask MacClade to check types for violation of the triangle inequality using the Check Δ button. If you wish, MacClade will automatically fix each violating type by setting the cost of going between any two states to be the minimum cost along any path between the two states. (One might imagine that this procedure would give different results depending upon the sequence in which the various costs in the matrix are adjusted. However, empirical studies on 2,000 random cost matrices violating the triangle inequality suggest that this is not the case [D. Maddison, unpublished].)

Character state tree types

The character state tree types appear in the **Type Edit** dialog box as dots containing state symbols, linked by lines (see figure, below). Under the large rectangular field containing the character state tree is a holding area for states not yet incorporated into the tree. There are three tools available for rearranging the tree: a hand tool for moving state dots around, a link/unlink tool for connecting and disconnecting them, and a reroot tool for choosing a new root state. Move the tool down to the row of circles with state symbols. Pick up a state dot and drop it into the large rectangular field. Go back down and pick up another state. Join the two states by clicking on one in the field, dragging, and dropping the line on the other state in the field. Disconnect states by repeating this using the link/unlink tool. Unnamed, unobserved states can be added by using the "•" state. Unnamed states cannot be left in terminal position in the tree; MacClade will warn you and remove these states.

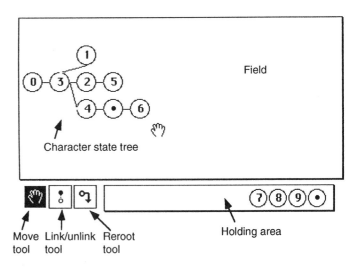

You cannot create a loop or circuit in a character state tree. Also, all states in the field must be connected to one another before you click on Clean Up or move to another type. (If not, MacClade will remove those not connected to the root.)

The first state placed in the field is drawn as the root of the character state tree. You can reroot the tree by touching on a new root with the reroot tool. The root has aesthetic value only, as MacClade 3's character state trees are undirected (effectively unrooted); root state is not implied to be ancestral, nor is it implied that evolution occurs only from the root to the tips. Character state tree types are fully reversible. In the tree figured above evolution can proceed from state 4 to 3 to 1, for example.

If you click on the Clean Up button, the character state tree will be re-drawn in an evenly spaced fashion.

If you originally define a type as a character state tree, you can see its matrix form by pressing on the "step matrix" radio button, but you cannot edit the matrix directly.

WARNING: *MacClade does not allow the unnamed, unobserved states, represented by spots, to be reconstructed as ancestral states. They are considered only as indications of how distant the observed states (e.g., A, C, G, T) are from one another. PAUP does not follow this convention, and instead allows the unobserved states to be reconstructed as ancestral states where this would allow a parsimonious reconstruction. This means that whenever a character state tree has unnamed, unobserved states in it, PAUP and MacClade may differ in the treelengths, reconstructions of character evolution, and other results that they report.*

Creating protein parsimony types

For protein data, MacClade will create a user-defined type based on the minimum number of amino acid substitutions required by the current genetic code. For details, see Chapter 19, p. 333.

Creating types based on reconstructed frequencies of change

If you have asked MacClade to chart the reconstructed frequency of state changes using the **State Changes & Stasis** menu item of the **Chart** menu, you can then ask MacClade to convert the reconstructed changes to a user-defined type, as described in Chapter 15.

Importing types from other files

The **Type Import** menu item in the **Assume** menu allows you to load in types from other NEXUS files. If, during the process of loading types from another file, MacClade encounters duplicate type names, it will ask you how to resolve the conflict. MacClade assumes that the other file will be using the same symbols (see p. 175). If it is not, problems may arise, and MacClade will give a warning and abandon importing the types.

Type sets

Type sets can be stored, retrieved, renamed, and deleted in the same fashion as weight sets (pp. 198–199), using the **Store Type Set** and **Type Sets** menu items.

Limitations on the use of various character types

Some character types cannot be used with some of the features of MacClade. For instance, with a polytomous tree no included characters can be of user-defined types. The following table indicates which features are available with which character types. Because of these limitations, you will notice that some options will be occasionally unavailable to you (for instance, you cannot change a character to a Dollo type if the current tree has polytomies), or that MacClade will give a warning when you try to use them.

Feature	Unordered	Ordered	Irreversible	Stratigraphic	Dollo	User-defined
Treelength Trace Character Branch swapping Equivocal Cycling	✓	✓	✓	✓	✓	✓
Tree changes Trace All Changes Branch length	✓	✓	✓		✓	✓
Consistency index shown	✓	✓	✓			
Retention index Rescaled consistency index	✓	✓				
Polytomies	✓	✓				
Observed taxa fixed as ancestors	✓	✓	✓	✓		
DELTRAN/ACCTRAN	✓	✓				

The only two fully supported types are unordered and ordered. Most limitations are a result of our not yet having implemented the feature for a particular character type. Users should consult the descriptions of each of these features for information on why certain character types cannot be handled.

12. TREES AND TREE MANIPULATION

It is in MacClade's tree window that the relationship between hypothesized phylogenetic trees or cladograms and the stored data is explored. The tree window is one of MacClade's two major windows; the other is the data editor. This chapter concerns the basic functions of the tree window, including those for manipulating trees.

SUMMARY OF FEATURES: *Trees can be manipulated using tools in the Tools menu. With the arrow cursor you can pick up and move branches to rearrange the tree. With the reroot tool you can reroot the tree or individual clades. Observed taxa can be forced into ancestral position on the tree using the make-ancestor tool. The collapse-branch tool collapses an individual branch to create a polytomy; the collapse-clade tool collapses all resolution within a clade to make a polytomous bush. Polytomies can be interpreted as uncertainty in resolution or as multiple simultaneous speciation. Observed taxa can be excluded or included from the current tree using the scissors tool and the Include-Exclude Taxa dialog box. The four branch-swapping tools examine alternative local rearrangements of the tree to see if any result in a tree with shorter treelength. A number of tools change the appearance of the tree without changing its fundamental structure: the rotate-branches tool, the polytomy-exchange tool, the lean-right and lean-left tools, and the magnifying-glass tool. Most tree changes can be undone.*

Trees can be displayed with slanted branches or rectangular branches. Branches can be numbered or not. On the tree, taxa can be labeled by their names, numbers, or their states in a traced character.

Trees can be stored and retrieved from the data file or from external tree files.

Trees in MacClade

Trees in MacClade can be dichotomous, polytomous, or have observed taxa placed as ancestors. They may include all or only some of the taxa in the data matrix. See Chapter 4 for a discussion of trees and their terms.

MacClade can show only one tree at a time in its tree window, but it can hold multiple trees in its memory and show them one at a time or cycle through them to perform calculations on each one, for instance for charts.

MacClade's tree window

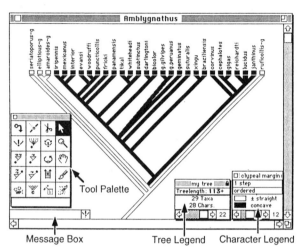

Tool Palette

Message Box   Tree Legend   Character Legend

MacClade's tree window displays a tree that can be manipulated and analyzed. The tree window is scrollable, resizable, and has several smaller windows that are associated with it: the tree legend, the trace legend (e.g., if a character is traced), and the tool palette (if it is torn off of the menu bar).

Getting to the tree window

You can move from the data editor to the tree window by choosing **Go To Tree Window** from the **Display** menu. If the tree window is hidden by another window, **Tree Window** will bring the tree window to the front.

NOTE: *If you hold down the Command key (⌘) as the file is being read in, you will be taken automatically to the tree window, even if the file was last saved with the editor on the screen.*

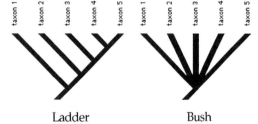

Ladder   Bush

The tree window and data editor cannot be open simultaneously. For this reason MacClade 3 is either in the tree window mode, or a data editor mode. Each of these modes has its own separate menu structure.

In moving to the tree window, MacClade will either take you to a previously saved tree, or ask you to choose a tree. If no trees have been stored in the data file, MacClade will ask that you choose between the two default trees (a ladder or a bush), or a randomly generated tree, or trees in an external tree file. The ladder is simply a comb in which taxa are arranged according to their position in the data matrix; the bush is a full polytomy with no cladistic structure.

Tree window structure and size

Tree name

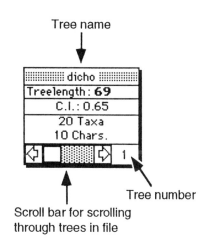

Scroll bar for scrolling
through trees in file

Tree number

Message icons

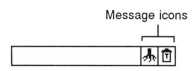

The message box

Legends

With a tree on the screen, you will see a small "tree legend" that gives various information about the tree on the screen, and allows you to scroll to other stored trees.

If a character is traced, there will be a legend for it (described in Chapter 13 for discrete characters, or Chapter 16 for continuous characters). If Trace All Changes is shown, it will also have a legend.

By default, these various legends are locked, that is, they hug the lower-right corner of the tree window. If you unlock them (turn off **Lock Legends** in the **Display** menu), you can then move them around independently of the tree window. If the legends are unlocked, they will automatically shrink and expand to accommodate the full length and width of character and state names and the treelength.

Message box

The message box on the lower left of the tree window gives information about many things. If the cursor is over top of a branch, it gives the name of the taxon or says how many taxa are in the clade above the branch.

On its right-hand side, icons may appear that indicate whether the DELTRAN or ACCTRAN options are in effect, if a branch has a fixed state, and so forth. The icons are:

Icon	Meaning
🄲	Some characters excluded
🅃	Some taxa excluded
🔍	Clade expanded
⚓	At least one character of a directed type
⬝	At least one branch with fixed state in traced character
⬝	DELTRAN option active in traced character
⬝	ACCTRAN option active in traced character
⬝	Polytomies in tree, assumed "soft" (uncertain resolution)
⬇	Polytomies in tree, assumed "hard" (multiple speciation)

NOTE: *To see amount of available memory, click on the message box.*

NOTE: *To hide the message box, hold down the Option key and choose the **Hide Message Box** from the **Display** menu. To recover the message box, hold down the Option key and choose the **Show Message Box** from the **Display** menu.*

The icons placed beside the message box can be used, in some circumstances, as buttons to perform actions. By double-clicking on the icon, the following actions are performed. (Actions in the right hand column are performed when the Option key is held down while double-clicking.)

Icon	Double-Click	Option-Double-Click
🗑		Includes all characters
🗑	Presents **Inc-Exc Taxa** dialog	Includes all taxa
🔍		Shows all clades
🌱		
✏️	Shows branches with states fixed	Unfixes all branches
☑	Presents **Resolving Options** dialog	Turns off DELTRAN
☑	Presents **Resolving Options** dialog	Turns off ACCTRAN
⬇	Presents **Polytomy Options** dialog	Arbitrarily resolves all polytomies
⬇	Presents **Polytomy Options** dialog	Arbitrarily resolves all polytomies

Tree window size

When MacClade first begins on a small-screened Macintosh the tree window fills the screen. It can be shrunk to expose the title bar at the top and grow box at the lower right by the **Reduce Window** menu item under **Display**. Once reduced, the window is moveable and resizable. On larger-screened Macintoshes, the tree window will be reduced so that the title bar and grow box will be visible.

If the window is reduced, choosing **Expand Window** from the **Display** menu will expand the window so that it fills the screen.

If you prefer an expanded tree window on a larger screen or reduced windows on a small screen, you can set those preferences using the **Save Preferences** dialog from the **File** menu.

Moving over the tree

If the tree is too big to fit into the window, you can move the view around using the hand tool from the tool palette. If the tree window is in "reduced" mode (i.e., you can see the title bar and scroll bars), then you can scroll through the tree using the scroll bars. If you grab a branch and try to drop it on a branch off the screen, the tree will automatically scroll. If the distance you want to move is too far for the window to quickly scroll automatically, you can use the branch storage feature (p. 225).

NOTE: *Whatever the current tool, you can temporarily turn it into the hand tool by holding down the Shift key.*

The Tool Palette

The palette provides a set of tools for manipulating the tree structure and for examining character evolution; it is available in the **Tools** menu. This menu is a tear-off menu; thus, you can move the palette to a preferred position on the screen.

You can use it in two ways. Using the standard arrow tool, you can grab a branch and drop it onto one of the icons of the torn-off palette. As you move the diamond cursor over each icon, the command that would be performed by that icon is listed in the small message box below the palette. If a command is illegal for a given branch, its icon may be dimmed. The other way to use the palette is exactly like the palette in many graphics programs: move the cursor over the palette and select the icon of your choice. The cursor will then become the tool pictured by that icon, and you can then move the tool over a branch and click. The command corresponding to that tool will be performed on the branch. The arrow tool is the tool to be used for picking up and moving branches.

NOTE: *As you hold the current tool over a branch, the message bar at the lower left of the tree window indicates what branch you are over — either by the name of the terminal taxon, or by the number of taxa in the clade above the branch. This message helps you know if the tool is over the branch intended.*

NOTE: *Whatever the current tool, you can temporarily turn it into the arrow tool by holding down the Command key (⌘).*

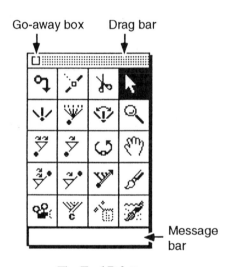

Go-away box   Drag bar

Message bar

The Tool Palette

The standard tools are shown below:

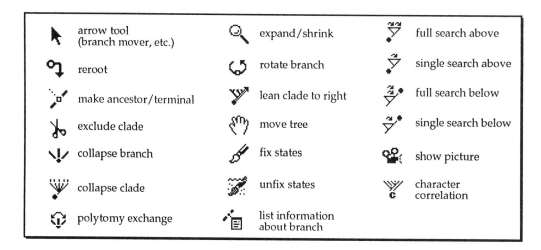

	arrow tool (branch mover, etc.)		expand/shrink		full search above
	reroot		rotate branch		single search above
	make ancestor/terminal		lean clade to right		full search below
	exclude clade		move tree		single search below
	collapse branch		fix states		show picture
	collapse clade		unfix states		character correlation
	polytomy exchange		list information about branch		

Six additional tools, available by holding down the Option key, are:

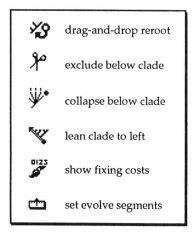

	drag-and-drop reroot
	exclude below clade
	collapse below clade
	lean clade to left
	show fixing costs
	set evolve segments

The "hot spot" or active area of each of these tools is pointed out by the H's in the figure below:

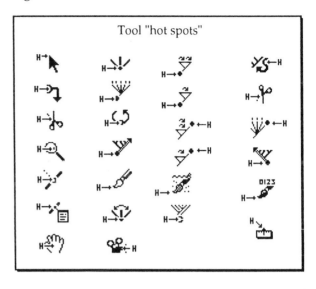

In the following sections, the action of each tool is documented.

Tree manipulation: Changing cladistic structure

The following commands substantively change the tree. You can Undo most of these commands; see "Undoing tree manipulations" at the end of this section.

Moving branches and clades around

With the arrow tool, a branch (and along with it any clade above it) can be picked up and moved to another part of the tree.

Unfix tool and diamond

Select a branch to be moved by clicking on it with the arrow tool and holding the mouse button down; the cursor will change from an arrow to a small diamond. Drag the diamond to the place you want the branch dropped, and drop it by releasing the mouse button.

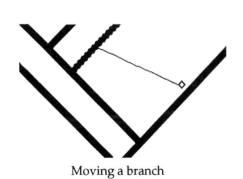

Moving a branch

If the tree is very large and extends over several screen widths, you may want to use the branch storage feature for a long distance branch move (see p. 225). In some circumstances MacClade will refuse to move a branch because it would be inappropriate (for instance, if you try to move a branch onto one of its descendants). After a branch move, MacClade will automatically recalculate treelength, consistency index, and so on, for the new tree. If any branches involved in the move have their states fixed in the traced character, their states will be unfixed by the move and a warning given.

Reroot tool and
drag-and-drop rerooting tool

Rerooting clades

Choose the reroot tool and click on the branch where the tree or clade is to be rerooted. For example, clicking on the branch leading to birds

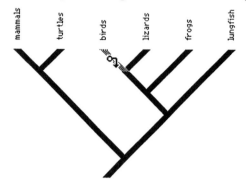

will cause the current root of the tree to be removed, the tree pulled down by the branch between birds and the other taxa, and a new root placed there.

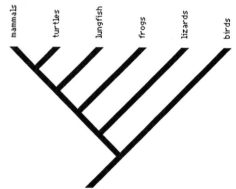

Rerooting may unfix fixed states at nodes and will make any observed taxa placed as ancestral terminal again (MacClade will give warnings if these occur).

Rerooting the entire tree will not change the treelength unless some characters are irreversible, stratigraphic, or of user-defined type with an asymmetrical step matrix. Rerooting can, of course, have an impact on the tracing of character evolution and other derived statistics.

EXAMPLE: *Try rerooting the tree presented in the example file "Rooting Example"; note that the treelength is the same under all rootings. Now choose the type set "All irreversible" from the* **Type Set** *dialog box in the* **Assume** *menu. Now try rerooting the tree. Note that the length of the tree varies between rootings.*

Rerooting within clades If you ask MacClade to reroot the following tree by clicking on birds, as shown below, then the entire tree will be rerooted at birds.

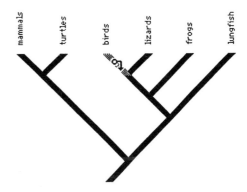

But what if you wish to reroot not the whole tree, but instead only the clade containing birds, lizards, frogs, and lungfish? This can be useful, for example, if you wish to try different rootings of the ingroup. MacClade provides two methods that can be used to reroot within individual clades (as opposed to rerooting the whole tree).

First, you can expand the clade of interest to fill the tree window, by using the expand tool:

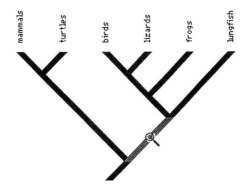

Once the clade has been expanded to fill the tree window (as indicated by the small magnifying glass (![]) near the lower-left corner of the tree window), then the rerooting tool reroots *only* the clade shown in the tree window; the rest of the tree below the clade remains untouched:

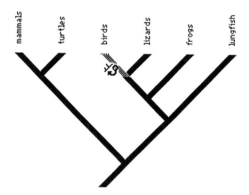

Second, you can use the **drag-and-drop rerooting tool**, available by choosing the reroot tool and holding down the Option key. Using this tool, you do not need to first expand the clade to fill the tree window. With this tool, if you click on a branch, such as birds

and drag the branch onto the root of a clade that contains birds,

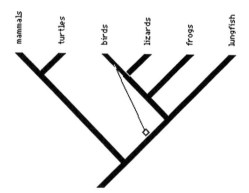

then that subclade will be rerooted, so that the new root intersects the bird branch:

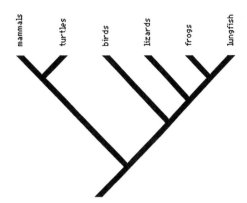

All possible rootings If you wish to save all possible rootings of a clade, then expand the clade to fill the tree window, hold down the Option key, and choose **All Rootings** from the **Trees** menu. MacClade will then store in the current data file (or tree file, if one is active) trees representing all possible rootings of the clade. To make this collection of trees, MacClade reroots the clade in turn at each of the branches of the clade. Each of the resulting trees is given a name whose suffix is the number of the branch at which the clade was rerooted. This allows you, for instance, to make a chart of the lengths of the rerooted trees, selecting the "length of each tree to text file" option, and then relating the text file output to the branch numbers (available in the **Display** menu) to see the cost of various rootings.

Polytomies

Polytomies can be produced using the collapse-clade and collapse-branch tools. Collapse clade makes the whole clade above the selected branch an unresolved bush; collapse branch destroys the resolution indicated by the selected branch, and thus yields a polytomy. These are undoable.

For example, clicking the collapse-branch tool as shown below

Collapse-branch and collapse-clade tools

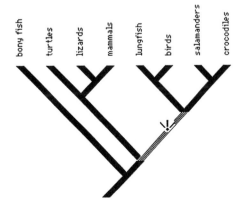

would destroy the branch, and yield the trichotomy shown below:

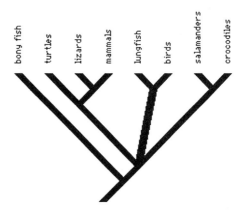

Clicking the collapse-clade tool on the same branch

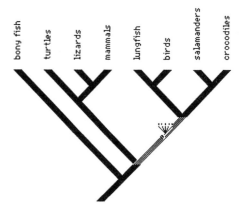

would destroy all resolution in the clade *above* the branch:

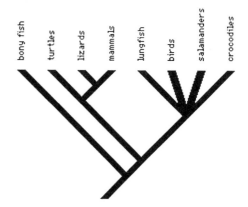

If you hold down the Option key while clicking the collapse-clade tool on a branch, the whole tree **below** the branch will collapse into an unresolved bush; the clade above the branch will be unaffected, as shown in the following figure.

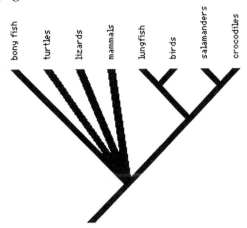

If you have expanded a portion of the tree to fill the tree window (as indicated by the small magnifying glass (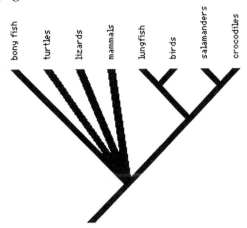) near the lower-left corner of the tree window), so that you are looking at just one clade, then Option-collapse-clade will collapse those branches *in the visible clade* below the branch.

Soft and hard polytomies

MacClade offers two ways to interpret polytomies: (1) as regions of ambiguous resolution ("soft" polytomies), or (2) as multiple speciation events ("hard" polytomies). The former is probably the more usual interpretation for phylogenetic trees. These two interpretations are discussed more in Chapter 5 and by W. Maddison (1989).

Before you fill your trees with an abundance of polytomies, you should understand clearly what they mean and their problems. (See W. Maddison, 1989, and Chapter 5 in this book; note that the interpretation of treelength is especially problematic.) Soft and hard polytomies differ in the interpretation of their display, as discussed in "Interpreting the character tracing", in Chapter 13. You may often find it best to examine various dichotomous resolutions of the polytomy, either by hand or generating them randomly using MacClade's random resolutions feature (Chapter 18).

The interpretation used by MacClade can be changed in the **Polytomies Options** dialog box in the **Tree** menu. Whether polytomies are soft or hard is indicated by an icon in the message box on the lower left of the tree window. The icon will appear if soft polytomies are present, the icon if hard.

Restrictions on polytomous trees MacClade prohibits polytomies when some characters are of a user-defined, irreversible, stratigraphic, or Dollo type or when some taxa are fixed as ancestors, because of computational difficulties. Note that PAUP does not make these prohibitions: user-defined, irreversible, and Dollo types are allowed with polytomies. The reason for this is that PAUP has only the "hard" variety of polytomies (multiple-speciation), for which algorithms are relatively easy to write. It has proven more difficult to write algorithms for these character types for "soft" polytomies, which are the default for MacClade. For instance, with a user-defined type character, soft polytomies would require a potentially difficult search for the best resolution of the polytomy for the character. To date, only the unordered and ordered characters have soft polytomy algorithms written.

MacClade also prohibits polytomies when continuous characters are traced, with one exception: it allows hard polytomies when squared-changed parsimony is used, as long as there is no basal polytomy with unrooted squared-changed parsimony.

Polytomies prohibit Equivocal Cycling and its uses (namely, Trace All Changes in maximum or minimum-average-maximum mode; State Changes & Stasis chart with mean or minimum and maximum number of changes; Character Steps/etc. chart with numbers of changes shown; **Tree Changes** from the Σ menu).

Including and excluding taxa

Trees do not have to include all of the taxa in the data matrix. You can exclude taxa or clades by using the scissors tool from the palette. Clicking the scissors on the branch below the clade will excise the whole clade from the tree. For example, if the 6 taxa on the right are excised

Scissors tool

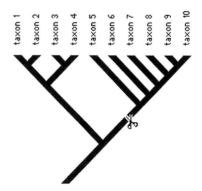

only the 4 taxa on the left will remain:

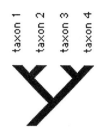

Excluding taxa from trees may cause problems with other computer programs that expect trees will include all taxa in the data matrix. However, it is often useful to be able to keep extra taxa in the data matrix (e.g., extra outgroups) that are only occasionally incorporated into the trees.

NOTE: *If you hold down the Option key while clicking on a branch, all taxa in the portion of the tree* **below** *that branch will be excised.*

If a single clade on the tree is expanded to fill the window (as indicated by the small magnifying glass (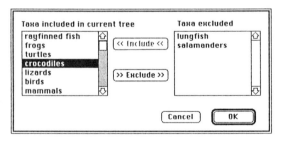*) near the lower left corner of the tree window), then Option-scissors will remove all taxa* **below** *the branch but within the expanded clade.*

You can include or exclude taxa from the tree using the **Include-Exclude Taxa** dialog box. If you wish to exclude taxa, then select them in the "Taxa included" list, and press Exclude; if you wish to include taxa, then select them in the "Taxa excluded" list, and press Include. Taxa newly included will always be added to the base of the tree in a ladder-like fashion.

The **Include-Exclude Taxa** dialog box

Branch storage

If you pick up a branch with the arrow tool, the arrow in the tool palette will change to a diamond or "storage tool". If you drop the branch onto this diamond in the palette, MacClade will temporarily remember the branch. Clicking the diamond onto another branch or a tool will be equivalent to dropping the stored branch onto the other branch or tool. This can be handy for moving branches on a very large tree: you can first store a branch at one end of the tree, then scroll to a second branch far off the screen at the other end of the tree, then drop the first branch on the second.

Searching for short trees

Searching tools

Use of a searching tool will tell MacClade to look for simple rearrangements of the tree that result in a shorter tree (i.e., a tree with a smaller treelength [p. 265]; a more-parsimonious tree). The full-search-above tool ( ) and the single-search-above tool ( ) perform local branch rearrangements in the clade *above* the branch selected. (To select the whole tree, click on the root.) The part of the tree below the clade is left untouched. The branch rearrangement algorithm visits each branch in the clade, and sees if a shorter tree would be obtained by rearranging relationships between its sister branch and its two descendant branches. At each branch three alternatives are examined (see figure below; the branch being visited is marked by a spot with question mark). The search-below tools ( ) perform local branch rearrangements in the region of the tree *below* the branch selected, while the clade above the branch is left untouched.

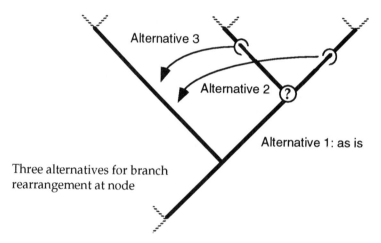

Three alternatives for branch rearrangement at node

NOTE: *Branch rearrangements are often called "swaps", even though there is no reciprocal exchange of branches.*

The **single-search** tool finds a rearrangement (swap) in the clade that shortens the tree. If the **steepest descent** option is chosen in **Search Options** in the **Tree** menu, then the search finds the single swap throughout the clade that shortens the tree the most. If the **quickest descent** option is chosen, the search chooses the first swap it finds that shortens the tree. (Only quickest descent is allowed if there are characters of user-defined or Dollo types.) The **full-search** tool does the same repeatedly until it can no longer find a local rearrangement that improves length. To help you track where the branch swapping is taking place, each time a branch is swapped, a spot (•) appears on the branch. In each case the branch with a spot has been moved onto its ancestor's sister branch. During full search, you can pause searching by holding down the mouse button, and you can abort searching, and show the tree obtained so far by swapping, by hitting Command-period (⌘-.) on the keyboard.

The **Search Options** dialog box also allows you to slow down the search and show its path, so as to make it easier to follow. The path is shown by a question mark placed over each branch as it is visited (like the question mark in the previous figure).

Single search and full search differ in a respect other than the number of swaps they will perform. If no rearrangements will improve length, and yet there is a rearrangement that will keep the same length, full search will make no change in the tree but single search *will* make that equally parsimonious rearrangement. Thus you can use single search to look for equally parsimonious trees.

Because the swapping algorithms visit the branches on the left side of the tree first, MacClade will preferentially make swaps on the left side. Also, beware that these algorithms may help you to fine-tune a tree, but you should not rely on them to find the shortest tree! Once we had a data matrix whose shortest tree was 36 steps, yet full search above could find no tree shorter than 72 steps, because the starting tree required more than just local rearrangements.

Because MacClade's forté is not in finding the shortest trees, it would be most profitably used in combination with the more sophisticated tree-finding programs such as PAUP (Swofford, 1991), HENNIG86 (Farris, 1988), or PHYLIP (Felsenstein, 1991). MacClade could be used initially to test favorite trees, explore the data set, explore different assumptions, and then the data set could be sent through one of the above programs for a more powerful tree search. The user could then return to MacClade to explore the newly found trees. See Chapters 7 and 9 for discussion of using MacClade with other programs.

Nonetheless, MacClade can be used to search for short trees. One way to proceed is to begin with a fairly reasonable tree (perhaps based on your experience with the group), and use local branch swapping on the whole tree. Try alternating between single and full searching (since single can find equally parsimonious alternatives that may allow you to escape from a local optimum). Next, examine the character state distributions (perhaps using the character Data Boxes), to see if any other rearrangements are suggested. After you've made some moves, try the branch-swapping tools again.

NOTE: *MacClade swaps only on dichotomous trees; thus, if your tree has polytomies, MacClade will ask you if you want to randomly resolve the polytomies into dichotomies before swapping. See Chapter 18 to learn more about the random resolution.*

NOTE: *If you hold down the Shift and Option keys while clicking on a branch with a search tool, MacClade will search for longer rather than shorter trees.*

Making an observed taxon ancestral

Make-ancestor tool

To push an observed taxon downward to be an ancestor, use the make-ancestor tool. (This tool is available only if there are no characters of user-defined or Dollo types, and can be used only on a terminal branch.)

This command forces the selected observed taxon to become an ancestor. The taxon is put in the place of the branch that used to be its immediate ancestor. The name of the taxon remains on top because it is easier to draw it there. From the name is a thin line pointing down to the taxon's actual position as ancestor. Of course, it doesn't make sense to use this tool if the observed taxon is a higher taxon including more than one species (e.g., a genus or family).

NOTE: *An observed taxon fixed as an ancestor can have only one descendant node in MacClade. That is, you cannot place an observed taxon directly onto a branching point from which descend two clades or species.*

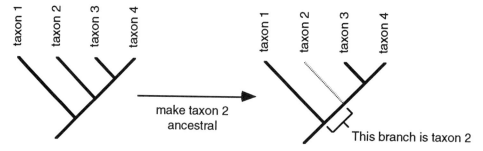

make taxon 2 ancestral

This branch is taxon 2

All of the character states of the taxon are forced down onto this ancestral branch. This is useful for paleontologists, because they can see the number of extra steps in character evolution required by supposing a fossil is an ancestor. It is also useful for neontologists to determine if a species might be paraphyletic according to the tree: if the treelength goes up when it is made an ancestor, then the species has autapomorphies. (Trace All Changes can also give a summary of autapomorphies.)

Even though a taxon made ancestral has only a line coming down from the taxon's name instead of a full terminal branch, this line can still be grabbed with the mouse. However, the only thing that can be done with this line is to apply the make-terminal tool to it.

A taxon fixed as ancestor remains so fixed even when another character is traced. The ancestral status of a taxon is stored when the tree is saved to the file.

A taxon fixed as ancestor can be made terminal again by reapplying the make-ancestor tool to it. All taxa fixed as ancestors can be made terminal by choosing **All Terminal** from the **Tree** menu.

WARNING: *If an observed taxon polymorphic for some character is forced down as an ancestor, the number of steps required is likely to be underestimated. A warning to this effect is given by MacClade in most circumstances. For example, when an observed taxon polymorphic for 0,1 is forced down as ancestor into a region of the tree with all state 0 surrounding, an extra step should be counted (gain, then loss, of 1) but isn't. The shading of branches indicating character evolution should be correct, however, except perhaps for irreversible characters. Note also that for Dollo and irreversible characters you can force the assumptions of the methods to be violated (for instance, if you make a taxon with state 1 ancestral to a clade with state 0 for an irreversible character). MacClade will not always give you a warning if you do this. Stratigraphic characters do not encounter such problems with polymorphisms.*

Undoing tree manipulations

After you make a change in tree structure, MacClade remembers the previous tree, so that you can undo the change and recover the old tree. To recover the old tree, choose the **Undo** command from the **Edit** menu. You can undo tree manipulations that had a substantive effect on the tree, but some cosmetic manipulations cannot be undone by the Undo command. The Undo command will reflect which type of move is to be undone; the menu item will read "Undo Branch Move", "Undo Rerooting", "Undo Branch Swap", "Undo Get Tree", "Undo Collapse", "Undo Inclusion-Exclusion", or "Redo". Calling Redo will get back the tree you just undid.

Undo will not always restore a tree exactly to its former appearance. Some nodes may have the left-to-right order of their descendants reversed, for instance. The important aspects of tree structure will be restored, however.

Tree display commands

The following commands change the appearance of the tree on the screen, but do not affect the tree in a substantive way. That is, tree-length, character tracing, and other such results will not be affected. (Subsequent use of the search tools may be affected, however, because these algorithms visit one side of the tree first.) For these changes, there is no Undo command available that would automatically reverse their action.

Rotating branches

Rotate tool

There may be times when you wish to change the order of sister groups on the screen. You can accomplish this by invoking the rotate-branches or rotate tool. For example, to reverse the position of crocodiles and birds in the following example, click the rotate tool on the branch below the clade:

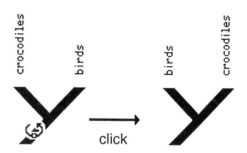

click

Exchanging elements of a polytomy

Polytomy-exchange tool

The rotate-branches tool will not work on a polytomy. In order to rearrange two elements of a polytomy, use the polytomy-exchange tool. Click on one element of the polytomy, and drop on another element of the same polytomy. The two elements will exchange places.

Ladderizing clades

Lean-right and lean-left tools

In the course of moving branches around, you might end up with a jagged clade, looking rather like a monkey-puzzle tree:

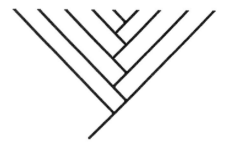

If you wish to tidy the clade up a bit, by reducing the jagged aspect, you could use the rotate-branches tool to reorganize the clade. But this can be very time consuming. A quicker method is to use the lean-right tool ( ), which automatically rotates branches to produce the arrangement that is maximally comb-like. Ladderizing the above jagged clade using the lean-right tool would yield the following arrangement:

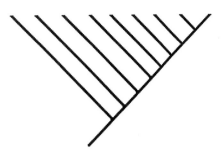

If you hold down the Option key, the lean-left tool (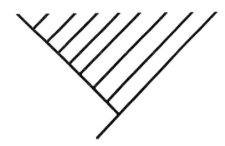) will become available, which will ladderize a clade with the backbone of the ladder directed toward the left:

Expanding and shrinking

Magnifying-glass tool

You can expand the tree to get a close up of a clade by clicking the magnifying-glass tool on the branch below the clade. This fills the tree window with the clade chosen. The remaining part of the tree, below and beside the displayed clade, is not visible. Although it is not visible, for the purposes of all calculations such as tracing character evolution, the remaining part of the tree is still attached to the displayed clade.

Expanding a clade does more than just allow you to look more closely at it. Some of MacClade's tree manipulation functions, such as rerooting, collapsing below, and cut below, apply to the whole tree except when a clade is expanded, in which case they are restricted to the clade. For instance, if you want to reroot a clade but leave the rest of the tree intact, expand that clade to fill the screen before using the reroot tool.

If the tree is expanded, you can shrink it back so that the whole tree fills the tree window by clicking the magnifying-glass tool on the basal branch on the screen. You can also shrink the tree by using the **Show All Clades** command in the **Display** menu.

NOTE: *Double-clicking on a branch is equivalent to using the magnifying glass on that branch.*

NOTE: *If you hold the Option key down while you shrink the tree using the mouse, the tree shrinks only enough so that the sister group of the viewed clade is included, rather than shrinking down so that the whole tree is visible.*

Display of taxon labels

You can change the display of labels used at the tips of the trees using the **Taxon Labels** dialog box in the **Display** menu. In this dialog box, the font, size, and style of the text shown can be chosen. (Although this allows you to italicize all the labels, you can individually italicize a taxon name if it is selected in the data editor and **Italics** is chosen from the **Display** menu.) Note that the font used in the tree window does not affect the font used in tree printing or saving of graphics files.

The state names of the currently traced character can be shown at the tips of the tree's branches instead of taxon names, if you so choose in the **Taxon Labels** dialog box. You can also ask MacClade to write the taxon numbers at the tips of the branches.

Square or angled trees

By default, MacClade draws trees on the screen with the diagonal branches, as shown at left, above. If you want square branches (consisting of only horizontal and vertical lines), then choose **Tree Shape & Size** in the **Display** menu. In the dialog box presented, you can choose the shape of tree, by selecting either of the two icons:

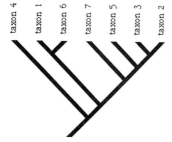

A tree with diagonal branches

Choosing the left-most icon will cause MacClade to draw trees with diagonal branches. Choosing the right-most icon will cause MacClade to draw trees with horizontal and vertical branches.

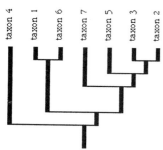

A tree with square branches

If you choose the centered branches option with square branches, then MacClade will adjust the horizontal position of the branch stems so that they are centered under the immediate descendants. This produces somewhat more pleasing trees but forces MacClade to redraw the entire tree more frequently.

Tree size

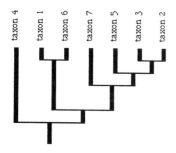

A tree with square, centered branches

You can change the size of the tree in the tree window using the **Tree Shape & Size** dialog box in the **Display** menu. In it you can set a scaling factor, which will increase or decrease the tree in both horizontal and vertical directions. This scaling factor is entered in the "Tree size: __ times normal size" box. You can further adjust the height/width ratio of square trees by entering the height/width ratio in the "__ times taller than wide" box. A height/width ratio of less than 1.0 is not allowed.

Numbering branches

The **Show Branch Numbers** command in the **Display** menu will draw small numbers over the branches of the tree. MacClade uses branch numbers to refer to branches or nodes when printing or saving text files. For instance, when you ask to print a Node List when a character is traced on the tree window, MacClade will list branch numbers, and beside each indicate the states reconstructed at the node at the top of the branch.

Trace labeling

Various options are available for altering the manner in which elements are traced upon the tree, using the **Trace Labeling** and **Patterns & Colors** dialog boxes in the **Display** menu. For full details, see Chapters 13 and 16.

Showing pictures and footnotes

Show-picture tool

To show (from the tree window) a picture of a taxon or character or character state that was attached to a cell in the data matrix, use the show-picture tool. To show a picture of the taxon, click the show-picture tool on the taxon name. Taxa with pictures are indicated by a bullet ("•") in the taxon name. To show a picture of a character state in a taxon, click the show-picture tool on the box just beneath the taxon's name when the character is traced, or click on the appropriate box in the Data Boxes display; the box will be outlined in black if a picture is stored.

To show a footnote attached to a taxon name, click the mouse pointer on the taxon name. Taxa with footnotes are indicated by an asterisk ("*") in the taxon name. To show a footnote of a character state in a taxon, click the arrow tool on the box just beneath the taxon's name when the character is traced, or click on the appropriate box in the Data Boxes display; the box will be outlined in gray if a footnote is stored.

Tree storage and retrieval

Trees in data files and tree files

Trees can be stored in the data file, or in an external tree file.

When you first start a data file, MacClade will presume that the trees are in the data file. If you store trees, they will be stored to the data file. If you request to get trees using **Trees** in the **Tree** menu, MacClade will look to the data file for trees.

However, you can specify an external tree file as the source and repository of trees. Do this in the tree window using **New** or **Open Tree File** in the **Tree** menu. If you choose **Open Tree File**, a dialog box will come up allowing you either to open an existing external tree file (for instance one saved as the result of a PAUP run), or to create a new one by clicking the New button. Once you have opened or created an external tree file, MacClade will place any stored trees in this external file, and will get trees from there when requested. Remember that the trees will be saved to the disk only when you ask to **Save Tree File**. If you do switch to an external tree file, the trees stored in the data file will not be lost. When you close the external tree file using **Close Tree File**, tree storage and retrieval reverts to the data file.

Thus, at any one time, MacClade uses only one **tree repository**. This repository is the tree file if a tree file is open, or the data file if no tree file is open.

W ARNING: *If you delete, add, or change the names of taxa in the data editor, then MacClade will automatically adjust the tree descriptions stored in the data file and any currently open external tree file. It will not, however, update the tree descriptions in any tree files that are not open when the taxon change is made, and these tree files might therefore be left with archaic taxon names that will cause problems in later reading those tree files. However, if you have tree files with archaic names, it is relatively easy to edit manually the files with a text editor to bring them into compatibility with the more newly modified data files.*

If you want to examine only some of the trees in a tree file, you can specify a range of trees for MacClade to read in the dialog box that appears when you click on the Options button in the **Open Tree File** dialog box.

MacClade can read tree files created by MacClade, PAUP 3.0, HENNIG86, and PHYLIP. If MacClade cannot detect the file format of the tree file, it will ask you to specify the kind of tree file it is.

A third file can be temporarily accessed by asking a chart to be made of some aspect of the trees in another tree file. This other tree file will be read only for the purpose of the chart; once the chart is calculated MacClade will revert to using whichever tree repository (data file or external tree file) it had been using. See Chapter 15 for more information.

Displaying a stored tree

To display a stored tree, choose **Trees** from the **Tree** menu. You will be presented with a dialog box listing the two default trees (ladder and bush) and the available trees stored in the current tree repository (data file or external tree file, whichever is active). Select a tree by clicking on its name, and then click on the Get Tree button. Simply double-clicking on a tree's name is another way to choose it. That tree will then be displayed.

You can scroll through trees stored in the file by using the scroll bar in the tree legend window.

NOTE: *The up arrow* (↑) *key will take you to the next stored tree; if no stored tree has been displayed, it will take you to the first stored tree; if a stored tree was displayed, but has since been modified, then it will take you to the next stored tree beyond the one previously displayed. The down arrow* (↓) *key will take you to the previous tree.*

Typing Option-esc will present a dialog box into which you can enter the number of a tree you wish to see.

NOTE: *Double-clicking on the title bar of the tree legend will bring up the* **Trees** *dialog box.*

Deleting or renaming stored trees

You can delete or rename trees in the **Trees** dialog box. To delete, select the trees to be deleted and click on the Delete button. To rename a tree, select its name then click on the Rename button. You will be presented with a dialog box in which you can enter the new name.

Storing trees

To store a tree for later retrieval, choose **Store Tree** from the **Tree** menu. You will be presented with a dialog box. Type in the name of the tree and press Store. Remember, this does not save trees to disk; it only stores them in memory. To save them to disk, you must then choose **Save File** or **Save Tree File** from the **File** menu.

Saving external tree files

You can save a tree file to disk using the **Save Tree File** and **Save Tree File As** commands from the **Tree** menu; both of these will save the tree files in NEXUS format. If you wish to save a tree file in a different format (HENNIG86 or PHYLIP), then use the **Export Tree File** menu.

Transferring trees between data files and tree files

If you have an external tree file open, the **Transfer Trees** dialog box (**Tree** menu) allows you to choose trees to transfer over to the current data file. If no tree file is open, then choosing **Transfer Trees** will transfer the selected trees from the data file to a new, unsaved tree file.

Adding notes about the trees

You can save notes and comments about the trees; use the **About Trees** window, available from the **Tree** menu. These notes are stored with the trees in the current tree repository (that is, either in the data file or tree file). If you do a tree search in PAUP and save the trees to a file, PAUP will store information in the tree file about the source of the trees; this information will appear in MacClade's **About Trees** window if you open that tree file.

13. TRACING CHARACTER EVOLUTION

In this chapter we describe MacClade's methods for reconstructing evolutionary history of discrete-valued characters (for continuous-valued characters, see Chapter 16). The reader is referred to Chapters 3 and 4 for discussion on the importance of such reconstructions, and to Chapter 5 for the theory of parsimony reconstructions of character evolution.

SUMMARY OF FEATURES: *Character evolution can be reconstructed parsimoniously and displayed on the tree by shading branches for discrete-valued characters. The states reconstructed at branches can also be indicated by labelling branches, and in lists printed or saved to text files. The shading of branches can use black-and-white patterns, colors, or shades of gray on the appropriate monitors. If more than one reconstruction is parsimonious, MacClade can show in sequence all parsimonious reconstructions using Equivocal Cycling. You can explore alternative reconstructions, including less-parsimonious ones, by fixing the state at branches. All characters can have their states reconstructed and shown using Trace All States; the changes occurring on different branches can be reconstructed and shown using Trace All Changes. In Trace All Changes, the tree can be shaded or marked to indicate the amount of change on each branch; alternately, which characters and states change on each branch can be displayed as ticks on the tree.*

Tracing the history of character evolution

In the tree window, MacClade will reconstruct the evolution of a character in the data matrix and display the reconstruction graphically by tracing (painting) onto the tree the inferred states of ancestors.

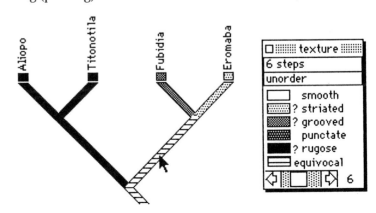

The tracing displays the ancestral character states that imply the smallest amount or number of character state changes. That is, the tracing shows, on each of the branches, the most-parsimonious (simplest) hypothesis of ancestral states. *Do not forget that these reconstructions are estimates based on parsimony considerations; they are not observed facts.* To be precise, each tree branch is shaded to indicate what states are most parsimoniously placed at the node terminating the branch. The set of states that can be parsimoniously placed at a node is the node's MPR set, as described in Chapter 5 (see also Swofford and Maddison, 1987). Each state in the MPR set occurs in at least one most parsimonious reconstruction (MPR) of character evolution. A box appears just under each terminal taxon's name, to show the state(s) observed in it. If the state was unknown for a taxon (coded in the data matrix as missing), no box appears. A legend is provided on the right of the screen showing what pattern, shade, or color represents what state.

Which states are reconstructed at the various ancestral branches depends on the shape of the tree, the observed states in the terminal taxa, and various background assumptions concerning the nature of changes from one state to another in the character. In particular, each character is assigned to a transformation type (e.g., unordered, ordered, irreversible) that indicates how many steps are counted for a change from each state to each other state. Thus with an unordered character, state i can change to state j in 1 step, whereas with an ordered character state i can transform to j in $|i - j|$ steps. The character tracing displays the reconstruction that is most parsimonious in the sense that it requires the fewest steps so counted.

Chapters 4 and 5 should be consulted for more information on the principles and assumptions underlying MacClade's ancestral state reconstructions.

When the tree has polytomies, there are two alternative interpretations of the polytomies (soft vs. hard polytomies) that affect the reconstruction of character evolution. Polytomies are difficult to deal with, and the reader should consult W. Maddison (1989) and the discussions of polytomies in Chapters 5, 12, and 15.

EXAMPLE: *Donoghue (1989) presents an analysis of the evolution of dioecy and dispersal mechanisms among the seed plants. With the aid of MacClade 2.1 he reconstructed, as one of several possibilities, the following scenario of phylogeny with propagule evolution overlain:*

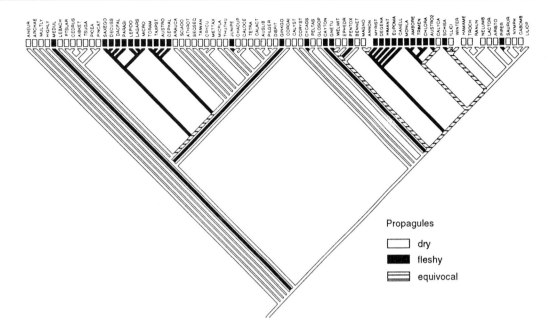

Propagules

☐ dry

■ fleshy

▤ equivocal

Donoghue sought a correlation between this character's evolution and the evolution of dioecy. Using W. Maddison's (1990) test, he found that reconstructed gains of dioecy may or may not be significantly concentrated in the phylogenetic context of fleshy fruit (= animal dispersal?), depending upon just how history is interpreted. This illustrates the important point that the sequence of events (which came first, which later) is critical to know if we are to distinguish various evolutionary processes.

Choosing a character to trace

To bring forth the dialog box that allows you to choose a character to trace, select **Choose Character** in the **Trace** menu. There are several ways to trace a character without going through the dialog box.

1. Choose **Trace Character** from the **Trace** menu. This will display the last character traced, or the first included character if none has yet been traced.

2. If character Data Boxes are visible, then double-click on the line of boxes of the character to be traced.

3. If the character status window is being shown, then double-click on the row of the character to be traced.

4. If Trace All Changes or All States are being shown, and you have queried about the changes along or states at a branch using the branch-information tool, then double-click on a line in the window

listing changes or states to turn off the summary mode and trace that character.

To revert back to the last character traced, choose **Previous Traced** from the **Trace** menu.

N O T E: *The right arrow (→) key will ask MacClade to trace the next included character, the left (←) arrow key the previous included character. If the tree window is front-most, and a character is traced, and you hit the Escape key (esc), MacClade will present a dialog box into which you can enter a character number; MacClade will trace that character.*

EXAMPLE: *In Donoghue's (1989) example of the evolution of dioecy and dispersal in seed plants described above, you could trace the character Dioecy, then trace the character Propagules. By selecting **Previous Traced**, Dioecy will be traced again. You can therefore continue to choose **Previous Traced** again and again in order to alternate back and forth between the two characters. This method allows close examination of any correlations in the evolution of the two characters.*

The character legend

If a character is traced, you will see a legend in the lower left corner of the tree window.

The number of evolutionary steps required in the character by the tree is shown below the character name. The number shown is simply the number of steps on the displayed (usually, the most parsimonious) ancestral state reconstruction according to the character's transformation type; it is not multiplied by the character weight. Thus if there are characters weighted differently from 1, when you add all the character steps you may not get the treelength. (Treelength is discussed in Chapter 14.) The number of steps is not necessarily the number of changes of state on the tree, if some changes are weighted, for instance by a step matrix. An asterisk (*) appears beside the number of steps when the character is of user-defined type and has a terminal taxon polymorphic for more than two states, signifying that MacClade's algorithms do not accurately count steps or reconstruct ancestral states in such a circumstance (see Chapter 5).

In the character legend is a series of smaller, shaded boxes, which show the patterns or colors used on the tree. The first several boxes show the patterns indicating the various character states. The lowest-valued state in the character (e.g., state 0) is shown at the top of the list, with higher-valued states below it. If you have named the states in the data file, then names of the states will appear beside the appropriate boxes (unless you request in the **Trace Labeling** dialog box in

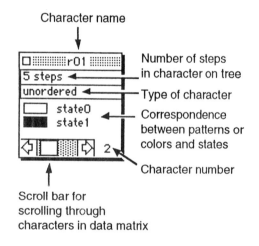

Character name

Number of steps in character on tree

Type of character

Correspondence between patterns or colors and states

Character number

Scroll bar for scrolling through characters in data matrix

The character legend

the **Display** menu that only symbols be used); if not, only the state symbols 0, 1, 2, or whatever, will appear.

The character legend is by default attached to the lower-right corner of the tree window, but you can unlock this attachment by using the **Lock Legends** item in the **Display** menu. This frees both the character legend and the tree legend to be moved independently of the tree window. When the character legend is unlocked, it will also widen to show any long character state names.

N O T E: *Double-clicking on the title bar of the character legend will bring up the* **Choose Character** *dialog box.*

Interpreting the character tracing

The shading of the branches indicates the reconstruction of ancestral states. It is important that you know how to interpret what states are reconstructed, and exactly to what points in the tree the reconstructions refer. The reconstruction of ancestral states determines what states are most parsimoniously placed at the branch-points or *nodes* of the tree, as defined in Chapter 4. However, as explained below, for graphical convenience MacClade shades the entire branch (node plus internode below it). Users must be aware that when MacClade shades an entire branch, and when this book refers to "state reconstructed at a branch", what is actually meant is the reconstructed state at the node at the top end of the branch.

Determining the states reconstructed at a branch

In general you can look to the character legend to see which shades correspond to which states, but the shades may be difficult to distinguish, or the character tracing may have the "equivocal", "uncertain" or "polymorphic" shadings. The equivocal pattern (▤) is used to indicate that more than one state can be equally parsimoniously reconstructed at a branch. For stratigraphic characters, a special pattern (▦) is used instead of equivocal, uncertain, or polymorphic shadings (see Chapter 5).

In order to determine exactly which states are reconstructed at a branch, you can use one of four methods:

1. If you place the cursor over top of the branch, asterisks or question marks appear in the character legend beside each of the states reconstructed at the branch.

2. If you ask to use text labels to indicate states (see the **Trace Labeling** dialog box in the **Display** menu), MacClade will place a label on each branch with a list of its reconstructed states.

3. If you touch a branch with the branch-information tool (⌘▤), MacClade will momentarily show a list of the reconstructed set of states.

4. A list of the states reconstructed at each of the branches can be printed or saved to a text file, using the **Node Lists** item in the **Print Other** or **Save Text File** submenus.

Boxes for terminal taxa

The box that appears just under each terminal taxon's name shows the state(s) observed in the taxon. If only a single state was observed in the taxon, then the pattern or color of the box will be that of the state. If the state was unknown for a taxon (coded in the data matrix as missing), or was coded as a gap, no box appears. If a terminal taxon is polymorphic (possesses more than one state), the box and the branch below it are shaded by a pattern designating polymorphism (▨▨). If there is partial uncertainty about the states of a terminal taxon, which you indicate by the use of the OR separator in the data editor, the box will be shaded by the pattern designating uncertainty (▨▨).

Shading of non-terminal branches

When a branch is shaded to indicate a particular state, it is important to realize to which part of the tree this reconstructed state refers. On a dichotomous tree, the branch shading is best thought of as indicating the reconstructed state at the branch point (node) at the top of the branch.

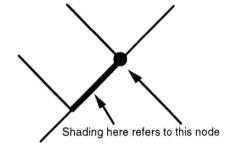

Shading here refers to this node

Thus, the figure at the start of this chapter is equivalent to the following:

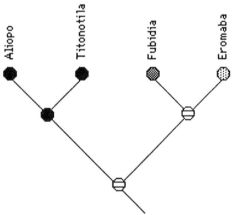

For instance, consider the basal branch of a clade that uniformly has state 1 while the rest of the tree has state 0:

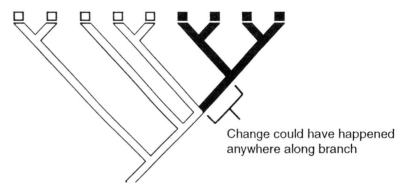

Change could have happened
anywhere along branch

The basal branch point of this clade is reconstructed as having state 1; the node just below this is reconstructed as having state 0. The change from state 0 to 1 might have occurred anywhere along the branch connecting the two nodes, as long as 1 is achieved before the basal node of the clade. MacClade, however, by convention shades the entire basal branch of the clade by state 1, from just above the node below it, up to and including the basal node of the clade.

When the node at the top of a branch is polytomous, the interpretation of the branch's shading depends on whether the polytomy is assumed to represent uncertainty (soft polytomy) or multiple speciation (hard polytomy). If it is assumed to represent multiple speciation, then the comments above apply: the shading of the branch below the polytomy indicates the reconstructed state at that polytomous node, that is, at the most recent common ancestor of the clade just above branch.

If the polytomy represents uncertainty, however, then MacClade attempts to reconstruct character evolution as if the polytomy were resolved dichotomously in the way most favorable for the character. In such a dichotomous resolution, the polytomy would be broken into two to many dichotomous nodes. One might expect that the basal branch of the polytomy in MacClade would be shaded according to the states at the most basal of these dichotomous nodes, but the states at this node can be difficult to calculate and to interpret, and instead MacClade invents an extra node just between the most basal dichotomous node resolved out of the polytomy, and the node just ancestral to the polytomy. It is to this intercalated node that the shading of the basal branch of a soft polytomy refers (figure at left).

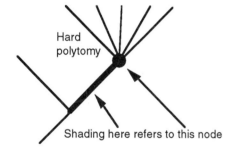

Hard polytomy

Shading here refers to this node

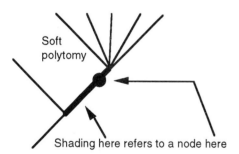

Soft polytomy

Shading here refers to a node here

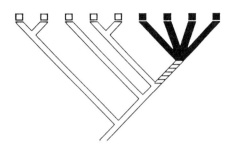

MacClade uses this convention because the context of the basal node varies with different resolutions of the phylogeny, and this can be difficult to deal with. As there can be changes between that extra node and the most basal node of the clade above, the shading of the basal branch therefore does not necessarily indicate the ancestral state of the clade. This can lead to puzzling results, such as that shown at left. The ancestral branch of the black clade, it would seem, should be reconstructed as being black. But since with a soft polytomy the shading of the branch refers to a node just below the most recent common ancestor of the black clade, and this node might be either just before or just after the change to black, it is shaded equivocal.

Shading of terminal branches

The shading of a terminal branch generally indicates the observed state in the corresponding terminal taxon. However, exceptions occur when the terminal taxon has uncertain state, or is polymorphic, or when the terminal branch's state is fixed.

If the terminal taxon's state is uncertain, then MacClade assigns to the terminal branch a state that represents the most-parsimonious choice, among those allowed by the uncertainty, for the taxon's state.

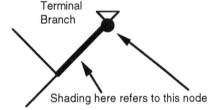

Terminal Branch

Shading here refers to this node

If the terminal taxon is polymorphic, then MacClade assigns a state to the terminal branch that represents the most-parsimonious estimate for *the ancestral state of the terminal taxon.* That is, MacClade treats the terminal taxon as a small clade whose internal structure is unresolved, and on the basis of the reconstructed states at nearby nodes, reconstructs what would have been the most-parsimonious estimate of the state at the most recent common ancestor of the terminal taxon.

That MacClade treats terminal taxa as unresolved clades is appropriate when the terminal taxa are genera or families, but when they are species, objections may be raised to this practice. For instance, we don't expect the internal structure of a species to be purely branching. However, there seems little else we can do given the lack of algorithms available to deal with reticulations and ancestral polymorphisms (see the discussion in Chapter 5). Note, however, that terminal polymorphisms can yield certain difficulties (see p. 47, and Nixon and Davis, 1991).

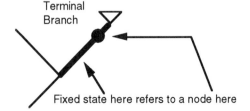

Terminal Branch

Fixed state here refers to a node here

The interpretation of a terminal branch's shading changes, however, when the user fixes the state at the terminal branch, as when using the paintbrush tool. When a terminal branch's state is fixed, it is treated as fixing a node *just below* the most recent common ancestor of the terminal taxon. This is done because of computational difficulties that arise when the fixing is considered as at the most recent common ancestor of the internal components of the terminal taxon. For instance, if the fixing is considered as at the most recent common ancestor of the components of the taxon, and the terminal taxon had state 1 and the terminal branch is fixed to 0, would we count 2 steps, one up the left and one up the right branches in the clade of the taxon's internal components? Note that MacClade 3's convention regarding fixed states differs from that in MacClade 2.1 and 1.0, in which fixing a terminal state was treated as if replacing the observed state. (See discussion of fixing the state at a branch, later in this chapter.)

A reminder about soft polytomies

Remember from the discussion in Chapter 5 that a soft polytomy represents ambiguity among alternative dichotomous resolutions. MacClade's algorithms find the reconstruction of character evolution on the resolution of the polytomy most favorable (parsimonious) to the character. There are various problems with such an approach (Chapter 5; W. Maddison, 1989), and you should avoid reconstructing character evolution on polytomous trees. Instead, examine alternative dichotomous resolutions. Be especially careful with polytomous consensus trees.

Display of character tracing

Changing patterns or shades or colors

You can change the default branch shading patterns or shades of gray or colors of traced characters, or the shadings used in the Trace All Changes mode, by double-clicking on the appropriate state box in the character legend. A dialog box will appear that lets you select a new pattern or color for that state.

For traced characters of standard or extended format data files, you will notice that MacClade uses the same two colors or patterns for all 0–1 two-state characters (e.g., 0 = white and 1 = black). MacClade decides what shades to use by the character's maximum observed state. All characters with maximum state 2 (or symbol corresponding to state number 2; see p. 175) would have the same shades for states 0, 1, and 2. Thus, if you change the shades for one character, you will be simultaneously changing the shades for other characters.

To change the shadings for several states all at once, or to switch between patterns, colors, or grays, you can choose **Patterns** or **Patterns & Colors** from the **Display** menu. (A character must be traced or Trace All Changes must be shown before you can change the branch shading.) A dialog box similar to this will appear:

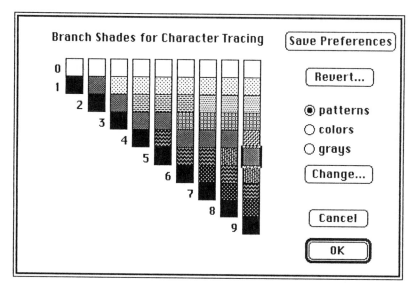

The first column on the left shows the patterns used for a character whose highest state is 1, the next column a character whose highest state is 2, and so on. To change a pattern, either select one of the squares in a column, and press **Change**, or simply double-click on the square. A dialog box will appear in which you select the new pattern for that square. If your Macintosh can display shades of gray, you can switch the shadings to various grays by choosing the grays radio button in the dialog box shown above. If your Macintosh can display color, you can switch the shadings to color by choosing the colors radio button. When you then ask to change a color, Apple's standard **Color Picker** dialog box will appear, allowing you to choose the color you prefer. Your chosen "palettes" can be saved to disk using the **Save Preferences** button.

N O T E : *Patterns used by MacClade are stored in the resource fork of MacClade (resource id 201 and 202). You can thus edit them using a resource editor such as Apple's ResEdit™.* **Do this on a back-up copy of MacClade, and only with caution.**

Labeling branches

You can, using the **Trace Labeling** dialog box in the **Display** menu, ask MacClade to write textual descriptions of the states at each branch in addition to the patterns and colors. If you wish, these textual descriptions can use full state names (as shown in the figure, left) or state symbols.

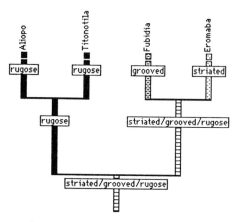

A traced character labeled with
full state names

Manipulating ancestral states

Manually assigning ancestral states ("fixing states") of a branch can be useful in a number of contexts. For example, you may want to see how much it would cost in number of steps to have an alternative state in a particular ancestor. It is also useful if the initial shading of the tree had equivocal areas (where more than one state could have been placed at a branch with equal parsimony). You can then see one of the reconstructions by fixing the branch to one of these equally parsimonious alternatives (for instance, the alternative least favorable to any evolutionary hypothesis you may be testing), after which MacClade will trace character evolution in the rest of the tree given this fixing.

For example, in a study of the constraints on the evolution of spider chromosomes, one of us (WPM) traced the evolution of the XXO and XXXY sex chromosome systems for a genus of jumping spiders on a tree provided by the work of Griswold (1987). On this tree, MacClade's tracing showed five or six independent derivations of the XXXY system. But two questions remained: How good is the evidence that there were independent derivations (instead of a single gain and multiple losses)? And, how much does this conclusion depend on the details of the tree? By fixing the states at branches, an alternative tracing on the same tree was made in which the XXXY was gained once and multiply lost. MacClade showed that this alternative was not supported, requiring seven more chromosome fusions than the one with multiple derivations. But, on another tree differing by only a few branch moves, the difference between the multiple-gain and multiple-loss hypotheses was reduced to only one fusion.

Fixing the state of a branch

Paintbrush tool

Initially, when MacClade traces a character on a tree, each branch will be shaded to indicate the states most parsimoniously placed on the branch. If there is more than one state that can be placed parsimoniously on the branch, then you can resolve the ambiguity by fixing the branch's state to one of these parsimonious states, and then examining character evolution with the ambiguity at that branch resolved. You can also examine alternative pathways of character evolution other than the most parsimonious, by fixing the state of a selected branch to any other desired state.

Fixing a state at a branch can be done in two ways: (1) by selecting the branch, and then dropping the diamond cursor over the top of one of the shaded boxes in the right-hand character legend, which indicate the shading used for a character state, or (2) by touching the paintbrush tool on a state in the character legend to fill the brush with that state, then touching those branches of the tree you wish to fix with that state. Any branch fixed is then forced to have that state regardless of what it costs in terms of number of steps. The surrounding branches will be reshaded as appropriate, and the number of the steps will be recalculated, given the fixing of the branch.

If character states are indicated by colors or shades of gray, then a "full" paintbrush will be the color of the state it contains; if character states are indicated by patterns, a full paintbrush will be black. An empty paintbrush is always white.

If any branch's state is fixed in the traced character, ✎ appears beside the message box in the lower-left side of the tree window. A small paintbrush appears beside each branch whose state is fixed (unless this has been turned off in the **Trace Labeling** dialog box available under the **Display** Menu).

WARNING: *Fixing the state at a branch affects only the character traced, and then only the tracing pictured on screen and one chart whose results are derived from it. The only chart that is affected by fixing states at branches is the chart of State Changes & Stasis that focuses only on the traced character on the current tree. All other charts, including the Character Steps/etc. and Treelength charts, ignore the fixing and use the original, unfixed reconstruction of the character's evolution. Trace All Changes, Trace All States, and search tools likewise use the original, unfixed reconstruction.*

WARNING: *If you fix the state of a terminal branch to a state other than that observed for its terminal taxon, you do not change the taxon's state in the data matrix. Rather, MacClade supposes that you are fixing the state of a just-subterminal node (see p. 244). Thus if the taxon had been observed to have state 1, and the terminal branch was fixed to state 0, one step would be counted to go from 0 to 1 in the terminal taxon, if the character was unordered. This convention differs from that in MacClade 2.1.*

WARNING: *For characters of some types, such as Dollo and irreversible, you can force the assumptions of the methods to be violated (for instance, you can fix state 1 at a branch below a clade with state 0 for an irreversible character). MacClade will not always give you a warning if you do this.*

EXAMPLE: *Open the file "Human mtDNA Fix States". The tree you see is among the most parsimonious based on the data on human mitochondrial DNA evolution of Cann et al. (1987); see D. Maddison (1991b) for details on the derivation of the tree. The right-most branch is labeled "all other individuals", and represents a clade of 121 individuals:*

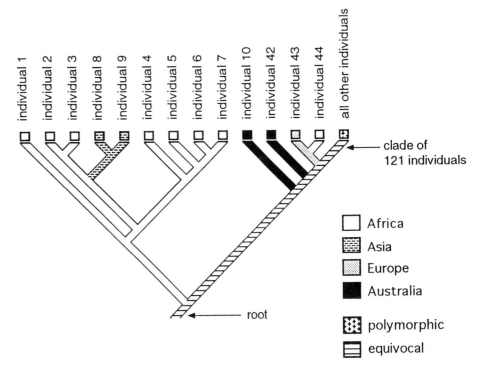

Move the cursor over the root branch, and note that question marks show up beside each geographic region in the character legend. This indicates that any of the five geographic regions is an equally parsimonious home of human mtDNA according to this tree. To show that this conclusion is independent of the ancestral state of the clade of 121 individuals, and thus independent of the relationships and states within the clade, you can use MacClade's paintbrush tool. First, fix the state of the branch labeled "all other females" to "Africa". Note that the root state is still fully equivocal. Now fix that branch to "Europe", then "Asia", and so on, each time noting that the root state is fully equivocal.

Examining the cost of alternative fixings of a branch

Try-all-fixes tool

If you wish to see quickly how the number of steps in the current character varies depending upon the state assigned to a particular branch, then hold down the Option key and click the paintbrush tool on the branch. Hold the mouse button down, and a small rectangle will appear, listing for each state the number of steps in the character if that branch were fixed to that state.

One can use this, for example, to see how much less parsimonious other assignments of ancestral state would be.

Unfix tool

Unfixing state of a branch

To unfix the state of a single branch, choose the unfix tool (the paint-brush under water, or turpentine) and touch the branch. To unfix states of *all* branches whose states have been fixed, choose **Unfix All** from the **Trace** menu, or double click on the unfix tool's icon in the palette, or hold down the Option key and double-click on the fixed branch icon (![fixed branch icon]) in the message box in the lower left (see p. 214).

The state of a fixed branch is unfixed automatically if another branch is moved onto it, or if a different character is traced, or if the character trace is turned off.

Seeing which branches are fixed

When labeling fixed branches is enabled using the **Trace Labeling** dialog box in the **Display** menu, MacClade will place the end of a paint-brush (![paintbrush]) beside branches whose states have been fixed. You can also see which branches have their character states fixed by touching on the fixed branch icon (![fixed branch icon]) in the message box. Those branches whose states have been fixed will be highlighted.

Resolving equivocal tracings

MacClade's default is to indicate *all* states that can be most parsimoniously assigned to a branch. Often there are several equally parsimonious assignments, thus yielding ambiguity. This is indicated in MacClade by the presence of some branches shaded with a horizontally striped pattern, called the equivocal pattern. For the unordered character shown traced onto the tree below, there are four branches shaded with the equivocal pattern:

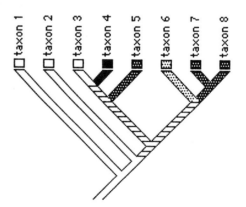

As noted in Chapter 5, there are six equally parsimonious ways to resolve this ambiguity; that is, there are six resolved reconstructions of character evolution for this example. You can ask MacClade how many parsimonious reconstructions there are by holding down the Option key and choosing **Number of Reconstructions** from the **Trace** menu, or by choosing **Number of Reconstructions** from the **Equivocal** menu in Equivocal Cycling mode (p. 252). If there are many reconstructions, it may take a while for MacClade to calculate the number; you can cancel the calculation by typing Command-period (⌘-.).

EXAMPLE: *The character presented in the file "Many Equivocal Reconstructions" has over 20,600,000,000 reconstructions on the tree!*

Several methods can be used to discover and explore these alternative reconstructions.

Using the paintbrush

The paintbrush can be used as described above to fix the state at an equivocal branch to one of the equally parsimonious assignments to that branch. The ambiguity at that branch will then be resolved, and MacClade will retrace the character assuming that the state at this branch is as fixed. Any other branches remaining equivocal can also have their states similarly fixed. In this way you can by hand obtain one of the most-parsimonious reconstructions of character evolution with no ambiguities. While such a method may make you intimately familiar with the alternatives, it can also be tedious. MacClade therefore has some features that resolve ambiguity automatically.

Reversals and parallelisms: ACCTRAN and DELTRAN

For characters of unordered and ordered type, MacClade can automatically resolve ambiguities in character tracings so as to choose the assignments that delay (DELTRAN) or accelerate (ACCTRAN) transformations (see Swofford and Maddison, 1987). ACCTRAN and DELTRAN are described, with warnings about their use, in Chapter 5.

MacClade will show you the ACCTRAN or DELTRAN reconstructions if you select these options in the **Resolving Options** dialog box available in the **Trace** menu. ACCTRAN and DELTRAN apply only to the character tracing shown on the screen and anything derived from it. These options do not apply to the Trace All Changes and Trace All States displays, nor to most of the other reconstructions of changes in the charts.

WARNING: *ACCTRAN and DELTRAN apply only to the character traced, and then only to the tracing pictured on screen and one chart whose results are derived from it. The only chart affected by ACCTRAN and DELTRAN is the chart of State Changes & Stasis that focuses only on the traced character on the current tree. All other charts and Trace All Changes and Trace All States ignore the ACCTRAN/*

DELTRAN *option. Apart from the tracing of a character on the tree on screen, ACCTRAN/DELTRAN does apply in the one other context in which single characters are graphically traced on trees: in printing. Thus for instance, when the Print All Characters option is selected under Print Tree, the ACCTRAN/DELTRAN option applies to all of the characters' tracings.*

Equivocal Cycling: All alternative reconstructions of character evolution

For characters of all transformation types MacClade can display, one after another, all equally parsimonious reconstructions of the ambiguity in the character tracing. This is accomplished with the **Equivocal Cycling** command, in the **Trace** menu. When this command is invoked, MacClade will give one of the possible reconstructions of the ancestral states of the character traced; then the user can step through the other reconstructions using the **Next Reconstruction** command in the **Equivocal** menu. Equivocal Cycling does respect the fixing of states at branches, and so you can ask, "What are all the parsimonious reconstructions of ancestral states given that these branches are fixed to have these states?" It should be noted that Equivocal Cycling is invoked automatically in calculations for some of the charting and **Trace All Changes** functions. Whenever you see the cursor of the Ediacaran organism *Tribrachidium* (⟨⟩), Equivocal Cycling is taking place.

While Equivocal Cycling is active on the traced character, most of MacClade's menus disappear and the other windows become inactive. Equivocal Cycling is therefore like a locked mode. You cannot access most of MacClade's features until you turn it off, or until Equivocal Cycling goes past the last reconstruction.

WARNING: *This cycling feature can be used only with dichotomous trees without observed taxa fixed as ancestors. It cannot be used if ACCTRAN or DELTRAN options are in effect. It cannot be used on stratigraphic characters.*

MacClade, in cycling through reconstructions, always follows a consistent order. It first sets the root state to the state with the lowest state number among those that are parsimonious at the root. For information about state numbers, see p. 175. It then sets the nodes higher in the tree sequentially to the lowest most-parsimonious state given what has already been set lower down in the tree. This yields the first reconstruction. Subsequent reconstructions are found by incrementing the states assigned to nodes, somewhat like counting, so that the terminal nodes are like the 1's digits and change most quickly, while the lower nodes are like the thousand's or million's digits, which change most slowly. All the while MacClade makes sure that only parsimonious reconstructions are allowed.

To go to a particular reconstruction, use **Go to** in the **Equivocal** menu. (The **Equivocal** menu appears only after you have chosen **Equivocal Cycling** from the **Trace** menu.) If you ask to go to the 200th reconstruction and there are only 50 reconstructions, MacClade will show you the 50th reconstruction.

When a clade is expanded to fill the screen using the magnifying-glass tool, Equivocal Cycling used on the character tracing on screen does not go through all character reconstructions over the whole tree. Instead, it leaves intact ambiguity in the character reconstruction below the clade, and examines alternative reconstructions only within the clade. For this reason, you may find that MacClade indicates that there are numerous different reconstructions in a character when the whole tree is shown, but when a clade is expanded, MacClade may indicate there are only a few reconstructions.

To turn off cycling, choose **Cycling Off** from the **Equivocal** menu. Cycling will automatically be turned off after the last reconstruction.

All equally parsimonious reconstructions can be printed in sequence using the **Print Tree** dialog box, if the **Print All Reconstructions** menu item of the **Options** pop-up menu is checked.

Character Data Boxes

You can get a graphical overview of the data matrix by selecting **Data Boxes** from the **Display** menu; reselect the **Data Boxes** menu item to remove the boxes. The Data Boxes look something like this:

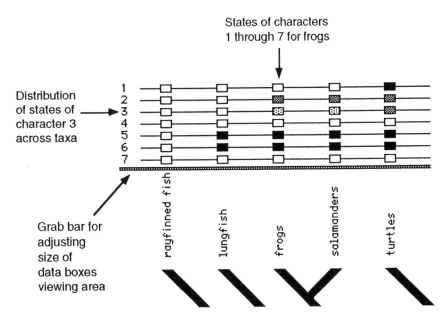

You can scroll through the Data Boxes using the scroll bar on the right.

In order to get an overview of more than the default number of characters, you can expand the Data Boxes area. Do this by placing the cursor over the grab bar at the bottom of the Data Boxes; when the cursor changes to ✛ , drag the bar down. You can also shrink the Data Boxes section by dragging the bar up.

Data Boxes can be printed from the **Print Other** submenu (in which case the order of taxa will match that in the data matrix) or the **Print Tree** dialog box (in which case the order of taxa will match that in the current tree). See Chapter 20 for details.

Summary of all changes on branches: Trace All Changes

MacClade has two methods for making a summary over all characters of the reconstructed changes in the tree: the **Trace All Changes** display on the tree, and the charting of **State Changes & Stasis** in the Chart menu. State Changes & Stasis shows the number of state i to state j changes in a table or bubble chart to give an indication of the relative frequency of various reconstructed changes, and is described in Chapter 15.

To activate **Trace All Changes**, choose that menu item from the **Trace** menu. Trace All Changes shows the number of characters changing on each branch or the amount of the tree's length on each branch (depending on whether changes are weighted or not). It can also show which characters are reconstructed as changing along each branch. It displays the results by shading the branches of the tree, listing the branches' lengths, or putting tick marks across them.

For a discussion of the relationship between the number of changes reconstructed on a branch and the evidential support for the clade above the branch, see pp. 258–259.

Stratigraphic characters are excluded from the calculations of Trace All Changes.

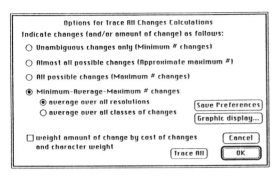

Options for Trace All Changes calculations

The **All Changes Options** dialog box (in the **Trace** menu) allows you to select options in the calculations of Trace All Changes. Two decisions must be made by the user: (1) how ambiguity in changes is to be dealt with (main four radio buttons in the upper part of dialog box), and (2) whether the amount of change is to be weighted or not (choice at bottom).

Dealing with ambiguity If several states may be placed with equally parsimony at a node, then whether a change is placed on the branch between this node and its ancestor may depend upon which of the alternative states is assigned to the node (see Chapter 5). Because ambiguity in the reconstruction yields ambiguity in changes, the **All Changes Options** dialog box gives four choices:

1. Show unambiguous changes only. An unambiguous change is counted as occurring on a branch if the sets of states reconstructed at a node and its ancestor do not overlap at all, because then there must be a change on the intervening branch regardless of which parsimonious states are assigned to these nodes. (Note: This option indicates a change whenever it is unambiguous that some change occurs, but it may be ambiguous as to exactly what change occurs; the "unambiguous changes" option of the State Changes & Stasis chart is different, since that indicates a change only when it is unambiguous as to exactly what change occurs.)

2. Show almost all possible changes (most ambiguous and unambiguous). This option counts a change if the state sets of a node and its ancestor are not identical. If the state sets are not identical, then there exists at least one parsimonious reconstruction in which a change occurs on the branch. This criterion will detect most but not all instances in which parsimony allows a change on the branch.

   Even when descendant and ancestor state sets are identical, there may exist a reconstruction placing a change on the branch between them. To discover these cases you need to use the third option.

3. Show the maximum amount of change allowed by parsimony. This choice finds all instances in which parsimony allows a change on the branch. If there exists a parsimonious reconstruction that places a change on the branch, MacClade will count a change.

4. Show minimum, average, and maximum amount of change allowed by parsimony. This option considers both unambiguous changes and all possible changes to calculate the minimum and maximum amounts, and at the same time calculates the average amount of change as measured over the various possible reconstructions. There are two options regarding averages: average over all reconstruc-

tions, and average over all classes of changes. These two options are discussed in Chapter 5. How the minimum, average, and maximum are displayed is discussed below under "How changes are indicated".

More information on how these calculations are done can be found in Chapter 5. The third and fourth options cannot be used if there are polytomies or other factors that prohibit Equivocal Cycling. (MacClade often has to use Equivocal Cycling to calculate maximum amount of change on each branch.)

Weighted changes By default, the total amount of change indicated on a branch by Trace All Changes is unweighted, and is simply the number of changes on the branch. One change is counted for each character that shows some change, from the node at the beginning of the branch, to the node at the end of the branch, regardless of the type of change or the character's weight. In contrast, if "weight amount of change..." in the **All Changes Options** dialog box is checked, then the amount is weighted by both the character's weight and by the cost of the change reconstructed according to the character's transformation type. Thus, a change from state 0 to 3 in an ordered character of weight 5 would add 15 to the amount of change on the branch. When the unambiguous changes option is selected, the minimum weighted amount of change is indicated. Weighting is not allowed when the second option above is selected ("Almost all possible changes").

How changes are indicated

The manner in which MacClade displays changes on the branches can be controlled by the **Trace Labeling** dialog box in the **Display** menu.

There are four ways that MacClade can show the changes on a branch.

First, the amount of change can be indicated by shading the branches, with the pattern or color indicating the number of changes (the option "Shade by amount of change"). You can change the patterns and colors used to shade the summary tree, using the same techniques as for changing the patterns and colors used to trace character evolution, as described above (p. 245). When the minimum-average-maximum option is selected in the **All Changes Options** dialog box, the shading indicates the average.

Second, the amount of change can be indicated directly by a numbered box (the option "Label by amount of change"). If minimum, average, and maximum changes are being shown, then all three of these will be written into the box:

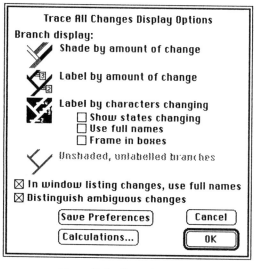

Trace Labeling dialog box

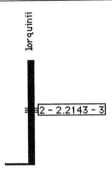

Third, the individual changes can be displayed directly on the tree by placing tick marks across the branches, one tick mark for each change, with the number of the character changing listed beside the tick (the option "Label by character changing"). You have the option of asking MacClade to write only the character number, or the character number plus the states changing:

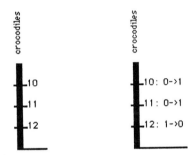

If you so request, MacClade will write the full names:

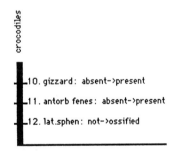

or draw a rectangle around the text. If you have selected "distinguish ambiguous changes", then any ambiguous changes will be italicized, or shown in green (if your screen is displaying color), or shown in gray (if your screen is displaying gray scales):

If you use tick marks, you may wish to adjust the shape and size of the tree, using the **Tree Shape & Size** dialog box in the **Display** menu, so that the markings on the branches are easier to see.

Fourth, you may request that the branches remain black and unlabeled. This option is available only from the **Print Tree** dialog box, and is intended for trees that are drawn with branch lengths proportional to the number of changes.

MacClade 3 does not differentially mark unique, parallel, and reverse changes as does CLADOS (Nixon, 1992).

Lists of changes occurring on branch

When Trace All Changes is in use, a more detailed indication of what changes are reconstructed on a branch can be obtained by using the branch-information tool, and clicking on the branch of interest. A small, scrollable summary window will then appear, listing the changes that occur along that branch.

Branch-information tool

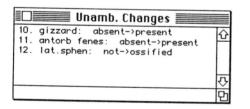

Summary window listing changes on a branch

Using the **Trace Labeling** dialog box in the **Display** menu, you can control whether full state names or state symbols are used in this window. If you are using one of the options to trace almost all possible, all possible, or minimum-average-maximum, and have asked MacClade to distinguish ambiguous changes, all ambiguous changes (i.e., all those other than the unambiguous changes) will be shown in parentheses.

If you double-click on a line in the list window, Trace All Changes will be turned off and the corresponding character will be traced on the tree.

A listing of the changes on all branches can be printed or saved to a text file using **Branch Lists** in the **Print Other** or **Save Text File** submenus. See Chapter 20 for details.

Is the number of changes indicative of support for a clade?

Even though the changes along a branch listed under the unambiguous changes option can often be considered apomorphies unambiguously supporting the clade above the branch, this is not always a good interpretation. For instance, if the character subsequently reverses in one taxon within the clade, it would be inappropriate to claim that the character supports the monophyly of the clade, except in the context of other characters that place the reversing taxon within the clade. Likewise, a tree with many unambiguous changes is not necessarily a good tree, for some of the unequivocal character state changes that occur on the tree might be avoided by a shorter tree. Thus whether or not a character changing on a branch gives support to the clade above the branch may depend upon the context of other characters.

If you want to know the support for a clade, it is more reasonable to compare the length of the shortest trees with that clade and without that clade (Bremer, 1988; Miyamoto and Boyle, 1989; Hillis and Dixon, 1989; Donoghue et al., 1992), or to use bootstrapping (Felsenstein, 1985c; Sanderson, 1989; Swofford and Olsen, 1990).

Problems with soft polytomies

When a tree has soft polytomies, Trace All Changes does not attempt to calculate changes occurring on the branches of a polytomy. Because the changes that would be calculated on these branches depend upon how the soft polytomy might be resolved, it is difficult to decide where to place changes upon them (Chapter 5, p. 114). These branches are shaded with an equivocal pattern, and a warning is given to the user that MacClade did not attempt to calculate changes on these branches.

Problems near the root

The root of the whole tree will never have changes indicated on it. A change on the root branch could be discovered only by assuming something about states in ancestral lineages below the root, or about the states in related groups. MacClade works with the states observed in taxa included in the data matrix, and does not assume anything about more distant relatives or ancestral states. MacClade, for instance, does not use ANCSTATES as does PAUP. MacClade assumes nothing about what is below the root, and thus will not indicate changes on the root branch.

The right and left branches descendant from the root cannot have unambiguous changes except in characters that are irreversible (or have step matrices that are asymmetrical or violate the triangle inequality). In most characters, if the two nodes descendant from the root node are reconstructed as having different states, then the root will be equivocal and it will be ambiguous as to whether the change occurred on the left or right side. For instance, if the right descendant branch of the root is reconstructed to have state 1, while the left branch has state 0:

then there is ambiguity as to whether the root had 0 changing to 1 up the right side or the root had 1 changing to 0 up the left side:

On the other hand, if the two nodes descendant from the root have the same state, then the root will share this state and no changes are required.

Even when no changes are indicated by Trace All Changes as occurring on the two branches descendant from the root, you might be interested in knowing how these two branches differ. The branch-information tool, when applied to either of these two branches, will list those characters in which there is an unambiguous or ambiguous difference between these branches.

Branch lengths

There is currently one statistic calculated by MacClade that might be considered a measure of branch length (see p. 54): the amount of change reconstructed on a branch by Trace All Changes. (MacClade does not yet allow users to specify their own branch lengths, except in the special context of Evolve Characters, p. 320.) It is important that you understand the ambiguity and problems involved in interpreting this reconstructed amount as a branch length.

First, there may be several equally parsimonious reconstructions of character evolution, some of which place a change on a branch, others of which don't. The options in Trace All Changes can be used to indicate the minimum and maximum amount of change allowed by parsimony on a branch.

Second, MacClade does not indicate any length on certain branches because of lack of information or calculation difficulties. Changes on the two branches coming off of the root of the tree are often shown with zero branch length, even when the two clades differ in the characters. This is a simple consequence of the ambiguity of where changes occur, and is

READ THIS BEFORE OPENING THIS PACKAGE

MacCLADE 3 LICENSE AGREEMENT

Sinauer Associates
108 North Main Street
Sunderland, MA 01375
Telephone (413) 665-3722
FAX (413) 665-7292

discussed under "Problems near the root", above. Zero branch length is also always indicated on any branch arising from a soft polytomy (discussed under "Problems with soft polytomies", above). Although many users may be disappointed with this, they should realize there is no simple solution to this problem. See Chapter 5 for more explanation of the difficulties in reconstructing changes with soft polytomies.

Third, the true amount of change that actually occurred on a branch may be different from that reconstructed. See Chapters 4 and 5 regarding error and confidence.

Fourth, the true amount of change may not itself be an accurate estimate of the length of time a branch existed.

Display and printing of branch lengths

The amount of change reconstructed on each branch can be displayed in the tree window as discussed in the preceding sections. There is also a special printing feature that prints trees with their branches having lengths proportional to the amount of reconstructed change. See Chapter 20 for a description of this feature.

Summary of all states along each branch

Choosing **Trace All States** from the **Trace** menu will cause MacClade to reconstruct ancestral states of all included characters. The results are visible by clicking on a branch of interest using the branch-information tool ( ). This brings up a scrollable summary window, listing the states reconstructed at the node at the top of the branch. There are two options, available under **All State Options**: first, the states of each character can be listed, one character after another; or second, the frequency of each state (0, 1, 2, or A, C, G, T, etc.) over all included characters at that branch can be listed. The latter is perhaps most useful for molecular data in which states are comparable between characters. When the reconstruction is equivocal for a character at a branch, then the frequency listing reflects this by showing the minimum and maximum frequencies allowed by the ambiguity. For stratigraphic characters, MacClade treats the state as equivocal whenever multiple states are placed at a node, even if they are placed there as a result of an observed polymorphic taxon fixed in ancestral position.

Confirming the validity of the parsimony algorithms

In programming MacClade, the proper functioning of the discrete-character parsimony algorithms was tested as follows.

— The source code was thoroughly checked and rechecked.

— Both ancestral state reconstructions and counts of treelength were examined by eye in a number of test data files, and also cross-checked against results from MacClade 2.1 and PAUP 3.0.

— In test versions and in the released version of MacClade 3, traced characters are checked to see that none of the final sets are empty, nor that they contain illegal values that should be cleared in the final sets. Faulty algorithms could express their errors by generating empty sets or adding illegal values.

— In test versions, a thorough consistency check was used that moved through all characters, comparing the calculated number of steps in the character with the number of steps recalculated as follows. If the tree had no polytomies nor observed taxa designated as ancestors, then Equivocal Cycling was used to make all most-parsimonious reconstructions, in each counting the number of steps and comparing to the number calculated with MacClade's usual step counting algorithms. This consistency check not only detects faulty reconstructions of character evolution, but also checks the Equivocal Cycling routines. If the tree had polytomies or observed ancestors, then the states at nodes were fixed successively from the root toward the tips to generate various reconstructions of ancestral states. First, the lowest-valued states allowed were fixed, and the number of steps in the resulting reconstruction compared with that previously calculated. Second, the highest-valued states were fixed, and the number of steps compared with the previous. This consistency check can detect faulty reconstructions, and also tests the algorithms dealing with the fixing of states at nodes (paintbrush tool) and how they interact with polytomies and observed ancestors.

— In test versions, a consistency check was incorporated that compared MacClade's two separate sections of code used in reconstructing characters (one in Pascal for the traced characters, the other in assembly language for Trace All Changes) whenever an unordered, ordered, or irreversible character was traced.

14. BASIC TREE AND CHARACTER STATISTICS

SUMMARY OF FEATURES: *Statistics related to the number of steps required in characters by the tree can be displayed in the tree legend and the character status window. These include the treelength, the number of changes, the consistency index, the retention index, and the rescaled consistency index. The minimum and maximum numbers of steps and treelength for the characters under any conceivable tree, used in the calculations of these indices, can also be displayed. The Σ menu is used to control the calculation of these statistics.*

Display of statistics

▦ Smith's Tree ▦ 🔒
Treelength: **653**
C.I.: 0.50
R.I.: 0.64
53 Taxa
85 Chars.

Tree legend displaying
treelength, CI, and RI

The most-parsimonious reconstructions of ancestral states imply a minimum number of steps in each character for the current tree. This minimum number of steps is one of the basic statistics used by many phylogenetic systematists as a measure of the fit between the character and the tree. By standardizing this number of steps in various ways, various indices like the consistency index can be obtained. By summing the number of steps over all characters, perhaps using weights as well, the **treelength** is obtained.

Those statistics that apply to the current tree as a whole (e.g., treelength, ensemble consistency index and retention index) are displayed in the tree legend. Those statistics that apply to each character can be displayed in various charts (p. 279) and seen in the character status window (available in the **Display** menu). In the following figure, note the columns for steps, CI, and RI.

	Character ▾	Type ▾	Weight ▾	States	Steps	CI	RI
☑	1. silver spots	ordered	1	2	1	1.00	1.00
☑	2. interval 3 micro.	ordered	1	4	10	0.40	0.89
☑	3. interval 4+5 micro.	ordered	1	4	20	0.70	0.87
☑	4. interval 6+7 micro.	ordered	1	4	14	0.79	0.86
☑	5. outer mirror	ordered	1	2	3	1.00	0.0
☑	6. silver spot	ordered	1	2	8	1.00	1.00
☑	7. elytral microsculpture	ordered	1	3	20	0.40	0.54
☑	8. suborbital setae	ordered	1	3	27	0.56	0.64
☑	9. midlat. pron. seta	ordered	1	2	11	0.36	0.46
☑	10. ed3 + ed5 + 3rd	ordered	1	2	5	0.80	0.95
☑	11. ed3 + ed5 pos.	ordered	1	2	9	0.89	0.0
☑	12. # eo4 – eo5 setae	ordered	1	4	7	0.43	0.33
☑	13. ed7 setae	ordered	1	2	1	1.00	0.0
☑	14. male adhes. setae	ordered	1	2	2	0.50	0.0
☑	15. protars. 4 setae	ordered	1	2	4	0.25	0.57

Character Status

263

Number of steps

The number of steps required for each character is shown in the legend of the character traced, as described in Chapter 13, and in the character status window. The number of steps in a character is the summed cost of all changes in a most-parsimonious reconstruction (Chapter 4). For character i, the number of steps, s_i, can be calculated by the following formula.

$$s_i = \sum_{j,k} c_{jki} n_{jki}$$

where c_{jki} is the cost of a change from states j to k in character i, and n_{jki} is the number of j to k changes on the tree in a most-parsimonious reconstruction of ancestral states for character i. If there are multiple equally parsimonious reconstructions, then any one could be used for the formula above, for if they are equally parsimonious they must give the same sum. (Compare the number of steps to number of changes, discussed below.) See Chapter 5 for descriptions of the algorithms used to count steps.

NOTE: *"Steps" may not be an entirely appropriate term to use, since the number of steps as defined above could be a number like 1.6 (two changes each with costs 0.8 according to the character's step-matrix transformation type), in apparent contradiction to the implication of "step" as a discrete change. The term "step" is a remnant from older computer programs in which it was more appropriate.*

The number of steps in each character is shown both in the character status window when treelength counting is turned on and in the Trace Character legend.

When terminal taxa are polymorphic, MacClade counts implicit changes within these terminal taxa. Thus for instance, suppose a terminal taxon has states 2 and 5 in an ordered character and MacClade reconstructs state 1 to be at the branch immediately ancestral to the terminal branch. MacClade would then count 1 step from state 1 to 2 along the terminal branch, then 3 steps from state 2 to 5 within the terminal taxon itself. Because MacClade does not have algorithms directly allowing ancestral polymorphisms in branches below the terminal taxa, the immediate ancestor is presumed to have a single state, and thus the diversity of states within the terminal taxon is evolved within the terminal taxon (see Chapter 5). MacClade assumes the most-parsimonious path of evolution possible within the terminal taxon. Because it is difficult to determine the most-parsimonious path when the taxon has three or more states in a character of user-defined type, the number of steps counted may be underestimated. The reason is that MacClade uses only the smallest distance between two observed states as an indication of the length within the taxon (as discussed in Chapter 5). In this case MacClade gives an error message, and puts an asterisk (*) beside the number of steps in the character status window to warn the user.

Treelength

The total treelength is calculated as the sum of the number of steps for the individual characters multiplied by their respective weights.

$$Treelength = \sum_{i=1}^{n} w_i \, s_i$$

It includes steps that must have occurred within polymorphic terminal taxa, except occasionally for characters of a user-defined type. For characters of user-defined types, changes within terminal taxa polymorphic for more than two states may not be counted accurately (see Chapter 5); in this case the treelength will be underestimated and MacClade will put a "+" in the treelength box to indicate that the actual treelength is higher than the number given. Similarly, treelength will be marked by a "+" if polytomies are in the tree and the soft polytomies option is chosen, for under this option the treelength listed will likely be an underestimate of the minimum possible treelength for any fully dichotomous resolution of the tree (Chapter 5).

To turn treelength counting off or on, choose **Treelength** in the Σ menu. Turning off the count is useful with large data sets when you want to make a lot of branch rearrangements and don't need to know treelength until you're done. Having the tree counted between each branch move can slow things down, especially if there are user-defined or Dollo characters.

WARNING: *Users moving between PAUP and MacClade may notice situations in which PAUP gives a different treelength. See Appendix 2 for details.*

Polytomies and treelengths

Uncertain-resolution ("soft") polytomies pose particularly difficult problems for calculating treelength as noted by W. Maddison (1989). See Chapter 5 for a discussion of the difficulties of calculating treelength with soft polytomies.

Number of changes

The number of changes required for a character differs from its number of steps in that the former is not weighted by the costs of the reconstructed changes. The number of changes for the different characters can be displayed in the Character Steps/etc. chart, or summed for all characters and shown as the Tree Changes (see below). The number of changes in each character is shown in the character status window when tree changes counting is turned on.

In a most-parsimonious reconstruction of character evolution, a change is required whenever a node has a different state from its immediate ancestor. The number of changes in a character on the tree is counted by MacClade as the number of instances in which a change is reconstructed as occurring on a branch. Implicit multiple changes within a branch are not counted separately. As noted in Chapter 5, if there is ambiguity in the tracing of character evolution, such that an equivocal assignment is given to some branches, then the alternative reconstruction of character evolution may have different numbers of changes (p. 113). Therefore MacClade may sometimes indicate a range of changes, for instance "5-7 changes". Changes within polymorphic terminal taxa are *not* counted (recall that their costs are counted into the number of steps). Because calculation of changes uses Equivocal Cycling, MacClade cannot calculate the number of changes with polytomous trees or trees that have observed taxa fixed as ancestors (p. 252).

Tree changes

A statistic related to treelength is the number of changes in the tree. It is the unweighted sum of the number of changes in all the characters. The number of changes differs from the treelength in that it is not weighted either by the cost of each change, nor by the weights of the characters. It can be requested by checking the **Tree Changes** item in the Σ menu. The results are presented in the tree legend. The calculations can be time consuming; the *Tribrachidium* cursor is shown spinning while they are being done. The calculations can be canceled by Command-period (⌘-.).

As noted above, the number of changes in a character may differ with alternative reconstructions of character evolution. MacClade sums all the minima, and all the maxima, for the various characters, and displays a minimum and maximum total value for tree changes (e.g., "95–102 changes"). Changes within polymorphic terminal taxa are *not* counted. Recall that their steps *are* counted in the treelength. If there are polymorphic terminal taxa, then MacClade puts a "*" beside the number of changes to indicate that changes were not counted within terminal polymorphisms. Because calculation of tree changes uses Equivocal Cycling, MacClade cannot calculate the tree changes for polytomous trees or trees that have observed taxa fixed as ancestors.

One context in which tree changes may be useful is to deal with missing characters, as suggested by W. Maddison (in press). If you had a character with states tail red, tail blue, tail absent, you might want to reconstruct character evolution first considering gains and losses of tails, then secondarily considering changes in tail color within those parts of the tree reconstructed as having tails. To do this, a step matrix could be created that counted one step for a change in tail color from red to blue or vice versa, but then 100 steps for a gain or loss of a tail (change from absent to red or blue, or vice versa). This would reconstruct character evolution as desired, but would count 100 steps for the gain or loss of a tail. If you wanted to give tail gain/loss primacy over tail color, but wanted all the changes to count equally, you could use tree changes instead of treelength (see W. Maddison, in press).

Minimum and maximum possible steps

You can ask MacClade to show the minimum and maximum conceivable number of steps in each character and the sum over all characters, by choosing the **Minimum Possible** or **Maximum Possible** items in the Σ menu. The values for the sum over all characters are displayed in the tree legend; those for individual characters are displayed in the character status window (obtainable in the **Display** menu).

The minimum conceivable number of steps in a character is the smallest number of steps that could be obtained in the character were the best tree found for that character by rearranging the terminal taxa. Thus if four taxa have states 0, 0, 1, and 1 for an unordered or ordered character, the fewest number of steps would be 1, by grouping the two taxa with 1's together. In calculating the minimum conceivable number of steps, polymorphic terminal taxa are not allowed to split up to avoid steps within the terminal taxa. That is, if one taxon has states 0 and 1, and the remaining three taxa have states 0, 1, and 1, then the smallest number of steps would be 2, because one step is required within the polymorphic terminal taxon and one in the remainder of the tree. Minimum number of steps are not calculated for characters of stratigraphic, Dollo, or user-defined types.

The number reported in the tree legend for the total minimum number of steps is the sum over all characters. This does *not* mean that there exists a tree with this number of steps that could be obtained by rearranging the branches, for the rearrangement required to yield the minimum for one character might not be the same as the minimum required for another character.

The maximum conceivable number of steps is the largest number of steps that could be obtained in the character were the worst tree found for that character by rearranging the terminal taxa. Thus, if four taxa have states 0, 0, 1, and 1 for an unordered or ordered character, the largest number of steps would be 2. Polymorphic terminal taxa are held intact, so that if one taxon has states 0 and 1, and the remaining five taxa have states 0, 0, 0, 1, and 1, then the largest number of steps would be 3. Maximum number of steps are not calculated for characters of irreversible, stratigraphic, Dollo, and user-defined types. As with the total minimum, the total maximum number of steps reported in the tree legend does not imply that there exists a tree with that number of steps.

Calculation of minimum and maximum steps

For unordered and ordered characters, MacClade uses its "soft" polytomy calculations (Chapter 5) to obtain the minimum number of steps conceivable for a character, by measuring the number of steps in the character in a tree that is an entirely unresolved bush. Irreversible characters are done using the soft polytomy calculations for ordered characters, since the smallest maximum to the largest minimum among the terminal node downpass sets is the minimum conceivable length for irreversible characters as well.

The maximum number of steps was defined above as the number of steps on the tree requiring the most steps for the character. A tree that is a hard polytomous bush is the least-parsimonious tree conceivable. On that basis, one could argue that it is appropriate to use the number of steps on a hard polytomous bush as the maximum conceivable number of steps for a character. In fact, MacClade uses the hard polytomy calculations to obtain the maximum number of steps conceivable for unordered and ordered characters. However, one might prefer to use as a standard the least-parsimonious *dichotomous* tree for the character. The distinction may be unimportant, for it is apparently the case that the least-parsimonious dichotomous tree for a given character has the same number of steps as a hard polytomous bush. This can be proven for ordered characters, as follows. Suppose we have 9 taxa named A through H, with observed state ranges diagrammed as follows (lower values to left, higher to right):

$$
\begin{array}{cccccc}
 & B & D & & F & \\
\hline
A & C & E & G & H
\end{array}
$$

A least-parsimonious dichotomous tree can be constructed that takes first the two terminals with most distant state sets, and places them as sister species. Then among the remaining terminals, choose the two most distant, and so on. Continue to make pairs until none or one terminal remains. We now have the taxa paired:

A H   B G   C F   D E
∨   ∨   ∨   ∨

These pairs of taxa can be joined together into a full tree in any way:

As one does a downpass (Chapter 5) on this tree for this character, all of the steps in the tree will be counted within these sister pairs, as (for each pair) the state set of one terminal taxon of the pair is combined with the state set of the other terminal taxon to yield the state set at their immediate common ancestor. The number of steps so counted will be the exact same as in a full hard polytomous bush. (Recall that these statements concern one character; this procedure does not necessarily yield the dichtomous tree that has the greatest treelength over all characters.) For unordered characters, we have no proof, but with many examples we have been able to find a dichotomous tree requiring as many steps as the hard bush, and we suspect that there will always exist one.

MacClade does not have algorithms for the minimum conceivable numbers of steps for stratigraphic, Dollo, and user-defined characters, nor for the maximum for irreversible, stratigraphic, Dollo, and user-defined characters. For characters of user-defined types, the minimum and maximum conceivable number of steps is in general very difficult to calculate. For this reason the consistency index is given only for unordered, ordered, irreversible, and stratigraphic characters, while the retention index and rescaled consistency index are given only for unordered and ordered characters.

Early versions of PAUP 3.0 calculated the minimum conceivable number of steps differently from MacClade. See Appendix 2 for details.

Consistency and retention indices

MacClade will calculate the consistency index (Kluge and Farris, 1969; Farris, 1989), retention index (Archie, 1989a,b [HERM]; Farris, 1989), and the rescaled consistency index (Farris, 1989) for the tree as a whole and for the characters individually. Calculations for these indices are requested in the Σ menu. The indices for the tree are displayed in the tree legend; those for individual characters are displayed in the character status window.

Character consistency and retention indices

The consistency index (CI) for each character i is calculated as:

$$\text{Character CI} = \frac{m_i}{s_i}$$

The retention index (RI) for each character i is calculated as:

$$\text{Character RI} = \frac{M_i - m_i}{M_i - s_i}$$

The rescaled consistency index (RC) for each character is calculated as:

$$\text{Character RC} = (\text{character CI}) \bullet (\text{character RI})$$

where m_i is the minimum conceivable number of steps for character i on any tree, M_i is the maximum conceivable number of steps, and s_i is the number of reconstructed steps for character i on the particular tree in question (for instance, that on the screen). Thus the CI would be 1 if the character had no homoplasy, 0.5 if there were twice as many steps as needed, and so on. By convention MacClade indicates an index of 0 if both the numerator and denominator are 0 (e.g., for invariant characters, the CI is 0/0).

Ensemble consistency and retention Indices

The CI, RI, or RC of a collection of characters is an ensemble index (Farris, 1989). MacClade calculates ensemble indices over all included characters, and presents this in the tree legend as the CI, RI, or RC of the tree. MacClade also calculates ensemble indices in the chart window, whenever the index for a collection of two or more characters is requested.

The consistency index CI for all characters on a tree is the minimum possible treelength divided by the observed treelength. To be exact, it is the weighted sum of the minimum conceivable number of evolutionary steps for each character of the n characters divided by the weighted sum of the observed number of steps for each character:

$$\text{Tree} \;\; CI = \frac{\displaystyle\sum_{i=1}^{n} w_i m_i}{\displaystyle\sum_{i=1}^{n} w_i s_i}$$

where w_i is the weight applied to character i. Characters of stratigraphic, Dollo, or user-defined type and invariant characters are not included in the CI. If the characters in the data set are perfectly congruent with each other and the tree, and thus there is no homoplasy, then the observed number of steps will equal the minimum, and the CI will be 1.00. The messier the data on the tree, and the greater the amount of homoplasy, the greater is the observed number of steps, and the more CI shrinks. CI lies between 0 and 1. MacClade does not remove the contribution of autapomorphies of terminal taxa from the overall CI. It is the responsibility of the user to avoid inflating the CI with autapomorphies. If you want to remove uninformative characters from the consistency index, use **Exclude Uninformative** (pp. 199–200).

The retention index RI for all characters on a tree is calculated as the (maximum possible treelength – actual treelength)/(maximum possible treelength – minimum possible treelength). To be specific:

$$Tree \ \ RI = \frac{\sum\limits_{i=1}^{n} w_i M_i - \sum\limits_{i=1}^{n} w_i s_i}{\sum\limits_{i=1}^{n} w_i M_i - \sum\limits_{i=1}^{n} w_i m_i}$$

Characters of irreversible, stratigraphic, Dollo, or user-defined type and invariant characters are not included in the RI. If the characters in the data set are perfectly congruent with each other and the tree, RI will have a value of 1. If the data are maximally homoplastic on the tree, RI will have a value of 0.

The rescaled consistency index RC for all characters on a tree is the CI multiplied by the RI. Characters of irreversible, stratigraphic, Dollo or user-defined type and invariant characters are not included in the RC. As with RI, RC ranges from 0 to 1, with higher RC values indicating that characters in the data set are more congruent with each other and the tree.

Notation used for indices

The **Index Notation** dialog box in the Σ menu allows you to alter how the consistency index, retention index, and rescaled consistency index are displayed. You can vary the number of significant digits displayed between one and four. You can also choose to have the indices displayed using exponential notation in the character status window.

15. Charting Tree and Character Statistics

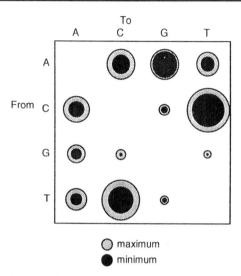

A State Changes & Stasis chart showing
the relative frequencies
of reconstructed changes

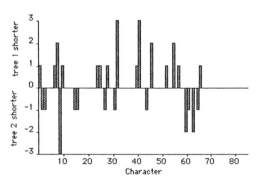

A Compare 2 Trees chart showing the
minimum difference in numbers of steps
between two trees

Various statistics concerning trees and characters can be plotted as bar charts, bubble charts, or tables. The charts can summarize, among other statistics, the numbers of steps or the types of changes reconstructed for one or more characters. The charts can be based on just the tree shown on the screen, or on multiple trees stored in tree files, or on randomly generated trees. Two example charts are shown at left. The charting features are available in the **Chart** menu. Examples of the use of the various sorts of charts are found both in this chapter, and in Chapter 19.

SUMMARY OF FEATURES: *The Character Steps/etc. chart summarizes information on one or more characters regarding their numbers of steps, consistency indices, retention indices, or numbers of changes. It can display information for one or more characters on one or more trees, including stored trees and randomly generated trees. The State Changes & Stasis chart displays a bubble chart or table indicating how many changes of different sorts (from one state to another) are reconstructed. It can display information for one or more characters on one or more trees, including stored trees and randomly generated trees. The Treelengths chart summarizes treelengths of stored or random trees. The States chart displays a histogram or table of the frequency of different character states among observed taxa in the current tree. The Compare 2 Trees chart compares two trees for the number of steps in each of the characters. The Compare 2 Tree Files chart indicates whether all trees in one file have consistently more or fewer steps required in each of the characters than all of the trees in another file.*

MacClade's chart windows can display their information in either graphic chart form, or in table form. A summary is also available. On the right-hand side of each chart is a series of buttons. These control the display of the chart, including font of text, patterns and colors, axes, etc., and are documented toward the end of this chapter.

General issues concerning chart calculations

This section discusses several issues that are relevant to the calculations and interpretation of most charts. For commands that allow you to alter the display of a chart, see the section "Chart display" toward the end of this chapter.

Multiple trees

In any inference of phylogeny, rarely is there only one acceptable tree. More often, there are multiple trees that are well-supported by the data. One of the main aims of the charting facilities in MacClade is to make easier the examination of multiple trees, so that one can see how the trees vary in their implications about character evolution.

In general, for those charts that summarize features of multiple trees, the trees can come either from the stored trees (in the data file or external tree file if one is active), from a different external tree file, or from MacClade's random tree generator.

The different trees will often differ in the values of the statistics calculated. For example, over 13 trees, there might be variation in treelength between 100 and 112:

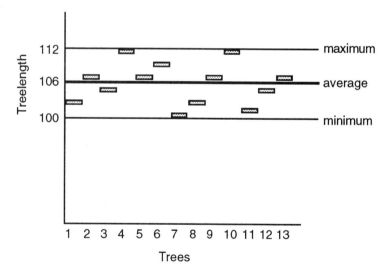

For treelength, each dichotomous tree will have a single value. Over all of the trees, there will be a minimum value (in this example, 100), a maximum value (112), and an average value (106).

For other statistics, each dichotomous tree may have more than a single value. For example, some of many equally parsimonious reconstructions of character evolution may involve several changes for character

1, whereas other reconstructions will involve few changes. If this is true, then MacClade will store the minimum and maximum values for that tree.

Thus, over multiple trees, there will be a minimum value of the minimum values, an average of minima, and a maximum value of minima; there will also be minimum, average, and maximum values of the maxima:

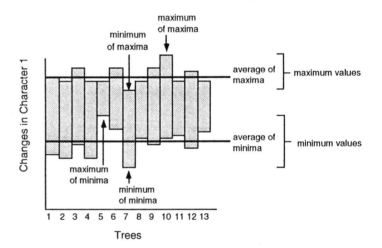

In these circumstances, there are six possible values MacClade could display to you: the minimum, average, or maximum of the minima or maxima. With this diversity of inferred values, MacClade can't display them all at once, but MacClade allows you to choose various subsets of these six values to be displayed (using the dialog box presented when you click on the ⊛ or ▪ buttons, as described toward the end of this chapter).

WARNING: *The interpretation of average values is problematical, as these are averages of a series of alternative hypotheses (e.g., different trees), not averages of a set of data values. Unless one is willing to assign equal probabilities to the alternative hypotheses, these averages* *are thus best thought of as descriptors of the acceptable hypotheses, rather than estimates.*

N O T E: *If you wish to make a chart from trees in a tree file, but do not need to open the tree file for any other purpose, then you will save memory by requesting the tree file from within the charting facility, rather than by first choosing* **Open Tree File** *from the* **Tree** *menu.*

N O T E: *The Compare 2 Tree Files chart reads the tree files off of the disk, even if one of the tree files is the tree storage currently in use by MacClade's tree window (whether an external tree file or the data file itself). If you request that the chart use the current tree storage file, the copy of the file on disk that is used will not contain any trees that you have recently asked MacClade to store, unless you have subsequently saved the file. These stored but unsaved trees will not be included in the chart calculations.*

Text files with values for each tree

When MacClade calculates statistics over multiple trees, in many charts only the minimum, maximum, and average values over those trees are presented in chart form. If you wish to know *all* of the values for each tree, not just the ranges, select the "text file" check box available in the dialog box that comes up when you choose the sort of chart to plot. MacClade will generate a text file with all of these values.

For example, imagine that you have a small data file with 8 characters, and you wish to examine how the number of steps for each of these characters varies over a collection of 5 stored trees. The chart presented by MacClade might look like the example chart on the left.

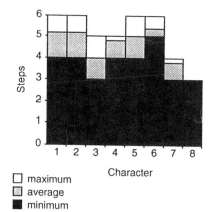

maximum
average
minimum

An example chart

Here we see that there is some variation between the trees. For example, the first character varies between 4 and 6 steps across the five trees. If we asked MacClade to write a text file detailing the values for each tree, by checking "text file" in the **Chart Options** dialog box, the text file would look something like that shown to the left. The first column in the table is the tree number, and the other eight columns contain the number of steps in each of the eight characters.

Some of the values written to these text files may be very large or very small, and MacClade may write these in exponential notation (e.g., 1,200,000 would be written 1.2 e 6). If you wish to edit these text files, and then read them in to some other program (perhaps a statistics application), you should make sure your other program can read exponential notation. If not, you may wish to force MacClade to avoid exponential notation. This can be done by making sure "use exponential notation in output files" is *not* selected in the **Other Options** dialog box in the **Options for Saving** submenu of the **File** menu.

```
MacClade version 3.0
Tuesday, July 1, 1992:  12:26 PM

Steps of characters in Trees

One column per character; one row per tree

tree  1   2   3   4   5   6   7   8

1     4   5   5   4   4   5   4   3
2     4   6   3   5   5   6   4   3
3     6   5   4   5   6   6   3   3
4     6   4   3   5   5   5   4   3
5     6   6   5   5   5   5   4   3
```

A text file recording results from a chart

Forbidden trees in chart window

When you request a chart summarizing features of multiple trees stored in the data file or a tree file, MacClade may find that some of the trees have features forbidden in the current situation.

Trees with polytomies or observed taxa in ancestral position will *not* be allowed if:

1. Equivocal Cycling is needed (for Character Steps/etc. chart with changes option specified; for State Changes & Stasis chart with average or minimum/maximum option),

2. Any characters being analyzed are of Dollo or user-defined types.

Additionally, trees with polytomies are not allowed if any characters being analyzed are of irreversible or stratigraphic types.

Should MacClade find any trees with forbidden features, it will warn you. If the forbidden features are polytomies, MacClade will give you the option to (1) ignore all trees with polytomies or (2) choose a random dichotomous resolution for any polytomies encountered (see Chapter 18). If the forbidden feature is observed taxa fixed in ancestral position, MacClade gives you no choice; it automatically ignores these trees when they are forbidden.

Polytomous vs. dichotomous trees in chart window

Even if polytomous trees are not forbidden, there may be reasons to avoid them, as discussed in Chapter 5. MacClade's chart window provides various ways to randomly sample from dichotomous resolutions of the tree, so as to avoid some of the problems of polytomies. This random sampling can be done either (1) in response to a request by MacClade after it has found forbidden polytomies, as discussed above, (2) by direct request of the user before any calculations start, using the Resolve Polytomies button in many of the chart dialog boxes, or (3) by asking for a special option of random trees that resolves the tree on screen randomly. When the Resolve Polytomies button is used and the choice is made to resolve polytomies, MacClade will resolve randomly any polytomies in trees processed.

Interval widths in bar charts

The interval width button

For charting functions that yield bar charts, the interval width button appears in the **Chart Options** dialog box. Click on this button to request a dialog box in which you can choose how values are grouped on the horizontal axis of the bar chart, and the maximum number of horizontal intervals.

For instance, if the chart window is to display a graph showing the number of steps in each character arranged in sequence, the default is to have one vertical bar for each character. However, by setting the bar chart interval width to 3 characters, the chart will sum every three characters, so that the first vertical bar is for characters 1–3, the second 4–6, and so on. Changing the value of the interval width will cause the entire chart to be recalculated.

As another example, consider a chart in which the number of steps per character is on the horizontal axis. By default, each bar will have a width of 1 step:

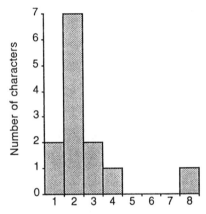

If you reset the interval for 2 steps, then the first interval will be for characters with 0-1 steps, the second interval 2-3 steps, and so on:

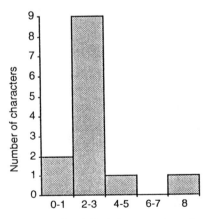

If the horizontal axis lists character numbers, and the statistic on the vertical axis is CI, RI, or RC, and two or more characters are grouped together for each bar of the chart, then the appropriate ensemble index (Chapter 14; Farris, 1989) will be calculated for the characters represented by each bar.

When MacClade recalculates charts

If you have a chart window on the screen, and you change a background assumption of the chart, MacClade will recalculate the chart. For example, a chart will be recalculated if the chart is for the current tree only, and you have changed the current tree, or if the chart is for the traced character only, and you have changed the type of the character, or changed the fixing of ancestral states. There is at least one exception; namely, if a chart was based on a tree file and that tree file was modified by deleting or storing trees, the chart is not recalculated. There may be other apparent exceptions, but they are not really exceptions. For example, changing the current tree does not affect a multiple trees chart even if the current tree had been read from a tree file, since you are not actually changing the tree file; or, fixing the state of a traced character affects State Changes & Stasis chart if it is for the current tree, but does not affect the chart if it is for multiple trees, since this chart is not based on the current tree or its fixing.

If the chart was based on multiple trees and you change a background assumption, MacClade will give you the choice of updating the chart or closing it. This allows you to avoid delays if you no longer want to keep the chart up-to-date. If **Quietly Recalculate** in the **Chart** menu is checked, then MacClade will recalculate charts without asking.

Changing the display of the chart by using the buttons on the right side of the chart will not cause the chart to be recalculated, but calling forth the **Chart Options** dialog box and pressing the Chart button will.

Determining the categories and values on a chart

For some bar charts and bubble charts, it can be difficult to determine what category a particular bar or bubble is referring to, or what the value is for a particular category. Clicking on the part of the bar or bubble chart in question will present a brief description of the category and associated value, as shown on the left.

Grayed horizontal axes

If a portion of the horizontal axes is dimmed or grayed, with no bars shown for these categories, then that means that those categories are not applicable for the current chart (e.g., if characters are plotted along the horizontal axis and some characters are excluded).

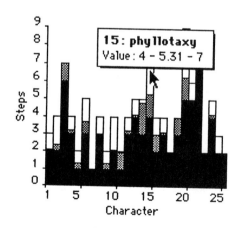

Clicking on a bar to determine
the category and value

Making the chart window front-most

If you have asked MacClade to calculate and display a chart, but the chart window has subsequently become hidden by another of MacClade's windows, you can bring the chart window to the front again by choosing **Chart Window** from the **Display** menu.

Printing and saving charts

Printing charts and saving charts as graphics and text files are described in Chapter 20.

Character Steps/etc.

Charts concerning the number of steps in characters and related statistics about characters are available under the **Character Steps/etc.** item in the **Chart** menu. The related statistics include consistency index, retention index, rescaled consistency index, and the number of changes. For each of these statistics, you can make various charts concerning the current tree or multiple trees that are stored, read from a file, or randomly constructed, and summarizing all included characters or only the currently traced one. The current data and assumptions are used to calculate these statistics.

For example, you could be interested in seeing the distribution of the steps in a character over stored trees, or the distribution along a DNA sequence of the number of transversions on the current tree. These are shown, respectively, in the following two charts.

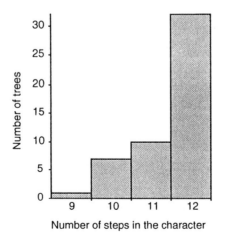

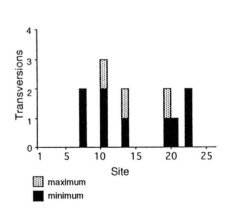

Options for charting statistics about characters are chosen in the following dialog box:

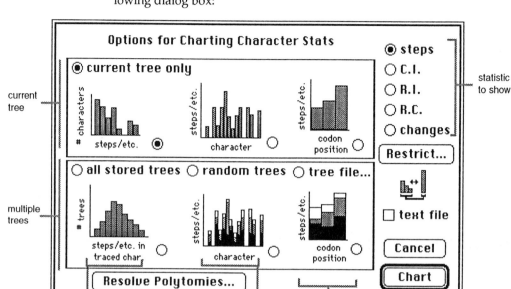

Statistic displayed: Steps, index, or changes

On the right of the above dialog box are listed the choices for the statistic displayed: the number of steps required by the tree for a character, the consistency index, retention index, rescaled consistency index, or the number of changes required in parsimonious reconstructions of character evolution. The meaning of each of these is described in Chapter 14.

If the statistic displayed is the number of steps, then it will be weighted by character weights, except if the chart displays the number of steps in the traced character over multiple trees, in which case the steps are unweighted.

If the statistic displayed is the number of changes, MacClade may indicate a range of numbers of changes for a single character on a single tree. The range indicates the minimum and maximum number of changes allowed in the various parsimonious reconstructions of character evolution (see pp. 75–78). When changes are shown, you can ask that only certain changes be shown. For instance, you might ask to show only transitions or only transversions for DNA data. The method to do this is described below under "Restricting changes to those of a given class", p. 282.

Number of characters with given number of steps/etc.

This option displays a bar chart showing the number of characters with given numbers of steps, consistency indices, and so on, on the current tree. Thus for instance one might ask for the number of characters with various values of the consistency index. If characters tend to be bimodal, either agreeing strongly with the tree or strongly against, this might lead to a different interpretation about the evidence for the tree than if the characters had had a more mixed set of consistency indices. If the statistic displayed is the number of changes, then there may be two superimposed bar charts, one for the minimum number of changes, the other for the maximum number.

Number of steps/etc. on each character in sequence

This option displays the number of steps, consistency indices, and so on, in each of the characters in sequence. The vertical axis is the number of steps or other statistic; the horizontal axis is the character number. This option is especially useful to see non-random distributions of change in molecular sequence data (see Chapter 19).

Number of steps/etc. by codon position

For DNA or RNA sequence data, you can chart by codon position. If this is chosen, then MacClade will sum all steps or changes in every first, second, and third codon position. If CI, RI, or RC are requested, then MacClade calculates the ensemble values (Chapter 14; Farris, 1989) for these indices over all first positions, second positions, and third positions. You might expect to see, for instance, that the number of steps in third positions is larger than in first and second positions in protein-coding regions. See Chapter 19 for a description of how codon position is defined and the options for altering the definition.

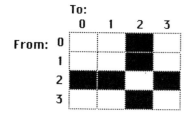

Number of trees with given number of steps/etc.

This option displays the number of trees, either stored in the data file or an external tree file or created randomly, that have various values for the statistics as they apply to the currently traced character. Thus, for instance, one might see how the traced character differs in its number of steps across the stored trees.

NOTE: *If you hold down the Option key as you press the* **Chart** *button in the* **Character Steps/etc.** *dialog box, and you request the number of steps in a traced character over multiple trees, and the character is of type unordered, ordered, irreversible, or stratigraphic, and text file is requested, then MacClade will also will write into the text file a list of the states assigned to the root branch for each tree examined.*

Restricting changes to those of a given class

If the statistic you are asking MacClade to graph is changes, by default MacClade will count or show all changes that are reconstructed. If you are not interested in all changes, but only changes of a particular sort, you can ask MacClade to include only changes of a particular class.

To do this, you first select changes as the index to be charted in the **Character Steps/etc.** dialog box, and then press the Restrict button. You will be presented with a dialog box, in which you select the sorts of changes you wish to include; you can also give a name to the class of changes you select.

For example, you could ask MacClade to chart only those changes to or from state 2. In the Restrict Changes Example file included with MacClade, if you ask to show a Character Steps/etc. chart, plotting changes over the current tree for each character, you will get a graph like the following:

Changes restricted
to and from state 2

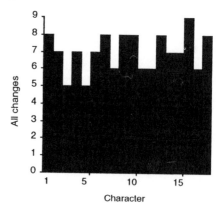

This graph shows all changes over each of the 18 characters. If you restrict it to just changes to or from state 2, you can see which of the changes in the above chart were changes to or from state 2:

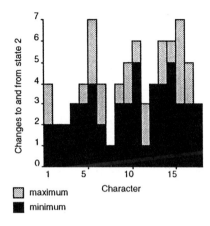

maximum

minimum

Because different equally parsimonious reconstructions of the evolution of single characters vary in the number of changes to and from state 2, there is a minimum and maximum value for many of the bars.

If your data are DNA or RNA sequences, then you can easily restrict changes to transversions or transitions, so that you can examine, say, the distribution of transversions along a DNA sequence.

Creation of weight sets based on a chart

If you create a chart of steps, changes, CI, RI, or RC for each character in sequence, or for codon positions for nucleotide data, you can ask MacClade to calculate weights for each character based on the value shown for each character, using the **Chart to Weight Set** menu item in the Σ menu. For example, if you had plotted RC on the vertical axis, character number on the horizontal, then asked MacClade to convert this to a weight set, MacClade would convert the RC for each character into a weight value. If codon position is on the horizontal axis, then MacClade will calculate a weight for each character according to its codon position, with all first positions receiving the same weight, and so on.

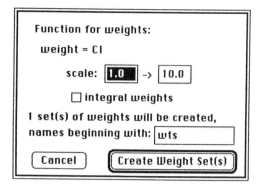

The **Chart to Weight Set** dialog box
for CI, RI, or RC charts

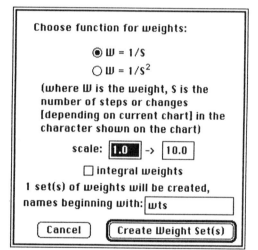

The **Chart to Weight Set** dialog box
for steps or changes charts

Note that MacClade does *not* invoke the created weight set or sets unless you so request using the **Weight Sets** dialog box.

If the statistic displayed is either CI, RI, or RC, then MacClade will convert the index values directly to weights, scaled as you specify in the dialog box.

You can ask MacClade to scale the weights so that they fit in to the range you request. For example, if you wanted the weights scaled so that a CI of 0 corresponded to a weight of 1.0, and a CI of 1 corresponded to a weight of 10.0, then enter 1.0 and 10.0 into the two scale boxes.

If you select integral weights, then MacClade will round the weights off to the nearest integer.

You can give a name to the weight set created by entering a name in the appropriate field in the dialog box. In the dialog box illustrated, the name is "wts". If for each character there is more than one value of the statistic (perhaps as there is more than one tree) then MacClade will calculate a weight set based on the minimum values (which, in this example, would be called "wts min"), another based on the average values ("wts avg"), and so on.

If the statistic being displayed is steps or changes, then the weights created will be a function of that statistic. Two functions are available: the inverse of the number of steps or changes, or the squared inverse (Williams and Fitch, 1989, 1990). You can choose these functions in the dialog box that appears when you choose **Chart to Weight Set**.

These weight sets can be used in a Successive Approximations Character Weighting analysis (Farris, 1969, 1988; Carpenter, 1988). SACW involves a search for the most-parsimonious tree(s), production of a weight set based on the CI, RI, RC, or whatever of each character on the tree(s), re-searching for the most-parsimonious tree(s) with each character weighted according to the weight set, and so on, until the trees found in two successive iterations are identical. Just as for Transformation Series Analysis, discussed in Chapter 4, an adequate justification for this procedure has yet to be provided. Some aspects of the method are not well defined, such as which of the multiple weight sets created by MacClade (due to multiple parsimonious trees, for example) one should use. We do not necessarily advocate use of SACW, but we have placed this capability in MacClade to allow you to explore the behavior of this method.

Treelengths of many trees

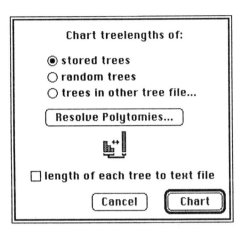

The **Chart Treelengths** dialog box

The **Treelengths** chart makes a bar chart or table of the numbers of trees with various numbers of treelengths. If the treelengths are charted over the stored trees in the current tree repository, the tree currently shown on screen is not included unless it has been explicitly stored. The current data and assumptions are used to calculate the treelengths.

Treelengths can also be charted over a set of randomly generated trees (including random resolutions of a displayed polytomous tree). If you choose this option, MacClade will present you with the dialog box to generate random trees (see Chapter 18 for a description of the **Random Trees** dialog box).

EXAMPLE: *The Bembidion example data file in your Examples folder contains a matrix of structural and cytogenetic characters for a group of ground beetles (D. Maddison, in press). There exist 545 equally parsimonious trees for this data matrix, if one considers all adult and larval characters included in the matrix. The trees are stored in the stored in the file Bembidion.trees. One can examine whether there is variation in how well the larval characters alone fit onto the 545 trees with MacClade's chart of treelengths. Open the Bembidion data file, go to the tree window, and choose the "larval only" inclusion set using the* **Inclusion Sets** *dialog box from the* **Assume** *menu. Then ask MacClade to chart treelengths. In the dialog box that is presented, choose "trees in other tree file...", and select the tree file "Bembidion.trees". Then click on the* **Polytomies** *button; in the dialog box that is presented, ask MacClade to resolve all polytomous trees; click* **OK** *on this dialog box. Then press* **Chart** *in the* **Treelengths** *dialog box. You should be presented with the following chart:*

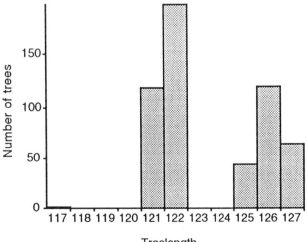

Note the one tree at length 117. Clearly, there is one tree among the 545 that is much more favored by the larval characters than the other 544 trees. This of course implies that there is more homoplasy on this one tree in adult characters than there is in the other 544 trees.

EXAMPLE: *Open the file "Polytomy Example". Go to the tree window. Note that the length of the tree is given as 91+ if the polytomy is presumed to represent uncertain resolution, and 109 if it is presumed to represent multiple speciation. (You can switch between these two modes using the* **Polytomy Options** *item in the* **Trees** *menu.) Now ask MacClade to chart the treelengths of random trees. In the dialog box that is presented, in which you are to specify the type of random tree, choose "randomly resolve current tree", and ask for a large number of trees. Choosing 10,000 random resolutions of the polytomous tree will yield a chart like the following:*

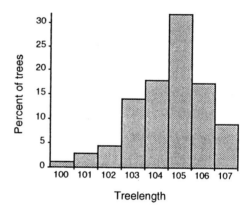

This is a more accurate picture of the treelength of a polytomous tree than the treelength of 91+ or 109. (As there are only 105 resolutions of this polytomous tree, clearly some of the resolutions are being sampled more than once, but with a large enough sample they should be sampled more or less equally.)

State Changes & Stasis

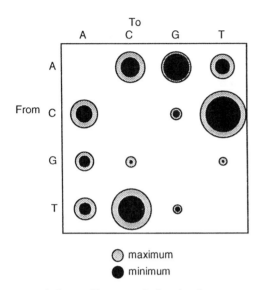

maximum
minimum

A State Changes & Stasis chart,
showing relative frequencies
of reconstructed changes
between nucleotides on tree

The State Changes & Stasis chart shows the number of *reconstructed* state i to state j changes in a table or "bubble" chart to give an indication of the relative frequency of various changes over all included characters or just the traced character, and over the current tree or multiple trees. A brief introduction to MacClade's bubble charts is given in Chapter 4 (see pp. 62–63). The discussion of counting changes in Chapter 5 should also be consulted.

Ancestral states are reconstructed for all included characters. Each branch in the tree is then visited and checked to see whether or not an i to j change is reconstructed as having occurred, either in one character or all characters depending on the option chosen. After MacClade visits all branches, it presents a matrix or bubble chart showing the total number of i to j changes in the tree for various i and j. (Actually, MacClade looks at all characters for one branch before moving to the next branch under the "unambiguous only" option, but it looks at all branches for one character before moving on to the next character under the "minimum and maximum" option.)

When **State Changes & Stasis** is selected, a dialog box is presented to give various choices:

Options for Charting Change and Stasis

This chart will display the numbers of changes of each sort (e.g., state i to state j) from one node to the next, and if requested the instances of stasis (state i to state i).

◉ **Count changes only**   ○ **Count changes & stasis**
☒ **Include changes within polymorphic terminals**

Count changes/stasis in: ○ **current tree only**
◉ **all included characters**   ◉ **stored trees** ○ **tree file...**
○ **traced character only**   ○ **random trees**
[**Resolve Polytomies...**]

For each sort   ◉ **Count unambiguous events only**
of event: ○ **Count minimum and maximum number**
○ **Count average number**

□ **text file**   [**Total...**]   [**Cancel**]   [**Chart**]

In the dialog box, you can choose which characters and trees to examine, and what sorts of events to show.

Reconstructions used in State Changes & Stasis charts

The State Changes & Stasis chart counts events of change and stasis based on a reconstruction of character evolution. The reconstruction used is the same sort of parsimony reconstruction of ancestral states shown in character tracings (see Chapters 5 and 13). It therefore depends on the tree, the distribution of character states, and the transformations types assigned to the characters (see Chapter 5).

The reconstructions used are not the ACCTRAN/DELTRAN reconstructions, even when one of these is the chosen option in the **Resolving Options** dialog box, except when the chart is restricted to the current tree and traced character only. The reason for this is that ACCTRAN/DELTRAN is used only for the character tracing displayed on the tree. Likewise, if states are fixed at branches in the current tree, this affects the chart only if it is restricted to the current tree and traced character, since only the character tracing in the tree window is affected by fixing states.

Users should be always aware that the reconstruction used as a basis for the State Changes & Stasis chart is only a reconstruction, and indeed is a parsimony reconstruction. Among other things, this means that the reconstruction will always yield a minimum estimate of the total amount of change.

EXAMPLE: *The difficulty that parsimony has in reconstructing change when evolutionary rates are high can be illustrated using MacClade's facility to evolve characters stochastically up the current tree (described in Chapter 18) and the State Changes & Stasis chart. 1,000 binary characters were simulated on a tree of 20 taxa in each of five cases, differing in the probability of change on each branch: 0.01, 0.1, 0.3, 0.5, and 0.9. For each case, parsimony was used to reconstruct the changes, and the results summarized in a State Changes & Stasis chart, as shown below. Note that as the probability of change rises to 0.3 or more, parsimony cannot detect these higher probabilities: even when each branch has a 0.9 probability of a change, parsimony's reconstruction minimizing change shows changes on only about 3 out of 10 branches.*

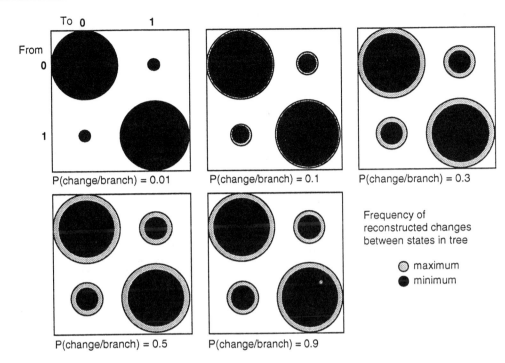

P(change/branch) = 0.01   P(change/branch) = 0.1   P(change/branch) = 0.3

P(change/branch) = 0.5   P(change/branch) = 0.9

Frequency of
reconstructed changes
between states in tree

○ maximum
● minimum

EXAMPLE: *The trees displayed and analyzed in MacClade are rooted
trees. If you wish to examine an unrooted tree (that is, a tree in which
the root is not specified), you need to follow several steps. An unrooted
tree is a kind of consensus tree, consisting of all trees that represent possible rootings of the tree. For example, in the file "Unrooted Chart
Example", the tree can be rooted along 17 different branches. If you
wished to analyze an unrooted tree, say, for relative frequencies of 0 to
1 and 1 to 0 changes, you should examine all 17 rootings (D. Maddison,
1990). You can ask MacClade to do this by first choosing* **New Tree File**
in the **Tree** *menu, then hold down the Option key and choose* **All
Rootings** *from the* **Tree** *menu. MacClade will store in the tree file 17
trees, representing each of the 17 possible rootings. If you then ask for a
State Changes & Stasis chart of all stored trees, counting minimum and
maximum number of changes, you should get a bubble chart like this:*

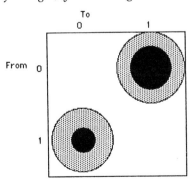

The size of the gray areas indicates that the rootings differ in their relative frequencies of 0 to 1 and 1 to 0 changes. This is in contrast to the chart you would see for just the current, rooted tree:

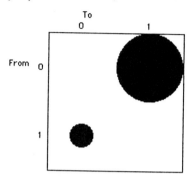

Change vs. stasis

If "Count changes and stasis" is requested, then instances where a state does not change from one node to the next (i.e., the state at a node and its descendant node are the same) are included in the chart. Otherwise, only changes are included.

Changes in terminal polymorphisms

If "Include changes within polymorphic terminals" is selected, implicit changes within polymorphic terminal taxa will be included in the chart. See Chapters 5 and 13 for details on how MacClade does this.

Character traced vs. all characters

If "traced character only" in the **Chart Options** dialog box is selected, then only the traced character is examined; if "all included characters" is selected, then all included characters are examined and the total number of i to j changes in all characters on the branches is counted. A discrete-valued character must be traced on the tree before "traced character only" can be selected.

Unambiguous vs. minimum/maximum vs. average

These choices are needed to deal with ambiguity in the reconstruction of character evolution. If several states can be placed at an ancestral node with equal parsimony, then exactly which changes occur may be ambiguous. For instance, there may be two equally parsimonious alternatives: two parallel 0 to 1 changes, or a 0 to 1 change followed by a 1 to 0 change.

When "unambiguous" is selected, an i to j change is counted as occurring on a branch only if parsimony requires i to be at the ancestral node below the branch, and j to be at the descendant node above the branch. Thus an i to j change is counted only when the ancestral and descendant nodes unequivocally have states i and j, respectively. In some situations there may definitely be an unambiguous change from 0 to 1, but where it occurred might be ambiguous. If the change could have occurred on a number of different branches, then it is not counted in the total number of unambiguous 0 to 1 changes. Thus, an i to j change is counted as unambiguous when it occurs on the same branch in all most-parsimonious reconstructions of character evolution.

When "minimum and maximum" is selected, all most-parsimonious reconstructions of character evolution are examined. MacClade's Equivocal Cycling algorithms are used to cycle through each unequivocal reconstruction of character evolution (p. 252). In each unequivocal reconstruction, the number of i to j changes is counted. Some of these reconstructions may have more i to j changes than others. The minimum number of i to j changes among these reconstructions is recorded, as is the maximum number. When each character is examined (if "all included characters" is selected), the minimum and maximum numbers of i to j changes are added to running totals. The minimum number of i to j changes over all characters would be obtained if all of those reconstructions were chosen that minimize these changes; similarly for the maximum. In the bubble chart for the minimum and maximum option, there may be black spots contained within gray spots:

The black spot indicates the minimum frequency of changes (that is, the changes that occur on all reconstructions and all trees); the gray spot the maximum frequency (that is the changes that occur on some but not all reconstructions or trees).

If several trees are examined, then for each tree there may be a minimum and maximum number of i to j changes, and over all trees there will be some tree that has the smallest minimum, and some other that has the largest maximum and average over all trees (see above, under "Multiple trees", pp. 273–275). You can choose to display various sorts of maxima and minima: the average of the maxima over all the trees, the smallest minimum and largest maximum, and so on. (MacClade's default is to show the smallest minimum and largest maximum.) MacClade can show no more than three of these values at once. The button ⊚ presents a dialog box in which you can choose which of them are to be displayed in a bubble chart (see below, under "Chart display").

When "average" is selected, all most-parsimonious reconstructions of character evolution are examined using Equivocal Cycling. The number of i to j changes in each of these reconstructions is recorded, and MacClade calculates the average number among these reconstructions. That is, if there were four reconstructions and they showed 2, 2, 3 and 3 i to j changes respectively, then the average number of i to j changes is (2+2+3+3)/4 = 2.5.

Because Equivocal Cycling is used for the minimum and maximum and the average options, these options cannot be used when certain factors, like the presence of polytomies, prohibit Equivocal Cycling.

EXAMPLE: *Open the Bembidion data file, and trace character 64 on the tree "1 of 4 common". Then ask MacClade to calculate a bubble chart, traced character only, showing only unambiguous changes. You should see a chart like this:*

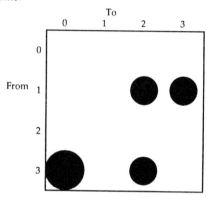

If you click on the largest circle, you will note that its area corresponds to 2 changes. If you then choose **Chart Options** *from the* **Chart** *menu, and ask MacClade to calculate minimum and maximum changes, you should see a chart like this:*

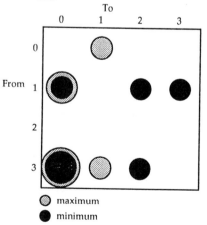

(The largest gray circle here corresponds to 3 changes, as can be seen by clicking on the table button ▦ *on the chart window.) The fact that the*

gray and black spots are not the same size shows that there is some ambiguity in the reconstruction of ancestral states that affects the reconstructed number of 0 to 1 and 1 to 0 transformations. Finally, the chart of average changes is:

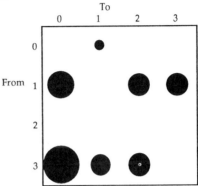

(The largest circle here corresponds to 2.6 changes).

Trees examined

The State Changes & Stasis chart can be calculated on the current tree in the tree window or for multiple trees (either those stored in the current tree repository, another tree file, or random trees, the latter including multiple random resolutions of a polytomous tree on the screen). If the "stored trees" option is checked, MacClade will examine trees in the current external tree file, if there is one active; otherwise it will examine trees stored with the data. If the "tree file" option is checked, MacClade will query you for the tree file you wish to examine.

Calculating total changes of a certain class

You can get a vague idea of the total number of changes of a certain sort by having a bubble chart displayed as a table (by clicking on the ▦ button on the chart window), and then summing the changes in the table. However, the sum can be misleading. For example, in the file "Total Changes Example", the single character in the matrix would be reconstructed like this:

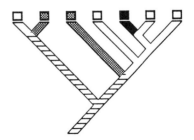

The State Changes & Stasis chart of minimum and maximum changes will yield the following table:

From:	To: 0	1	2
0		0-2	1-1
1	0-2		0-0
2	0-0	0-0	

The sum of the minimum values in the To State 1 column, and the minimum values in the From State 1 column is 0; the sum of the maximum values is 4. This implies that there are between 0 and 4 changes to or from state 1, with variation due to the multiple equally parsimonious reconstructions of character evolution on the tree. But if you looked at each reconstruction of the character on the tree, it would be clear that each of them has exactly 2 changes to or from state 1. You can ask MacClade to calculate total changes of a particular class for you using the Total button in the **Chart Options** dialog box. The Total button will present you with a dialog box much like the **Restrict Changes** dialog box, described on p. 282. You then define a class of changes in the **Total** dialog box. In this example, you want to define the class of changes to be all changes to or from state 1:

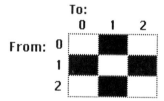

Once this class of changes is set, then MacClade will total the number of changes of the defined class. To see the total, press on the text display button ($\overline{\mathbf{x}}$) in the chart window. In this example, MacClade will calculate the number of changes to or from state 1 to be between 2 and 2.

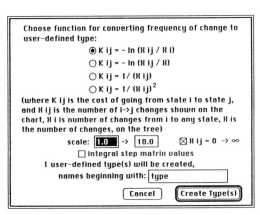

Choose function for converting frequency of change to user-defined type:

- ⊙ K ij = - ln (H ij / H i)
- ○ K ij = - ln (H ij / H)
- ○ K ij = 1/ (H ij)
- ○ K ij = 1/ (H ij)²

(where K ij is the cost of going from state i to state j, and H ij is the number of i->j changes shown on the chart, H i is number of changes from i to any state, H is the number of changes, on the tree)

scale: [1.0] -> [10.0]   ☒ H ij = 0 -> ∞
☐ integral step matrix values
1 user-defined type(s) will be created,
names beginning with: [type]

(Cancel)   (Create Type(s))

The **Chart to Type** dialog box

Creation of a transformation type based on a chart

Choosing **Chart to Type** from the **Chart** menu presents you with a dialog box in which you choose options to convert a State Changes & Stasis chart to a transformation type.

In general, these four functions are of the form: cost of an i to j change in the step or cost matrix is equal to a function of the inferred frequency of that change on the tree(s). The four functions are all monotone decreasing; that is, the higher the observed frequency, the lower the cost. The first two functions provided are similar to those proposed by W. Wheeler (1990); the latter two by Williams and Fitch (1989, 1990).

You can set the scale of the values in the user-defined type that will be created. By default, the costs are scaled to fit in to the range 1 to 10, so that the least frequent kind of change will be given a weight of 10.0, and the most frequent a cost of 1.0. If you set "Xij = 0 -> ∞", then any change with zero frequency will be set to a cost of infinity (that is, it will be presumed impossible); otherwise it will be set to the maximum value of the range. If "integral step-matrix values" is chosen, then the values in the step matrix will be rounded to the nearest integer.

You can name the type to be created in the box provided. If there is a range of values for an i to j change, then MacClade will produce more than one user-defined type. For example, if there were minimum, average, and maximum values of each change, then MacClade would produce three types, by default named "type min", "type avg", and "type max".

These types can then be applied to the characters, new trees found, new types created based on the frequency of changes on those new trees, and so on. This is a variant of Williams and Fitch's (1989, 1990) method of Dynamic Weighting. In their Dynamic Weighting, they simultaneously infer a probabilistic model and a tree, using an iterative process. A step matrix is derived from an initial estimate of relative frequencies of change, a tree is then inferred using parsimony, new estimates of relative frequencies of change are made based on that tree, from these a new step matrix is formed, a tree is inferred assuming this step matrix, and so on, until the estimate of the step matrix in one iteration is the same as in the next. This method has been justified primarily by empirical studies (Fitch and Ye, 1992). MacClade's algorithms differ in that node numbing is not performed, and that equally parsimonious reconstructions of character evolution are weighted equally in calculating the weights based on average number of changes over all reconstructions. Rather than using node numbing, we recommend asking MacClade to fix violations of the triangle inequality (see p. 82) if you want to avoid the triangle inequality. Some aspects of Dynamic Weighting are not well defined. For example, should one use the user-defined type created from the minimum values across multiple reconstructions and trees, the average values, or the maximum values? We do not necessarily advocate use of Dynamic Weighting, but we have placed this capability in MacClade to allow you to explore the behavior of the method.

States

This chart shows the frequency that various states occur among the terminal taxa of the current tree. If no character is traced, the frequency in all (included) characters will be calculated. If a character is traced, you will be presented with a choice to calculate over the frequency in the character traced, or all (included) characters of the matrix. If the state of a taxon is uncertain, its possible states are not counted into the frequency. An example of use of a States chart is given in Chapter 19.

Comparing two trees

Choosing **Compare 2 Trees** from the **Chart** menu allows you to see quickly how two trees differ in the number of weighted steps assigned to each character. The two trees to compare are selected from the current tree repository (data file or tree file). In the first dialog that appears, select a stored tree. MacClade will beep; then you select another tree. MacClade will then present you with a graph of the difference in number of steps in each character between the first tree and second tree.

EXAMPLE: *Open the file Bembidion. Ask MacClade to Compare 2 Trees. In the dialog box that is presented, request automatic resolution of polytomies. In the next dialog box that is presented, choose tree "from Island 1"; in the following dialog, choose "from Island 8". You will be presented with the following chart:*

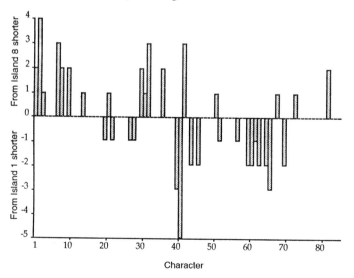

The bars above the center line indicate that those characters exhibit less steps on the tree "from Island 8" than on the other tree; the bars below the center line indicate that those characters exhibit fewer steps on the tree "from Island 1". Note that character 41 is 5 steps shorter on tree "from Island 1" than on "from Island 8".

Comparing two tree files

This chart displays, character by character, whether and by how much all the trees in one tree file differ from all the trees in another tree file. That is, it calculates whether the number of weighted steps required for a character by all of the trees in one tree file is consistently more or less than the number of steps required by all of the trees in another tree file.

This chart is requested by selecting **Compare 2 Tree Files** in the **Chart** menu. You will be presented with a dialog box to choose the first tree file, then a dialog box to choose the second tree file.

EXAMPLE: *Open the file Hamamelidae. Go to the tree window. Ask MacClade to do a Compare 2 Tree Files chart. In the dialog box that is presented, request automatic resolution of polytomies. In the next dialog box that is presented, choose tree file Ham.island2 from the Hamamelidae Trees folder; in the following dialog, choose Ham.island47. These tree files contain two of the islands (D. Maddison, 1991a) of most-parsimonious trees for this data matrix. You will be presented with the following chart:*

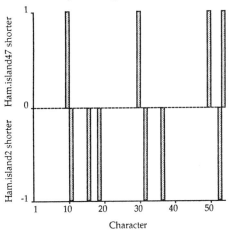

Bars above the center line indicate those characters that are shorter on all Ham.island47 trees than all Ham.island2 trees; thus, there are four characters that are at least one step shorter on each Ham.island47 trees than on any Ham.island2 trees. Bars below the center line indicate characters that are shorter on Ham.island2 trees.

Chart display

Various options alter the manner of the presentation of the charts. Some of these options can be specified in the **Chart Options** dialog box that appears when you request the chart, as described above; others can be specified using the buttons along the right hand margin of the chart window itself. These buttons include:

Button	Meaning
▮▮▮	Display as bar chart
⊞	Display as table
⦙∶∙	Display as bubble chart
x̄	Display summary text
⦗←2→⦘	Adjust sizes of circles
◉ ▮	Choose which of multiple values for each category to show
TITLE	Display a title on the chart
A	Adjust the type font, size, and style of the text in the chart
▦	Options for displaying a State Changes & Stasis table using percentages
⦙↔⦙	Adjust vertical axes of a bar chart
⦙↓⦙	Adjust horizontal axes of a bar chart
⬗▨	Change color or patterns in chart
▦	Display a grid on the chart

Viewing charts, tables, or textual summaries

The buttons ▮▮▮, ⊞, ⦙∶∙, and x̄ choose the basic form in which information is displayed: as a bar chart, table, bubble chart, or as a textual summary. All charts have at least one graphic view (bar chart or bubble chart) and one table view. The bubble chart is available only for the State Changes & Stasis chart. The textual summary presents information (such as number of characters and trees examined, and so on) not available in the other views.

Choosing the values to show

Ambiguity in character reconstruction and multiple trees can yield more values for an interval of a bar chart or for changes from state i to j than can be displayed on one chart. In these instances there are six possible values that can be shown:

1. The minimum value across trees of the minimum value across reconstructions.

2. The average value across trees of the minimum value across reconstructions.

3. The maximum value across trees of the minimum value across reconstructions.

4. The minimum value across trees of the maximum value across reconstructions.

5. The average value across trees of the maximum value across reconstructions.

6. The minimum value across trees of the maximum value across reconstructions.

The ⊛ or ▮ buttons bring forth a dialog box in which you can choose which two or three of these values are to be shown at once. You have the choice to show:

a. The two extreme values (the minimum of minima and maximum of maxima, values 1 and 6 above).
b. The average values of the minima and maxima across reconstructions (values 2 and 5, above).
c. The three values for the minima across reconstructions (values 1–3, above).
d. The three values for the maxima across reconstructions (values 4–6, above).

Displaying a title

To have MacClade include a small descriptive title above the chart, select the TITLE button.

Changing fonts

The **A** button requests a dialog box in which you can choose the type font, size, and style of the text used in the chart window.

Adjusting the size of circles

By default, MacClade adjusts the size of the circles such that the cell with the largest number of changes visible on the chart has a circle that exactly fills the cell, and scales the areas of the other circles in proportion to their values. You can alter MacClade's choice of circle sizes using the dialog box presented by clicking on the 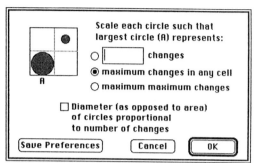 button.

If multiple trees were examined, and you ask MacClade to scale the circles such that the size of each cell represents the maximum value over trees of the maximum number of changes over all reconstructions, then MacClade will shrink the circles so that even the maximum maximum number of changes would fit into the cells, even if this maximum maximum is not displayed on the current chart.

Either of these options may make it difficult to compare different charts, as the scales of the circles may vary from chart to chart. You can force a uniform scale across charts by manually specifying to scale the cell size to represent, say, 4 changes. MacClade will then adjust the sizes of the circles so that the width of the cells is equivalent to 4 changes. If there are more changes than this in some cells, the circles in those cells will be large, and will overlap adjacent cells.

By default, the area of each circle is proportional to the number of changes; this can be changed so that the diameter is proportional to the number of changes.

Adjusting the vertical axes

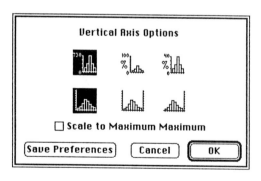 requests a dialog box in which the user chooses options for vertical axes.

The top three buttons determine whether the vertical axis shows (1) numbers or (2) percentages scaled from 0 to 100 or (3) percentages scaled from 0 to the highest observed. The bottom three buttons determine whether vertical axes are displayed on the left, both sides, or right.

If multiple trees were examined, and you ask MacClade to scale the vertical axis to accommodate the maximum value over all reconstructions over all trees, then MacClade will set the axis so that even the maximum maximum values would fit on the chart, even if this maximum maximum is not displayed on the current chart.

Adjusting the horizontal axis

requests a dialog box in which the user chooses the horizontal scaling of the bars in a bar chart. MacClade automatically calculates a particular horizontal scaling, but the user can set a manual scaling if so desired. Width is measured in points (1/72 of an inch).

Changing display of State Changes & Stasis tables

For State Changes & Stasis tables, the entries can be displayed either as absolute numbers, or as percentages. You can adjust this using the dialog box presented when you click on the ▨ button.

Changing patterns and colors

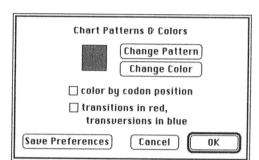 presents you with a dialog box in which you choose the patterns and colors of a chart's bars or bubbles. You cannot change the patterns of the bars or bubbles if the chart is showing both minimum and maximum values.

In the State Changes & Stasis chart, for DNA or RNA sequence data, transitions will be shown in red, and transversions in blue if this option is selected. In the Character Steps/etc. chart, for DNA or RNA sequence data, if site number is shown on the horizontal axis, then you can ask MacClade to color the bars blue, green, or red for the first, second, and third codon positions respectively. Non-coding regions will be shown in black.

MacClade will allow you to change color even if the Macintosh you are using does not currently display color on the screen, if the machine is capable of displaying or printing colors (as is, for example, the Macintosh SE/30).

Displaying a grid

▦ chooses whether a grid is to be displayed on a chart.

Confirming the validity of the charting calculations

In programming MacClade, the proper functioning of the charting calculations was tested as follows:

— The source code was thoroughly checked and rechecked.

— For several test cases, the results of the charts were compared against results calculated by hand, and as calculated by other parts of MacClade (e.g., the results presented in the character status window).

16. Continuous Characters

The preceding several chapters dealt with characters with a finite number of discrete states (0, 1, 2, etc.). MacClade can deal directly with continuous-valued character data, though its features are relatively limited.

SUMMARY OF FEATURES: *Four continuous-valued characters can be stored in the file. They are edited in a small dialog box. Their evolution can be reconstructed and traced on the tree, using either linear parsimony or squared-change parsimony. Continuous characters do not contribute to the treelength or changes shown by Trace All Changes, and cannot be analyzed using the charting facility.*

To make discrete or not?

Continuous characters have often been recoded as discrete characters for use in phylogenetic analysis (Archie, 1985; Mickevich and Johnson, 1976; Felsenstein, 1988b; Baum, 1988; Goldman, 1988; Chappill, 1989; Stevens, 1991), though at least for the purpose of reconstructing character evolution there exist methods that can handle continuous characters without recoding (Farris, 1970; Rogers, 1984; Swofford and Berlocher, 1987; Swofford and Maddison, 1987; Huey and Bennett, 1987; W. Maddison, 1991). MacClade allows both options, recoding to discrete or treating continuous characters in their native form.

Continuous characters can be recoded as discrete and entered into MacClade's data editor, and treated as ordered characters. If each distinct observed value of the continuous character receives a different discrete state in the recoding, and the order of values is preserved in the order of states 0, 1, 2, ..., then the reconstruction of ancestral states will not be affected by the recoding, at least if one is using Wagner or linear parsimony (Maddison and Slatkin, 1990). That is, the reconstruction of character evolution obtained with the discretely recoded character treated as an ordered character would be the same as the reconstruction obtained using the Wagner/linear parsimony option for continuous characters (see below). Discrete recoding in MacClade allows you to take advantage of several features such as charting, Equivocal Cycling, fixing of states at branches, and soft polytomies that are available only with discrete characters, but it has several disadvantages. First, the recoding has to be done. Second, squared-change parsimony cannot be used on discrete characters. Third, although the reconstruction of character evolution may not be changed by recoding, the character's length required by the tree may change because the distance between two adjacent states in an ordered discrete character is counted as one step, whereas values in a continuous character may be separated by varying distances. (This last problem may be solved if the discrete character is assigned a user-defined transformation type with state-to-state distances reflecting the distances in the original continuous form.) Fourth, MacClade can handle only 26 discrete states in a character. If a continuous character has more than 26 different values in a set of taxa, then it cannot be recoded to discrete without loss of information.

MacClade's features for treating continuous characters in their native form are described below.

Editing continuous characters

Select **Edit Continuous** in the **Edit** menu to obtain a dialog box listing the taxa in the data matrix and their assigned values in the continuous characters. At the top are four radio buttons to choose which of the four continuous characters is being edited.

The **Edit Continuous** dialog box

Select one or more taxa whose values you wish to change (using the standard methods for selecting elements in a list), type in the new value in the box below the list, and click on the Enter button. You can type in a range (e.g., "0.89 – 0.94"), though only the lowest value will be used when squared-change parsimony is in effect. To expedite entry of data for many taxa, you can hit Tab to simultaneously enter the value you have typed and move to the next taxon. Click on OK when you are done editing.

No missing data are allowed when a continuous character is traced on the tree. Thus, MacClade will indicate an error if you try to trace a continuous character on the tree and it finds a missing value. In the **Edit Continuous** dialog box, missing values are indicated by blank spaces beside the taxon names. MacClade indicates "Complete" at the bottom when there are no missing values in the character shown.

The Deselect button changes all taxa in the list from selected to unselected.

Continuous characters are saved in a special block of the data file, resembling the data matrix for the discrete characters. Even if you have only continuous characters you must still work with the discrete-character data editor, if only to create the taxa and their names.

Tracing continuous characters

The tracing of continuous characters can use two different parsimony criteria to reconstruct ancestral states:

1. "Linear", "Manhattan", or "Wagner parsimony" minimizes the sum of the (absolute value of the) changes on the branches of the tree (Farris, 1970; Swofford and Maddison, 1987). This often yields a range of equally parsimonious values at each branch. MacClade will display the full range, or only the minimum (MINSTATE) or maximum (MAXSTATE) values at each branch according to choices made in the **Trace Continuous** dialog box. Linear parsimony can be used only with dichotomous trees. MacClade uses Swofford and Maddison's (1987) algorithm for linear parsimony. See p. 109 for a discussion of MINSTATE and MAXSTATE.

2. "Squared-change parsimony" minimizes the sum of the squared changes on the branches of the tree (Rogers, 1984; Huey & Bennett 1987). This yields a single value at each branch. With squared-change parsimony, terminal taxa are not allowed to be polymorphic. If a range is indicated, only the minimum value will be used. Whether or not the root of the tree is considered a true node in the tree will affect the reconstruction (W. Maddison, 1991). Thus, rooted or unrooted options can be chosen. If the tree has a basal polytomy, then the unrooted option cannot be chosen. Squared-change parsimony can be used with dichotomous trees and trees with hard polytomies. MacClade uses W. Maddison's (1991) algorithm for squared-change parsimony. As noted by W. Maddison (1991), the squared-change reconstruction can also be considered a Bayesian probability estimate under a Brownian motion model of evolution.

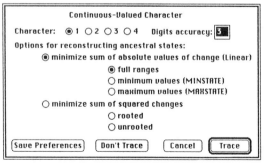

The **Trace Continuous** dialog box

These options are specified in the **Trace Continuous** dialog box, available in the **Trace** menu. If a continuous-valued character has been read or entered, its evolution can be reconstructed by requesting this dialog box. Choose continuous character 1, 2, 3, or 4 and click on **Trace**. If a taxon in the tree has not been assigned a continuous value, a warning is given and the continuous tracing is turned off. To turn off the trace, call up the dialog box and click on **Don't Trace** or, alternatively, click on the go-away box in the upper left of the continuous character legend. To trace a different continuous character, either go back to the **Trace Continuous** dialog box and choose a different character, or click on the left and right arrow keys to scroll from one continuous character to the next.

The tracing will automatically break the observed range of the character into 10 subranges and assign each a color, shade, or pattern, indicated in the legend at right. If a node is reconstructed to have a range of values spanning two or more subranges, it is shaded by the equivocal pattern. When the cursor is held over a branch, the exact value or range of values reconstructed for that branch is shown in the character legend. Using the **Trace Labeling** dialog box in the **Display** menu, you can ask MacClade to place labels on each branch to indicate textually the states reconstructed.

The continuous character tracing can be printed using **Print Tree**, and a listing node-by-node of the reconstructed ancestral states can be printed by selecting **Branch List** in the **Print Other** submenu, or saved to a text file using the **Branch List** item in the **Save Text File** submenu.

Confirming the validity of the parsimony algorithms

In programming MacClade, the proper functioning of the continuous-character parsimony algorithms was tested as follows.

— The source code was thoroughly checked and rechecked.

— Ancestral state reconstructions and counts of treelength were examined by eye in a number of test characters.

— Using the principle described by Maddison and Slatkin (1990), the discrete-character algorithms were used as a check against the linear parsimony algorithms for continuous characters.

— The results of the squared-change parsimony algorithms were checked against the results from an alternative algorithm, the iterative averaging algorithm (Rogers, 1984; Huey and Bennett, 1987), for a number of test cases.

17. PATTERNS OF CORRELATED CHARACTER EVOLUTION

Among the various applications of phylogenies discussed in Chapter 3, one that has attracted much attention recently is the use of phylogenies to uncover patterns of correlated character evolution. MacClade provides a number of features to aid in applying tests of correlated character evolution.

The one correlation test that is directly implemented in MacClade is W. Maddison's (1990) concentrated-changes test. It can test whether changes in one binary character are more concentrated than expected by chance in certain regions of the phylogeny.

SUMMARY OF FEATURES: *The concentrated-changes test uses a null model of changes occurring equiprobably on any branch. Exact calculations are available to derive probabilities for varying numbers of changes occurring in specified regions of the tree. Simulations are also available to handle cases with larger trees and greater numbers of changes. With the simulations, probabilities can be based either on the actual changes as they are simulated, or with reconstructions of changes based on the end products of the simulated actual changes.*

Using reconstructed histories to test correlation

One function of MacClade that is relevant to seeking patterns of character evolution is its tracing of character evolution. A number of proposed tests of character correlation involve first reconstructing the ancestral states in the characters of interest (Ridley, 1983; Huey and Bennett, 1987; W. Maddison, 1990). Both for discrete and continuous characters MacClade supplies parsimony reconstructions of ancestral states. When the exact reconstruction is equivocal, MacClade's various features for examining alternative reconstructions can be used. Equivocal Cycling for discrete characters allows one to examine all most-parsimonious reconstructions of ancestral states. This can be important, for example, if some reconstructions would be favorable to the correlation hypotheses, and others not.

Applying correlation tests to reconstructions of character evolution is a practice that can pose some problems. The reader is advised to see the comments on pp. 65–66 in Chapter 4 regarding reliance upon ancestral state reconstructions.

The concentrated-changes test

The concentrated-changes test of W. Maddison (1990) is designed for testing the association of changes in a binary character with some other binary variable within a selected clade. For instance, it can test whether gains (0 to 1 changes) in one character are more concentrated than expected by chance on those branches of the clade selected that are reconstructed to have a particular state in a second variable. A significant concentration might indicate that this state in the second character may enable or select for gains in the first character. Note that in MacClade's implementation of the test, a 0 to 1 change is called a gain; a 1 to 0 change a loss. If you want to assume the reverse, recode the character (pp. 186–188.)

Calculations are requested by touching the ⅄ tool on the branch below the clade over which the test will be performed. Before requesting the calculations, there must be a binary character traced on the tree to serve as the independent variable.

The calculations determine the probability that various numbers of gains and losses would occur in certain distinguished areas of the clade selected, given a certain number of gains and losses occur in the whole clade, and given the null model that changes are randomly distributed among the branches of the clade. One can imagine the test scattering changes randomly around the clade many times, and counting the fraction of replicates in which certain numbers of gains and losses are located in the distinguished area of the clade. If the null model suggests that the number of gains or losses actually reconstructed in this area should only rarely occur by chance, then a large number reconstructed in this area would suggest the null model is false. That is, changes are not distributed randomly, and they are significantly concentrated either within or outside of the distinguished area. For more information see W. Maddison (1990) and Harvey and Pagel (1991:88).

To perform the test, trace the evolution of a binary (two-state, 0-1) character representing the independent variable. MacClade uses this character's tracing to decide what you intend to be the distinguished branches. That is, the tracing in this character will indicate those branches on which a significant concentration of the other (dependent variable) character is sought. By choosing 0, 1, or equivocal in the **Correlation Test Parameters** dialog box (see below), you indicate whether the distinguished branches are those having state 0, 1, and/or equivocal in the character traced.

Thus, if the hypothesis tested is that proximal chiasma localization is a constraint against the evolution of chromosome fusions, chiasma localization (distal versus proximal) is traced on the clade. Use proximal=state 0 and distal=state 1, and indicate that the distinguished branches are those with state 1. You would then ask MacClade to calculate the null distribution for the number of gains of fusions falling in the distinguished area. If gains appear more concentrated than by chance, then there would appear to be an association between fusion and the supposedly unconstrained condition.

If needed, you can use the paintbrush tool to fix the state at various branches, for instance to resolve ambiguity. You can even create a fictitious character and trace it purely to define distinguished branches. For instance, if you want to ask whether changes in the dependent character are concentrated on branches on which the independent character changes, you could invent a character with all state 0's, then fix to state 1 just those branches on which the independent character changes, and set 1 to be the distinguishing state. Remember that the character traced must be the independent variable, and be a binary character (states 0 and 1 only).

N O T E : *The concentrated-changes test can be applied only to dichotomous trees. If your tree is polytomous, then you will have to resolve it manually or examine one or more random resolutions. Trees also cannot have any observed taxa fixed as ancestors.*

Once you have prepared the character tracing as you wish, the character-correlation tool ( ) is then applied to the base of the clade over which the calculations are to be done. MacClade will present the following dialog box, in which you specify options for the calculations.

Concentrated-Changes Test

In these calculations the independent variable is the character traced, the dependent variable is a second character. The calculations determine the probability of various numbers of gains and losses in the second character occurring in the distinguished areas of the clade selected, given a total number of gains and losses over the whole clade selected, under the null hypothesis that gains and losses are randomly distributed over the branches (Concentrated changes character correlation test; W. Maddison 1990). The "distinguished areas" are defined as those branches with the indicated state in the character traced.

Define the "distinguished branches" as those having,
☐ 0
☒ 1
in the character traced, state (choose one or more): ☐ equivocal

Determine probabilities by:
○ **EXACT COUNT** ☒ check abort often

◉ **SIMULATION** Sample size: 1000   of ○ 0 ○ 1 ◉ either ancestral

○ actual changes
◉ MINSTATE reconstruction   Initial state: Compensation:
○ MAXSTATE reconstruction   ◉ 0 ○ 1   ◉ 0 ○ 1 ○ 2 ○ 3

In the other (dependent) character,
number of gains: 3   **losses:** 2   (Cancel) (Calculate)

Correlation Test Parameters dialog box

The next several sections outline how you set up the test using this dialog box.

Choosing the branches distinguished by the independent character

With the choice of "distinguished branches" you indicate the character state(s) in the traced character indicating the area of the clade in which a concentration is sought. Thus, if equivocal and 1 were checked, the concentration test would determine the probabilities of various numbers of gains and losses falling on those branches of the clade reconstructed as have state 1 or an equivocal (0,1) assignment.

Methods to calculate probabilities

Two methods can be used to determine probabilities. The exact count uses the formulae presented by W. Maddison (1990). If the problem is too large for exact calculations, simulations can be used.

Exact count In order to make the exact count calculations reasonably fast, four-byte integers are used instead of real numbers. Because the calculations can yield very large numbers if there are many observed changes in the dependent character or taxa in the clade selected, and because four-byte integers can be only as high as 2,147,483,647, the calculations may exceed this value and therefore cannot proceed further. Approximate overflow conditions are as follows: with 130 taxa, the highest number of gains or losses in the dependent character that does not overflow is 2; with 80 taxa, 3; with 40 taxa, 4; with 30 taxa, 5; with 20 taxa, at least 6. If overflow occurs, MacClade will stop the calculations and give a warning. The exact calculations, if there are more than 5 or 6 observed gains or losses in the clade, can be very slow.

Simulations If the exact calculations overflow or are too slow, the simulations are a reasonable alternative. The simulations generate changes randomly on the clade selected and the number of gains and losses within the area of interest and in the clade as a whole are counted. Only those replicates that match the observed total number of gains and losses (entered at the bottom of the **Correlation Test Parameters** dialog box) are examined to see where the gains and losses are distributed. The simulation continues until the requested sample size is reached, or the user hits Command-period (⌘-.).

In the simulations, MacClade first decides how many changes it will throw onto the clade. If the simulation is of actual changes, then it will determine number of changes to be the sum of the "observed" total number of gains and losses indicated at lower left in the **Correlation Test Parameters** dialog box. Then, that many branches are randomly chosen using uniform random numbers. *Note that the root branch of the clade selected is never chosen for a change.* MacClade then supposes 0 is ancestral, and moves up the tree interpreting the changes as either gains or losses. If the total number of gains and losses each match the requested "observed" number, then MacClade accepts this as an instance of the requested number of gains and losses, given 0 is ancestral. If the simulated number of gains matches the requested number of losses, and vice versa, then MacClade accepts this as an instance of the requested number of gains and losses, given 1 is ancestral. In either case MacClade counts how many of the gains and how many of the losses are in the distinguished areas of the clade selected. One is added to the appropriate cell in a matrix storing the observed frequency of each possible combination of gains and losses in the distinguished areas. At the end of the simulations the frequencies in this matrix, divided by the sample sizes simulated, are taken as estimates of the probabilities of various numbers of gains and losses in the distinguished areas.

If the simulations are of reconstructed changes, then MacClade will throw onto the clade a number of changes equal to the requested "observed" number of gains plus losses plus the compensation (see below). Assuming the indicated initial state at the root of the clade selected (see below), these changes imply states in the terminal taxa. Using these terminal states, the ancestral states in the clade selected are reconstructed using the typical parsimony algorithms. Ambiguity in these states is resolved using either MINSTATE or MAXSTATE; this is done instead of ACCTRAN/DELTRAN, which can leave ambiguities unresolved (see p. 108). If the reconstructed number of gains and losses matches the requested number of gains and losses, then MacClade accepts this as an instance of the requested number of gains and losses given the reconstructed ancestral state is ancestral; the calculations proceed as for the actual changes. Note that the reconstructed ancestral state in the simulation is based entirely on simulated states at the terminal taxa in the clade selected; it is assumed that no information is available from outside the clade.

Option for simulations

Sample size In case you intend to focus on cases with a particular ancestral state in the dependent character, MacClade allows you to qualify the sample size requested. Thus you may ask to simulate 1,000 replicates in which state 0 is ancestral. Along the way, other replicates will be found with 1 ancestral, but the simulation will stop when 1,000 replicates with 0 ancestral have been found. The maximum sample size is 1,000,000.

Actual vs. MINSTATE/MAXSTATE With simulations, there are three options: the actual changes can be examined, or the changes as reconstructed by parsimony using MINSTATE or MAXSTATE ambiguity reduction (see p. 109) can be examined. By using reconstructed changes, one is using the null model as stated (equal probability of change on each branch), but in deriving the probability distributions, one is accounting for possible biasing effects of the use of parsimony reconstructions (W. Maddison, 1990:553). With the reconstructed change options one asks the question "What are the probabilities of reconstructing changes in various places given the null model?" rather than "What are the probabilities of changes actually occurring in various places given the null model?". The former might be considered in general better, because in practice we only have reconstructions, and are never certain we know the actual changes. However, the MINSTATE and MAXSTATE options present two extra parameters to specify, initial state and compensation.

Initial state For simulation of reconstructed changes (MINSTATE or MAXSTATE) you need to assume an initial state (at the root of the clade selected) in the simulation so that MacClade can interpret whether changes are gains or losses, and so assign states to terminal taxa from which to reconstruct changes.

In the exact count, one does not need to pre-specify an ancestral state. By assigning certain numbers of gains and losses randomly to the branches, as a side consequence one ends up implying an ancestral state at the root node of the clade selected. This state will be sometimes 0, sometimes 1. It should be noted that (a) the probability of 0 or 1 being implicitly ancestral depends on the shape of the tree and other factors, and (b) the probability distribution of numbers of gains and losses falling in the distinguished areas conditional upon 0 ancestral may be different from that conditional on 1 ancestral. Recall that when we say 1 ancestral, we mean at the root node of the clade selected, that is, at its "ingroup node" (Maddison et al., 1984), not the next node lower.

In the simulations, the initial state need not be specified when actual changes are counted but it needs to be specified when reconstructed changes are counted. With actual changes, it is not clear whether a change is a gain or a loss until one moves up the tree with an ancestral state assumed. However, suppose that one assigned changes to branches, and then tried both 0 and 1 ancestors. If the number of gains and losses desired were different, and the appropriate number of total gains and losses (requested by the user) occurred assuming 0 was ancestral, then this could be counted as an instance of the correct numbers and ancestor. This is what MacClade does. It can be shown that the various probabilities, including that of choosing ancestor 0 versus 1, match those from the exact calculations.

After simulating reconstructed changes you will note that you can still ask a question such as "Given that we have reconstructed 4 gains 2 losses and 0 at the base, what is the probability of so many gains in the distinguished areas?" even though in the **Correlation Test Parameters** dialog box you specified 1 as the initial state. The distinction here arises because you might reconstruct state 0 as ancestral even if 1 actually was ancestral. However, one must realize that the assumed simulation ancestral state is not necessarily the reconstructed one, and you may get different probabilities asking the above question depending upon whether you had set the initial state to 0 or 1.

Compensation When one is simulating reconstructed changes with the MINSTATE or MAXSTATE options, compensation needs to be specified. Compensation is a variable indicating how many extra changes are desired. It is needed because parsimony reduces the number of changes. If you need to generate 6 changes on the clade selected, then by having a compensation of 1 or 2, one would throw down 7 or 8 actual changes, and this would yield a better chance of parsimony reconstructing 6 than if you had thrown down only 6 actual changes. Note that this is not just an issue of speed; it could affect probabilities. Generally, you can leave the compensation at 0 unless the total number of changes is more than one-quarter of the number of taxa in the clade. MacClade monitors the simulation periodically to check if changing compensation would appear to speed the simulation; if so, the user is given the option of stopping the current simulation.

Setting changes in the dependent character

At the bottom of the dialog box, one enters the number of gains and losses reconstructed in the character whose concentrated evolution is being examined. This is the number of gains and losses in the whole clade selected. The calculations will then derive the probabilities of various numbers of gains and losses in the area of interest, given the indicated number of gains and losses in the whole clade selected. Note that even if you put 3 gains and 1 loss in this dialog box, after the calculations are done you can ask about probabilities given there are *other* numbers of gains and losses in the whole clade selected (up to 3 gains and 3 losses) *as long as* the calculations are done by exact count. If the calculations are done by simulation, you can ask only about the same total number of gains and losses indicated initially.

Stopping calculations

The calculations can be stopped by hitting Command-period (⌘-.). MacClade checks fairly frequently to see if you have requested a stop, but this checking slows down the calculations. To speed up the exact calculations, but therefore check less frequently, turn off "check abort often".

Viewing probabilities

After the calculations, a dialog box will be presented that allows you to ask about the results, as shown in the following figure.

> **Results from Concentrated-Changes Test**
>
> Given that there are [3] gains and [0] losses in the selected clade,
>
> and that ○ 0   ○ 1   ⦿ either is at the ancestral node,
>
> the probability of having
>
> ☐ more   ☒ as many   ☐ fewer than [3] gains and
>
> ☐ more   ☒ as many   ☐ fewer than [0] losses
>
> on branches distinguished by state 1 in character traced,
>
> is: [0.0922]
>
> under the null hypothesis that gains and losses   [Output to file]
> are randomly distributed.
>
>   (**Done**)

Correlation Test Results dialog box

You can ask what is the probability of having more than, as many as, or fewer than an indicated number of gains and losses in the area distinguished in the traced character, given the number of gains and losses over the whole clade specified at the top, and given that 0 or 1 is assumed ancestral in the character of interest. For instance, if you want to ask what is the probability of having 4 or more gains (and any number of losses) in the distinguished area, given 5 gains 2 losses overall, then you should indicate 5 gains 2 losses at the top, select "either" for ancestral state; indicate "more" and "as many" and "4" under gains; and "more", "as many", and "fewer" under losses.

When the exact calculations are used, the **Correlation Test Results** dialog box allows you to change the total number of gains and losses at the top, as long as the higher of the number of gains or losses does not exceed the higher of the number of gains or losses you entered for the total in the lower left of the **Correlation Test Parameters** dialog box. With simulations, the **Correlation Test Results** dialog box does not allow you to change the overall gains and losses.

By clicking on Output to file, a text file will be written showing the probability of various numbers of gains and losses occurring in the distinguished area, given the number of gains and losses overall, and the ancestral state that you have indicated at the top of the dialog box.

EXAMPLE: *Consider the following phylogeny, in the file Concentrated Changes Example, with character 1 traced upon it:*

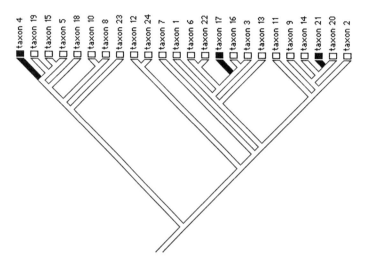

You note that "black" has arisen three separate times. Upon examining character 2, you notice that the three arisals of black in character 1, above, all occur within groups that have black in character 2:

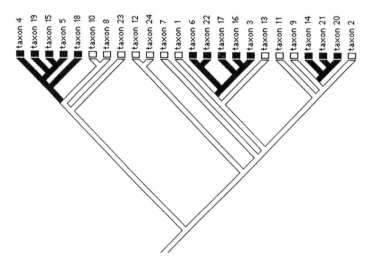

This suggests that there might be some sort of correlated evolution of characters 2 and 1; perhaps something about character 2 being white prevents the evolution of black in character 1; when this constraint is freed, black can evolve in character 1.

But are the three changes in character 1 overly concentrated in the black regions in character 2? MacClade's concentrated-changes test allows one to test the following hypothesis: The changes in character 1 are randomly distributed about the clade selected. To do this, we ask the question: What is the probability, under this null hypothesis, that three gains of black in character 1 would occur on black lineages in character 2?

Click the character-correlation tool ( ) on the root of the tree. In the dialog box that comes up, type 3 for gains and 0 for losses, and click on OK (exact calculations will be done). In the dialog box that comes up after calculations are done, specify as many or more than three gains, and 0 losses. The probability listed is 0.120671, the probability of having all three gains fall in the black area were they distributed by chance.

The assumption of equal branch lengths

One assumption behind the concentrated-changes test is that all branches are alike; the null hypothesis supposes change is equally likely on each branch. W. Maddison (1990) discusses when this assumption could cause problems.

Pagel and Harvey (1989) have described a phylogenetic correlation test that attempts to generalize Ridley's (1983) and W. Maddison's (1990) method by correcting for varying branch lengths. Is their test a version of the concentrated changes test that is sensitive to branch lengths? Not quite. Because Pagel and Harvey's test standardizes the "observed" change on branches using the branch lengths, the two characters being examined will have standardized changes that vary in concert whenever no change is reconstructed in either character on the branches, merely because both characters are being standardized by the same branch lengths. This means that the Pagel and Harvey correlation test is almost guaranteed to yield highly significant correlations whenever there is little change on the tree and branches have different lengths, regardless of how the character states are distributed in the terminal taxa. One could randomize the character-state distributions of the two characters with respect to each other, and the characters would still be judged to be highly correlated. The evolution of the characters would be judged especially highly correlated if both characters were invariant. Perhaps the test is telling us that both characters are similarly failing to change. Harvey and Pagel (1991) have noted this problem with their earlier test and suggest restricting the test to branches on which a change is reconstructed, but this modification remains incompletely justified. It is fair to say that we still lack an appropriate branch-length-sensitive version of W. Maddison's (1990) test.

Confirming the validity of the correlation test algorithms

In programming MacClade, the proper functioning of the correlation-test algorithms was tested as follows.

— The source code was thoroughly checked and rechecked.

— The exact and simulations calculations provide a natural cross-check for each other. For numerous test cases, simulations calculations were shown to provide accurate estimates of the exact results.

— Both simulations and exact calculations were shown to give correct results in a few small test cases that could be calculated by hand.

— The simulations keep track of how many changes were assigned to each branch. Each branch should get approximately the same number of changes assigned. If more than 100 changes are assigned to at least one branch, and another branch has less than half as many, then a warning is given. This is a weak test but is effective if the algorithm is misbehaving badly. In addition, if you save the results to a file, then included in the file is a branch-by-branch list of how many changes were assigned. In test cases, the changes were assigned evenly enough.

— The probability shown on the **Correlation Test Results** dialog box when it first appears to the user should be 1. In tests it was consistently close enough to 1.

18. GENERATING RANDOM DATA AND RANDOM TREES

MacClade has several tools for generating data or trees randomly. These could be used, for example, to determine if the observed values of some statistic differ from those obtained under a particular random model. These tools all use a random number generator, which will be described first.

SUMMARY OF FEATURES: *A block of the data matrix can be selected and filled entirely with randomly generated data, or the states of taxa can be randomly reshuffled. Characters can be generated randomly also by a simulation of evolution on the branches of the tree. Trees may be generated randomly using various models, including a simple model of speciation or coalescence.*

Random number generator and its seed

To generate random data or trees, MacClade uses a random number generator. This generator begins with a number called a "seed", and from it calculates a pseudo-random number. If it is to generate more than one random number, MacClade uses the previous random number as the seed for the next step. Given the same starting seed, the generator will generate the same sequence of numbers.

The random number generator is the same as in PAUP 3.0, translated from Swofford's C source code (Swofford, 1991) into assembly language. It is a linear congruential random number generator, where the next number x_i is calculated from the previous in the sequence x_{i-1} by the formula $x_i = 397204094 * x_{i-1} * \mod (2^{31} - 1)$. (For discussion of the random number generator, see Payne, Rabung and Bogyo, 1969; Fishman and Moore, 1982; Swofford, 1991.)

If left to itself, the generator will choose its own starting seed, based on the current time and date. To see or change the seed used by MacClade (e.g., to make a sequence of random data or trees reproducible), press the seed button ( ), present in any of the **Random Trees** or **Random Data** dialog boxes.

The following dialog box will appear:

You can set a new seed with the dialog box. Setting the seed to the seed used in a previous randomization will allow you to duplicate the previous randomization exactly (with the exception noted below). We suggest that you touch the seed button to see and record the seed before you begin a randomization, in case you want to duplicate the randomization exactly.

There is one circumstance in which it will be difficult to duplicate a randomization. This occurs when you are making random dichotomous resolutions of a polytomous tree on the screen. Even if you have the same polytomous tree on the screen, and set the seed to be the same, regenerating a set of random dichotomous resolutions may result in a different set each time. The reason for this is that MacClade stores polytomous trees internally as being dichotomous with some nodes marked as being "ghost" nodes that don't actually exist. This hidden "ghost" dichotomous resolution affects the random dichotomous resolutions obtained, and at different times you can have different ghost resolutions residing inside a polytomy. The best way to eliminate variations in this ghost resolution is to **Store Tree**, then choose **Trees** from the **Tree** menu to get the polytomous tree from storage just before use, because on processing from storage, the hidden resolution in a polytomy is always a ladder-like arrangement.

Random data

MacClade can generate new random data, or it can randomly shuffle existing data.

Data can be generated randomly in two ways: either states are assigned randomly to the taxa without reference to a tree, or states are evolved using a stochastic model of change on the current tree.

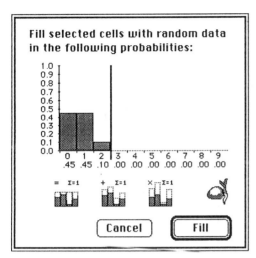

The **Random Fill** dialog box

Randomly assigning states to taxa

To generate random data without reference to a tree, select a portion of the matrix in the editor and choose **Random Fill** from the **Utilities** menu to have MacClade fill the selection with data generated randomly using the indicated frequencies of states.

On the horizontal axis of the bar chart in the dialog box are the states, indicated by their current symbols (in this case, 0 – 9). Each cell will be filled with a state with the probabilities shown on the bar chart. In the example illustrated above, each cell would be filled with either 0, 1, or 2, with probabilities 0.45, 0.45, and 0.10. To alter the frequency with which a state will be generated, move the top of the bar for that state up or down. Move the black vertical bar to indicate the maximum state. This is necessary to include states of higher value; for example, in the above example, if one wanted to set the probability of state 6 to be 0.2, one would first have to move the black vertical bar over to the right of state 6. It is also important for the norming functions, as described in the next paragraph.

Remember, the frequencies must sum to 1! The three **norming buttons** can be used to make frequencies sum to 1. They have the following actions:

 Makes frequencies equal (from state 0 through to the maximum state indicated by the vertical bar)

Scales frequencies to sum to 1 by adding or subtracting a constant amount to each

Scales frequencies to sum to 1 by multiplying or dividing, thus maintaining their proportions

The norming buttons act on all states between 0 and the vertical black bar. For example, pressing on the equal-frequencies norming button

( ) with the vertical bar set to be just above state 3 will set states 0 to 3 at equal frequency. If the vertical bar is just above state 4, then states 0 through 4 will be set to have equal frequency.

Once you have chosen the desired frequencies, press Fill to fill the selected cells with random data.

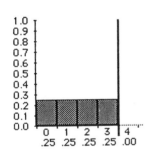

Effect of the equal-frequencies norming button with vertical bar above state 3

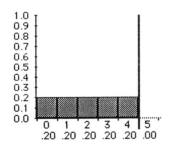

Effect of the equal-frequencies norming button with vertical bar above state 4

Shuffling existing data

To randomly shuffle existing data, select a portion of the matrix and choose **Shuffle** from the **Utilities** menu in the data editor. MacClade will scramble the selected portion. For each character, the states assigned to the taxa in the selected portion are scrambled so that they are now assigned randomly to (possibly different) taxa within the selected portion.

When you choose **Shuffle**, a dialog box is presented, letting you choose the random number seed, and asking if you wish to remove all footnotes and pictures from the shuffled block of data. If you choose not to remove footnotes and pictures, they will not be shuffled, and will remain stuck to the same cell in the editor they were attached to before shuffling.

This data shuffling can be used, for example, to calculate Archie's (1989a,b) homoplasy excess ratio.

Evolving characters up a tree

To generate data by a stochastic model of change on the current tree, you need to be in the tree window. Select **Evolve Characters** in the **Edit** menu. The following dialog box allows you to enter the parameters of the stochastic model.

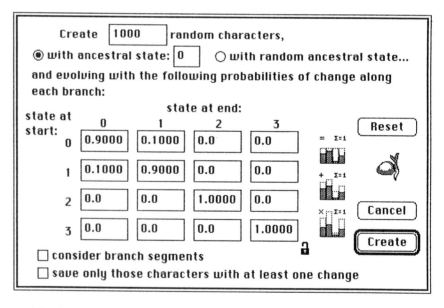

MacClade will randomly evolve the requested number of characters, according to the model, and add these on to the end of the data matrix. The probabilities shown indicate, for instance, that if a branch begins with state 0 that there is a 0.1 = 10 % probability the lineage will be at state 1 at the end of the branch.

By default, there is an equal probability of change along each branch in the tree. You can make some branches longer than others, thus increasing the probability of change, by increasing the number of **segments** on the branches. On branches with more than one segment, MacClade will perform one round of evolution (with the probabilities chosen in the dialog box above) along each segment of the branch. The dividing of a branch into segments is a special way to indicate branch length that is used currently only by the Evolve Characters feature. It is not connected to the branch lengths arising from Trace All Changes and is not used in the correlation test nor in reconstructing the evolution of continuous characters.

You can set branches to have more than one segment, using the set-segments tool (available in the **Tools** menu when the Option key is held down). With this tool, click on a branch, and choose a value from the pop-up menu. This will set the number of segments on the branch. (You can see the number of segments on each branch by choosing **Show Evolve Segments** from the **Display** menu.) You can reset all the branches to one segment by holding down the Option key and choosing **All One Segment** from the **Edit** menu.

WARNING: *The segments feature is still in preliminary form. The number of segments on a branch is not remembered when the tree is rebuilt from its stored description. This happens when you do Get Tree, when you move to the editor and back to the tree window, when you use a chart or print with multiple trees, when the file is closed and reopened, and in other circumstances. Therefore if you are using Evolve Characters with segments, you should check to see that the segments are as you want them just before using them.*

If some branches have more or less than one segment, then a check box will appear in the **Evolve Characters** dialog box, entitled "consider branch segments". If this is checked, then the probabilities given in the matrix will be per branch segment, not per branch, so that on a branch with three segments MacClade will perform three rounds of evolution on the branch. Thus, a 3-segmented branch might start out with state 0, change to state 1 on the first segment, remain at state 1 through the second segment, and then change to state 2 on the third segment.

The buttons on the right-hand side are the norming buttons; that is, they will cause the probabilities to be adjusted so that the sum in each row is 1.00. The norming buttons by default adjust all values in a row, including the value on the diagonal. If you want the values on the diagonals to be unaffected by the norming buttons, you can lock the diagonals by clicking on the lock at the lower-right corner of the matrix. If you click on the lock again, the diagonals will be unlocked.

The norming buttons work in the following ways:

 = Σ=1   Makes frequencies within in each row of the probability matrix equal. If the diagonal elements of the matrix are not locked, then this button will set all probabilities to 0.25. If the diagonal is locked, then this button will set the three off-diagonal probabilities in each row to equal (1-prob diagonal element)/3. For example, if the probability of a 0 to 0 change is set to 0.70, and the diagonals are locked, then this norming button will set the probabilities of 0 to 1, 0 to 2, and 0 to 3 all equal to 0.10.

 + Σ=1   Scales frequencies in each row to sum to 1 by adding or subtracting a constant amount to each.

× Σ=1   Scales frequencies in each row to sum to 1 by multiplying or dividing, thus maintaining their proportions.

The ancestral state for each created character will be 0 or another fixed state chosen by you, or you can ask MacClade to generate randomly ancestral states according the frequencies you set when you click on "with random ancestral state". The dialog box in which you set the ancestral frequencies behaves exactly like the one described in the preceding section.

If you choose "save only those characters with at least one change", then characters that did not change during their simulated evolution will be discarded.

Press **Create** to create the characters.

While MacClade is evolving these characters, it keeps track of the actual changes between states that take place in the simulated evolution. When it has finished creating all of the characters, a dialog box comes up, asking if you wish to save this information and other aspects of the simulation to a text file.

Confirming the validity of the random data algorithms

In programming MacClade, the proper functioning of the random data algorithms was tested by comparing the outcome of the randomization with the parameters of the model used; several different parameter values were tested. The frequency of states produced by **Shuffle** and **Random Fill** match those expected, as calculated by the States chart, and the frequency of changes produced by Evolve Characters in the tree window as written in the Simulation Report file match those of the model.

Random trees

MacClade can generate random dichotomous trees in various contexts, for instance in charts. MacClade can also generate and save random trees into the current data file or tree file, if you choose **Random Trees** from the **Edit** menu.

There are four options for generating trees. The first three of these relate to different probability distributions of completely random trees (Maddison and Slatkin, 1991):

Equiprobable trees: The probability of picking any given tree out of all possible dichotomous rooted trees is equal. Random trees so generated sample evenly all possible dichotomous trees. This might be useful, for instance, to examine the shape of the bar chart of treelengths over all possible trees (e.g., Fitch, 1979; Huelsenbeck, 1991), without actually enumerating all possible trees.

Random joining: Trees are formed by successively joining taxa randomly. Thus, two terminal taxa are chosen at random and made into a new clade, and this clade is treated as if it were a terminal taxon for purposes of further joining. The taxa are randomly joined until all have been clustered. Such random joining trees are useful to model the coalescent process in a panmictic population (see example, pp. 333–335), or to model a random speciation process in which each species has an equal chance of speciating (Harding, 1971; Simberloff et al., 1981; Maddison and Slatkin, 1991).

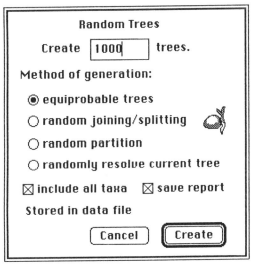

The **Random Trees** dialog box

Random partition: Trees are formed by successive random partitions of the taxa. A random partition of all taxa into two subsets is first made, with each terminal taxon having a 0.5 chance of falling into the left-hand subset. Then within each subset, again a random partition is made, and so on until a fully resolved tree is created. Such random partitioning trees might be useful to examine trees generated by a divisive clustering method whose decisions are taken randomly. Although no biological process has been proposed that yields tree distributions of this sort, random partition trees provide a heuristic extreme emphasizing symmetrical trees.

Random dichotomous resolution of polytomous tree: There is a fourth option that does not create a fully random tree. It appears only when the tree in the tree window has polytomies, and it allows the user to create random dichotomous resolutions of this polytomous tree. The tree on screen is kept as is, except that a dichotomous resolution of each polytomy is chosen randomly (equiprobably for each possible resolution) to yield a dichotomous tree. This option is useful to sample from among all possible dichotomous resolutions consistent with a given polytomous tree. It is discussed further in the section on "Looking at alternative resolutions", in Chapter 5 (p. 121), although such dichotomous resolutions are also accessible in the other contexts in which random trees are generated.

Comparatively, samples of random partition trees are most biased toward symmetrical trees and equiprobable trees toward asymmetrical trees. Random joining trees are intermediate in their bias.

If taxa are excluded from the current tree on the screen, and the "include all taxa" box is not checked, then trees will be formed of only the taxa in the current tree (all taxa in the tree, not just those visible if a clade happens to be expanded). If the "include all taxa" box is checked, then all taxa in the data matrix will be included in each random tree.

Just above the Create button, MacClade lists where the created trees will be stored — in the current tree repository, either the data file or a external tree file — if they are to be stored.

Confirming the validity of the random tree algorithms

In programming MacClade, the proper functioning of the random tree algorithms was tested as follows.

— The source code was thoroughly checked and rechecked.

— MacClade will keep track of the basal split in the tree and compare observed basal clade size asymmetries with those theoretically expected for the type of random tree being generated. Theoretical expectations are given by the equations for R given by Maddison and Slatkin (1991), except that the equation for equiprobable trees is not correctly listed in their paper: each expression should be divided by 2. (The results of their paper were calculated using the correct expressions.) In test cases, MacClade gave observed asymmetries very close to those expected. If you want to use this check, select "save report" in the dialog box where you request random trees to be generated.

— The random tree algorithms yielded the appropriate probability distributions expected in theory for the number of steps in characters (Maddison and Slatkin, 1991).

19. USING MACCLADE WITH MOLECULAR DATA

MacClade was designed for use with morphological, behavioral, molecular, or other classes of character data. In this chapter we describe some of the special features in MacClade for use with molecular data.

SUMMARY OF FEATURES: *MacClade has three data formats for molecular data: DNA, RNA and protein. These formats predefine symbols for character states and provide other features. In DNA and RNA formats, coding and non-coding regions can be distinguished, and sites labeled as first, second and third positions in codons. DNA and RNA data can be translated into protein data using a predefined or user-specified genetic code. Special editing features include complementing and reversal. Blocks of sequence can be pushed for manual alignment. The matrix can be displayed with a special symbol to indicate a match with the first sequence. Step matrices can be generated for amino acids to reflect distances suggested by the genetic code. A number of charts distinguish transitions and transversions or different codon positions. Charts are available that can reveal biases in character evolution, including hot spots along a sequence.*

DNA, RNA, and protein data formats

Three of MacClade's data formats (DNA, RNA, and protein) come preformatted with appropriate symbols defined (e.g., "A", "C", "G", and "T"). The symbols used are the standard IUPAC symbols (see Chapter 10, p. 175).

Some features in MacClade are available only if DNA or RNA formats are chosen (e.g., tabulations of transitions and transversions in some charts, translation of nucleotide sequence to amino acid sequence, and so on).

Specifying coding regions and codon positions

For DNA or RNA sequence data, sites are specified as to whether or not they are in protein-coding regions. Sites in coding regions are designated as being either in the first, second or third position of a codon. You can assign such positions manually, or ask MacClade to calculate them automatically. The coding status and position of a site is shown in the Pos column in the character status window. The symbol "-" indicates a non-coding site.

When you start a new DNA or RNA data file, or add new sites to an existing matrix, MacClade assumes the new sites are non-coding. You can designate sites as coding either by indicating their codon positions as first, second or third, or by asking MacClade to calculate codon positions automatically. To set a site manually as first, second, or third position, or non-coding, selecting it in the character status window or data editor and select the appropriate the menu item in the **Change Codons** submenu.

To have MacClade calculate positions automatically, select a contiguous block of characters in either the character status window (p. 196) or in the data editor. Then choose **Calculate Positions** from the **Change Codons** submenu of the **Assume** menu. In the dialog box, choose whether or not you want MacClade to reset bases currently designated as noncoding to be coding, and then set the position of the first selected base. If you then press Calculate, MacClade will automatically assign bases to first, second, and third positions. If the first base in the selected block is part of a coding region, then MacClade will assign to it the position number you have requested. For example, if the first site is designated a second position and is in a coding region, then MacClade will set the positions to 2, 3, 1, 2, 3, 1, 2, 3, ... and so on. If you so choose, the first base past a non-coding block will be designated a first position:

```
sequence              ACCCGACGACATGACAGTACAGTTA
coding/non-coding     ccccccc-------cccccccccc
calculated position   3123123--------1231231231
assigned position     3123123--------1231231231
```

Otherwise, MacClade will continue the numbering through the noncoding block:

```
sequence              ACCCGACGACATGACAGTACAGTTA
coding/non-coding     ccccccc-------cccccccccc
calculated position   3123123123123123123123123
assigned position     3123123--------3123123123
```

The purpose of the codon position designation is for display and selection in the character status window, for DNA/RNA-to-protein translation, and for various charting options. The **Select** submenu in the **Edit** menu, available if the character status window is front-most, will contain, for example, an **Every 2nd** menu item, the selection of which will cause every second position in the character status window to be selected. This allows one to exclude all second and third codon positions to focus on the evolution of nucleotides in the first codon position, or to give all third-position nucleotides low weight in a phylogenetic analysis, and so on. Codon position can be used in the chart window, to distinguish first, second, and third positions regarding the statistical results presented. For instance, the By Codon Position option in the Character Steps/etc. chart can indicate the number of steps in nucleotides at the first, second and third positions (see Chapter 15). Codon position designations are important for DNA/RNA-to-protein translation, as they specify the codons that get translated to amino acids.

Translating nucleotide sequences to amino acid sequences

If your data are of DNA or RNA sequences, and you select the **Translate to Protein** item in the **Format** menu in the data editor, then MacClade will transcribe and translate the nucleotide sequence into an amino acid sequence according to the current genetic code. (If in doubt about the nature of the genetic code and therefore of the translation used by MacClade, open the **Genetic Code** dialog box from the **Format** menu, which specifies the correspondence between nucleotide triplets as they appear in the matrix and amino acids.)

When you ask MacClade to translate nucleotide data to amino acid data, you will be presented with the **Translate to Protein** dialog box.

If gaps are considered, then three consecutive gaps in positions 1, 2, and 3 are taken to mean that there is a gap in the amino acid sequence; other gaps are considered equivalent to missing data. In translating a triplet containing missing data, MacClade will convert to all possible amino acids consistent with the partially specified triplet. For example, "CA?" will be treated as equivalent to "CAA or CAC or CAG or CAT", and will be converted to Gln/His. If gaps are ignored, then MacClade will skip over gaps during translation. Considering gaps essentially preserves some of the information in the alignment of nucleotides; ignoring gaps essentially removes the alignment.

> Are you sure you want to translate DNA/RNA data to protein data using standard nuclear genetic code? This cannot be undone; you may wish to save a copy of the nucleotide file first.
>
> ⦿ consider gaps
>   AAG---CCT = AAG---CCT,
>   AA-G-C-CT = AA?G?C?CT
>
> ◯ ignore gaps & push to end of sequence
>   AAG---CCT = AAGCCT???,
>   AA-G-C-CT = AAGCCT???
>
> [Cancel] [Translate]

The **Translate to Protein** dialog box

MacClade's translation is the same whether the data file is RNA or DNA; it does not invert the sense of the codons for one or the other. When in doubt, check the **Genetic Code** dialog box to see how the translation will be performed.

Some sequences cannot be translated by MacClade. For example, if three consecutive sites are designated as positions 1, 2, and 2, then MacClade will recognize that adjacent sites do not have adjacent codon positions and will refuse to translate. MacClade will also refuse to translate if a non-coding site is followed by a site designated as position 2 or 3.

In translating the data, all type sets, weight sets, and inclusion sets are destroyed, as are all footnotes and pictures (except those attached to taxon names), and all character names. All characters are reset to the default type.

Data editor features for sequence data

Naming sites

You may wish to provide character names to the sites along the sequence, so that you can track the sites even as you delete or add new sites. MacClade's **Fill** command (**Utilities** menu) allows rapid entry of sequentially numbered character names.

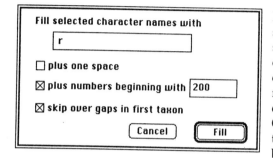

For example, imagine that you have an aligned set of sequences, 450 sites in length, one sequence of which corresponds to sites 200-600 of some reference sequence (with 50 gaps added into the reference sequence during the alignment). To assign character names based on this reference sequence, move that reference sequence to be taxon 1, and select the full set of character names. The easiest way to do this would be to touch on the character name of the first site, then hold down the Shift and Option keys and press the right arrow (→) key (down arrow [↓] key if the matrix is transposed). You are now ready to call up the Fill dialog box, and set it up as shown on the left. With the "skip over gaps in first taxon" selected, MacClade will number the sites based on the reference sequence:

```
          r200
          r200a
          r200b
          r201
          r201a
          r202
          r203
          r204
          r205
          r206
reference A - - C - G T G C T
sequence2 A G G C - G T G C T
sequence3 A - - C C G T G C T
```

Changing nucleotides to their complements

To convert all nucleotides in a selected block of cells to their complements, choose **Complement** from the **Utilities** menu. This will convert all A→T, all T→A, all G→C, and all C→G, as illustrated in the example below:

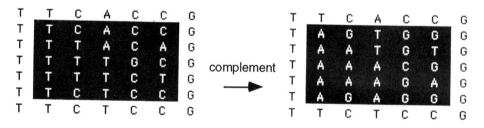

Reversal of sequences

To reverse a selected block of cells, choose **Reverse** from the **Utilities** menu. For example, if bases 2 through 6 are selected, then base 6 will exchange places with base 2, and base 5 with base 3:

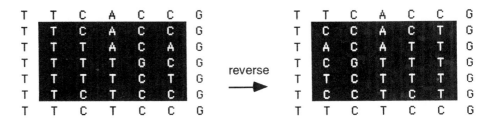

Sequence alignment

Primitive ways to manually align sequences are built into MacClade's data editor. If Block Moves are enabled (by selecting the **Block Moves** item in the **Edit** menu), you can quickly move blocks of cells around the matrix.

To move blocks of data a short way, one can use MacClade's nudging feature. Select a block of cells to move, and with Block Moves enabled, hit any of the four arrow keys. The selected block will be nudged one cell over in the direction of the arrow.

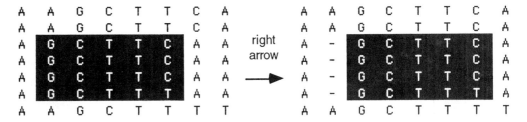

Gaps will be left in the wake of the nudged block. The leading edge of the nudged block will overwrite the character states it covers.

N O T E: *As the leading edge of a moved block overwrites any sequence data it covers, you may wish to make sure the leading edge of the block is at the edge of the matrix, so that there is no data for it to overwrite. You can then move the leading edge of the block out of the matrix using the Option key, as described below. (To quickly extend a block to include the edge of the matrix, type Shift-Option-Arrow key.)*

If one wishes to move blocks of data large distances, you can use the mouse. First, make sure Blocks Moves are enabled, and then select the block to be moved. When the pointer is moved over the selected block of cells, it changes to a hand, with arrows on it indicating the directions you can move the block. (Cells can be moved only within taxa, not between taxa.) You can then simply drag the block to the new location:

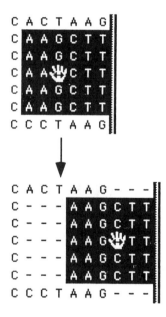

You cannot push blocks off the edges of the matrix, unless you hold down the Option key. If you do hold down the Option key and you push a block off the edge, then the matrix will be expanded to accommodate the block:

As an additional aid for sequence alignment, MacClade will output a file in the NBRF format (see Chapter 9), which can then be read into a sequence alignment program.

Match first

This matrix display option, described in "Editor display options" in Chapter 10, uses the first taxon as a standard and displays cells in the rest of the matrix with a chosen symbol (for instance, ".") whenever the state matches that in the first taxon.

If "match first mode" is on in the editor, you can type the matching symbol into any data cell and MacClade will interpret that to mean you are entering the same state as in the first taxon. This, of course, does not work for entering data into the first taxon.

Uninformative sites

You may want to have MacClade ignore or delete uninformative sites so that they do not get involved in the various calculations performed. Chapter 10 describes the features for including, excluding, and deleting characters. If you want to exclude the uninformative characters, you can use **Exclude Uninformative** in the **Assume** menu while in the tree window. However, this does not save any memory usage, because MacClade (unlike PAUP) does not pack the data matrix according to assumptions and exclusions. (It does not pack in part because MacClade's tree window maintains a "live" display of results even as you change assumptions.) If you want to get rid of the uninformative characters to save memory, you need to delete them from the data file entirely. The **Filter Characters** command can be used to permanently delete characters that are excluded (for instance, by **Exclude Uninformative**).

Before deleting any characters, you may want to assign the characters names corresponding to their positions in the sequence, so that their original positions will still be indicated even after other sites are deleted. The **Fill** command will allow you to name the characters automatically in sequence (see "Naming sites", earlier in this chapter).

Setting the genetic code

The **Genetic Code** dialog box

MacClade allows the user to specify a genetic code, which MacClade uses for DNA/RNA-to-protein conversion and to create user-defined types of the minimum number of nucleotide changes underlying amino acid substitutions (Swofford and Olsen, 1990; Felsenstein, 1991).

The genetic code can be specified in the **Genetic Code** dialog box from the **Format** menu. The "universal" genetic codes are provided by pressing the nuclear and mtDNA buttons. To change the amino acid corresponding to a particular nucleotide triplet, select the nucleotide triplet in the table, then touch on the amino acid name (the little buttons on the right) to which you wish the triplet to correspond. ("*" refers to the termination codon.) Multiple nucleotide triplets can be selected if you hold down the Shift key while clicking on additional triplets.

Changing TCG so that it codes for Lys

An amino acid can be said to be disjunct if there exist at least two triplets that code for the amino acid, such that there is no chain of triplets linking them, with adjacent elements in the chain differing by only one single nucleotide mutation, and with all elements of the chain coding for that amino acid. Note that serine is disjunct in the standard nuclear code (as the serine codons AGC and AGT are at least 2 mutational steps away from serines TCA, TCC, TCG, and TCT). Evolutionary changes between serine AGC and serine TCT therefore must go through an intermediate amino acid. To check to see if the code as you have it currently defined has any disjunct amino acids, touch on the Disjunct? button. Even though serine is disjunct, the Disjunct? button will not indicate this for the standard nuclear code because the two disjunct pieces have been coded as distinct states 1 and 2. (Serines AGC and AGT are coded as 1.Ser, and TCA, TCC, TCG, and TCT are coded as 2.Ser.)

If you create a custom genetic code, there may be disjunct amino acids other than serine. You may wish to code the disjunct pieces of an amino acid as distinct states, as is done automatically for serine with the standard nuclear code. This can be of value if you wish to analyze your data using protein parsimony (see next section). To do this, you need to first define extra amino acid states. You can define extra states by clicking on a box below the title "AA" beside "Extra State", then clicking on the list of amino acids to indicate what amino acid the extra state represents. Once these extra amino acids are defined, you can then apply them to the genetic code.

If some elements of the code specify extra states (as is the case for AGC, AGT, TCA, TCC, TCG, and TCT in the standard nuclear code), then when you ask MacClade to convert from nucleotide to amino acid sequences, it will use those extra states in the conversion. Thus, if you are using the standard nuclear code, your converted matrix may have some "1" and "2" entries, indicating the two serine states.

If you modify the genetic code, your new code will be stored in the data file when you save it. There is currently no easy way to make a central storage place for various genetic codes you have created, but if you regularly work with data files that use codes other than MacClade's built-in codes, you may want to make a series of stationery pads (Chapter 8), each one of which has stored in it a different genetic code appropriate for the different molecules on which you work.

WARNING: *If you wish to export your data matrix to a program that doesn't understand that the symbols 1 and 2 mean serine, then use **Recode** in the **Utilities** menu to convert 1 and 2 to S before you export your file.*

Creating protein-parsimony user-defined types

To create a user-defined type, in which the cost of a change between two amino acids is the minimum number of amino acid changes required to convert between the two amino acids, press the **New** button in the **Type Edit** dialog box in the **Assume** menu. Check the box "Protpars type based on genetic code". If you then press **Create**, MacClade will use the current genetic code to calculate the minimum number of changes between amino acids, and create a user-defined type based on these changes. Such a type can be used to implement protein parsimony (Felsenstein, 1991).

WARNING: *Your data matrix may contain amino acids that are no longer defined in the current genetic code, perhaps to avoid disjunction. For example, in the standard nuclear code, serine (symbolized by "S") is replaced by serine.1 ("1") and serine.2 ("2"), as there are two disjunct sets of triplets coding for serine (see previous section). If MacClade detects any serine ("S") in your data matrix, or other similar amino acids, as it creates a protein parsimony type, it will ask if you wish to convert these to their non-disjunct equivalents. For serine, this will involve converting all S to 1/2. In the process, any cells containing such amino acids that were polymorphic will be converted to uncertainty (e.g., V&S will be converted to V/1/2).*

Importing data from molecular data bases

For information about importing data from non-NEXUS files, see Chapter 9.

File saving options

You have some flexibility over how MacClade writes its NEXUS files. Some of the available features are specifically designed for molecular sequence data. See Appendix 1 for details.

Examples using molecular data

Testing panmixis using gene phylogenies

Suppose that you have sampled individuals from four nearby localities and reconstructed a phylogenetic tree relating their mitochondrial DNA sequences, as follows:

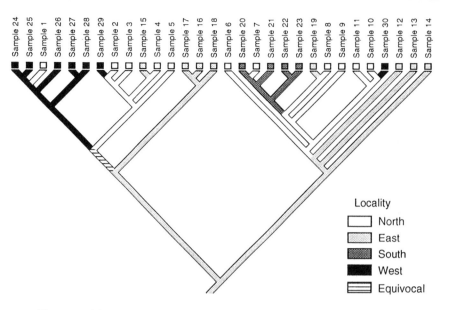

How would you use this to test whether there is some restriction of gene flow among these populations? Slatkin and Maddison (1989) have suggested using the number of migration events required by a tree as a statistic to measure gene flow. Construct a MacClade data file listing all of the specimens and treat locality as a four-state unordered character. Trace this character to determine the minimum number of interlocality migration events allowed by the tree. In this case, it is 10. Then create a chart for the number of trees with various numbers of steps for the traced character, using random trees. Construct 1,000 random joining trees. The chart should look something like this:

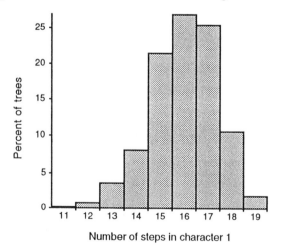

Were these four localities part of a single panmictic population, the minimum number of interlocality migration events should have the same probability distribution as the number of steps on random joining trees (Slatkin and Maddison, 1989; Maddison and Slatkin, 1991). Note that the 10 interlocality migrations on the reconstructed tree would be highly unlikely under panmixis, suggesting that there are indeed restrictions to gene flow.

Molecular data and MacClade's charts

Open up the primate mtDNA data file (from Hayasaka et al., 1988). It should open up to show the tree window. Choose **Character Steps/etc.** menu item of the **Chart** menu. Click the upper-middle chart icon (charting by sequence for the current tree). Click on the ⬛ button, and set the interval width to 5 using the dialog box that comes up; press OK in this dialog box. Then press Chart in the **Character Steps/etc.** dialog box. You should see the following chart.

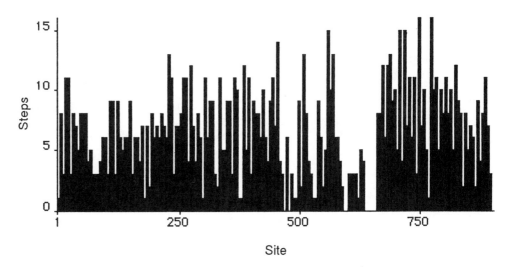

On the horizontal axis is the base position. On the vertical axis is the number of steps *on the tree* for each site in the DNA sequence. There is clearly a more conserved region around site 650. (This region codes for a leucine tRNA.)

If you choose **Chart Options** from the **Chart** menu, select the "changes" radio button on the right side, then click on Restrict, press the Transversions and OK button in the dialog box that appears, then press Chart. MacClade will show you the distribution of transversions along the sequence:

Calculated over current tree

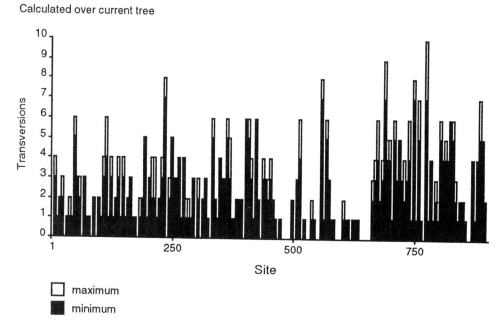

If you choose **Chart Options** from the **Chart** menu, and select the upper right icon, so that MacClade will chart steps by codon position, the chart MacClade will present is:

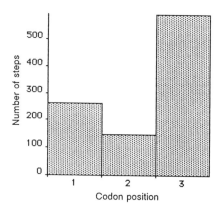

As expected, most of the changes on the tree are at the third position. Recall that these are changes reconstructed on the tree, not merely calculated from pairwise distances.

Choose **State Changes & Stasis** from the **Chart** menu. In the dialog box that appears, choose "count minimum and maximum number", and press Chart. You should see the following chart.

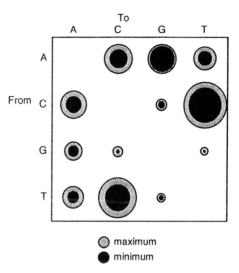

This chart is calculated over all sites, coding and non-coding, as no characters have been excluded. Note that the largest spots in each row are for the transitions A to G, G to A, C to T, and T to C. If you click on the table view button ▦, you will see these results in numerical rather than graphical form:

Frequency of possible changes between states (minimum– maximum)

	To: A	C	G	T
From: A		72-179	136-186	41-116
C	56-149		10-31	234-419
G	24-72	3-26		1-14
T	30-100	147-334	5-18	

If you click on the text view button $\overline{\mathbf{X}}$, you will see the following summary:

Number of transitions: 712–777
Number of transversions: 376–441
Number of all changes: 1153–1153

The number of reconstructed transitions is about twice as high as the number of transversions. Let us see if the results are similar when we focus only on second positions of codons. If you then choose the inclusion set "only 2nds" from the **Inclusion Set** dialog box from the **Assume** menu, MacClade will present you with similar results for just second positions:

```
Number of transitions : 116-120
Number of transversions : 26-30
Number of all changes  : 146-146
```

With second positions we can see that the bias for transitions is stronger, with about four times as many transitions as transversions reconstructed.

If you then choose the inclusion set "All Included" from the **Inclusion Set** dialog box from the **Assume** menu, and ask MacClade to show a **States** chart, you should see:

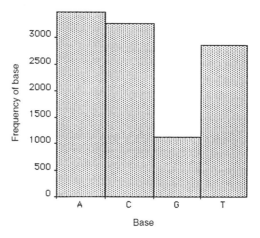

Note the low frequency of G.

Click on the text view button, and you will get a summary of the frequency of each base:

A	**Mean** : 0.3232	**Range** : 0.3040 - 0.3474
C	**Mean** : 0.3031	**Range** : 0.2527 - 0.3440
G	**Mean** : 0.1052	**Range** : 0.0979 - 0.1158
T	**Mean** : 0.2655	**Range** : 0.2360 - 0.2895

The mean frequency of each base across taxa is listed in the first column, and the ranges of base frequency across taxa is listed after that.

Now let us consider alternative hypotheses about the closest relatives of *Homo sapiens*, using charts that compare hypothetical phylogenetic trees. Notice that the treelength of the tree in the tree window is 1153. Try rearranging the tree to give all three possible rearrangements of the *Homo-Pan-Gorilla* clade. Two of these, the one linking *Pan* with *Homo* and that linking *Pan* with *Gorilla*, both have a treelength of 1153, while the third arrangement linking *Gorilla* with *Homo* has a treelength of 1160. The first two equally parsimonious arrangements are stored in the data file as "*Homo-Pan*" and "*Pan-Gorilla*". To compare them, ask for the chart **Compare 2 Trees**. Choose one tree, then the other. You will notice that *Homo-Pan* requires one fewer step of each of 12 characters, while *Pan-Gorilla* requires one fewer step of a different 12 characters. By excluding first, second or third codon positions one could examine whether one of the trees was supported by more first or second positions than the other. Now, go to the character status window, select all characters, and assign them all the user-defined step-matrix type "ttbias". As you can see in the **Type Edit** dialog box, this type assigns six steps to a transversion, one step to a transition. When this assumption is applied to all characters, the treelengths of *Homo-Pan* and *Pan-Gorilla* are 3033 and 3048 respectively. As can be seen in the Compare 2 Trees chart, there are still 12 characters preferring *Homo-Pan* and 12 preferring *Pan-Gorilla*, except that in three of these characters, *Pan-Gorilla* requires a transversion. The chart shows these characters at positions 88, 340, and 625. In the character status window the first two can be seen to be third positions, the last in a non-coding region. If a step matrix is used that gives a higher cost to transversions than transitions, then *Homo-Pan* is preferred.

20. Recording Your Work: Printing, Graphics, and Text Files

SUMMARY OF FEATURES: *The data matrix, tree, character status window, and chart can be printed while their windows are front-most on the screen.*

Trees can be printed with slanted, rectangular, or partly slanted branches, or in a circular format. Branch thicknesses can be changed. Trees can be resized or repositioned on the page. Multiple trees can be printed, either on successive pages or sharing one page. A single tree can be printed to span multiple pages. Taxon names can be angled and printed in various styles. The printed tree can also show the name of the tree, the tree number, tree statistics, the legend for any tracing, and a comment.

Character tracings can be printed with the tree. Tracings of all characters or all equally parsimonious reconstructions of a single character can be printed. When a tree showing Trace All Changes is printed, the lengths of printed branches can be made proportional to the number of reconstructed changes. Lists of the states reconstructed at the nodes of the tree can be printed. Data Boxes can be printed with taxa arranged on the tree or in data matrix sequence.

Instead of printing the tree or a chart, MacClade can also create a graphics file for editing in a graphics program. Text files summarizing reconstructed states at nodes or other information can be saved.

Saving a record of your work

With some phylogenetic computer programs it was relatively easy to save a record of your work, because a formatted data file was processed by a program that generated an output tree. One needed only print out the data file, the options in effect at the time of tree reconstruction, and a log file, and a complete record was saved. However, MacClade's interactive nature means that results large or small are constantly being generated against a changing background of assumptions. Although this encourages free exploration of alternatives, it makes saving a record of your work particularly difficult, especially as many of the results are presented in graphical, not textual, forms. MacClade's features for

340

printing and saving graphics files provide the user with record-keeping ability, but it is largely up to the user to remember to keep records.

The first and most basic method to save records is to use **Save As** in the **File** menu to store archive copies of your data file (with its trees, assumptions, options, and so on) at critical points in the analysis. Remember, **Save As** will leave the last-saved version on disk with its old name and create a new file with the new name you specify. The new file will store the current options and data.

Second, various results, data, and assumptions can be printed. Trees and charts can be printed to store a record of results, and the data matrix to print a record of data. However, likely to be forgotten are the assumptions and options that can affect the results and yet which don't appear in the data matrix. The character status window, which contains a list of which characters are included, their weights and transformation types, can be printed. A summary of current options and assumptions, the transformation-type definitions, footnotes, pictures, and character and state names can be printed using the **Print Other** submenu in the **File** menu.

There is no facility in MacClade to print all aspects of the data file with a single command. For this reason, if you select a file in the Finder and give the **Print** command, MacClade will start, open that file, but not print (as MacClade doesn't know what aspect of that file you wish to print). If you want an archival printout of the exact form of your data file as saved, you can open it in any word processor and print it (because MacClade files are stored as text files).

Third, images of trees and charts can be saved to graphical PICT files so that you can later edit and print them in graphics programs.

Fourth, general information about current assumptions, and tables such as the character status window and chart window can be saved as text files using the **Save Text File** submenu of the **File** menu. Text files can also store information generated by chart calculations, the character-correlation test, and by character tracings.

Choosing fonts for printing

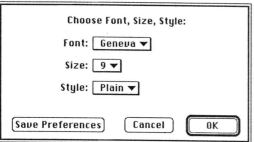

Choose Font, Size, Style:

Font: Geneva ▼

Size: 9 ▼

Style: Plain ▼

[Save Preferences]   [Cancel]   [OK]

For printing the data matrix, chart window, and character status window from within MacClade, the font used is the font visible on the screen. For printing the tree, control over fonts is provided in the **Print Tree** dialog box.

For the About *filename* and About trees windows, and the items in the **Print Other** submenu, MacClade gives you a choice of fonts to use when you request printing, in the dialog box pictured on the left. Choose the font, size, and style of the text to be printed, and press **OK** to continue printing.

Printing data and assumptions

Printing the data matrix

The data matrix can be printed when it is the front-most window on the screen, by calling **Print Matrix** from the **File** menu. It will be printed more or less as it appears on the screen. It will therefore be rather crude. You might be better served by using the **Simple Table** item of the **Export File** submenu of the **File** menu to create a text file of the data matrix that can be formatted in a word-processing, page-layout, or spreadsheet program (see Chapter 9, p. 157), or by editing and printing a copy of the NEXUS file itself from within a word-processing program.

Printing current options

By choosing **General Notes** from the **Print Other** submenu, MacClade will print a sheet with the current time and date, version of MacClade, and the status of various options:

```
Wednesday, July 1, 1992: 9:02 PM
MacClade  Version 3.0
Status Notes
=======================
Data file: Hamamelidae
28 taxa

CHARACTERS
54 characters
54 characters included
No characters excluded
Character Transformation types:
      Types currently in use: unordered
      Directed types in use: no
```

```
TREES
Current tree repository: external tree file
(Ham.island4)
Polytomies assumed to represent uncertain resolu-
tion
Current tree:
        Includes all 28 taxa in data file
```

Upon your request to print these general notes, MacClade will present you with a dialog box that allows you to choose the font of the printed notes.

Printing other components

Other components of the data file, such as the user-defined transformation type definitions, the footnotes, pictures, a list of character and state names, the current genetic code, Data Boxes, and continuous data can be printed using the **Print Other** submenu in the **File** menu.

Upon your request to print these general notes, MacClade will present you with a dialog box that allows you to choose the font of the printed information.

If you ask to print the Data Boxes from the **Print Other** submenu, then the taxa will appear in the Data Boxes in the order of appearance in the data matrix, not their order in the current tree. To have Data Boxes printed in the order of appearance in the current tree, you must print Data Boxes from within the **Print Tree** dialog box in the **File** menu.

Printing the character status table

The character status window can be printed when it is front-most on the screen, by calling **Print Table** from the **File** menu. It will be printed more or less as it appears on the screen.

Printing trees

MacClade's tree printing facility allows you to print trees in a wide variety of forms. Characters can be traced or not, changes indicated, and branches may be slanting, square, or proportional to branch length. Taxon names may be written diagonally at varying angles and with varying fonts and styles. Five examples follow.

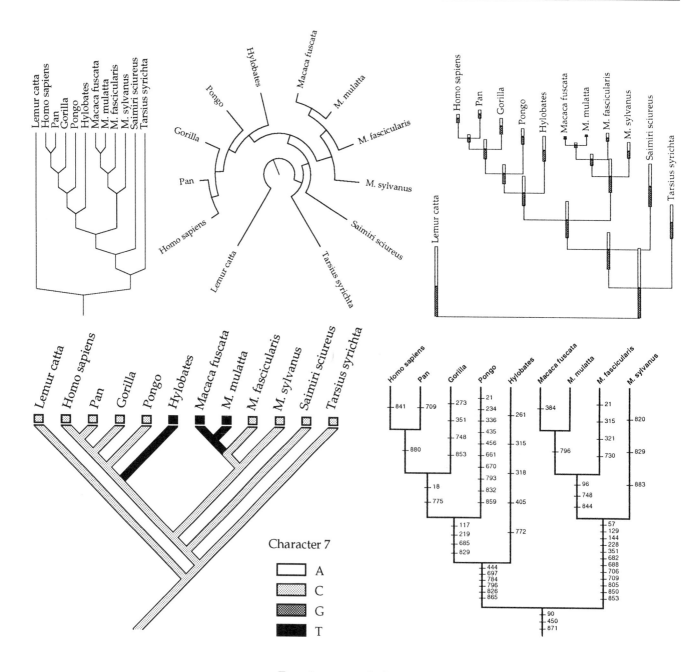

Character 7

☐ A

▨ C

▓ G

■ T

To print a traced character, it must be traced already in the tree window. To print the branch lengths according to Trace All Changes, Trace All Changes must be displayed already in the tree window.

Trees can be printed when the tree window is on screen and it (or one of its accessory windows) is the front window. Select **Print Tree**, in the

File menu, and MacClade will present a dialog box that has an image of the tree on the page, as it will be printed, in the center:

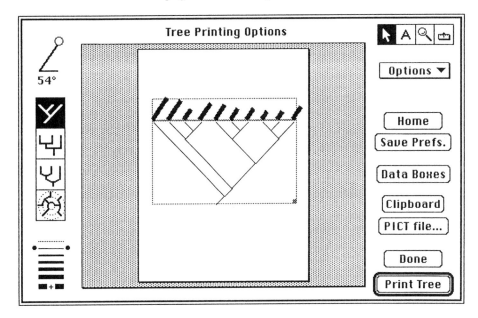

The tree can be printed using the Print Tree button. The PICT file button will cause the tree image to be saved as a PICT graphics file, rather than to the printer. For a more complete discussion of graphics files, see "Savings graphics files", later in this chapter. If you click on the Clipboard button, then the image of the tree will be saved to the Clipboard for pasting into a graphics, word-processing, or other program.

If you click on the Data Boxes button, the Data Boxes (a graphical overview of the data matrix) will be printed.

Some display features, such as the shape of the tree, fonts of taxon names, and the manner of labeling traced branches, are controlled separately in the tree window and the **Print Tree** dialog box. For example, one can request angled branches for printing, and square branches for screen display. Other features, such as display of branch numbers, are controlled solely from within the tree window.

Preview tools

At the top right of the dialog box is a palette of four tools — an arrow, an "A", a magnifying glass, and a ruler. These tools are used to edit the preview of the tree image, or to obtain information about it. The functions of the tools are as follows:

The arrow is the basic tool that allows you to move boxes, resize the tree box, and so on. This tool will change to a hand when you move it over parts of the preview that you can move.

If the magnifying-glass tool is touched on the image of the previewed tree, a close-up of the tree will be shown. Click again to return to the regular view. Another way to obtain a close-up view is to double-click on the tree.

The text tool allows you to change the font and style of text on the tree and legends. With the tool touch on the portion whose text you want to change, and a menu will pop up. Choose the font, size, and style.

The ruler provides information about the positions of each of the boxes in the preview window. If you touch on a box with the ruler, the top left coordinates of the box will be written at the bottom of the dialog box. By recording these numbers, you can duplicate the exact positions of boxes the next time you print. You can see the size of the tree box by clicking on its grow box with the ruler.

NOTE: *Holding down the Option key will temporarily make the text tool the current tool, holding down the Command key (⌘) will make the ruler the current tool, and holding down the Shift key will make the arrow tool the current tool.*

Adjusting tree shape

Trees can be printed in the same form as in the tree window, with diagonal branches, or with square branches, with an intermediate form in which the branches are slanted at the base but vertical near their tips, or in a circular fashion.

Circular trees print much better on PostScript® printers than on other printers. If you do ask to print circular trees on a non-PostScript® printer, but have Angle Names (PostScript®) checked, the taxon names will not print properly. Any feature of MacClade that entails tracing or labeling branches is not compatible with circular trees. There is currently a bug in circular tree printing, which prevents MacClade from properly printing multiple circular trees per page on a PostScript® printer.

Angle of gap in circular trees For circular trees, the angle of the gap at the bottom of the tree can be adjusted. For example, in the tree below, *half* the angle of the gap is 45°. To adjust the angle, grab and move the white ball on the end of the stick.

45°

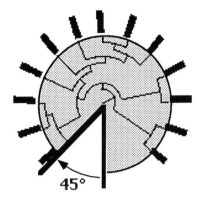

Adjusting size and position of tree on page

The central window with the image of the tree shows a preview of how the tree will appear when printed. The central window looks something like this:

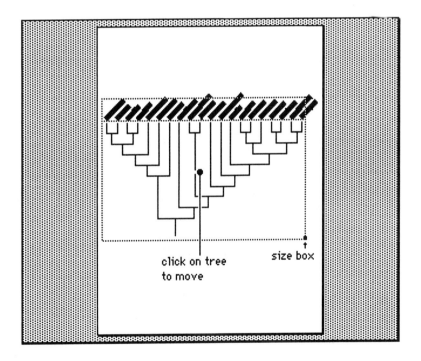

To move the tree on the page, click on the tree and drag it using the arrow tool (which will change to a hand when the pointer is over the tree). To adjust the width or height of the tree, then click on the size box on the lower right-hand side of the tree, and drag it.

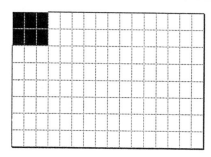

Choosing an image that is
3 pages wide by 2 pages high

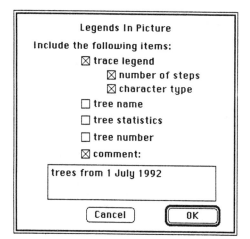

If you press the Home button, the tree will be returned to its default position on the page.

Drawing size The **Drawing Size** item of the **Options** pop-up menu presents a dialog box, in which one can choose the number of pages the tree image occupies. In the dialog box the size of the selected area indicates the size of the image. For example, the selection shown on the left indicates an image 3 pages wide by 2 pages high.

Multiple trees per page The **Trees Per Page** item of the **Options** pop-up menu allows you to specify the number of trees to be printed horizontally and vertically on each page. This option is available only if the tree image occupies one page (see "Drawing Size", above).

Altering text and legends

You may see other boxes in the preview window (such as the legend for a traced character); you can move these around the page simply by dragging them.

These items can be removed or added from the page using the **Legends** dialog box from the **Options** pop-up menu. This dialog box allows you to choose whether the tree name, calculated tree statistics (e.g., CI, treelength), trace legend, or comment are to be displayed.

The comment is a piece of text you can add to the image. To add a comment, enter the text and check the "comment" box. If you wish to have the number of steps or character types included in the trace legend, then check those boxes.

The type font, size, and style of text on the image can be adjusted by clicking the text tool (**A**) on the portion of the image, and choosing the appropriate items from the pop-up menus that are presented.

Adjusting taxon names The angle of the taxon names for all trees except circular trees can be changed by grabbing and moving the white ball on the end of the stick in the upper left corner of the dialog box. This can be done only if the **Angled Names (PostScript®)** menu item from the **Options** pop-up menu is checked. This will work on any PostScript® printer, but is unlikely to work on non-PostScript® printers. For non-PostScript® printers, MacClade will in general print vertical taxon names. (We say "unlikely" and "in general" as some printer drivers for non-PostScript® printers may provide some of the facilities of PostScript®, including angled text in MacClade trees.) If you turn off the Angled Names (PostScript®) option, then the names will always be printed vertically for non-circular trees.

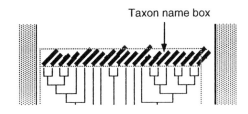

Taxon name box

For circular trees, you can ask MacClade either to print the names horizontally (by turning off **Angled Names**), or to print each name at the same angle as the branch to which it connects.

To change the font of the taxon names, touch the text tool (**A**) on the taxon name box immediately above the box surrounding the tree. A pop-up menu will drop down, from which you can choose the font, size, and style of the text.

Branch Appearance

Branch widths   Branch width can be varied by choosing one of the widths shown in the icon at left. If the upper, dotted line is chosen, then the tree will be printed using very thin lines (1/288 of an inch) on PostScript® printers, and single-point (1/72 of an inch) width lines on non-PostScript® printers. If the bottom bar, with the "+", is chosen, a dialog box is presented allowing you to specify a width in points (one point is 1/72 of an inch).

Branch lengths   When Trace All Changes is active on the current tree, and trees are square, MacClade can print trees that have branches longer or shorter to show the amount of reconstructed change on each branch; the length of the branch is drawn proportional to the amount of change. The amount of change is either the number of changes, or the weighted length that the branch contributes to treelength. The branch length is taken directly from the number of changes or length shown in Trace All Changes. Branch lengths cannot be shown on soft polytomies (and thus the branches involved in a polytomy will always be shown of zero length; see p. 259). To adjust how MacClade displays branch lengths, choose the **Branch Lengths** item of the **Options** pop-up menu.

Branch Lengths

᠘ᒷ Cladogram   ○ draw all branches to same height

᠘ᒷ Phylogram   ◉ draw branch length proportional
                        to the number of changes on
  □ Show scale   branch
  □ set length of one change to: [2   ] pixel(s)

show minimum-average-maximum changes as:
  ◉ rectangles ○ tick marks ○ don't show

make internal branch lengths proportional to:
  ○ minimum ◉ average ○ maximum

[Cancel]   [**OK**]

The **Branch Lengths** dialog box

In the dialog box that is presented, you can alter the scale of the branches, and have a scale bar printed on the right side of the tree, if you wish.

If minimum-average-maximum changes are calculated, then all three will be visible on each branch, with gray and white bars indicating the minimum, average, and maximum lengths over all equally parsimonious reconstructions of character evolution:

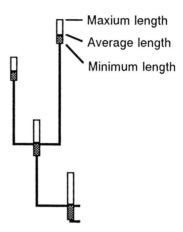

If you prefer, the display can be altered to use tick marks rather than rectangles:

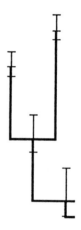

By default, the length of internal branches is proportional to the average branch length. If you prefer, you can adjust the length to match the minimum or maximum branch lengths:

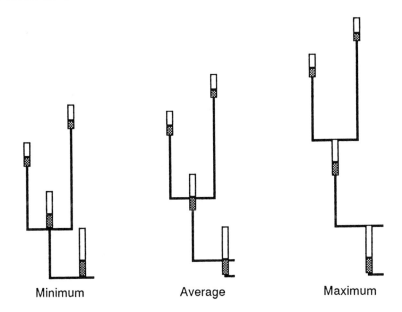

| Minimum | Average | Maximum |

Trace labeling When Trace All Changes is displayed or a character is traced in the tree, the **Trace Labeling** item in the **Options** pop-up menu allows you to choose how the trace is to be displayed. For full details on the options, see p. 256 if Trace All Changes is shown, or p. 246 if a character is traced on the tree. If Trace All Changes is shown, and minimum-average-maximum changes are calculated, then you cannot trace the changes using a pattern or color if you also ask MacClade to draw the length of branches proportional to the number of changes.

Branch shading The **Branch Shading** submenu of the **Options** pop-up menu allows you to choose whether patterns, colors, or grays are used in tracing characters or Trace All Changes on the tree.

Printing multiple trees

The **Multiple Trees** item in the **Options** pop-up menu allows you to select multiple trees to print. Pressing the Print Tree button will then cause MacClade to print just those trees selected. Note that if you did not select the tree currently on the screen, it will not be printed when multiple trees are selected. To turn off multiple-tree printing, select this menu item again.

Print trace for all characters

If the **Print All Characters** item in the **Options** pop-up menu is activated when a character is traced in the tree window, then a tracing for each included character will be printed. You may want to print multiple trees per page so as not to use too much paper.

Printing all reconstructions of a traced character

If the **Print All Reconstructions** item in the **Options** pop-up menu is activated then all equally parsimonious reconstructions of evolution of the traced character are printed in sequence. You may want to print multiple trees per page so as not to use too much paper.

Printing information for each branch

The **Branch Lists** or **Node Lists** item in the **Print Other** submenu prints a list of information about each of the branches. When a character is traced, whether discrete or continuous, it will indicate the state(s) reconstructed at the node above each branch. When **Trace All States** is displayed, a list of the states at the node above each branch is printed, or the frequencies of states, depending on the options selected under **All States Options** in the **Trace** menu. When **Trace All Changes** is displayed, a list of changes along each branch is printed. Branches are referred to by their numbers, which will be printed on the tree if **Show Branch Numbers** is chosen from the **Display** menu.

Printing charts

Charts can be printed when they are on the screen by choosing **Print Chart** in the **File** menu when the chart window is front-most.

If you wish to have the chart fill the printed page, turn on **Full Page Print** in the **Chart** menu. If **Full Page Print** is unchecked, MacClade will print a chart of the size seen on the screen.

Saving graphics files

As noted already in the discussion of tree printing, output that might normally go to the printer can instead to be saved to graphics files of type PICT for later editing in a graphics program. This can be done for the chart window and other windows using the **Save Graphics File** command in the **File** menu.

Ideally, you could then go into a graphics program that could understand PICT files, open the graphics file saved by MacClade, and edit the image to your heart's content. Unfortunately, graphics programs treat PICT files in different ways. We have tested out MacClade's PICT files on MacDraw 1.9.5, MacDraw II, Cricket Draw 1.0, Canvas 2.1, 3.01, 3.02, SuperPaint 1.0, 1.1, and 2.0, and 2.0a. The only programs to correctly deal with the rotated text (with **Angle Names (PostScript®)** turned on) are MacDraw II, Cricket Draw 1.0, SuperPaint 2.0a, and Canvas 3.02; all others ignore the rotation, or deal with it improperly. If **Angle Names (PostScript®)** is turned off, all of the programs understand the rotated text. MacDraw II, Canvas 2.1, 3.01, and 3.02, and SuperPaint deal with the basic branches correctly; Cricket Draw and MacDraw 1.9.5 do not. Canvas and SuperPaint deal with character tracings correctly; Cricket Draw and MacDraw II do not. Thus, the only programs that we know of that work for all elements of the image are SuperPaint 2.0a and Canvas 3.02; newer versions of other programs might also treat the image properly.

You may want to save the PICT file so that the Macintosh thinks it was created by MacDraw or some other graphics program, so that it will be easier to open directly from the Finder. To do this, set the creator of saved PICT files using the **Other Options** dialog box in the **Options for Saving** submenu of the **File** menu. To use this feature safely, you need to understand the concept of file creator and to know what the appropriate four-symbol code is. (For example, the four-letter creator code for Canvas 2.1 and 3.0 is DAD2, for Illustrator 88 is ARTZ, for MacDraw II is MDPL, and for SuperPaint 2.0 is SPNT.)

Saving text files

The **Save Text File** submenu in MacClade provides a means to save information to disk as text files. You can save a text file version of the General Notes, described above under "Printing data and assumptions" (p. 342). You can save a list of the states reconstructed at the nodes of the tree, or changes reconstructed along the branches, described above under "Printing list of information for each branch" (p. 352). You can also save a text version of the character status window.

A chart can be saved as a text file for later editing and examination. For all charts, **Save Chart As Text** can be called from the **Save Text File** submenu of the **File** menu to save a textual version of the chart. An example chart is:

```
MacClade version 3.0
Wednesday, July 1, 1992;  11:43 AM

Changes in all characters in Tree

          mean
numbers
0       4       5       2
5       0       8       6
2       1       0       0
4       6       7       0

frequencies, whole matrix normed
0.0     0.080   0.100   0.040
0.100   0.0     0.160   0.120
0.040   0.020   0.0     0.0
0.080   0.120   0.140   0.0
```

```
frequencies, rows normed
0.0      0.364   0.455   0.182
0.263    0.0     0.421   0.316
0.667    0.333   0.0     0.0
0.235    0.353   0.412   0.0
```

As well, if the Character Steps/etc. or State Changes & Stasis chart is requested, the "text file" check box can be selected in the **Chart Options** dialog box before the chart is calculated, and a detailed text file will be saved. This is described in Chapter 15 (see p. 275).

If the columns in the text file do not align, you may need to adjust tabs and switch to a font like Courier or Monaco in your word processor.

Text files can be saved in various other places in MacClade, such as a report on random tree generation, as described elsewhere in this book.

Appendix 1: File Format

The NEXUS format

For basic MacClade use, you don't have to learn the NEXUS file format, as MacClade saves the information from the data editor, trees, type definitions, type sets, weights sets, character and state names, and so on, and writes it as a NEXUS formatted file. Space does not permit more than a brief outline of that format here. A full description is in preparation (Maddison, Swofford, and Maddison, in preparation); see also the PAUP manual (Swofford, 1991).

The file must begin with "#NEXUS". The rest of the file consists of BLOCKS, containing data, assumptions, trees, and so on. In general, the data matrix is bounded by "MATRIX" and ";" and further is enclosed within the data block, which begins with "BEGIN DATA;" and ends with "END;". There must be a DIMENSIONS statement indicating the number of taxa and characters.

```
#NEXUS
BEGIN DATA;
DIMENSIONS NTAX=4 NCHAR=2;
MATRIX
A    00
B    01
C    10
D    11
;
END;
```

The words of a NEXUS file consist of tokens. A token is a string of characters surrounded by whitespace (that is, blanks, tabs, carriage returns, or line feeds). Tokens cannot contain any NEXUS punctuation ([ ] ( ) { } = , ; : - \ / * " ') or whitespace, or if they do, they must be surrounded by single quotes (e.g., 'A token', 'Species 1; west'); any contained single quotes should be duplicated (e.g., 'Jane''s Wren').

If you have data in some format other than NEXUS and want to change it to a form that MacClade will accept, see Chapter 9.

The states of characters will be saved to the data matrix in the NEXUS file as symbols (as shown in the **Symbols** dialog box in the **Display** menu), or using the standard IUPAC codes for DNA, RNA, or protein data. No matter which symbols are used, the matrix in the data file is stored using these symbols regardless of whether you have defined full names for the character states (e.g., "red", "blue"). Thus even though MacClade's data editor may display the matrix using the full state names, when saved to a file on disk the matrix will not be saved with the full state names; these are stored in another part of the data file.

Cursors

Organismal cursors displayed as the data file is being read indicate which part of the file is being read; this can be handy if MacClade crashes while reading in a file. For the curious, and for debugging purposes, the correspondence between cursor and file is:

Cursor	Organism	File
	amoeba	initial commands in DATA block
	jumping spider	first half of matrix
	ground beetle	second half of matrix
	flower	various calculations
	DNA	CODONS block
	owlfly	CHARACTERS block for continuous data
	trilobite	USERTYPEs
	anemone	TYPESETs
	mouse	WTSETs
	flatworm	EXSETs
	bacteriophage	CHARSETs
	tree	TREES block
	starfish	NOTES block
	scallop	MACCLADE block
	fish	information foreign to MacClade

Changing the way MacClade writes NEXUS files

Imagine a DNA sequence matrix written by MacClade consisting of 80 sites for five taxa. If the match-first facility is turned on in the data editor, MacClade will write the data matrix in the file something like this:

```
[                    10        20        30        40        50        60        70        80]
[                     .         .         .         .         .         .         .        .]
Hylobates  AAGCTTTACAGGTGCAACCGTCCTCATAATCGCCCACGGACTAACCTCTTCCCTGCTATTCTGCCTTGCAAACTCAAACT  [80]
Homo       ......C..C..C...GT.A.T...................R..T..A..C..AT.A..........A............  [80]
Pan        ......C..C..C....TTA.....................T..A..C..AT.AT.........A............T.  [80]
Gorilla    ......C..C..C...GTT..T..T.....T..........T..A..A..AT.AT.........A............  [80]
Pongo      ......C..C..C......AC......G..T.....T.....C..A..C.....A..G........A............  [80]
```

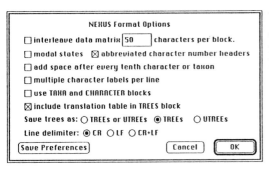

You can control some aspects of this by changing the display in the data editor (e.g., transposing the matrix, choosing not to use the match-first facility, and so on). Some changes in the editor will also affect how MacClade writes the NEXUS file. A few other aspects can be controlled using the **NEXUS Format** menu item of the **Options for Saving** submenu in the **File** menu.

Turning on the interleave option in the **NEXUS Format** dialog box, and setting for 40 characters per block, will cause MacClade to write the matrix in more than one block:

```
[                    10        20        30        40]
[                     .         .         .        .]
Hylobates  AAGCTTTACAGGTGCAACCGTCCTCATAATCGCCCACGGA  [40]
Homo       ......C..C..C...GT.A.T.................R  [40]
Pan        ......C..C..C....TTA...................  [40]
Gorilla    ......C..C..C...GTT..T..T.....T.........  [40]
Pongo      ......C..C..C......AC......G..T.....T...  [40]

[                    50        60        70        80]
[                     .         .         .        .]
Hylobates  CTAACCTCTTCCCTGCTATTCTGCCTTGCAAACTCAAACT  [80]
Homo       ..T..A..C..AT.A..........A............  [80]
Pan        ..T..A..C..AT.AT.........A............T.  [80]
Gorilla    ..T..A..A..AT.AT.........A............  [80]
Pongo      ..C..A..C.....A..G........A............  [80]
```

In typical files written by MacClade, the character number is written above every tenth character. This is an abbreviated character number header. It is placed within square brackets, and so has no impact on MacClade's or PAUP's reading of the file (as elements in square brackets are ignored), but is useful to help you look at the file. If abbreviated headers are turned off in the **NEXUS Format** dialog box, then character numbers will be written above each character:

```
[                   1         2         3         4         5         6         7         8]
[          12345678901234567890123456789012345678901234567890123456789012345678901234567890]
Hylobates  AAGCTTTACAGGTGCAACCGTCCTCATAATCGCCCACGGACTAACCTCTTCCCTGCTATTCTGCCTTGCAAACTCAAACT  [80]
Homo       ......C..C..C...GT.A.T...................R..T..A..C..AT.A..........A............  [80]
Pan        ......C..C..C....TTA.....................T..A..C..AT.AT.........A............T.  [80]
Gorilla    ......C..C..C...GTT..T..T.....T..........T..A..A..AT.AT.........A............  [80]
Pongo      ......C..C..C......AC......G..T.....T.....C..A..C.....A..G........A............  [80]
```

Headers are only written for molecular sequence data and for standard or extended standard data in which no entries are polymorphic or partially uncertain.

If you request the sequence of modal states in the **NEXUS Format** dialog, then MacClade will write above the first taxon the most common state for that character:

```
[                1         2         3         4         5         6         7        8]
[       12345678901234567890123456789012345678901234567890123456789012345678901234567890]
[Modal  AAGCTTCACCGGCGCAATCATCCTCATAATCGCCCACGGACTTACATCCTCATTACTATTCTGCCTAGCAAACTCAAACT]

Hylobates AAGCTTTACAGGTGCAACCGTCCTCATAATCGCCCACGGACTAACCTCTTCCCTGCTATTCTGCCTTGCAAACTCAAACT  [80]
Homo      ......C..C..C...GT.A.T.................R..T..A..C..AT.A..........A............  [80]
Pan       ......C..C..C....TTA....................T..A..C..AT.AT.........A............T.  [80]
Gorilla   ......C..C..C...GTT..T..T.....T.........T..A..A..AT.AT.........A............  [80]
Pongo     ......C..C..C......AC......G..T.....T.....C..A..C.....A..G........A............  [80]
```

If more than one state is equally common, and the data are not nucleotide sequences, then MacClade arbitrarily chooses the state among the most common with the lowest numerical value (as defined by the order of the states in the symbols list — see Chapter 10, p. 175, for details). If the data are of nucleotide sequences, then MacClade uses the IUPAC ambiguity codes to indicate several equally common modal states.

If you request "add space after every tenth character or taxon", then MacClade will add a blank column after every tenth character (or taxon for a transposed matrix):

```
[                 1          2          3          4]
[        1234567890 1234567890 1234567890 1234567890]

[Modal   AAGCTTCACC GGCGCAATCA TCCTCATAAT CGCCCACGGA]

Hylobates AAGCTTTACA GGTGCAACCG TCCTCATAAT CGCCCACGGA  [40]
Homo      ......C..C ..C...GT.A .T........ .........R  [40]
Pan       ......C..C ..C....TTA .......... .........  [40]
Gorilla   ......C..C ..C...GTT. .T..T..... T........  [40]
Pongo     ......C..C ..C......A C......G.. T.....T...  [40]
```

If there are characters named in the matrix, and the matrix is not transposed, then MacClade will by default write up to 10 character labels on one line:

```
CHARLABELS
[1] eye_color  [2] head_size  [3] number_of_toes
;
```

If you turn off "multiple character labels per line", then each character label will be placed on a separate line:

```
CHARLABELS
[1] eye_color
[2] head_size
[3] number_of_toes
;
```

By default, MacClade writes the discrete data matrix in one single DATA block, not in separate TAXA and CHARACTERS blocks. If you check the "use TAXA and CHARACTERS blocks" in the **NEXUS**

Format dialog box, then MacClade will write instead separate blocks. Use of a single DATA block will make the program compatible with earlier versions of PAUP (version 3.0r and before), but less compatible with Rod Page's forthcoming version 2.0 of COMPONENT.

By default, MacClade writes TREES blocks with a translation table; you can ask MacClade to omit the translation table by unchecking the appropriate box in the **NEXUS Format** dialog.

As MacClade treats all trees as rooted trees, by default it labels all trees it writes as rooted TREEs. Users will notice that PAUP, on reading a MacClade file with all trees saved as TREEs, requests to unroot these trees whenever no directed transformation types are in use. If you want MacClade to write unrooted UTREEs when no directed transformation types are in use, and TREEs when they are, then select the TREEs or UTREEs option. With this option, PAUP will not complain, but the user should be aware that the rooting as shown by MacClade may be lost in the process, and that PAUP may substitute, in a sense, an alternative root. In most respects PAUP's UTREEs are not rooted, except that something like a root is arbitrarily chosen to be between the first taxon in the matrix and the rest (if no outgroups are designated). This root position will influence both ACCTRAN/DELTRAN reconstructions and any subsequent true root that is designated for the trees if directed transformation types are reapplied (see Appendix 2). If you select the UTREEs option, MacClade will always write UTREEs.

By default, MacClade writes carriage returns (CR) at the end of each line of the file. However, carriage returns may not be the appropriate end-of-line marker if the file is to be moved to some other computer system, such as an MS-DOS machine, for which both a carriage return and line feed (LF) may be the most appropriate line delimiters (see p. 151). You can choose whether MacClade writes carriage returns, line feeds, or both carriage returns and line feeds.

APPENDIX 2:
USING MACCLADE AND PAUP TOGETHER

In developing MacClade we have worked closely with David Swofford, the developer of PAUP (Swofford, 1991), to ensure that the two programs are compatible and complementary. Our hope is that the two programs will be used together: MacClade to edit files, to set up constraint trees and assumptions, PAUP to do automatic searches for parsimonious trees, and MacClade to explore the trees further and analyze character evolution upon them. In this appendix we discuss some of the issues in using the two programs together. Among the most important are the incompatibilities and inconsistencies that still exist between PAUP and MacClade, most of which concern differences in the features supported by the two programs.

If you use PAUP and MacClade, we recommend that you acquire the latest version of both programs, as they will be most compatible with one another. MacClade's data files will be more acceptable to PAUP version 3.0s and later than to earlier versions. The description of incompatibilities between MacClade and PAUP apply to versions 3.00 and 3.0s respectively. PAUP changes relatively rapidly; some of the incompatibilities may be eliminated in the near future. Check the addendum to this book for the latest news on any changes to the incompatibilities described herein.

A scenario of using MacClade and PAUP

Here we present a typical scenario of using MacClade and PAUP together. It presumes you are using the two programs together on a Macintosh with 4 megabytes or more of memory, running System 7 or Multifinder. Of course, in your own work you would be unlikely to perform the exact same actions in the same order, but we present this example to indicate how the programs can interact.

In MacClade, open a new file and enter a data matrix and some user-defined types. Apply weights and types to some of the characters. Then save the file as "My genus". Start PAUP, open and execute this file. The assumptions (such as weightings) last in effect when you saved MacClade will be in effect in PAUP when the file is executed. Now do a branch-and-bound search to find parsimonious trees, and use **Save Trees to File** to save these trees to a tree file named "My genus.trees". Go back to MacClade, and go to its tree window, asking for the tree file you just saved in PAUP. Scan through the trees to see how they look, tracing the evolution of particular characters of interest. Now close the tree file and rearrange the tree on screen to match a previously published tree. Store the tree with the name "published". Save the file. Now go to the chart **Compare 2 Tree files** and select the data file (containing the published tree) and "My genus.trees" (containing the PAUP trees) to see if the published tree has consistent differences with PAUP's trees. Now build a new tree that is mostly unresolved but indicates as monophyletic one special group that was not monophyletic in PAUP's trees. Store the tree with the name "constraint" (it will be stored in the data file). Save the data file. Go back to PAUP, *close and reread the data file*, and invoke **Load Constraints**, choosing the data file itself. Do another tree search, this time enforcing the topological constraints tree "constraint". This will find the shortest trees that have this special group monophyletic. After saving the resulting trees, go back to MacClade and analyze evolution of important characters on the various trees, summarizing the reconstructed character evolution using the charts.

Using both programs simultaneously

In the scenario described above there were a number of steps of saving files that may have seemed superfluous. They were not, even if you are using MacClade and PAUP simultaneously under Multifinder or System 7. MacClade reads a data file from disk and operates on it while it is in the computer's RAM memory. Any changes you make to the data file are not written to the disk until you give the **Save File** or **Save File As** command. If you are editing a data file in MacClade and want to move to PAUP and work on the same data file, remember to save the data file to disk before moving from MacClade to PAUP, where you must then reread the data file from the disk. Otherwise, PAUP won't know about the most recent changes to the data file. Since PAUP does not have access to MacClade's RAM copy of the data file, it must access the data file via the disk. This principle works in reverse — if PAUP has done a tree search, don't expect MacClade to have access to the trees stored in PAUP's memory. You must save the trees to a file on disk first, after which MacClade can read the trees from the file. Always remember that the files *as they are saved on the disk* are the means by which all information is currently passed between MacClade and PAUP.

Incompatibilities between MacClade and PAUP

The programs are not fully compatible. That is, there are slight differences in defaults or in the ways that certain calculations are done, and there are some differences in the data file formats used by the two programs. The differences in data files concern different capabilities of the programs: thus, for instance, MacClade does not support the interpretation of gaps as extra character states, while PAUP does not support the stratigraphic character type.

If you find an incompatibility other than those described below, especially in calculations, it may represent a bug in one of the programs. Reread the instructions for both programs to see if the incompatibility is an intentional difference in the features of the programs. If it appears to be a bug, please report it to the authors of the programs.

Data

PAUP 3.0 requires that all multistate entries in the data matrix be uncertainties, or all be polymorphisms; mixtures are not allowed. If you do type in some cells as 0/1 in MacClade, and others as 0&1, PAUP will default to assuming all are 0/1, unless you alter the data file appropriately (see PAUP manual). The difference between uncertainty and polymorphism does not make an important difference in finding parsimonious trees for unordered and ordered characters, but could affect what are the parsimonious trees for other character types such as irreversible, Dollo, and step-matrix types.

Assumptions

MacClade does not support GAPMODE = NEWSTATE. That is, in MacClade gaps are treated as missing data.

PAUP's Ignore Uninformative and MacClade's **Exclude Uninformative** may not ignore the same characters, for several reasons. First, PAUP has algorithms to calculate what might be uninformative for characters of unordered, ordered, irreversible, and Dollo types; MacClade only finds uninformative characters when they are unordered or ordered. Second, when some terminal taxa are polymorphic, PAUP may fail to exclude some characters that are actually uninformative. Third, MacClade's **Exclude Uninformative** excludes characters that are uninformative over the set of taxa *in the current tree*, which may be only a subset of the file's taxa.

PAUP does not support weights with decimals. You should convert weights to integral values for use with PAUP.

User-defined types

MacClade cannot handle step matrices with values above 999; PAUP allows higher ones. When MacClade finds a matrix with higher values, it divides the matrix by 10's until all values are under the limit. This affects steps counted and possibly the character reconstruction.

MacClade and PAUP differ in how they treat terminal taxa polymorphic for three or more states in a user-defined type character.

MacClade and PAUP also differ in how they treat unnamed states in character state trees. These differences are describe under Treelength.

PAUP does not support the stratigraphic type. If you use the stratigraphic type in a data file, earlier versions of PAUP will give a warning about the illegality of "STRATTYPE" or "strat" and stop processing the data file; later versions will give a warning and convert the assignment of any stratigraphic characters to the default type.

PAUP does not support user-defined step matrices that contain numbers with decimal points (REALTYPEs). Convert these decimal values to integers for use in PAUP.

Trees

MacClade can store trees in a data file or tree file with different numbers of taxa. For example, some of the trees might contain taxa 1–7, others 4–9. PAUP, however, on reading the file, automatically adds taxa to trees until they contain all currently available taxa (either all taxa in the data matrix or fewer if you have explicitly told PAUP to delete taxa).

MacClade can treat polytomies as uncertainty of resolution ("soft" polytomies) or multiple speciation ("hard" polytomies); PAUP treats polytomies always as hard. This can generate differences in treelengths and character reconstruction.

MacClade treats all trees as rooted trees, as required by a number of MacClade's features. The State Changes & Stasis chart, for instance, needs a root to determine whether a change was a 0 to 1 or a 1 to 0 change. Users will notice that PAUP, on reading a MacClade file with all trees saved as TREEs, requests to deroot these trees whenever no directed transformation types are in use. If you ask MacClade to write trees as UTREEs, or if you allow PAUP to deroot the trees, you should be aware that the rooting as shown by MacClade may be lost in the process, and that PAUP may substitute, in a sense, an alternative root. PAUP's unrooted trees are not purely unrooted, for something like a root is arbitrarily chosen to be between the first taxon in the matrix and the rest (if no outgroups are designated). This "root" is used both to polarize PAUP's ACCTRAN/DELTRAN reconstructions and to orient branch swapping. It also may become the true root if directed transformation types are reapplied and the trees rerooted.

These differences between PAUP and MacClade tree rooting can cause confusion. Under the following section, we describe how one can, by mistakenly rerooting trees, obtain different treelengths under MacClade and PAUP. One can also obtain unexpected results in interpreting character evolution. For instance, if you have a tree (0,(0,((1,1),(1,0)))) with a single unordered character, MacClade will show ambiguity as to whether there was a gain and loss or two independent gains. If you read the file into PAUP, you get the request to deroot the trees. If you say yes and then in the **Show Reconstructions** dialog box ask for character changes, PAUP will indicate a switch from 0 to 1 to 0 *if* the first taxon in the data matrix happened to be one of the first two taxa in the tree above. If you then go to MacClade's editor and move rows around to put one of the taxa with state 1 into the first row, save the file, and move back into PAUP and reread the file (not having changed the tree or the data, only the sequence of taxa in the matrix), PAUP will now indicate a switch from 1 to 0 to 1. PAUP indicates different character changes before and after the moving of rows because (1) PAUP uses as default reconstruction for its "character change" display the ACCTRAN reconstruction, and the ACCTRAN reconstruction depends on some sort of root, and (2) PAUP chooses the first taxon in the matrix as the implicit "root" for purposes of ACCTRAN when rooting is not specified otherwise. PAUP also uses an implicit root when presenting lists of changes and apomorphies, which may not be accurate if PAUP's implicit root does not match the explicit root chosen in MacClade.

Treelength

Users moving between PAUP and MacClade may notice situations in which the two programs give a different treelength. Some possible causes are as follows:

1. You may have been using different versions of the data file. See the comments above (p. 361) regarding the caution needed when using MacClade and PAUP simultaneously.

2. MacClade and PAUP may be using different sets of assumptions because of the different commands and parts of the data file supported by the two programs. MacClade does not read the PAUP block where you may have specified assumptions such as which characters are excluded. MacClade does not process the IGNORE=UNINFORM command in the OPTIONS line of the DATA block; PAUP does so, and may therefore automatically exclude uninformative characters, yielding a lower treelength. When you change assumptions in PAUP using menu items (for instance, using **Set Character Types**), these assumptions are not saved with the data file when you save it. They are only ephemeral changes unless you ask PAUP to save the assumptions to a separate file (which MacClade will not process). The only way to ensure that such changed assumptions are saved to the data file is to place them by hand into the ASSUMPTIONS block of the file in PAUP's editor, or by specifying them in MacClade and saving the file, since MacClade automatically writes the newly changed assumptions into the file.

3. MacClade allows integral values in step matrices to be only as high as 999; PAUP allows values up to 32767. When MacClade encounters higher values, it will divide all values in the step matrix by 10's until the highest value is within MacClade's limit. This may result in MacClade's reporting not only a lower number of steps for the character but also accuracy will be lost as MacClade reduces the number of digits to 3. If only a subset of characters are assigned a user-defined type that was so reduced, these characters will effectively have their relative weights reduced by a factor of 10 or more.

4. Unnamed states in character state trees cannot be assigned as states at ancestral nodes in the tree by MacClade, in contrast to PAUP. This means MacClade may not get as low treelengths as will PAUP. If it were important to allow unnamed states to be assigned in MacClade, you could manually create a step matrix that corresponds to the costs implied by the character state tree and that uses named states for the formerly unnamed states.

5. MacClade does not support the PAUP character types dollo.dn and irrev.dn; MacClade will convert characters of these types to dollo.up and irrev.up, which may affect the treelength.

6. MacClade always treats gaps like missing data for calculations; PAUP has the additional option to treat gaps like an extra character state (GAPMODE=NEWSTATE). These different options can yield different treelengths.

7. If ancestral states (ANCSTATES) are defined in PAUP, they effectively add an ancestral taxon to the tree and may reorient the direction of irreversible or Dollo characters. MacClade does not use ANCSTATES.

8. Recall that MacClade and PAUP both add to the treelength implicit changes within polymorphic terminal taxa. When a terminal taxon is polymorphic with three or more states in a character of user-defined type, MacClade and PAUP cannot accurately estimate the number of steps required within this terminal taxon for each state that might be ancestral to it, but MacClade does make an attempt to judge at least part of the cost, by adding the smallest change to one of the other states observed for the taxon (see Chapter 5). MacClade does this in part to prevent assigning impossible states to a terminal node. PAUP does not do this, and so reports a smaller treelength.

9. MacClade allows the user to mix taxa with polymorphisms (e.g., "0&2") and taxa with uncertain state (e.g., "0/2") together in the same data matrix; PAUP prohibits a data matrix from mixing

polymorphisms and uncertainties, and will therefore interpret all multiple-state listings as one or the other.

10. PAUP does not have the option to treat polytomies as soft polytomies, that is, as uncertain resolution. If MacClade is considering polytomies to be soft (which is MacClade's default mode), then PAUP (which always considers polytomies as hard, as if they were multiple speciation) will sometimes yield a higher treelength. If the polytomies arose because PAUP collapsed zero-length branches, there will be no problem if the characters and assumptions being analyzed in MacClade are the same as those used in the PAUP analysis. Problems will arise, however, with consensus trees, or if the characters and assumptions being analyzed are different from those used in the PAUP analysis.

11. If the length of a rooted tree was measured by MacClade for irreversible (or otherwise directed) characters, then the rooted tree is read into PAUP, and characters are then assigned non-directed transformation types (e.g., unordered), PAUP will ask to deroot the tree. If it does, and you later reroot the tree for use with directed characters again, PAUP may place the root in a different place from where it was on the originally read rooted tree. Thus it may get a different treelength on directed characters than MacClade had obtained originally. These problems can be avoided, of course, if you are careful to reread the trees after the directed characters are once again in use.

12. PAUP automatically adds taxa to fill any tree to include all taxa in the data matrix (except for those explicitly deleted within PAUP). MacClade allows different trees in the file to contain different subsets of the taxa, and displays them without alteration.

13. MacClade always checks all character states in a step matrix, even those not observed in any taxa, in doing step-matrix calculations. PAUP can do this, but the default option uses an alternative time-saving measure. Namely, it examines only states in the matrix and any shortcuts identified as such by the 3+1 test. These time-saving measures can in certain circumstances give only approximate treelengths, and therefore PAUP's treelength will differ from MacClade's. This may be a common problem if the step matrix violates the triangle inequality, but uncommon otherwise.

14. If MacClade saves a tree with observed taxa fixed as ancestors, it places these taxa in the tree description as named ancestral nodes. PAUP does not support trees with observed taxa fixed as ancestors. If MacClade saves such a tree, PAUP will pop out the observed ancestors to terminal position, and therefore may yield a different treelength.

Character reconstructions

The reconstructions of character state evolution shown by MacClade's Trace Character and PAUP's Show Reconstructions may differ for the following reasons:

1. Discrepancies described under "Treelength" can also be reflected in differences in character reconstructions between PAUP and MacClade.

2. The character-changes option of PAUP's Show Reconstruction implicitly uses one of the ambiguity-resolving methods, ACCTRAN, DELTRAN, or MINF; in contrast, the possible-state-assignments option does not resolve ambiguity. MacClade's **Trace Character** does not resolve ambiguity unless explicitly requested in **Resolving Options**. Even if both MacClade and PAUP are using the same resolving method, they may still differ in their character reconstructions because of PAUP's choice of only one of the ACCTRAN or DELTRAN reconstructions (see Chapter 5) and PAUP's derooting of trees (see pp. 363–364).

3. ACCTRAN/DELTRAN in MacClade apply *only* to the traced character, not to **Trace All Changes** or **Trace All States**; in PAUP the ambiguity-resolving method is used for branch length, change lists, and so on.

4. PAUP provides no facility for fixing character states at nodes. If states are fixed at nodes in the character tracing in MacClade, the fixing may not be reflected in the reconstructions shown by PAUP.

Consistency and retention indices

Users moving between PAUP and MacClade may notice situations in which the two programs give different consistency and retention indices. Some possible causes are as follows:

1. The treelength or number of character steps may differ (see the two previous sections).

2. MacClade's ensemble consistency indices do not include stratigraphic, Dollo, and user-defined type characters; its ensemble retention indices do not include irreversible, stratigraphic, Dollo and user-defined characters. PAUP's ensemble indices include unordered, ordered, irreversible, and Dollo characters.

3. PAUP versions 3.0a – 3.0g calculated the minimum conceivable number of steps differently from MacClade. PAUP asked, "What is the smallest number of steps that could be obtained with the observed character states?" and thus it effectively allowed polymor-

phic terminal taxa to be split up into their component states. This approach yields a lower smallest number of steps, and thus lower consistency index than MacClade, which takes the terminal taxa as indivisible and asks: "What is the smallest number of steps that can be obtained for the character by rearranging the terminal taxa?" MacClade maintains the terminal taxa intact partly because the user's choice to maintain a polymorphic terminal taxon intact implies that the monophyly of the taxon is not to be questioned, and partly because a directly analogous maximum conceivable number of steps can be easily formulated. As with the minimum, MacClade asks for the maximum: "What is the largest number of steps that can be obtained for the character by rearranging the terminal taxa?" PAUP did not ask for the maximum a question analogous to its question for the minimum because the largest number of steps that could be obtained for the observed states in the observed taxa is not a well-defined question when terminal taxa are allowed to break up. Instead, PAUP maintained terminal taxa intact for the maximum, and broke them up for the minimum. A consistency index based on PAUP's minimum is a more complete measure of homoplasy, whereas MacClade's measure can indicate better how consistent characters are to each other. As a result of this distinction, PAUP versions 3.0h and subsequent calculate a "homoplasy index" equal to one minus the "consistency index" of earlier versions. The consistency index is now calculated in the same way as does MacClade.

Differences in data file format

Though the NEXUS format was designed to make MacClade and PAUP data-file compatible, there are some parts of data files that will be accepted by PAUP but will either not be accepted or not be fully read by MacClade, and vice versa.

Several features in PAUP NEXUS files are not allowed or are ignored in MacClade:

1. MacClade does not allow abbreviation of tokens.

2. MacClade will not accept all-digit character or taxon names. PAUP allows them, but warns that taxon/character names have precedence over numbers (e.g., If the tenth character is named "5", MacClade will not read the file; PAUP will, but the command "EXSET *no_5 = 5;" causes character number 10 to be excluded by PAUP.) Do not use all-digit names in PAUP if you intend to use the data file in MacClade (and it's not advisable in PAUP, in any case).

3. MacClade does not pay attention to uppercase and lowercase; thus, RESPECTCASE will be ignored.

4. MacClade will abort reading a file if you use LABELPOS=RIGHT.

5. MacClade will ignore GAPMODE=NEWSTATE.

6. If you use types Dollo.dn or irrev.dn in MacClade, it will convert them to Dollo.up and irrev.up.

7. MacClade does not process the PAUP block.

8. MacClade does not allow you to add extra symbols to DNA and RNA data files.

9. PAUP allows any number of DATA/TAXA/CHARACTERS BLOCKS within a file to allow batch processing of multiple data sets. MacClade allows at most one DATA block, or one TAXA and one CHARACTERS block, and ignores all others.

Several features in MacClade NEXUS files are not allowed or are ignored in PAUP:

1. Versions 3.0s and earlier of PAUP will not accept the stratigraphic transformation type ("strat"). Later versions will automatically convert any characters of this type to the default character type, which is unordered unless overridden by a DEFTYPE option setting.

2. PAUP will not accept transformation types with decimal values ("REALMATRIX").

3. PAUP will not accept weight sets with decimal values ("REAL").

4. PAUP will not accept matrices in which some elements represent uncertainties, others polymorphisms. It therefore does not accept the option MSTAXA=VARIABLE.

5. PAUP does not process the CONTINUOUS, CODONS, NOTES, or MACCLADE blocks.

6. PAUP does not process MacClade's [*] comments, which indicate, among other things, which taxa are to have italicized names.

7. As PAUP treats polytomies only as hard polytomies, PolyTcount=MINSTEPS will be ignored.

8. PAUP does not allow trees in a trees block to have varying numbers of taxa; to resolve the problem it adds taxa to the trees until each includes all non-deleted taxa.

9.   PAUP does not allow UTREEs and TREEs in the same TREES block.

10. Versions 3.0s and earlier of PAUP will not process a data file with TAXA and CHARACTERS blocks

There may be other differences we hadn't expected; these should be considered bugs.

REFERENCES

Archie, J. 1985. Methods for coding variable morphological features for numerical taxonomic analysis. *Syst. Zool.*, 34:326–345.

Archie, J. 1989a. A randomization test for phylogenetic information in systematic data. *Syst. Zool.*, 38:239–252.

Archie, J. 1989b. Homoplasy excess ratios: New indices for measuring levels of homoplasy in phylogenetic systematics and a critique of the consistency index. *Syst. Zool.*, 38:239–252.

Avise, J. C. 1989. Gene trees and organismal histories: A phylogenetic approach to population biology. *Evolution*, 43:1192–1208.

Avise, J. C., J. Arnold, R. M. Ball, E. Bermingham, T. Lamb, J. E. Neigel, C. A. Reeb, and N. C. Saunders. 1987. Intraspecific phylogeography: The mitochondrial DNA bridge between population genetics and systematics. *Ann. Rev. Ecol. Syst.*, 18:489–522.

Ball, G. E., and D. R. Maddison. 1987. Classification and evolutionary aspects of the species of the New World genus *Amblygnathus* Dejean, with description of *Platymetopsis*, new genus, and notes about selected species of *Selenophorus* Dejean (Coleoptera: Carabidae: Harpalini). *Trans. Amer. Entomol. Soc.*, 113:189–307.

Barry, D., and J. A. Hartigan. 1987. Statistical analysis of hominoid molecular evolution. *Stat. Sci.*, 2:191–210.

Baum, B. R. 1988. A simple procedure for establishing discrete characters from measurement data, applicable to cladistics. *Taxon*, 37:63–70.

Baum, D. A. and A. Larson. 1991. Adaptation reviewed: A phylogenetic methodology for studying character macroevolution. *Syst. Zool.*, 40:1–18.

Bell, G. 1989. A comparative method. *Am. Nat.*, 133:553–571.

Bremer, K. 1988. The limits of amino acid sequence data in angiosperm phylogenetic reconstruction. *Evolution*, 42:795–803.

Bremer, K., and H.-E. Wanntorp. 1979. Hierarchy and reticulation in systematics. *Syst. Zool.*, 28:624–627.

Brooks, D. R. 1981. Hennig's parasitological method: A proposed solution. *Syst. Zool.*, 30:229–249.

Brooks, D. R. 1985. Historical Ecology: A new approach to studying the evolution of ecological associations. *Ann. Missouri Bot. Gard.*, 72:660–680.

Brooks, D. R. 1988. Macroevolutionary comparisons of host and parasite phylogenies. *Ann. Rev. Ecol. Syst.*, 19:235–259.

Brooks, D. R. 1990. Parsimony analysis in historical biogeography and coevolution: Methodological and theoretical update. *Syst. Zool.*, 39:14–30.

Brooks, D. R., and D. A. McLennan. 1991. *Phylogeny, Ecology and Behavior: A Research Program in Comparative Biology*. Univ. Chicago Press, Chicago.

Brooks, D. R., R. T. O'Grady, and E. O. Wiley. 1986. A measure of the information content of phylogenetic trees and its use as an optimality criterion. *Syst. Zool.*, 35:571–582.

Bulmer, M. 1991. Use of generalized least squares in reconstructing phylogenies from sequence data. *Mol. Biol. Evol.*, 8:868–883.

Burt, A. 1989. Comparative methods using phylogenetically independent contrasts. Pp. 33–53 in P. H. Harvey and L. Partridge (eds.), *Oxford Surveys in Evolutionary Biology*, Vol. 6. Oxford Univ. Press, Oxford.

Cameron, H. D. 1987. The upside-down cladogram: Problems in manuscript affiliation. Pp. 227–242 in H. M. Hoenigswald and L. F. Wiener (eds.), *Biological Metaphor and Cladistic Classification: An Interdisciplinary Perspective*. Univ. Pennsylvania Press.

Camin, J. H., and R. R. Sokal. 1965. A method for deducing branching sequences in phylogeny. *Evolution*, 19:311–326.

Cann, R. L., M. Stoneking, and A. C. Wilson. 1987. Mitochondrial DNA and human evolution. *Nature*, 325:31–36.

Carpenter, J. M. 1988. Choosing among multiple equally parsimonious cladograms. *Cladistics*, 4:291–296.

Carpenter, J. M. 1989. Testing scenarios: Wasp social behavior. *Cladistics*, 5:131–144.

Cavalli-Sforza, L. L., and A. W. F. Edwards. 1967. Phylogenetic analysis: Models and estimation procedures. *Evolution*, 32:550–570.

Cavender, J. A. 1978. Taxonomy with confidence. *Math. Biosci.,* 40:271–280.

Cavender, J. A. 1981. Tests of phylogenetic hypotheses under generalized models. *Math. Biosci.,* 54:217–229.

Cavender, J. A. 1989. Mechanized derivation of linear invariants. *Mol. Biol. Evol.,* 6:301–316.

Cavender, J. A., and J. Felsenstein. 1987. Invariants of phylogenies in a simple case with discrete states. *J. Class.,* 4:57–71.

Chappill, J. A. 1989. Quantitative characters in phylogenetic analysis. *Cladistics,* 5:217–234.

Cheverud, J. M., M. M. Dow, and W. Leutenegger. 1985. The quantitative assessment of phylogenetic constraints in comparative analyses: Sexual dimorphism in body weight among primates. *Evolution,* 39:1335–1351.

Clutton-Brock, T.H. and P. H. Harvey. 1977. Primate ecology and social organization. *J. Zool., London,* 183:1–39.

Clutton-Brock, T. H., and P. H. Harvey. 1984. Comparative approaches to investigating adaptation. Pp. 7–29 in J. R. Krebs and N. B. Davies (eds.), *Behavioural Ecology: An Evolutionary Approach,* 2nd Ed. Sinauer Associates, Sunderland, Mass.

Coddington, J. A. 1986. The monophyletic origin of the orb web. Pp. 319–363 in W. A. Shear (ed.), *Spiders, Webs, Behavior, and Evolution.* Stanford Univ. Press, Stanford, California.

Coddington, J. A. 1988. Cladistic tests of adaptational hypotheses. *Cladistics,* 4:3–22.

Cracraft, J. 1981. Pattern and process in paleobiology: The role of cladistic analysis in systematic paleobiology. *Paleobiology,* 7:456–468.

Cracraft, J. 1985. Species selection, macroevolutionary analysis, and the "hierarchical theory" of evolution. *Syst. Zool.,* 34:222–229.

DeBry, R. W., and N. A. Slade. 1985. Cladistic analysis of restriction endonuclease cleavage maps within a maximum-likelihood framework. *Syst. Zool.,* 34:21–34.

de Queiroz, K. 1988. Systematics and the Darwinian revolution. *Phil. Sci.,* 55:238–259.

de Queiroz, K., and M. J. Donoghue. 1988. Phylogenetic systematics and the species problem. *Cladistics,* 4:317–338.

de Queiroz, K., and M. J. Donoghue. 1990. Phylogenetic systematics or Nelson's version of cladistics? *Cladistics,* 6:61–75.

Dobson, F. S. 1985. The use of phylogeny in behavior and ecology. *Evolution,* 39:1384–1388.

Donoghue, M. J. 1989. Phylogenies and the analysis of evolutionary sequences, with examples from seed plants. *Evolution,* 43:1137–1156.

Donoghue, M. J., and J. A. Doyle, 1989. Phylogenetic analysis of angiosperms and the relationships of Hamamelidae. Pp. 17–45 in P. R. Crane and S. Blackmore (eds.), *Evolution, Systematics and Fossil History of the Hamamelidae, Volume 1: Introduction and 'Lower Hamamelidae'.* Systematics Assoc., Special Vol. No. 40A, London.

Donoghue, M. J., and M. J. Sanderson. 1992. The suitability of molecular and morphological evidence in reconstructing plant phylogeny. Pp. 340-368 in P. S. Soltis, D. E. Soltis, and J. J. Doyle (eds.), *Molecular Systematics of Plants.* Chapman and Hall, N.Y.

Donoghue, M. J., R. G. Olmstead, J. F. Smith, and J. D. Palmer. 1992. Phylogenetic relationships of the Dipsacales based on rbcL sequences. *Ann. Missouri Bot. Gard.,* 79:333–345.

Doolittle, R. F., D. F. Feng, K. L. Anderson, and M. R. Alberro. 1990. A naturally occurring horizontal gene transfer from a eukaryote to a prokaryote. *J. Mol. Evol.,* 31:383–388.

Doyle, J. A. and M. J. Donoghue. 1986. Seed plant phylogeny and the origin of angiosperms: An experimental cladistic approach. *Bot. Rev.,* 52:321–431.

Doyle, J. A. and M. J. Donoghue. In press. Phylogenies and angiosperm diversification. *Paleobiology.*

Doyle, J. A., S. Jardiné, and A. Doerenkamp. 1982. *Afropollis,* a new genus of early angiosperm pollen, with notes on the Cretaceous palynostratigraphy and paleoenvironments of Northern Gondwana. *Bull. Centres Rech. Expl. Prod. Elf-Aquitaine,* 6:39–117.

Edwards, A. W. F. 1970. Estimating the branch points of a branching diffusion process. *J. Roy. Statist. Soc.,* B32:154–174.

Edwards, A. W. F., and L. L. Cavalli-Sforza. 1964. Reconstruction of evolutionary trees. Pp. 67–76 in V. H. Heywood and J. McNeill (eds.), *Phenetic and Phylogenetic Classification.* Systematics Assoc., Publ. No. 6, London.

Eldredge, N., and J. Cracraft. 1980. *Phylogenetic Patterns and the Evolutionary Process: Method and Theory in Comparative Biology.* Columbia Univ. Press, N.Y.

Eldredge, N., and S. J. Gould. 1972. Punctuated equilibria: An alternative to phyletic gradualism. Pp. 82–115 in T. J. M. Schopf (ed.), *Models in Paleobiology.* Freeman, Cooper and Co., San Francisco.

Engelmann, G. F., and E. O. Wiley. 1977. The place of ancestor-descendant relationships in phylogeny reconstruction. *Syst. Zool.,* 26:1–11.

Estabrook, G. F., C. S. Johnson Jr., and F. R. McMorris. 1976. A mathematical foundation for the analysis of cladistic character compatibility. *Math. Biosci.* 29:181–187.

Farrell, B., and C. Mitter. 1990. Phylogenesis of insect/plant interactions: Have *Phyllobrotica* leaf beetles (Chrysomelidae) and the Lamiales diversified in parallel? *Evolution,* 44:1389–1403.

Farrell, B., D. E. Dussord, and C. Mitter. 1991. Escalation of plant defense: Do latex and resin canals spur plant diversification? *Am. Nat.,* 138:881–900.

Farris, J. S. 1969. A successive approximations approach to character weighting. *Syst. Zool.,* 18:374–385.

Farris, J. S. 1970. Methods for computing Wagner Trees. *Syst. Zool.,* 19:83–92.

Farris, J. S. 1972. Estimating phylogenetic trees from distance matrices. *Am. Nat.,* 106:645–668.

Farris, J. S. 1977. Phylogenetic analysis under Dollo's Law. *Syst. Zool.,* 26:77–88.

Farris, J. S. 1978. Inferring phylogenetic trees from chromosome inversion data. *Syst. Zool.,* 27:275–284.

Farris, J. S. 1982. Outgroups and parsimony. *Syst. Zool.,* 31:328–334.

Farris, J. S. 1983. The logical basis of phylogenetic analysis. Pp. 7–36 in N. I. Platnick and V. A. Funk (eds.), *Advances in Cladistics,* Vol. 2. Proceedings of the Second Meeting of the Willi Hennig Society. Columbia Univ. Press, N.Y.

Farris, J. S. 1986. On the boundaries of phylogenetic systematics. *Cladistics,* 2:14–27.

Farris, J. S. 1988. *HENNIG86, version 1.5.* Distributed by the author, Port Jefferson Station, N.Y.

Farris, J. S. 1989. The retention index and the rescaled consistency index. *Cladistics,* 5:417–419.

Felsenstein, J. 1973. Maximum-likelihood estimation of evolutionary trees from continuous characters. *Am. J. Hum. Genet.,* 25:471–492.

Felsenstein, J. 1978a. The number of evolutionary trees. *Syst. Zool.,* 27:27–33.

Felsenstein, J. 1978b. Cases in which parsimony or compatibility methods will be positively misleading. *Syst. Zool.,* 27:401–410.

Felsenstein, J. 1979. Alternative methods of phylogenetic inference and their interrelationship. *Syst. Zool.,* 28:49–62.

Felsenstein, J. 1981a. A likelihood approach to character weighting and what it tells us about parsimony and compatibility. *Biol. J. Linn. Soc.,* 16:183–196.

Felsenstein, J. 1981b. Evolutionary trees from DNA sequences: A maximum likelihood approach. *J. Mol. Evol.,* 17:368–376.

Felsenstein, J. 1982. Numerical methods for inferring evolutionary trees. *Q. Rev. Biol.,* 57:379–404.

Felsenstein, J. 1985a. Phylogenies and the comparative method. *Am. Nat.,* 125:1–15.

Felsenstein, J. 1985b. Confidence limits on phylogenies with a molecular clock. *Syst. Zool.,* 34:152–161.

Felsenstein, J. 1985c. Confidence limits on phylogenies: An approach using the bootstrap. *Evolution,* 39:783–791.

Felsenstein, J. 1988a. Phylogenies from molecular sequences: Inference and reliability. *Ann. Rev. Genet.,* 22:521–565.

Felsenstein, J. 1988b. Phylogenies and quantitative characters. *Ann. Rev. Ecol. Syst.,* 19:445–471.

Felsenstein, J. 1991. *PHYLIP (Phylogeny Inference Package), version 3.4.* Distributed by the author, Univ. Washington, Seattle.

Felsenstein, J. 1992. Phylogenies from restriction sites: A maximum-likelihood approach. *Evolution,* 46:159–173.

Felsenstein, J. In press a. Estimating effective population size from samples of sequences: Inefficiency of pairwise and segregating sites as compared to phylogenetic estimates. *Genetical Research.*

Felsenstein, J. In press b. Estimating effective population size from samples of sequences: A bootstrap Monte Carlo approach. *Genetical Research.*

Felsenstein, J., and E. Sober. 1986. Parsimony and likelihood: An exchange. *Syst. Zool.,* 35:617–626.

Feng, D. F., and R. F. Doolittle. 1987. Progressive sequence alignment as a prerequisite to correct phylogenetic trees. *J. Mol. Evol.,* 25:351–360.

Fink, W. L. 1982. The conceptual relationship between ontogeny and phylogeny. *Paleobiology,* 8:254–264.

Fink, W.L. 1985. Phylogenetic interrelationships of the stomiid fishes (Teleostei: Stomiiformes). *Misc. Pub. Mus. Zool., Univ. Michigan,* 171:1–127.

Fisher, D. C. 1982. Phylogenetic and macroevolutionary patterns within the Xiphosurida. *N. Amer. Paleont. Conv. III, Proc.,* 1:175–180.

Fisher, D. C. 1988. Stratocladistics: Integrating stratigraphic and morphologic data in phylogenetic inference. *Geol. Soc. Amer., Abst. Prog.,* 20:A186.

Fisher, D. C. 1991. Phylogenetic analysis and its application in evolutionary paleobiology. Pp. 103–122 in N. L. Gilinsky and P. W. Signor (eds.), *Analytical Paleobiology*. Short Courses in Paleontology, No. 4, Paleontological Society.

Fisher, D.C. 1992. Stratigraphic parsimony. Pp. 124–129 in W.P. Maddison and D.R. Maddison, *MacClade: Analysis of Phylogeny and Character Evolution*. Sinauer Associates, Sunderland, Mass.

Fishman, G. S., and L. R. Moore. 1982. A statistical evaluation of multiplicative congruential random number generators with modulus $2^{31} - 1$. *J. Amer. Stat. Assoc.*, 77:129–136.

Fitch, W. M. 1971. Toward defining the course of evolution: Minimal change for a specific tree topology. *Syst. Zool.*, 20:406–416.

Fitch, W. M. 1979. Cautionary remarks on using gene expression events in parsimony procedures. *Syst. Zool.*, 28:375–379.

Fitch, W. M. 1986. A hidden bias in the estimate of total nucleotide substitutions from pairwise differences. Pp. 315–328 in S. Karlin and E. Nevo (eds.), *Evolutionary Process and Theory*. Academic Press, Orlando, Florida.

Fitch, W. M., and J. J. Bientema. 1990. Correcting parsimonious trees for unseen nucleotide substitutions: The effect of dense branching exemplified by ribonuclease. *Mol. Biol. Evol.*, 7:438–443.

Fitch, W. M., and M. Bruschi. 1987. The evolution of prokaryotic ferredoxins — with a general method correcting for unobserved substitutions in less branches lineages. *Mol. Biol. Evol.*, 4:381–394.

Fitch, W. M., and J. S. Farris. 1974. Evolutionary trees with minimum nucleotide replacements from amino acid sequences. *J. Mol. Evol.*, 3:263–278.

Fitch, W. M., and E. Margoliash. 1967. Construction of phylogenetic trees. *Science*, 155:279–284.

Fitch, W. M., and J. Ye. 1992. Weighted parsimony: Does it work? Pp. 147–154 in M. M. Miyamoto and J. Cracraft (eds.), *Phylogenetic Analysis of DNA Sequences*. Oxford Univ. Press, Oxford.

Fukami-Kobayashi, K., and Y. Tateno. 1991. Robustness of maximum likelihood tree estimation against different patterns of base substitutions. *J. Mol. Evol.*, 32:79–91.

Funk, V. A. 1985. Phylogenetic patterns and hybridization. *Ann. Missouri Bot. Gard.*, 72:681–715.

Futuyma, D. J. 1988. *Sturm und Drang* and the evolutionary synthesis. *Evolution*, 42:217–226.

Futuyma, D. J., and S. S. McCafferty. 1991. Phylogeny and the evolution of host plant associations in the leaf beetle genus *Ophraella* (Coleoptera, Chrysomelidae). *Evolution*, 44:1885–1913.

Gilinsky, N. L. 1991. Cross sections through evolutionary trees: Theory and applications. *Syst. Zool.*, 40:19–32.

Gillespie, J. H. 1986. Rates of molecular evolution. *Ann. Rev. Ecol. Syst.*, 17:637–665.

Gillespie, J. H. 1989. Lineage effects and the index of dispersion of molecular evolution. *Mol. Biol. Evol.*, 6:636–647.

Gingerich, P. D. 1979. Stratophenetic approach to phylogeny reconstruction in vertebrate paleontology. Pp. 41–77 in J. Cracraft and N. Eldredge (eds.), *Phylogenetic Analysis and Paleontology*. Columbia Univ. Press, N.Y.

Gittleman, J. L. 1988. The comparative approach in ethology: Aims and limitations. *Perspect. Ethol.*, 8:55–83.

Gittleman, J. L., and M. Kot. 1990. Adaptation: Statistics and a null model for estimating phylogenetic effects. *Syst. Zool.*, 39:227–151.

Gojobori, T., W.-H. Li, and D. Graur. 1982. Patterns of nucleotide substitution in pseudogenes and functional genes. *J. Mol. Evol.*, 18:360–369.

Golding, B., and J. Felsenstein. 1990. A maximum likelihood approach to detection of selection from a phylogeny. *J. Mol. Evol.*, 31:511–523.

Goldman, N. 1988. Methods for discrete coding of morphological characters in numerical analysis. *Cladistics*, 4:59–71.

Goldman, N. 1990. Maximum likelihood inference of phylogenetic trees, with special reference to a Poisson process model of DNA substitution and to parsimony analysis. *Syst. Zool.*, 39:345–361.

Goodman, M. 1981. Globin evolution was apparently very rapid in early vertebrates: A reasonable case against the rate-constancy hypothesis. *J. Mol. Evol.*, 17:114–120.

Goodman, M., J. Czelusniak, G. W. Moore, A. E. Romero-Herrera, and G. Matsuda. 1979. Fitting the gene lineage into its species lineage, a parsimony strategy illustrated by cladograms constructed from globin sequences. *Syst. Zool.*, 28:132–163.

Gould, S. J., and E. S. Vrba. 1982. Exaptation — the missing term in the science of form. *Paleobiology*, 8:4–15.

Grafen, A. 1989. The phylogenetic regression. *Phil. Trans. R. Soc. London, Ser. B*, 326:119–157.

Greene, H. 1986. Diet and arboreality in the Emerald Monitor, *Varanus prasinus*, with comments on the study of adaptation. *Fieldiana Zool.*, New Series, 31:1–12.

Griswold, C. E. 1987. A revision of the jumping spider genus *Habronattus* F. O. P.-Cambridge (Araneae; Salticidae), with phenetic and cladistic analyses. *Univ. Calif. Publ. Entomol.*, 107:1–344.

Guyer, C., and J. B. Slowinski. 1991. Comparisons of observed phylogenetic topologies with null expectations among three monophyletic lineages. *Evolution*, 45:340–350.

Hafner, M. S., and S. A. Nadler. 1990. Cospeciation in host-parasite assemblages: Comparative analysis of rates of evolution and timing of cospeciation events. *Syst. Zool.*, 39:192–204.

Harding, E. F. 1971. The probabilities of rooted tree-shapes generated by random bifurcation. *Adv. Appl. Prob.*, 3:44–77.

Harrison, R. G. 1991. Molecular changes at speciation. *Ann. Rev. Ecol. Syst.*, 22:281–308.

Hartigan, J. A. 1973. Minimum mutation fits to a given tree. *Biometrics*, 29:53–65.

Harvey, P. H., and G. M. Mace. 1982. Comparisons between taxa and adaptive trends: Problems of methodology. Pp. 343–361 in King's College Sociobiology Group (eds.), *Current Problems in Sociobiology*. Cambridge Univ. Press, Cambridge.

Harvey, P. H., and M. D. Pagel. 1991. *The Comparative Method in Evolutionary Biology*. Oxford Univ. Press, Oxford.

Hasegawa, M., H. Kishino, and N. Saitou. 1991. On the maximum likelihood method in molecular phylogenetics. *J. Mol. Evol.*, 32:443–445.

Hayasaka, K., T. Gojobori, and S. Horai. 1988. Molecular phylogeny and evolution of primate mitochondrial DNA. *Mol. Biol. Evol.*, 5:626–644.

Hein, J. 1989. A new method that simultaneously aligns and reconstructs ancestral sequences for any number of homologous sequence, when the phylogeny is given. *Mol. Biol. Evol.*, 6:649–668.

Hein, J. 1990a. Reconstructing evolution of sequences subject to recombination using parsimony. *Math. Biosci.*, 98:185–200.

Hein, J. 1990b. TreeAlign. Source code for a program, distributed by the author.

Hendy, M. D. 1989. The relationship between simple evolutionary tree models and observable sequence data. *Syst. Zool.*, 38:310–321.

Hendy, M. D., and D. Penny. 1982. Branch and bound algorithms to determine minimal evolutionary trees. *Math. Biosci.*, 59:277–290.

Hendy, M. D., and D. Penny. 1984. Cladograms should be called trees. *Syst. Zool.*, 33:245–247.

Hendy, M. D., and D. Penny. 1989. A framework for the quantitative study of evolutionary trees. *Syst. Zool.*, 38:297–309.

Hennig, W. 1966. *Phylogenetic Systematics*. Univ. Illinois Press, Urbana.

Hey, J. 1991. The structure of genealogies and the distribution of fixed differences between DNA sequence samples from natural populations. *Genetics*, 128:831–840.

Hey, J. 1992. Using phylogenetic trees to study speciation and extinction. *Evolution*, 46:627–640.

Hillis, D. M. 1987. Molecular versus morphological approaches to systematics. *Ann. Rev. Ecol. Syst.*, 18:23–42.

Hillis, D. M., and M. T. Dixon. 1989. Vertebrate phylogeny: Evidence from 28S ribosomal DNA sequences. Pp. 355–367 in B. Fernholm, K. Bremer, and H. Jörnvall (eds.), *The Hierarchy of Life*. Elsevier Press, Amsterdam.

Hillis, D. M., J. J. Bull, M. E. White, M. R. Badgett, and I. J. Molineux. 1992. Experimental phylogenetics: Generation of a known phylogeny. *Science*, 255:589–592.

Holmquist, R. 1979. The method of parsimony: An experimental test and theoretical analysis of the adequacy of molecular restoration studies. *J. Mol. Biol.*, 135:939–958.

Hudson, R. R., and N. L. Kaplan. 1985. Statistical properties of the number of recombination events in the history of a sample of DNA sequences. *Genetics*, 111:147–164.

Huelsenbeck, J. P. 1991. Tree-length distribution skewness: An indicator of phylogenetic information. *Syst. Zool.*, 40:257–270.

Huey, R. B. 1987. Phylogeny, history and the comparative method. Pp. 76–98 in M. E. Feder, A. F. Bennett, W. Burggren, and R. B. Huey (eds.), *New Directions in Ecological Physiology*. Cambridge Univ. Press, Cambridge.

Huey, R. B., and A. F. Bennett. 1987. Phylogenetic studies of coadaptation: Preferred temperatures versus optimal performance temperatures of lizards. *Evolution*, 41:1098–1115.

Hull, D. L. 1967. Certainty and circularity in evolutionary taxonomy. *Evolution*, 21:174–189.

Hull, D. L. 1979. The limits of cladism. *Syst. Zool.*, 28:416–440.

Iwabe, M., K. Kuma, M. Hasegawa, S. Osawa, and T. Miyata. 1989. Evolutionary relationship of archaebacteria, eubacteria and eukaryotes inferred from phylogenetic tree of duplicated genes. *Proc. Natl. Acad. Sci. USA*, 86:9355–9359.

Janson, C. H. 1992. Measuring evolutinary constraints: A markov model for phylogenetic transitions among seed dispersal syndromes. *Evolution,* 46:136–158.

Jin, L., and M. Nei. 1990. Limitations of the evolutionary parsimony method of phylogenetic analysis. *Mol. Biol. Evol.,* 7:82–102.

Kidwell, M. G. In press. Horizontal transfer of *P* elements and other short inverted repeat transposons. *Genetics.*

Kimura, M. 1981. Doubt about studies of globin evolution based on maximum parsimony codons and the augmentation procedure. *J. Mol. Evol.,* 17:121–122.

Kingman, J. F. C. 1982. The coalescent. *Stochast. Proc. Appl.,* 13:235–248.

Kishino, H., T. Miyata, and M. Hasegawa. 1990. Maximum likelihood inference of protein phylogeny and the origin of chloroplasts. *J. Mol. Evol.,* 31:151–160.

Kluge, A. G., and J. S. Farris. 1969. Quantitative phyletics and the evolution of the anurans. *Syst. Zool.,* 18:1–32.

Koop, B. F., D. Siemieniak, J. L. Slightom, M. Goodman, J. Dunbart, P. Wright, and E. Simons. 1989. Tarsius delta- and beta-globin genes: Conversions, evolution, and systematic implications. *J. Biol. Chem.,* 264:68–79.

Lake, J. A. 1987. A rate-independent technique for analysis of nucleic acid sequences: Evolutionary parsimony. *Mol. Biol. Evol.,* 4:167–191.

Lanave, C., G. Preparata, C. Saccone, and G. Serio. 1984. A new method for calculating evolutionary substitution rates. *J. Mol. Evol.,* 20:86–93.

Langtimm, C.A., and D.A. Dewsbury. 1991. Phylogeny and evolution of rodent copulatory behavior. *Anim. Behav.,* 41:217–225.

Larson, A. 1984. Neontological inferences of evolutionary pattern and process in the salamander family Plethodontidae. *Evol. Biol.,* 17:119–217.

Lauder, G. V. 1981. Form and function: Structural analysis in evolutionary morphology. *Paleobiology,* 7:430–442.

Lauder, G. V. 1982. Historical biology and the problem of design. *J. Theor. Biol.,* 97:57–67.

Lauder, G. V. 1988. Phylogeny and physiology. *Evolution,* 42:113–114.

Lauder, G. V. 1990. Functional morphology and systematics: Studying functional patterns in an historical context. *Ann. Rev. Ecol. Syst.,* 21:317–340.

Lee, A. R. 1989. Numerical taxonomy revisited: John Griffith, cladistic analysis and St. Augustine's *Quaestiones in Heptateuchum. Studia Patristica,* 20:24–32.

Lemen, C. A., and P. W. Freeman. 1989. Testing macroevolutionary hypotheses with cladistic analysis: Evidence against rectangular evolution. *Evolution,* 43:1538–1554.

Le Quesne, W. J. 1974. The uniquely evolved character concept and its cladistic application. *Syst. Zool.,* 23:513–517.

Liebherr, J. K., and A. E. Hajek. 1990. A cladistic test of the taxon cycle and taxon pulse hypotheses. *Cladistics,* 6:39–59.

Losos, J. B. 1990. A phylogenetic analysis of character displacement in Caribbean *Anolis* lizards. *Evolution,* 44:558–569.

Lynch, J. D. 1989. The gauge of speciation: On the frequencies of modes of speciation. Pp. 527–553 in D. Otte and J. A. Endler (eds.), *Speciation and Its Consequences.* Sinauer Associates, Sunderland, Mass.

Lynch, M. 1989. Phylogenetic hypotheses under the assumption of neutral quantitative-genetic variation. *Evolution,* 43:1–17.

Lynch, M. 1991. Methods for the analysis of comparative data in evolutionary biology. *Evolution,* 45:1065–1080.

Mabee, P. M. 1989. Assumptions underlying the use of ontogenetic sequences for determining character-state order. *Trans. Am. Fish. Soc.,* 118:151–158.

Maddison, D. R. 1990. Phylogenetic inference of historical pathways and models of evolutionary change. PhD. thesis, Harvard Univ.

Maddison, D. R. 1991a. The discovery and importance of multiple islands of most-parsimonious trees. *Syst. Zool.,* 40:315–328.

Maddison, D. R. 1991b. African origin of human mitochondrial DNA reexamined. *Syst. Zool.,* 40:355–363.

Maddison, D. R. In press. Systematics of the Holarctic ground-beetle subgenus *Chrysobracteon* Netolitzky and related *Bembidion* Latreille (Coleoptera: Carabidae). *Bull. Mus. Comp. Zool.*

Maddison, D. R., M. Ruvolo, and D. L. Swofford. 1992. Geographic origins of human mitochondrial DNA: Phylogenetic evidence from control region sequences. *Syst. Biol.,* 41:111–124.

Maddison, W. P. 1982. XXXY sex chromosomes in males of the jumping spider genus *Pellenes* (Araneae: Salticidae). *Chromosoma (Berlin),* 85:23–37.

Maddison, W. P. 1986. *MacClade 1.0.* Distributed by the author, Cambridge, Mass.

Maddison, W. P. 1989. Reconstructing character evolution on polytomous cladograms. *Cladistics,* 5:365–377.

Maddison, W. P. 1990. A method for testing the correlated evolution of two binary characters: Are gains or losses concentrated on certain branches of a phylogenetic tree? *Evolution,* 44:539–557.

Maddison, W. P. 1991. Squared-change parsimony reconstructions of ancestral states for continuous-valued characters on a phylogenetic tree. *Syst. Zool.,* 40:304–314.

Maddison, W. P. In press. Missing data versus missing characters in phylogenetic analysis. *Syst. Biol.*

Maddison, W. P., and D. R. Maddison. 1987. *MacClade 2.1.* Distributed by the authors, Cambridge, Mass.

Maddison, W. P., and M. Slatkin. 1990. Parsimony reconstructions of ancestral states do not depend on the relative distances between linearly-ordered character states. *Syst. Zool.,* 39:175–178.

Maddison, W. P., and M. Slatkin. 1991. Null models for the number of evolutionary steps in a character on a phylogenetic tree. *Evolution,* 45:1184–1197.

Maddison, W. P., M. J. Donoghue, and D. R. Maddison. 1984. Outgroup analysis and parsimony. *Syst. Zool.,* 33:83–103.

Marshall, C. R. 1990. Confidence intervals on stratigraphic ranges. *Paleobiology,* 16:1–10.

Martins, E., and T. Garland 1991. Phylogenetic analyses of the evolution of continuous characters: A simulation study. *Evolution,* 45:534–557.

Maynard Smith, J., R. Burian, S. Kauffman, P. Alberch, J. Campbell, B. Goodwin, R. Lande, D. Raup, and L. Wolpert. 1985. Developmental constraints and evolution: A perspective from the Mountain Lake Conference on development and evolution. *Q. Rev. Biol.,* 60:265–287.

Mayr, E. 1963. *Animal Species and Evolution.* Harvard Univ. Press, Cambridge, Mass.

McDade, L. 1990. Hybrids and phylogenetic systematics. I. Patterns of character expression in hybrids and their implications for cladistic analysis. *Evolution,* 44:1685–1700.

McDonald, J.H., and M. Kreitman. 1991. Adaptive protein evolution at the *Adh* locus in *Drosophila. Nature,* 351:652–654.

McLennan, D. A. 1991. Integrating phylogeny and experimental ethology: From pattern to process. *Evolution,* 45:1773–1789.

Meacham, C. A. 1984. The role of hypothesized direction of characters in the estimation of evolutionary history. *Taxon,* 33:26–38.

Meacham, C. A., and G. Estabrook. 1985. Compatibility methods in systematics. *Ann. Rev. Ecol. Syst.,* 16:431–446.

Mickevich, M. F. 1981. Quantitative phylogenetic biogeography. Pp. 209–222 in V. A. Funk and D. R. Brooks (eds.), *Advances in Cladistics.* Proceedings of the First Meeting of the Willi Hennig Society. The New York Botanical Garden, N.Y.

Mickevich, M. F. 1982. Transformation series analysis. *Syst. Zool.,* 31:461–478.

Mickevich, M. F., and M. S. Johnson. 1976. Congruence between morphological and allozyme data in evolutionary inference and character evolution. *Syst. Zool.,* 25:260–270.

Mickevich, M. F., and C. Mitter. 1981. Treating polymorphic character in systematics: A phylogenetic treatment of electrophoretic data. Pp. 45–58 in V. A. Funk and D. R. Brooks (eds.), *Advances in Cladistics.* Proceedings of the First Meeting of the Willi Hennig Society. The New York Botanical Garden, N.Y.

Mickevich, M. F., and S. J. Weller. 1990. Evolutionary character analysis: Tracing character change on a cladogram. *Cladistics,* 6:137–170.

Mindell, D. P., J. W. Sites, Jr., and D. Graur. 1989. Speciational evolution: A phylogenetic test with allozymes in *Sceloporus* (Reptilia). *Cladistics,* 5:49–61.

Mitter, C. 1981. "Cladistics" in botany. *Syst. Zool.,* 30:373–376.

Mitter, C., and D. R. Brooks. 1983. Phylogenetic aspects of coevolution. Pp. 65–98 in D. J. Futuyma and M. Slatkin (eds.), *Coevolution.* Sinauer Associates, Sunderland, Mass.

Mitter, C., B. Farrell, and B. Wiegemann. 1988. The phylogenetic study of adaptive zones: Has phytophagy promoted insect diversification? *Am. Nat.,* 132:107–128.

Miyamoto, M. M., and S. M. Boyle. 1989. The potential importance of mitochondrial DNA sequence data to eutherian mammal phylogeny. Pp. 437–450 in B. Fernholm, K. Bremer, and H. Jörnvall (eds.), *The Hierarchy of Life.* Elsevier Press, Amsterdam.

Mooi, R. 1989. The outgroup criterion revisited via naked zones and alleles. *Syst. Zool.,* 38:283–290.

Moore, G. W., Barnabas, J. and M. Goodman. 1973. A method for constructing maximum parsimony ancestral amino acid sequences on a given network. *J. Theor. Biol.*, 38:459–485.

Navidi, W. C., G. A. Churchill, and A. von Haeseler. 1991. Methods for inferring phylogenies from nucleic acid sequence data by using maximum likelihood and linear invariants. *Mol. Biol. Evol.*, 8:128–143.

Neff, N. A. 1986. A rational basis for a priori character weighting. *Syst. Zool.*, 35:110–123.

Nei, M. 1987. *Molecular Evolutionary Genetics*. Columbia Univ. Press, N.Y.

Nei, M. 1992. Relative efficiencies of different tree-making methods for molecular data. Pp. 90–128 in M. M. Miyamoto and J. Cracraft (eds.), *Phylogenetic Analysis of DNA Sequences*. Oxford Univ. Press, Oxford.

Nelson, G. 1974. Classification as an expression of phylogenetic relationships. *Syst. Zool.*, 22:344–359.

Nelson, G. 1983. Reticulation in cladograms. Pp. 105–111 in N. I. Platnick and V. A. Funk (eds.), *Advances in Cladistics*, Volume 2. Proceedings of the Second Meeting of the Willi Hennig Society. Columbia Univ. Press, N.Y.

Nelson, G., and N. I. Platnick. 1981. *Systematics and Biogeography: Cladistics and Vicariance*. Columbia Univ. Press, N.Y.

Nixon, K. C. 1992. *CLADOS, version 1.2*. Distributed by the author, Ithaca, N.Y.

Nixon, K. C., and J. I. Davis. 1991. Polymorphic taxa, missing values and cladistic analysis. *Cladistics*, 7:233–241.

Nixon, K. C., and Q. D. Wheeler. 1990. An amplification of the phylogenetic species concept. *Cladistics*, 6:211–223.

Norell, M. A. 1992. Taxic origin and temporal diversity: The effect of phylogeny. Pp. 89–118 in M. J. Novacek and Q. D. Wheeler (eds.), *Extinction and Phylogeny*. Columbia Univ. Press, N.Y.

Novacek, M. J., and M. A. Norell. 1982. Fossils, phylogeny, and taxonomic rates of evolution. *Syst. Zool.*, 31:366–375.

O'Grady, R. T., and G. B. Deets. 1987. Coding multistate characters, with special reference to the use of parasites as characters of their hosts. *Syst. Zool.*, 36:268–279.

O'Hara, R. J. 1988. Homage to Clio, or, Toward an historical philosophy for evolutionary biology. *Syst. Zool.*, 37:142–155.

Olsen, G. J. 1991. Systematic underestimation of tree branch lengths by Lake's operator metrics: An effect of position-dependent substitution rates. *Mol. Biol. Evol.*, 8:592–608.

Packer, L. 1991. The evolution of social behavior and nest architecture in sweat bees of the subgenus *Evylaeus* (Hymenoptera: Halictidae): a phylogenetic approach. *Behav. Ecol. Sociobiol.*, 29:153–160.

Page, R. D. M. 1988. Quantitative cladistic biogeography: Constructing and comparing area cladograms. *Syst. Zool.*, 37:254–270.

Page, R. D. M. 1989. *COMPONENT User's Manual (Release 1.5)*. Distributed by the author, Univ. Auckland, Auckland, New Zealand.

Page, R. D. M. 1990a. Temporal congruence and cladistic analysis of biogeography and cospeciation. *Syst. Zool.*, 39:205–226.

Page, R. D. M. 1990b. Component analysis: A valiant failure? *Cladistics*, 6:119–136.

Page, R. D. M. In press. *COMPONENT 2: Tree comparison software for Microsoft Windows*. Natural History Museum, London.

Pagel, M. D., and P. H. Harvey. 1988. Recent developments in the analysis of comparative data. *Q. Rev. Biol.*, 63:413–440.

Pagel, M. D., and P. H. Harvey. 1989. Comparative methods for examining adaptation depend on evolutionary methods. *Folia Primatologica*, 53:203–220.

Pamilo, P., and M. Nei. 1988. Relationships between gene trees and species trees. *Mol. Biol. Evol.*, 5:568–583.

Patterson, C. 1982. Morphological characters and homology. Pp. 21–74 in K. Joysey and A. Friday (eds.), *Problems of Phylogenetic Reconstruction*. Academic Press, London.

Patterson, C., and A. B. Smith. 1987. Is the periodicity of extinctions a taxonomic artifact? *Nature*, 330:248–251.

Payne, W. H., J. R. Rabung, and T. P. Bogyo. 1969. Coding the Lehmer pseudo-random number generator. *Comm. ACM*, 12:85–86.

Platnick, N. I. 1977. Cladograms, phylogenetic trees, and hypothesis testing. *Syst. Zool.*, 26:438–442.

Platnick, N. I. 1986a. On justifying cladistics. *Cladistics*, 2:83–85.

Platnick, N. I. 1986b. "Evolutionary Cladistics" or Evolutionary Systematics? *Cladistics*, 2:288–296.

Platnick, N. I., and H. D. Cameron. 1977. Cladistic methods in textual, linguistic and phylogenetic analysis. *Syst. Zool.*, 26:380–385.

Platnick, N. I., and G. Nelson. 1978. A method of analysis for historical biogeography. *Syst. Zool.*, 27:1–16.

Platnick, N. I., C. E. Griswold, and J. A. Coddington. 1991. On missing entries in cladistic analysis. *Cladistics*, 7:337–343.

Pogue, M. G., and M. F. Mickevich. 1990. Character definitions and character state delineation: The bête noire of phylogenetic inference. *Cladistics*, 6:319–361.

Reidl, R. 1978. *Order in Living Organisms*. Wiley, N.Y.

Rempe, U. 1988. Characterizing DNA variability by stochastic matrices. Pp. 375–384 in H.H. Bock (ed.), *Classification and Related Methods of Data Analysis*. Elsevier, North Holland.

Ridley, M. 1983. *The Explanation of Organic Diversity*. Oxford Univ. Press, Oxford.

Ridley, M. 1986. The number of males in a primate troup. *Anim. Behav.*, 34:1848–1858.

Ridley, M. 1989. Why not to use species in comparative tests. *J. Theor. Biol.*, 136:361–364.

Rieseberg, L. H., and D. E. Soltis. 1991. Phylogenetic consequences of cytoplasmic gene flow in plants. *Evolutionary Trends in Plants*, 5:65–84.

Rinsma, I., Hendy, M., and Penny, D. 1990. Minimally colored trees. *Math. Biosci.*, 98:201–210.

Ritland, K., and M. T. Clegg. 1987. Evolutionary analysis of plant DNA sequences. *Am. Nat.*, 130:S74–S100.

Rogers, J. S. 1984. Deriving phylogenetic trees from allele frequencies. *Syst. Zool.*, 33:52–63.

Ronquist, F., and S. Nylin. 1990. Process and pattern in the evolution of species associations. *Syst. Zool.*, 39:323–344.

Rosen, D. E. 1976. A vicariance model of Caribbean biogeography. *Syst. Zool.*, 24:431–464.

Rosen, D. E. 1978. Vicariant patterns and historical explanation in biogeography. *Syst. Zool.*, 27:159–188.

Saitou, N. 1989. A theoretical study of the underestimation of branch lengths by the maximum parsimony principle. *Syst. Zool.*, 38:1–6.

Saitou, N., and T. Imanishi. 1989. Relative efficiencies of the Fitch-Margoliash, maximum-parsimony, maximum-likelihood, minimum-evolution, and neighbor-joining methods of phylogenetic tree construction in obtaining the correct tree. Mol. Biol. Evol., 6:514–525.

Saitou, N., and M. Nei. 1987. The neighbor-joining method: A new method for reconstructing phylogenetic trees. *Mol. Biol. Evol.*, 4:406–425.

Sanderson, M. J. 1989. Confidence limits on phylogenies: The bootstrap revisited. *Cladistics*, 5:113–129.

Sanderson, M. J. 1990. Estimating rates of speciation and evolution: A bias due to homoplasy. *Cladistics*, 6:387–391.

Sanderson, M. J. 1991. In search of homoplastic tendencies: Statistical inference of topological patterns in homoplasy. *Evolution*, 45:351–358.

Sanderson, M. J., and M. J. Donoghue. 1989. Patterns of variation in levels of homoplasy. *Evolution*, 43:1781–1795.

Sankoff, D. 1975. Minimal mutation trees of sequences. *SIAM J. Appl. Math.*, 28:35–42.

Sankoff, D. 1990. Designer invariants for large phylogenies. *Mol. Biol. Evol.*, 7:255–269.

Sankoff, D., and R. J. Cedergren. 1983. Simultaneous comparison of three or more sequences related by a tree. Pp. 253–263 in D. Sankoff and J. B. Kruskal (eds.), *Time Warps, String Edits, and Macromolecules: The Theory and Practice of Sequence Comparison*. Addison-Wesley, Reading, Mass.

Sankoff, D., and P. Rousseau. 1975. Locating the vertices of a Steiner tree in arbitrary space. *Math. Progr.*, 9:240–246.

Savage, H. M. 1983. The shape of evolution: Systematic tree topology. *Biol. J. Linn. Soc.*, 20:225–244.

Sawyer, S. 1989. Statistical tests for detecting gene conversion. *Mol. Biol. Evol.*, 6:526–538.

Sessions, S. R., and A. Larson. 1987. Developmental correlates of genome size in plethodontid salamanders and their implications for genome evolution. *Evolution*, 41:1239–1251.

Sidow, A., and A. C. Wilson. 1990. Compositional statistics: An improvement of evolutionary parsimony and its application to deep branches in the tree of life. *J. Mol. Evol.*, 31:51–68.

Sidow, A., and A. C. Wilson. 1992. Compositional statistics evaluated by computer simulations. Pp. 129–146 in M. M. Miyamoto and J. Cracraft (eds.), *Phylogenetic Analysis of DNA Sequences*. Oxford Univ. Press, Oxford.

Sillén-Tullberg, B. 1988. Evolution of gregariousness in aposematic butterfly larvae: A phylogenetic analysis. *Evolution*, 42:293–305.

Simberloff, D. 1987. Calculating probabilities that cladograms match: A method of biogeographical inference. *Syst. Zool.*, 36:175–195.

Simberloff, D., K. L. Heck, E. D. McCoy, and E. F. Connor. 1981. There have been no statistical tests of cladistic biogeographical hypotheses. Pp. 40–63 in G. Nelson and D. E. Rosen (eds.), *Vicariance Biogeography: A Critique*. Columbia Univ. Press, N.Y.

Simpson, G. G. 1961. *Principles of Animal Taxonomy*. Columbia Univ. Press, N.Y.

Slatkin, M., and W. P. Maddison. 1989. A cladistic measure of gene flow inferred from the phylogenies of alleles. *Genetics,* 123:603–613.

Slatkin, M., and W. P. Maddison. 1990. Detecting isolation by distance using phylogenies of alleles. *Genetics,* 126:249–260.

Slowinski, J. G., and C. Guyer. 1989. Testing the stochasticity of patterns of organismal diversity: An improved null model. *Am. Nat.,* 134:907–921.

Smith, A. B., and C. Patterson. 1988. The influence of taxonomic method on the perception of patterns of evolution. *Evol. Biol.,* 23:127–216.

Sneath, P. H. A. 1975. Cladistic representation of reticulate evolution. *Syst. Zool.,* 24:360–368.

Sneath, P. H. A., and R. R. Sokal. 1973. *Numerical Taxonomy: The Principles and Practice of Numerical Classification.* W. H. Freeman, San Francisco.

Sneath, P. H. A., M. J. Sackin and R. P. Ambler. 1975. Detecting evolutionary incompatibilities from protein sequences. *Syst. Zool.,* 24:311–332.

Sober, E. 1983. Parsimony methods in systematics. Pp. 37–47 in N. I. Platnick and V. A. Funk (eds.), *Advances in Cladistics,* Vol. 2. Proceedings of the Second Meeting of the Willi Hennig Society. Columbia Univ. Press, N.Y.

Sober, E. 1988. *Reconstructing the Past: Parsimony, Evolution, and Inference.* MIT Press, Cambridge, Mass.

Sokal, R. R., and P. H. Sneath. 1963. *Principles of Numerical Taxonomy.* W. H. Freeman, San Francisco.

Sourdis, J., and C. Krimbas. 1987. Accuracy of phylogenetic trees estimated from DNA sequence data. *Mol. Biol. Evol.,* 4:159–166.

Sourdis, J., and M. Nei. 1988. Relative efficiencies of the maximum parsimony and distance-matrix methods in obtaining the correct phylogenetic tree. *Mol. Biol. Evol.,* 5:298–311.

Stearns, S. C. 1983. The influence of size and phylogeny on life history patterns. *Oikos,* 41:173–187.

Stephens, J. C. 1985. Statistical methods of DNA sequence analysis: Detection of intragenic recombination or gene conversion. *Mol. Biol. Evol.,* 2:539–556.

Stevens, P. F. 1991. Character states, morphological variation, and phylogenetic analysis: A review. *Syst. Bot.,* 16:553–583.

Strauss, R. In press. Optimal mapping of continuous characters onto evolutionary trees for studies of character evolution. *Paleobiology.*

Swofford, D. L. 1991. *Phylogenetic Analysis Using Parsimony (PAUP), version 3.0s.* Illinois Natural History Survey, Champaign.

Swofford, D. L., and S. H. Berlocher. 1987. Inferring evolutionary trees from gene frequency data under the principle of maximum parsimony. *Syst. Zool.,* 36:293–325.

Swofford, D. L., and W. P. Maddison. 1987. Reconstructing ancestral character states under Wagner parsimony. *Math. Biosci.,* 87:199–229.

Swofford, D. L., and W. P. Maddison. In press. Parsimony, character-state reconstructions, and evolutionary inferences. In R. L. Mayden (ed.), *Systematics, Historical Ecology, and North American Freshwater Fishes.* Stanford Univ. Press, Stanford, California.

Swofford, D. L., and G. J. Olsen. 1990. Phylogeny reconstruction. Pp. 411–501 in D. M. Hillis and G. Moritz (eds.), *Molecular Systematics.* Sinauer Associates, Sunderland, Mass.

Tajima, F. 1983. Evolutionary relationships of DNA sequences in finite populations. *Genetics,* 123:229–240.

Tajima, F. 1992. Statistical method for estimating the standard errors of branch lengths in a phylogenetic tree reconstructed without assuming equal rates of substitution among different lineages. *Mol. Biol. Evol.,* 9:168–181.

Takahata, N. 1989. Gene genealogy in three related populations: Consistency probability between gene and population trees. *Genetics,* 122:957–966.

Takahata, N. 1991. Genealogy of neutral genes and spreading of selected mutations in a geographically structured population. *Genetics,* 129:585–595.

Tateno, Y. 1990. A method for molecular phylogeny construction by direct use of nucleotide sequence data. *J. Mol. Evol.,* 30:85–93.

Tavaré, S. 1984. Line-of-descent and genealogical processes, and their applications to population genetic models. *Theor. Pop. Biol.,* 26:119–164.

Templeton, A. R. 1983. Phylogenetic inference from restriction endonuclease cleavage site maps with particular reference to the evolution of humans and the apes. *Evolution,* 37:221–244.

Templeton, A. R., E. Boerwinkle, and C. F. Sing. 1987. A cladistic analysis of phenotypic associations with haplotypes inferred from restriction endonuclease mapping. I. Basic theory and an analysis of alcohol dehydrogenase activity in *Drosophila. Genetics,* 117:343–351.

Templeton, A. R., C. F. Sing, A. Kessling, and S. Humphries. 1988. A cladistic analysis of phenotype associations with haplotypes inferred from restriction endonuclease mapping. II. The analysis of natural populations. *Genetics*, 120:1145–1154.

Thomas, R.H., W. Schaffner, A.C. Wilson, and S. Pääbo. 1989. DNA phylogeny of the extinct marsupial wolf. *Nature*, 340:465-467.

Thompson, E. A. 1975. *Human Evolutionary Trees*. Cambridge Univ. Press, Cambridge.

Thompson, E. A. 1986. Likelihood and parsimony: Comparison of criteria and solutions. *Cladistics*, 2:43–52.

Thorpe, R. S. 1984. Primary and secondary transition zones in speciation and population differentiation: A phylogenetic analysis for range expansion. *Evolution*, 38:233–243.

Valdez, A. M. and D. Piñero. 1992. Phylogenetic estimation of plasmid exchange in bacteria. *Evolution*, 46:641–656.

Vrba, E.S. 1980. Evolution, species and fossils: How does life evolve? *South African J. Sci.*, 76:61–84.

Wagner, H.-J. 1981. The minimum number of mutations in an evolutionary network. *J. Theor. Biol.*, 91:621–636.

Wagner, W. H., Jr. 1983. Reticulistics: The recognition of hybrids and their role in cladistics and classification. Pp. 63–79 in N. I. Platnick and V. A. Funk (eds.), *Advances in Cladistics*, Vol. 2. Proceedings of the Second Meeting of the Willi Hennig Society. Columbia Univ. Press, N.Y.

Wake, D. B. 1991. Homoplasy: The result of natural selection, or evidence of design limitations? *Am. Nat.*, 138:543–567.

Wake, D. B., and A. Larson. 1987. Multidimensional analysis of an evolving lineage. *Science*, 238:42–48.

Wanntorp, H.-E. 1983a. Historical constraints in adaptation theory: Traits and non-traits. *Oikos*, 41:157–160.

Wanntorp, H.-E. 1983b. Reticulated cladograms and the identification of hybrid taxa. Pp. 81–88 in N. I. Platnick and V. A. Funk (eds.), *Advances in Cladistics*, Vol. 2. Proceedings of the Second Meeting of the Willi Hennig Society. Columbia Univ. Press, N.Y.

Wanntorp, H.-E., D. R. Brooks, T. Nilsson, S. Nylin, F. Ronquist, S. C. Stearns, and N. Wedell. 1990. Phylogenetic approaches in ecology. *Oikos*, 57:119–132.

Watrous, L. E., and Q. D. Wheeler. 1981. The out-group comparison method of character analysis. *Syst. Zool.*, 30:1–11.

Weir, B. S. 1990. *Genetic Data Analysis*. Sinauer Associates, Sunderland, Mass.

Wheeler, Q. D. 1986. Character weighting and cladistic analysis. *Syst. Zool.*, 35:102–109.

Wheeler, W. C. 1990. Combinatorial weights in phylogenetic analysis: A statistical parsimony procedure. *Cladistics*, 6:269–275.

Wiley, E. O. 1981. *Phylogenetics. The Theory and Practice of Phylogenetic Systematics*. Wiley, N.Y.

Wiley, E. O. 1988. Parsimony analysis and vicariance biogeography. *Syst. Zool.*, 37:271–290.

Wiley, E. O., and R. L. Mayden. 1985. Species and speciation in phylogenetic systematics, with examples from the North American fish fauna. *Ann. Missouri Bot. Gard.*, 72:596–635.

Williams, P. L., and W. M. Fitch. 1989. Finding the minimum change in a given tree. Pp. 453–470 in B. Fernholm, K. Bremer, and H. Jörnvall (eds.), *The Hierarchy of Life*. Elsevier Press, Amsterdam.

Williams, P. L., and W. M. Fitch. 1990. Phylogeny determination using dynamically weighted parsimony method. *Methods in Enzymology*, 183:615–626.

Wu, C. 1991. Inferences of species phylogeny in relation to segregation of ancient polymorphisms. *Genetics*, 127:429–435.

ANNOTATED INDEX ORGANIZED BY MENU AND PALETTE

The following list includes the standard MacClade menus. Special menu items that are available if you hold down the Option key are listed in the Alphabetical Index. Some menus are available only in the tree window, and others only in the data editor.

| About MacClade... | Information about MacClade, including Help, 137 |

File

New File	⌘N	Begins new data file with empty matrix, 143
Open File...	⌘O	Opens data file on disk, 143
Close File	⌘W	Closes current data file, 148
About filename...		Displays comments about data file, 145
Save File	⌘S	Saves to disk current data file, overwriting old copy, 145
Save File As...		Saves copy of data file, not overwriting old, 145
Export File	▶	Saves copy of data file under non-NEXUS format, 149–158
Save Graphics File...		Saves image in current window as PICT file, 352
Save Text File	▶	Saves various text files, 353
Options for Saving	▶	Options for saving NEXUS and other files, 147, 357–359
Page Setup...		Macintosh Page Setup for printing
Print Tree...	⌘P	Prints current window, 340–352
Print Other	▶	Prints miscellaneous items, 342–343, 352
Save Preferences...		Sets currents options as program defaults, 139–141
Quit	⌘Q	Quits MacClade, 142

(Submenu of File menu)

HENNIG86 1.5...	Saves data file in HENNIG86 1.5 format, 155
PHYLIP 3.3...	Saves data file in PHYLIP 3.3 format, 153–155
PHYLIP 3.4...	Saves data file in PHYLIP 3.4 format, 153–155
NBRF...	Saves data file in NBRF format, 155–156
Simple Table...	Saves data matrix as a text table, 156–158
Descriptions...	Saves data matrix as set of descriptions, 158

Format	
	(Available in data editor)
Standard	Chooses standard data format (10 char. states maximum), 163
Extended Standard	Chooses extended format (26 char. states max.), 163
DNA	Chooses DNA format (symbols A,C,G,T predefined), 163
RNA	Chooses RNA format (symbols A,C,G,U predefined), 163
Translate to Protein...	Chooses protein format (amino acid symbols predefined), 163, 327
Genetic Code...	Edits genetic code, 331

Assume	
Change Type ▶	Changes types of selected characters, 201
Change Weight ▶	Changes weights of selected characters, 197–198
Change Inc Exc ▶	Designates selected characters as included or excluded, 199
Change Codons ▶	Designates codon positions of selected characters, 325–327
Type Sets...	Gets, renames, or deletes already-stored type sets, 209
Store Type Set...	Stores current type set, 209
Type Import...	Imports user-defined types from other file, 209
Type Edit...	Edits user-defined types, 204–209
Weight Sets...	Gets, renames, or deletes already-stored weight sets, 198–199
Store Weight Set...	Stores current weight set, 198–199
Inclusion Sets...	Gets, renames, or deletes already-stored inclusion sets, 200
Store Inclusion Set...	Stores current inclusion set, 200
Exclude Uninformative	Excludes characters that must have same number of steps on all trees with currently included taxa, 199–200

Change Type ▶	
	(Submenu of Assume menu)
• **unordered**	One step any change (Fitch parsimony), 202
ordered	States in sequence (Wagner parsimony), 202
irreversible	Gain only (Camin-Sokal parsimony), 202
stratigraphic	Fisher's stratigraphic debt, 202–203
Dollo	Gains only occur once, 203
	(User-defined — You add these), 204

Change Weight ▶

(Submenu of Assume menu)

Set Weights...	Sets weights of selected characters, 198
Decimal Weights	Converts weights from integral to decimal, 198
0	Changes weight of selected character to 0 through 9, 198
1	
2	
3	
4	
5	
6	
7	
8	
9	

Change Inc Exc ▶

(Submenu of Assume menu)

Include	Includes selected characters, 199
Exclude	Excludes selected characters, 199
Reverse	Excludes if included and vice versa, 199

Change Codons ▶

(Submenu of Assume menu)

Calculate Positions...	Calculates codon positions for selected sites, 326
Set To 1st Position	Sets selected sites to 1st position, 326
Set To 2nd Position	Sets selected sites to 2nd position, 326
Set To 3rd Position	Sets selected sites to 3rd position, 326
Non-Coding	Sets selected sites as not protein-coding, 326

Tree

(Available in tree window)

Trees... ⌘Y	Gets, renames or deletes already stored trees, 235
Store Tree...	Stores current tree to active tree repository, 235
About Trees...	Displays comments about current tree repository, 236
Random Trees...	Creates trees randomly and stores them, 323–324
New Tree File	Begins new external file for storing trees, 234
Open Tree File...	Opens existing external file for storing trees, 234
Close Tree File	Closes current external tree file, 234
Save Tree File	Saves current external tree file, overwriting old copy, 235
Save Tree File as...	Saves external tree file, not overwriting old copy, 235
Export Tree File ▶	Saves copy of tree file under other format, 235
Transfer Trees...	Transfers trees between data file and tree file, 236
Include-Exclude Taxa...	Includes or excludes taxa from current tree, 225
Search Options...	Chooses options for search tools, 226–227
Polytomy Options...	Chooses soft or hard polytomies, 223
All Terminal	Makes any taxa fixed as ancestors terminal again, 229

Chart

Chart menu	Description
Character Steps/etc...	*(Available in tree window)*
Treelengths...	Charts steps, CI, etc. of characters, 279–284
State Changes & Stasis...	Charts lengths of trees, 285–286
States...	Charts number of reconstructed changes between states, 287–296
Compare 2 Trees...	Shows frequencies of various states, 296
Compare 2 Tree Files...	Compares two trees in current tree repository, 296
	Compares all trees in two tree files, 297
Chart Options... ⌘J	Displays dialog box adjusting options for current chart, 279–298
Chart To Weight Set...	Converts chart to a weight set or user-defined type, 283–284, 295
Full Page Print	Option to print chart to fill page or as shown on screen, 352
Quietly Recalculate	Chooses option to recalculate chart whenever needed, without asking, 278

Display

(As appears in data editor)

Go To Tree Window ⌘T	Goes to tree window, or brings tree window to front, 212
Data Editor ⌘E	Goes to data editor, or brings data editor to front, 162
Character Status ⌘I	Opens character status window, or brings it to front, 196
Font ▶	Changes text font of data editor, 191
Size ▶	Changes text size of data editor, 191
Italic	Makes style italic/plain of selected taxon in data editor, 191
Symbols...	Specifies symbols of character states, 175
State Names...	Specifies names of characters and character states, 174
Display State Names	Shows states by their names in matrix, 189–190
Match First...	Puts special symbol if taxon has same state as first taxon, 190
Show or Hide...	Shows or hides elements of data editor, 191
✓Footnotes	Allows one to show/edit footnotes in footnote area below matrix, 192
Footstates	Allows one to show states and symbols in footnote area, 190

Tools

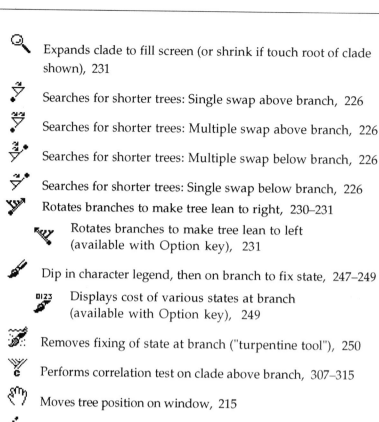

Chart window buttons

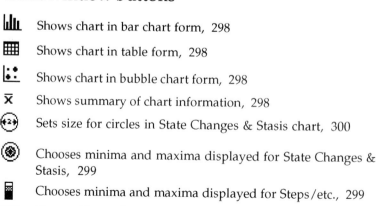

A   Chooses font, style, and size of text in chart, 299

Shows State Changes & Stasis chart using percentages, 301

Chooses options for vertical axes, 300

Chooses scaling of horizontal axis, 300

Changes shading of chart, 301

Adds grid on chart, 301

Editor Buttons

   Adjusts column width, 191

    Transposes matrix, 191

    Autotabs right, down, 165

ALPHABETICAL INDEX

Entries for standard menu items and tools will be found in the Menu and Tools index. Entries for menu items that are visible by holding down the Option key are in this index.